Alaska Native Education

Views From Within

ALASKA NATIVE EDUCATION

VIEWS FROM WITHIN

⊰⊱

EDITED BY

RAY BARNHARDT

ANGAYUQAQ OSCAR KAWAGLEY

ALASKA NATIVE KNOWLEDGE NETWORK
CENTER FOR CROSS-CULTURAL STUDIES
UNIVERSITY OF ALASKA FAIRBANKS

Alaska Native Knowledge Network
Center for Cross-Cultural Studies
University of Alaska Fairbanks
PO Box 756730
Fairbanks, AK 99775-6730
www.ankn.uaf.edu

ISBN 978-1-877962-43-1

Library of Congress Cataloging-in-Publication Data

Alaska native education : views from within / edited by Ray Barnhardt,
Oscar Kawagley.
     p. cm.
  Includes bibliographical references.
  ISBN 978-1-877962-43-1 (alk. paper)
  1. Indians of North America—Education—Alaska. 2. Eskimos—
Education—Alaska. I. Barnhardt, Ray. II. Kawagley, A. Oscar
(Angayuqaq Oscar), 1934-
  E97.65.A4A45 2009
  371.829710798--dc22
                              2009051259

This publication was printed on acid-free paper that meets the minimum
requirements for ANSI / NISO Z39.48–1992 (R2002) (Permanence of
Paper for Printed Library Materials).

Text and cover design by Paula Elmes, ImageCraft Publications & Design

Snow goggles on the cover carved by and used with permission of Linc
Qimiq Hill.

TO ALL THE ALASKA NATIVE ELDERS WHO HAVE SHARED
THEIR KNOWLEDGE, INSIGHTS, AND WISDOM FOR THE
BENEFIT OF SUCCEEDING GENERATIONS.

In Memory of

Frank Hill

1939–2007

THERE ARE FEW EDUCATORS in Alaska who have left a more enduring mark than did Frank Hill. He was a leader among leaders who grew up as a hunter and fisherman in the Bristol Bay region and went on to become a teacher, principal, and superintendent in the region, as well as to assume several statewide leadership roles. Throughout his career he inspired others to pursue their educational aspirations, but not to forget who they are in the process.

In the summer of 2003, Frank, along with his brothers Pete and Lary and Pete's wife BJ, took a nine-day hiking and camping trip along the length of the Telaquana Trail to explore their Dena'ina heritage. When they returned, Frank wrote an article (published in *Sharing Our Pathways* vol. 9, no. 4) about their experience, which included the following comments.

> There are many aspects of cultural knowledge that form the basis for Alaska Native peoples' ability to thrive in their respective environments, among these are the traditional trails . . . In sharing this story, it is our hope that it will encourage others to visit with Elders about important trails in their cultural area and hear stories or events associated with those trails. Perhaps you will travel on some of those trails as your ancestors did. Doing so will enrich your lives, honor those who established and used those significant trails and, in the process, reconnect you to your ancestral lands and lifeways.
>
> The last traditional chief of Batzunletas in the Ahtna Region, "Iizin Ta" or Charley Sanford (1876–1945) said: "After I die, burn all my material wealth; the only thing of true value to pass to future generations is a trail, a song and a story."

There is no doubt that Frank left a wide trail, an uplifting song, and an inspiring story for all to follow. We offer this book in his memory.

CONTENTS

Part V
Strengthening Native Languages

Part VI
Education for Self-Determination

Appendices

Acknowledgments

As EDITORS OF THIS VOLUME, we wish to express our appreciation to all the contributing authors for granting permission to include their essays in this collection of seminal writings on issues related to education, as viewed from Alaska Native perspectives. Many of these essays have been in limited circulation for years as readings for college classes or passed on from person to person, but most have not been readily available to a broad general audience. We hope that this publication will help bring them the attention they deserve.

Since the initial version of these essays came in many forms ranging from speeches and informal reflections to formal reports and scholarly articles, we have sought to retain as much of the original tone, format, and writing conventions as possible, so elements such as citations, vernacular language, spelling, and grammatical forms may vary from essay to essay. We have also attempted to include essays from different Alaska Native cultural perspectives, though the regions are not equally represented. We invite readers to let us know of writings not included in this collection that could be considered for future publications.

We also extend our appreciation to Paula Elmes for taking the rough material we provided and making it into a visually attractive and readable publication, as well as helping to work through the technical processes required to produce a document ready for final printing. Finally, we express our appreciation to the North by 2020 program at the University of Alaska Fairbanks, the Arctic Social Science Program at the National Science Foundation, and the Alaska Center for Ocean Science Education Excellence for providing the financial support to bring this publication to fruition.

Ray and Oscar

FOREWORD

—•••••—

Angayuqaq Oscar Kawagley

I RECENTLY WATCHED A TELEVISION PROGRAM titled *You Own Alaska*. My first reaction was that this was an expression motivated by political and economic interests. But the more I thought about it the more it grated on my worldview. How could anyone "own" Alaska? According to my ancestral traditions, the land owns me! Thus began my reflections on how my Yupiaq worldview differs from that of the dominant society.

The cold defines my place. Mamterilleq (now known as Bethel, Alaska) made me who I am. The cold made my language, my worldview, my culture, and my technology. Now, the cold is waning at a very fast rate and as a result, it is changing the landscape. The changing landscape in turn is confusing the mindscape of the Yupiat, as well as other indigenous people. Some of the natural sense makers of Mother Nature are out of synchronization with the flora and fauna.

We, the Yupiat of the Kuskokwim River, used the leafing of the alder tree to tell us when the smelts would be journeying up the river and we could begin dip-netting for them. When the alder leaves emerge from the bud, the king salmon will be arriving, and so on. But these indicators are no longer reliable when spring arrives two to four weeks earlier than usual. This is just one example of the changes that are taking place in the Yukon-Kuskokwim Delta.

In the times past, the landscape formed our mindscape, which in turn formed our identity. I grew up as an inseparable part of Nature. It was not my place to "own" land, nor to domesticate plants or animals that often have more power than I as a human being.

We know that Mother Nature has a culture, and it is a Native culture. This is why we as a Native people have to emulate Her. We know that the

Ellam Yua, the Person or Spirit of the Universe, lives in Her. That is why she serves as our guide, teacher, and mentor.

We need to spend time in Nature to commune with the Great Consciousness. This gives balance to the Native person. Nature encourages us to become altruistic, showing the utmost respect for everything around us, including the flora, fauna, and all the elements of Mother Earth, including the winds, the rivers, the lakes, the mountains, the clouds, the stars, the Milky Way, the sun, the moon, and the ocean currents. Mother Earth gives me everything I need to know and be able to do to solve problems. But times have changed, making living a life in concert with Mother Earth more difficult.

Missionaries and the educational system had the first impact on changing our lives. In the late 1800s and early 1900s, schools were introduced to the Yupiat people by the Christian churches under contract with the U.S. government. Boarding schools were established for Alaska Native youngsters. By this time the United States had become very adept at organizing and administering boarding schools for American Indians. Native children were taken away from their parents and villages for long periods of time. They would return to their home villages but no longer fit in. Their wants and desires became averse to village life. The education provided was organized to assimilate the Native people to the techno-mechanistic and consumerist worldview. The education system was oppressive and suppressive of the Native language and culture. The assimilative education was so effective it caused many Native youngsters to suppress their own Nativeness.

From the late 1960s and up to the present, Native people have been working diligently to change education so that it accommodates their languages, worldviews, culture, and technology. This is a slow healing process for the villages. Our educational mission is to produce human beings at home in their place, their environment, their world. This is slowly being brought to fruition through the efforts of the Native people themselves, with support from others of like thinking.

The Yupiat have been proactive in reorienting the education system for their children and are now proving to be equally proactive in dealing with the effects of climate change. They are looking at how our ancestors dealt with climate change in the past and applying what they learn to the present. Once they have an idea of what might be done, they devise a plan and ask for technical assistance from engineers, hydrologists, geographers, and other scientists whose knowledge and skills will contribute to the local efforts.

Native people realize that the traditional ways of knowing and doing can benefit from technical assistance provided by the various disciplinary sciences to strengthen their locally based plans. The working together of the two ways of knowing is much more powerful and, hopefully, more conducive to doing the right thing. It is through such collaborations that the historic clash of worldviews as reflected in the phrase "You Own Alaska" can become a force for new understandings and solutions to the many challenges we face together.

INTRODUCTION

Ray Barnhardt

ON AUGUST 7, 1999 at the 5th World Indigenous People's Conference on Education held in Hilo, Hawai'i, the Coolangatta Statement on Indigenous Peoples' Rights in Education (see Appendices) was formally adopted and forwarded to the United Nations as an outgrowth of the First International Decade of the World's Indigenous Peoples (1995–2004). The following Preamble accompanied the Coolangatta Statement:

> The Coolangatta Statement represents a collective voice of Indigenous peoples from around the world who support fundamental principles considered vital to achieving reform and transformation of education for Indigenous peoples. The need for such an instrument is self-evident. Over the last 30 years, Indigenous peoples throughout the world have argued that they have been denied equity in non-Indigenous education systems which have failed to provide educational services that nurture the whole Indigenous person inclusive of scholarship, culture and spirituality. Most all Indigenous peoples, and in particular, those who have suffered the impact and effects of colonization, have struggled to access education that acknowledges, respects and promotes the right of Indigenous peoples to be indigenous—a right that embraces Indigenous peoples' language, culture, traditions, and spirituality. This includes the right to self-determination

It is in the spirit of the Coolangatta Statement that this collection of speeches, essays, and articles has been assembled from writings by Alaska Native authors and educators over the past forty years. The assertion of the right to be indigenous is both implicit and explicit in all the essays that follow, with each providing an indigenous perspective reflecting an insider's viewpoint. Most salient and intractable in the task of reconciling the underlying differences in insider and outsider perspectives are the differences in worldviews between those of the relative newcomers to Alaska (i.e. the miners, loggers, oil -field workers, seasonal fishermen, tourists, and scientists) and the Native people with roots in the land that go back millennia.

But no longer can these differences be cast in simplistic either/or terms, implying some kind of easily definable dichotomy between those who support subsistence versus cash economies, or traditional versus modern technologies, or anecdotal versus scientific evidence, or indigenous versus Western curricula. These lines have been blurred with the realities that Native cultures are not static, and Western institutional structures are no longer dominant. Instead, we now have a much more fluid and dynamic situation in which once-competing views of the world are having to seek reconciliation through new structures and frameworks that foster coexistence rather than domination and exploitation, one over the other.

The current state of affairs in the relationship between Native and non-Native people is still very tentative, however, and the negotiations are ongoing, with legislators, commissions, task forces, working groups, conferences, workshops, symposia, and seminars convening throughout Alaska to craft new laws, principles, guidelines, strategies, and structures to fit the much-maligned "new world order." The essays in this collection outline some of the critical features of the current landscape that illustrate the contributions that Native people are making to the institutional and cultural fabric of contemporary Alaska.

So what is it that Native people bring to the examination of these issues that differs from the work and perspectives of other interested parties, besides an intrinsic dependence on the sustainability of their worldviews, knowledge systems, and ways of knowing for their physical and cultural survival? I will touch on a few of the contributions that Native people are bringing to the table, all of which serve to complement and add to, rather than contradict or diminish, the knowledge base that continues to be generated by Western scientific and educational means.

One of the most important contributions that Native people are bringing to the research, policy-making, and educational arenas across Alaska is an extended temporal dimension, that is, a long-term perspective spanning many generations of observation and experimentation which enriches the relatively short-term, time-bound observations of the itinerant observers. As a result, patterns and cycles that are not evident in the outsider's database of detailed in-depth, short-term observations can be factored into the equation for analytical and decision-making purposes. One Inuit Elder chided fish and game biologists who were proudly displaying charts showing 30 years of data on polar bear observations along a stretch of the Beaufort Sea indicating that the Iñupiaq record went back 300 years, and that just because it hadn't been written down didn't mean it was any less reliable. A Yup'ik hunter triggered scientists' interest in research linking industrial pollution from factories as far away as Central Europe and China to "acid snow" through his detection of changes in the coloration of tundra plants in western Alaska which he had observed over a period of 40 years. As a result, he was invited to participate in an international conference on "Arctic haze" at Cambridge University to provide a dimension that was not readily available through conventional scientific observation.

Coupled closely with this long-term temporal dimension of indigenous knowledge is another important contribution that Native ways of knowing provide, that of linking human interaction with the environment in ways that demonstrate and exemplify the interconnectedness of all the elements that make up the social and ecological systems in which we live. While Western scientists tend to specialize and conduct research in one component of an ecosystem at a time, Native observers are immersed in the system in its totality and thus are more likely to recognize how the various components interact with and depend upon one another over time and across species.

Another important contribution that Native people are making to our understanding of sustainable living is in the recognition of the dynamic nature of cultural systems. Unlike the Western observers' tendency to freeze indigenous cultural systems in time, as though they exist in some kind of idealized static state destined never to change, Native people themselves, as a matter of cultural survival, have been quick to adapt new technologies and to grasp the "new world order." While retaining a keen sense of place and rootedness to the land they occupy, they have not hesitated to take advantage of new opportunities to improve their quality of life and the efficiency of their lifestyle. This is done, however, within their own framework of values, priorities, and worldviews, so that the development trajectory they choose is not always the same as what outsiders might anticipate, or even recognize.

The recognition of cultural systems as being dynamic and ever-changing in response to new conditions has enormous implications for education, especially where climatic changes, technological innovations, and external policy mandates have combined to create a rapidly changing social, political, and cultural milieu. Nowhere has this been more contentious than in the federal and state educational policy mandates imposed by the No Child Left Behind legislation. Which brings us to another dimension in illustrating the contributions that Native people are making to educational issues in Alaska, and that is the qualitative dimension. Defining and assessing the role of culture in the curriculum and pedagogy associated with formal education has taken on national and international dimensions as indigenous people have joined together to assert their own definitions of educational success.

On September 7, 2007, the United Nations General Assembly formally adopted the Declaration on the Rights of Indigenous Peoples (see Appendices), following over 15 years of deliberations among indigenous peoples from around the world, including Alaska. Contained within the Declaration are three articles addressed specifically to the rights of indigenous peoples with regard to education, including Article 14.1, which states:

> Indigenous peoples have the right to establish and control their educational systems and institutions providing education in their own languages, in a manner appropriate to their cultural methods of teaching and learning.

Indigenous people are no longer willing to be passive recipients of educational policies and practices derived in arenas far from their own, but are now taking an active role in reshaping educational systems to meet their unique needs. For example, building on the principles outlined in the Coolongatta Statement and the U.N. Declaration, Alaska Native Elders and educators responded to the focus on content standards in education by developing a set of "Alaska Standards for Culturally Responsive Schools." These Cultural Standards were developed to address the missing cultural elements in the state standards, and elements of the Cultural Standards are now imbedded in state regulation (http://www.ankn.uaf.edu/standards).

As indigenous people have begun to assert their acknowledged rights to self-determination and self-government and assume control over various aspects of their lives, one of the first tasks they have faced has been to reconstruct the institutional structures and practices that were originally established by distant bureaucrats. In so doing, they have sought to make them more suitable to their needs as a people with their own worldviews, identities, and histories. In addition to seeking to influence the established institutional structures related to education, Native people have played an active role in creating new structures under their own control to address issues directly from an indigenous perspective. Most prominent in that regard has been the Alaska Federation of Natives, which in addition to its many other advocacy activities, has developed a set of "Guidelines for Research" that apply to all forms of research impacting Alaska Native people (see Appendices). Other examples of politically and educationally active Native institutions include the First Alaskans Institute, the Alaska Native Science Commission, the Inuit Circumpolar Conference, Ilisagvik College, and the Consortium of Alaska Native Higher Education.

The incongruities between Western institutional structures and practices and traditional cultural forms have not always been easy to reconcile. The complexities that come into play when two different cultural systems converge present a formidable challenge. The specialization, standardization, and compartmentalization that are inherent features of Western bureaucratic forms of organization are often in direct conflict with practices in indigenous societies, which tend toward collective decision-making, extended kinship structures, ascribed authority vested in elders, flexible notions of time, and traditions of informality in everyday affairs. It is little wonder then that educational structures, which often epitomize Western bureaucratic forms, have been found wanting in addressing the educational needs of traditional societies.

This picture is not as bleak as it once was, however, as indigenous people themselves, including the authors of the following essays, have begun to rethink their role and seek to blend old and new practices in ways that are more likely to fit the contemporary conditions of the people being served. Regardless of whether the educational goals of a community are directed toward internal quality of life issues or external economic considerations, the steps being taken to improve cultural and community sustainability point toward greater involvement of indigenous people in everything from policy making to curriculum development and from research to management practices. As more Alaska Native educators, scientists, researchers, and community advocates move into leadership roles, the human and natural landscapes of Alaska will take on new meaning within the context of old traditions. This will benefit us all.

The actions currently being taken by indigenous people themselves in communities throughout the world clearly demonstrate that a significant "paradigm shift" toward the revaluation of indigenous knowledge systems and ways of knowing is well underway, with the emphasis shifting consistently toward the utilization of local knowledge and local people in the decision-making processes. The essays that make up this book provide clear guidance in those endeavors.

PART I

ALASKA NATIVE EDUCATION—PAST, PRESENT, AND FUTURE

———◆◆◆◆———

66 Indigenous peoples throughout the world survive policies and practices ranging from extermination and genocide to protection and assimilation. Perhaps more than any other feat, survival is the greatest of all Indigenous peoples' achievements. 99

From the *Coolongatta Statement on Indigenous Rights in Education*

ALASKA NATIVE EDUCATION

PAST, PRESENT, AND FUTURE

———◆◇◆———

Doreen Andersen-Spear and Eben Hopson

The following article was the keynote presentation at the 2003 Native Educators' Conference banquet in Anchorage. The first portion of the presentation consists of excerpts from a speech given by Eben Hopson to the people of the North Slope Borough in 1975 and published by UAF in *Cross-Cultural Issues in Alaskan Education* in 1977. Doreen was born in Barrow and is the granddaughter of Eben Hopson, who was the founding mayor of the North Slope Borough and the cofounder of the Inuit Circumpolar Conference.

WE IÑUPIAQ ARE A NATION OF PEOPLE occupying the circumpolar Arctic from Siberia through Alaska, Canada, and Greenland. We share common values, language, culture, and economic systems. Our culture has enabled us to survive and flourish for thousands of years in the Arctic where no other man or culture could. Among our entire international Iñupiaq community, we of the North Slope are the first Iñupiaq who have achieved true self-government with the formation of the North Slope Borough. We have the greatest opportunity to direct our own destiny as we have for the past millennia.

Possibly the greatest significance of home rule is that it enables us to regain control of the education of our children. For thousands of years, our traditional method of socializing our youth was the responsibility of the family and community.

1

From the first, visitors of the Arctic universally commented on the warm disposition of our children. Corporal punishment was absolutely unknown. Boys and girls began their education with their parents, and by the time they reached their teenage years, they had mastered the skills necessary to survive on the land. From that time forward the youth—with their family and within their community—devoted their education to their intellectual and social growth.

For 87 years, the Bureau of Indian Affairs tried to destroy our culture through the education of our children. Those who would destroy our culture did not succeed. However, it was not without cost. Many of our people have suffered. We all know the social ills we endure today. Recently, I heard a member of the school personnel say that many of our Iñupiaq children have poor self-concepts. Is it any wonder, when the school systems fail to provide the Iñupiaq student with experiences which would build positive self-concepts, and the Iñupiaq language and culture are almost totally excluded?

My children and yours spend many hours in school each day, 180 days each year for 12 years. We must have teachers who will reflect and transmit our ideals and values. We must have Iñupiat-centered orientation in all areas of instruction. I do not want my children to learn that we were "discovered" by Columbus or Vitus Bering. I do not want to hear that we were barbaric or uncivilized. I do not want our children to feel inferior because their language and culture are different from those of their teacher. I do not want to see school planning surveys which list hunting, fishing, whaling, or trapping as "social" or "recreational" activities.

The land-claims movement and the self-determination attitude of the Alaska Natives were largely responsible for the removal of the suppression of our Native languages and culture. Bilingual instruction became the new education policy. However, this has generally meant that we use English as our primary language of instruction and somehow integrate Iñupiat into the curriculum.

The North Slope Borough schools must implement a program that is bilingual and bicultural. Our children must be taught in our Iñupiat language, with English as the secondary language. To attain this goal, we must have teachers who are bilingual and bicultural, knowledgeable in our Iñupiat culture and values. This can be achieved either with instructors who are Iñupiat or who have been trained in Iñupiat.

What can we do about this problem?

- We must develop a teacher recruitment and training program to satisfy our needs.

- Foremost we must encourage and train our own Iñupiaq to become teachers.
- Recruit responsive teachers who are willing to learn both the Iñupiat language and our cultural values.
- Train teachers and offer financial incentives to those who become proficient in our language and culture, in addition to Iñupiat history and ideologies.
- Evaluate current teachers to insure Iñupiat educational philosophies are being implemented.

Americans are beginning to assess their own values and are finding them compatible with our own. We can now afford to be selective in our teachers. We should select teachers who are willing to become contributing members of the community. We must strive to break down the barrier between the community and the school. Rather than being an integral part of the community, the schools and teacher housing resemble a colonial fort. We must end teacher segregation.

We must rid ourselves of these temporary residents who are here merely for financial gain. A number of teachers have already demonstrated their willingness to live among us as neighbors and friends. They have become permanent members of the community. They identify with us and share our concerns.

Our teachers are the highest-paid teachers in the entire United States. What are we getting for our money? We should be able to hire the best bilingual-bicultural teachers in the world. We should have teachers who can teach well in Iñupiat schools. We should have the best schools in the nation, surpassing any of the elite prep schools in the east. We should have teachers who earn their keep by effectively teaching our children.

I feel certain that the school board members share my frustration and concerns. It is important to remember the lessons of the past. In addition, we must research and master the new changes if we are to continue to dominate the Arctic. We have demonstrated we can survive the trespasses that have been perpetrated upon us. We have been successful in establishing our own home-rule government. We have been able to achieve self-government. We must strive to insure that our borough, our city governments, and our school systems reflect our Iñupiat ideals. We are Iñupiaq.

COMMENTARY BY DOREEN ANDERSEN SPEAR

My name is Doreen Andersen-Spear. My *aaka*, Rebecca Hopson, named me Maligian. My presentation this evening was a word-for-word recital of parts of a speech my *aapa*, Eben Hopson, Sr., gave on December 19, 1975, at the Teachers Affiliation Union's contracting meeting in Barrow. His words still ring true today. They mean so much to me. They are part of my roots and I keep them strong and alive by remembering them.

My *aapa* was the founding mayor of the North Slope Borough. He was denied a high school education by the BIA, which only motivated him to build high schools and improve the educational system on the North Slope. Now there is a middle school in Barrow named after him and a life-size statue with an inscription that reads "Education is the key to success. Do not let anything stand in your way in your pursuit of education."

I'm a product of a racially mixed marriage. My dad, Ralph Andersen, is Yupik and Danish. My mom, Flossie Hopson Andersen, is Iñupiat and English. I don't know much about my Yupik heritage, and I know nothing about my Danish and English roots. I claim my Alaska Native heritage. Barrow is the only home I know. I was born and raised there.

I have seen our Iñupiat culture start to lose its strength within the younger generations. Living among Iñupiat Elders is a life experience and to learn anything of my Iñupiat culture is dear to my heart. I do not speak Iñupiaq but this does not discourage me to learn more. As I grow older, my desire to acquire the knowledge of my Elders also grows. I only hope the younger generations also consider strengthening our culture—keeping our roots strong—as a priority.

From my earliest childhood memories my parents stressed the importance of education. They are both college graduates and are my role models. My mom and dad enrolled me in early childhood education when I was four years old. They also taught me the need to know my family, my culture ,and my roots. I know they are proud of me.

My mom and dad encouraged me to participate in bilingual and bicultural activities while I was growing up. Mom taught me some of my Iñupiaq language at home. I learned how to sing and motion dance in the Iñupiat way. But this does not make me any less proud of my other cultural roots.

I am only one person and I cannot represent those who chose not to learn about their Native traditions and Native heritage. I observed my peers who chose not to participate actively in bilingual and bicultural classes, dances, and community activities. I was always curious why many parents did not encourage their children to learn their Native culture.

I like the theme for this conference—Keeping Our Roots Strong—because it made me really think hard about my roots and my generation in the context of education.

The formal education of Alaska Natives is a classic example of a clash between cultures. The values of the Western educational system of speaking, reading, and writing in the English language and studying Western history, concepts, and ideas conflict with the values, beliefs, and traditions of Alaska Natives. For generations, it was more important for our people to gather and harvest subsistence foods than it was to learn how to read and write English.

Educating Alaska Natives in the ways of Western society is a continuing problem today. Contributing factors include the lack of Alaska Native teachers, inadequate criteria and delivery of bilingual and bicultural curricula, and students who are not taught their Alaska Native cultures at home.

Many of our people suffered physically and emotionally from being forced to not practice their cultures in school. They suffered corporal punishment for speaking their Native language and personal humiliation and embarrassment for not being able to speak the English language fluently and write it correctly.

Some Native students also had to leave their homes to attend BIA boarding schools when they were only small children in their middle school years. I can't even imagine what that must have been like. At the boarding schools, attempts were made to integrate them into the American mainstream with military living conditions and military rules. Many slowly lost touch with important parts of their traditional ways and beliefs and many lost their Native language.

Natives who were fortunate enough to complete their education returned home and had children of their own. Their situation was a frustrating dilemma. On one hand, they were not fully accepted by their people because they no longer spoke their language or were able to practice their cultural ways. On the other hand, they were not accepted by Western society because of their skin color. While many wanted to teach their children the ways and traditions of their ancestors, they simply could not.

My generation is facing a similar dilemma and problems with cultural identity. We feel pressures to advance and succeed in Western ways, yet keep solid footing in and strengthen our cultural roots. We face cultural identity issues and hard decisions.

Many, like me, are from mixed cultures. Which culture are we supposed to choose for the foundation of our lives? Is it wrong to choose one over another? Which roots do we keep strong without neglecting others? Will we be accused of favoring one culture over another when, in fact, combined together they make us who we are? Those are not new questions and there are no easy solutions. Your challenge as educators is to broaden our minds and vision to help us find answers.

The main barrier between the younger generations and our traditional cultures is an educational system that completely satisfies our cultural well-being. I was involved in bilingual and bicultural studies and activities throughout elementary and high school. My formal education has led me to college, but I still lack the cultural knowledge of my ancestors.

In order for the younger generations to be great leaders, we must strive to be flexible enough to live in two worlds. We need to seriously consider our cultures to be the most important parts of our lives. We need the security to make important decisions to build the foundation for our lives. We need to pursue our educational dreams not only in the Western way, but also to gain the cultural knowledge and understanding of who we are and where we came from. We need to know what our roots are and we need to keep them alive so they can grow stronger. We need your help.

Thank you very much for inviting me to speak here this evening. Thank you, *quyanakpak*!

ALASKA NATIVE EDUCATION

———◆→※←◆———

Report of the Education Task Force
Alaska Natives Commission/Alaska Federation of Natives, 1995

I. INTRODUCTION AND HISTORICAL BACKGROUND

THIS STUDY PROVIDES BASELINE INFORMATION for recommendations of the Commission for improving federal and state policies affecting the education of Alaska Natives. The information includes a recounting of the evolution of federal and state educational policy and programs affecting Alaska Natives, a description of the educational situation of Alaska Natives using 1990 data, a summary of concerns about that situation as revealed by hearings conducted by the Commission and its task forces, and recommendations as to how federal and state governments can improve the educational situation of Alaska Natives.

A. WESTERN EDUCATION OF ALASKA NATIVES PRIOR TO 1867

Attempts to impose "Western" education on Alaska Natives began in 1784 when a Russian fur trader, Gregorii Shelikhov, established a trading post at Three Saints Bay on the southwest coast of Kodiak Island. After killing a large number of Alaska Natives and taking others hostage to gain a foothold on Kodiak, Shelikhov opened a school for young Natives. He taught them "the precepts of Christianity," arithmetic, and the Russian language.[1]

Shelikhov's school for young Natives gave way to mission schools operated by the Russian Orthodox Church after its first priests arrived in Alaska in 1796. The Russian American Company, which received a monopoly to exploit Alaskan resources from the Tsar in 1799, supported the mission schools. The company also provided technical training for some Alaska Natives and Creoles (children of mixed Russian and Native parentage) in return for periods of indentured service. Russian schooling of Alaska Native children had three goals: to "Christianize" them; to "civilize" or "Westernize" them; and to make them more useful servants of the Russian American Company.[2]

Russian American Company vocational schools in Alaska closed with the 1867 ceremonies transferring Alaska from Russian to American jurisdiction. The Russian mission schools continued after 1867 with support from the Russian government. The last of them did not close until 1916.[3]

B. WESTERN EDUCATION OF ALASKA NATIVES AFTER 1867

The Russian mission schools were supplemented, or in some cases supplanted, by American Protestant and Roman Catholic mission schools. A Methodist missionary began the first of them at Wrangell in 1877. A Presbyterian missionary began the second of them at Sitka in 1878. Army and Navy administrators of Alaska supported them on an informal basis. Again, the schools intended to "Christianize" and "civilize" their Native students.[4]

Although Congress in 1869 had appropriated $100,000 for education among "Indian tribes not otherwise provided for" with the expectation that some or all of the money would be spent on education of Alaska Natives, not a dollar of the money reached Alaska. About this time the government compelled the Alaska Commercial Company, which had acquired an exclusive government lease to harvest the fur seal herds of the Pribilof Islands, to operate schools for the children of St. George and St. Paul Islands.[5]

Formal government support for education of Alaska Native children began only in 1884 with passage of the Alaska Organic Act. This established the "District of Alaska." It authorized limited civil government for Alaska and directed the United States Secretary of the Interior to establish an educational system for school-age children in Alaska "without reference to race." At this time 99 percent of the school-age children in Alaska were Alaska Natives.[6]

In 1885 the Secretary of the Interior assigned his department's Bureau of Education the responsibility for education in Alaska. The director of the

Bureau of Education then appointed Sheldon Jackson, a Presbyterian missionary, as General Agent for Education in Alaska. By 1895 the Bureau of Education was operating 19 grade schools in Alaska. Many were initially contract schools run by and taught by Protestant and Roman Catholic missionaries. Concern over church-state separation resulted in secularization of the schools in 1894.[7]

The education objectives assigned to these schools were that:

> The children must be kept in school until they acquire what is termed a common-school education, also practical knowledge of some useful trade. . . . We believe in reclaiming the Natives from improvident habits and in transforming them into ambitious and self-helpful citizens.[8]

In connection with schooling, Christianity was seen as a "powerful lever in influencing them (Alaska Natives) to abandon their old customs."[9]

The schools were segregated, either by intention or circumstance. In Juneau and Sitka, where there were substantial numbers of non-Native children, Native and non-Native schools operated concurrently. An attempt to consolidate the Native and non-Native schools at Juneau was foiled by local resistance. In other areas of Alaska the schools served mostly, if not all, Native children because there were few non-Native children. The schools stretched from Metlakatla at Alaska's southern tip to Gambell on St. Lawrence Island in the Bering Sea.[10]

The growing non-Native population brought to Alaska in the wake of the Klondike Gold Rush of 1898 expressed growing dissatisfaction with a school system that seemed to focus on the education of Native children. In response, Congress included in a 1900 Civil Code for Alaska authorization for incorporated towns to establish and operate schools for White children. In 1904 Congress passed the Nelson Act. The act directed the District of Alaska to assume responsibility for education of "white and colored children and children of mixed blood who live a civilized life." It further specified that the Secretary of the Interior would retain direction and control of schools for Eskimos and Indian children.[11]

Although the Russian American Company was no longer a factor in Alaska, the goal of education for Alaska Native children remained much the same as it had in the Russia era: "so that the White man can use these men for things that are useful for his civilization." Harlan Updergraff replaced Jackson as director of Native education in Alaska, working under the title of Chief of the Alaska Division, Bureau of Education.[12]

Under Updergraff, bureau educational objectives continued to reflect assimilationist philosophy. In 1910 the bureau desired to mold the future development of Native villages and the Natives "by their guidance in all phases of life, in the schoolroom, industrial room, kitchen, bathroom, home, and herd." But for the first time the bureau recognized the unique requirements of Alaska Natives. While still grounded in assimilationist philosophy, the new objectives recognized a need to develop Native industries adapted to the region and to the Natives' abilities.[13]

Congress passed Alaska's Second Organic Act in 1912. This established Alaska as a territory, with a territorial legislature. Although prohibited by the act from changing existing school laws, the 1915 Territorial Legislature tried to establish a uniform school system. The legislation for this purpose excluded schools for Natives "which are now or may hereafter come under the control of the Federal Government.[14]

The Solicitor of the Interior Department ruled the legislation invalid when it reached Washington. It made clear, nevertheless, the intent of the Territory not to be responsible for the education of Alaska Natives. When Congress amended the Second Organic Act to allow the Territorial Legislature to pass school laws, the 1917 Legislature restated the exclusion of Alaska Natives from the territorial school system.[15]

Thus, 1917 gave official sanction to a mostly segregated school system in Alaska. In that year 46 territorial rural schools enrolled 1,162 pupils. The federal Bureau of Education concurrently operated 71 rural schools that enrolled 3,500 pupils. Children, mostly non-Native, in incorporated municipalities continued to be served by city-operated schools. There were exceptions. The Territorial Commissioner of Education wrote in his 1920 report:

> no objection is made (to attendance of Natives at Territorial Schools) where the admission of Natives does not interfere seriously with the progress of the school and where their admission does not precipitate a quarrel because of divided sentiment. In other words, the question of admission of Native children has been left very largely in the hands of the local school boards.[16]

Despite the intention to maintain racially segregated schools, this did not happen. Neither the territorial government nor the Bureau of Education had enough money to establish schools in each rural community. Over time duplicate schools disappeared and de facto integration occurred to the extent that small community schools occasionally included both Native and non-Native children. By the time of statehood in 1959, there would be 6,144 Native students in territorial schools and 4,300 Native students in federal schools.[17]

Throughout the years the territorial school system, regardless of the number of Native students it served, continued to offer a Western curriculum. The federally operated system, in contrast, included Native games and dances in its 1926 curriculum. Other curriculum elements for the Bureau of Education–operated schools included Health and Sanitation; Agriculture and Industry; Decencies, Safety, and Comforts of Home; Healthful Recreation and Amusements; and Basic Education and Industrial Schools. To further this curriculum the Bureau of Education established three vocational schools for Alaska Natives. The schools were at Eklutna, Kanakanak, and White Mountain.[18]

In 1931 the Secretary of the Interior transferred responsibility for education of Alaska Natives from the Bureau of Education to the Bureau of Indian Affairs (BIA). With appointment of John Collier as Commissioner of Indian Affairs in 1934, the BIA adopted dual-purpose education for Native Americans, including Alaska Natives. Collier said when taking office:

> Indians whose culture, civic tradition, and inherited institutions are still strong and virile should be encouraged and helped to develop their life in their own patterns, not as segregated minorities but as noble elements in our common life. At the same time, the individual Indian is entitled to every opportunity which the nation offers to any citizen. This means that he is entitled to the fullest educational privileges, not in sequestrated institutions but in the schools and colleges which serve us all.[19]

Congress reflected some of the concerns expressed by Collier in 1934 when it authorized financial assistance to territories and states operating public schools on tax-exempt Native-occupied lands. Practice failed to fulfill policy, however. When Alaskan officials were unable to obtain federal funding for territorial schools with mostly Native student bodies, they began to transfer the schools to the BIA. By 1939 19 schools had been transferred from territorial to BIA jurisdiction.[20]

Evaluations of the era revealed that BIA schools were not meeting the federal education policy goals of (1) integrating Natives in White culture and (2) preserving Native culture. A 1935 survey concluded that the curricula in rural schools in Alaska were an inept patchwork of various American textbooks quite unsuited to an Eskimo environment. A 1941 study reached similar conclusions: "this academic type of curriculum is especially ill-suited to the needs of Native children, who constitute a large majority in the rural schools."[21]

When World War II came to Alaska in the early 1940s, Native and non-Native contact intensified throughout the territory. As a result BIA adopted a new policy for assimilation. Instead of converting entire Native groups to White culture, individual Natives would be prepared for assimilation. At the same time the Territorial Attorney General issued an opinion which stated that the Territory was obligated to provide education for Native children either in traditionally White schools or in separate but equal segregated schools.[22]

At the close of World War II, the Territorial Commissioner of Education proposed a single territorially operated school system for Natives and non-Natives alike. He also insisted on a common curriculum for all students. This initiative was unsuccessful. The BIA continued to operate a separate school system for Alaska Natives.[23]

To facilitate its new policy of individual assimilation, the BIA in 1947 opened a high school for Natives at the site of a World War II Naval Air Station at Sitka. Known as Mount Edgecumbe, the school took Native students from all over Alaska. It offered both academic and vocational instruction. If Mount Edgecumbe was full, Alaska Native students were sent to boarding schools operated by the BIA in other states. The bureau also operated an elementary school at Wrangell for children from communities with no school facilities at all. The philosophical emphasis of the BIA program changed from keeping Native children in their home communities to taking them out of their communities and encouraging them not to return.[24]

In 1951 the BIA began to transfer some of the schools it had been operating to the Territory of Alaska for operation as contract schools. This process continued after Alaska became a state in 1959 and was completed in 1985.[25]

With statehood in 1959 came formation in 1965–1966 of a State Operated School System designed to provide centralized management of schools in rural Alaska. By the 1960s the generally agreed-upon goal of the education system was to equip Alaska Native youth to function in either Native or non-Native cultures. In 1975 the state disbanded the State Operated School System. Twenty-one regionally controlled school districts were set up to provide local control of schools. Community School Committees supplemented regional school boards to further emphasize local participation in school management.[26]

Federal policy also changed in the mid-1970s and placed emphasis on local control of schools. Public Law 95–561 assigned most control over BIA schools to tribal governing bodies or to school boards appointed by tribal governing bodies. These tribal entities had more control than that delegated by the state to regional school boards and Community School Committees.[27]

State Operated Schools, when in existence, also provided education in grades 8 through 12 at several regional high schools. Established as a result of studies in the 1960s, the regional high schools were discontinued in the 1970s. Students' inability to fit comfortably back into village life after attending the regional high schools plus appalling alcohol abuse and suicide rates in the student populations led policy makers to reevaluate the regional high school concept.[28]

State-funded village high schools became a reality in the late 1970s. Taken into court by plaintiffs who argued a constitutional right to K–12 education in a student's home community, the state settled out of court in 1975. In the settlement the state agreed to provide a high school in every community that has an elementary school. One hundred and ten communities out of 126 eligible chose to have a local high school. Later, 10 of the 16 that originally chose not to have a local high school reversed their original decisions.[29]

In the words of the most thorough study to date of the federal and state school systems operated in Alaska from 1867 to 1970:

> Policy makers over the years have vacillated between attempted assimilation of the Native population into white society and protection of their cultural identity.[30]

That study goes on to report that throughout the history of these systems, non-Natives determined policy and developed programs under the premise that they knew what was best for Native education.[31]

II. Contemporary Background

A. Current Western Education and Alaska Natives, K–12

1. Alaska Native Students in the 1990s
In the 1989–1990 school year, 68 percent of Alaska's K–12 students were White; 21 percent were Alaska Native; and 11 percent were from other

ethnic groups. Twenty-two of Alaska's 54 school districts had student populations of 75 percent or more Alaska Natives. Twenty-nine districts (over half) had student populations of 50 percent or more Alaska Natives.[32] These percentages did not change dramatically in 1990–1991 school year when, of Alaska's 110,982 K–12 students, 24,453 or 22 percent were Alaska Natives.[33]

In some school districts up to 30 percent of Native children in elementary school are below grade level. In grades 7 through 12 the figure jumps up to over 40 percent.[34] Despite this failure of the school system, some students are passed from grade to grade and finally graduated without achieving academic competency. According to one Native Alaskan who testified before the Alaska Natives Commission:

> Education in the Bush for our students is nothing but social passing. A kid in school; he doesn't read or write well; he's passed along; he's old—too old to be in school; he's too big; he's whatever; he('s) disruptive; so we're not going to educat(e) him; we're going to pass him through.[35]

Another observer noted that many Alaska Native high school graduates can't read at the sixth-grade level or do sixth-grade math.[36]

Overall, about 30 percent of Alaskan students entering high school wind up not graduating. In urban areas, about 60 percent of Alaska Natives entering high school do not graduate, while in rural areas only 12 to 15 percent do not graduate. However, the high rural graduation rate is countered by much lower-than-average student achievement levels.[37]

Students in over one-third (20 of 54) of Alaska's school districts scored on average below the 22nd percentile in either reading, mathematics, or language arts at the 4th, 6th, or 8th grade. On average, Natives constituted 87 percent of the children in these districts. Nineteen of the 20 lower-performance districts had populations that were 60 to 98 percent Native students.[38]

The failure of the schools to adequately prepare Alaska Natives is also reflected in tests such as the American College Test (ACT) and Scholastic Aptitude Test (SAT) taken by students preparing to graduate from high school. According to a 1989 address by a former chancellor of the University of Alaska Fairbanks:

> Caucasian Alaskans had an average composite score of 20.7 (on the ACT), almost two points above the national average; American Indian groups (outside Alaska) had

an average score of 14.9, while Alaska Natives had an average score of 12.2.[39]

This means that Alaska Natives had ACT scores about 40 percent, on average, lower than those of White students. As the following table shows, this inadequate preparation of Alaska Natives for pre-college testing is also confirmed by SAT results.

Table 1: Scholastic Aptitude Test Scores by Ethnicity

Race	Math Average Score	Verbal Average Score	Total Average Score
Alaska Natives/ Native Americans	430	370	800
All Students in Alaska	476	438	914

Source: Riverside Publishing Co., Report of State Averages and Responses to Student Questionnaire, Iowa Tests of Basic Skills, November 1990.

In the instance of the ACT, and presumably the SAT, however, these statistics have been illuminated by more investigation. A 1987 questionnaire sent to students taking these tests revealed that only a small percentage of Alaska Natives taking them had studied subjects such as chemistry, American history, second-year algebra. Fifty-three percent of all Alaska students had taken second-year algebra versus only 11 percent of Alaska Native students. Forty-eight percent of all Alaska students had taken chemistry versus 8 percent of Alaska Native students. Sixty-seven percent of all Alaska students had taken American history versus 15 percent of Alaska Native students. These are among the studies that help students to acquire the habits of critical thinking and concepts necessary to do well on the college screening tests. Alaska Native students who reported taking these courses had ACT scores resembling those of non-Natives.[40]

In addition to Alaska Native students who are short-changed by the instruction they receive, there are others who leave school prior to graduation. On a statewide basis, only about 67 percent of Alaska Native students complete high school. This compares to a total statewide completion rate of 75 percent. The drop-outs who do not complete high school suffer many adverse consequences. Generally, they are left with low academic skills, lack of employment opportunities, limited opportunities of further education or training, and high potential for development of mental and physical health and social problems.[41]

Surveys conducted for the 1990–1991 school year indicate that Alaska Native students leaving school before graduation did so for a variety of reasons. Of the 914 Alaska Native drop-outs interviewed for the survey, 267 (almost 30 percent) had been dropped either administratively or for truancy, or they had been expelled. The second largest group, about 20 percent, said that they had dropped out due to family reasons. Another 11 percent left school early due to medical reasons (including pregnancy), and 8 percent indicated they left school because they were failing academically.[42]

2. Factors Contributing to Educational Success and Failure

Many reasons are cited for Alaska Native students' lack of academic success. The reasons include the economic situation in which many find themselves; endemic medical and social problems; the difficulty of succeeding in a system based on values of another culture and managed to a large extent by people from another culture; and, for rural Alaska Natives, limitations thought to be inherent in small schools.

a. **General.** A recent study of lower-performance school districts found them to have these common characteristics:

> rural and remote; small with low pupil/teacher ratios; cultural and linguistic differences (from the predominate White culture); high rate of poverty and low per capita income; high rates of students classed as learning disabled; and high rates of teacher turnover.[43]

Alaska, with an area of 586,000 square miles, and its population scattered over those miles, necessarily has a number of rural and remote school districts. As a result of the *Tobeluk v. Lind* settlement of 1976, state school regulations require that a school district must provide local secondary education if the local school committee wants it, if the community has an elementary school, and if one or more children are available to attend secondary school. As a result, there are over 100 small rural and remote high schools in Alaska.[44]

These 100-plus small rural schools are included in 31 predominately rural school districts that serve over 19,000 students. Of these students, over 14,000 are Alaska Natives. Only 7 percent of the instructional staff serving these students are themselves Alaska Natives. Another 9,500 Alaska Native students attend nonrural schools. In these schools, less than 2 percent of the instructional staff are Alaska Natives.[45]

In the rural schools, over 12 percent of the student population are classified as Chapter I pupils. This means that their educational attainment is below the level appropriate for children of their age according to regulations of the United States Department of Education. In nonrural schools, less than 4 percent of the student population are classified as Chapter I pupils. In rural and nonrural schools combined, Alaska Native students make up over 49 percent of Chapter I students. Also, in the rural schools, nearly 40 percent of the students are classified as bilingual/bicultural, as compared to less than 4 percent for students in nonrural schools.[46]

Nearly all rural Alaska schools recognize and attempt to accommodate the bilingual/bicultural nature of their students. Bilingual programs designed to help with English are offered in 53 percent of Alaska's small schools. Bilingual programs designed to maintain Native languages are offered in 62 percent of Alaska's small schools. Eighty percent of these schools offer instruction in community history and cultural traditions. Eighty-five percent of these schools offer instruction in local economic skills such as trapping. Eighty-nine percent offer instruction in subjects such as land claims and Native corporations that are of particular relevance to Alaska Natives.[47]

b. Teacher Turnover. High teacher turnover is a fact of life in Alaska's rural schools. Nationally, and also in Alaska, teacher retention in rural schools plots as a U shape. Rural schools tend to have some teachers with little experience, some teachers with much experience, and few teachers with a midrange of experience.[48]

Rural schools in Alaska have an approximate 30 percent teacher turnover rate. This means that at the end of any given school year, about 500 of the 1,600 teachers employed in rural Alaska leave for other jobs.[49]

The high turnover means that teachers often do not have enough time to adjust to the schools and communities in which they find themselves and that school-community communications must begin anew each year. As a result, students in rural schools are placed at a disadvantage. Responsibility for this condition can be apportioned among institutions that train teachers, agencies that certify teachers, school administrators that hire teachers, and teachers themselves.

Institutions that produce teachers frequently do not produce the generalists that rural schools need. They also often do not provide student teaching and internships that acquaint their students with the unique challenges and rewards of teaching in a rural, multicultural setting. These institutions also need to expand opportunities for professional development of teachers who are on the job in rural schools.[50]

Agencies that certify teachers also bear some responsibility for high teacher turnover in rural areas. By not establishing different criteria for rural and metropolitan teaching certificates, they fail to alert candidates to the differing requirements of rural and metropolitan teaching and do not give school officials knowledge that they need to make good hiring decisions.[51]

School officials also contribute to the problem of high teacher turnover. Some turn to the institutions in which they were trained or Outside school districts in which they have worked as sources of candidates for teaching positions. In many cases, excellent, newly graduated teachers or outstanding teachers from other areas are simply not prepared for the exigencies of teaching in rural Alaska.

Teachers sometimes set themselves up as agents of high teacher turnover. Some fail to understand the differing conditions of rural and metropolitan teaching. They may not have prepared themselves academically for those conditions and be frustrated once on the job by finding themselves ill-equipped for the tasks they are asked to perform.[52]

c. **Size of Student Population.** Despite the seeming association between small rural schools and low performance, specialists in rural education point out that they can offer several advantages to their students. These advantages include:

> low student-teacher ratios; opportunities for teachers to get to know students and their families; opportunities for teachers to significantly influence the lives of their students; relative freedom from burdensome bureaucracy; and, economies of scale.[53]

The small schools are, some investigators have noted, similar to the alternative schools offered in nonrural areas. They offer a personalized atmosphere, a sense of community, and individualized instruction tailored to students' academic background.[54]

The same specialists admit that small rural schools cannot be comprehensive. They lack the diversity of teachers, pupils, and courses as well as the extracurricular activities. On the other hand, they point out, small rural schools have a wealth of advantages that make them among the most promising educational opportunities to be found anywhere.[55]

Thus, there is some evidence that simply being rural and remote and having low teacher-student ratios are not necessarily ingredients of low performance.

d. **Poverty and Student Performance.** Children living in poverty are one-third less likely to graduate from high school than other children,[56] and Alaska Natives were the largest group of the Alaska population to live in poverty. In 1989, one in every five Alaska Natives lived in poverty versus one in 15 Alaskans generally.[57]

In Alaska's rural school districts, over 47 percent of the students lived in poverty as of the 1990–1991 school year. This compares to 17 percent in nonrural schools districts. Rural districts did not, however, have significantly higher proportions of learning-disabled students than did nonrural school districts (15.33 percent versus 12.39 percent).[58]

School-age Alaska Native children, like Native American children throughout the United States, are bored, burned out, unhappy, and worried, according to a recent report. A national survey of Indian and Native youth revealed that 21 percent of the girls and 12 percent of the boys have attempted suicide; 46 percent of the girls and 56 percent of the boys have used hard liquor; and 26 percent of the girls and 9 percent of the boys have been sexually abused. Less than 50 percent of the Indian and Native youth lived with both parents.[59]

e. **The Cultural Divide.** Another reason cited for Alaska Native students' lack of academic success is a dearth of Native teachers. Native teachers, it is believed, are better able to understand Native ways of learning and to establish bridges between schools and the communities in which they are located.

Native ways of learning are different than traditional Western ways of learning. Much of this is attributable to the high value placed on cooperation by Native culture as opposed to the high value placed on individualism by Western culture. In the words of Mr. John Active, a Yupik who spoke at a University of Alaska Faculty Convocation in 1992, Native students have to become another person, an opposite of their natural selves, to succeed in a traditional American school setting. Traditional Native learning emphasizes quiet observation as opposed to the questioning and active participation emphasized by American-trained educators.

The gaps that the bridges must cross are illustrated by a recent incident in a rural Alaska community. A federal official who had been in the community on non related business for only a few hours was asked by residents of the predominately Native village to talk with the school principal. The principal needed to know, they said, that the instructor hired to teach Native language was teaching their children the wrong dialect. When the federal official asked why the parents did not talk with the principal themselves, the parents replied that the principal would not listen to them because they were Natives.[60]

The cultural differences between students and teachers in Alaska's rural schools are exacerbated by a lack of Native teachers and administrators. In 1991 Alaska Natives made up less than one-tenth (9.5 percent) of the workforce within Alaska's elementary and secondary schools. More than two-thirds of them were instructional aides based mainly in rural schools. Of the nearly 7,000 elementary and secondary teachers statewide, less than 4 percent (1990: 3.2 percent; 1991: 3.7 percent) were Alaska Natives. Out of about 250 certificated Alaska Native teachers, a total of 244 were employed as instructional staff in the 1990–1991 school year. This included 164 in rural schools and 80 in nonrural schools. Only a small percentage of school administrators, however, were Alaska Natives.

B. CURRENT WESTERN EDUCATION AND ALASKA NATIVES, POST-SECONDARY

Alaska had 30,793 students enrolled in all of its colleges in 1990. The 2,793 Alaska Natives enrolled in the colleges constitute 9 percent of the total in-state population enrolled in post-secondary institutions. Comprehensive figures are not available, but at least another 280 Alaska Native students were enrolled in colleges outside Alaska.

Table 2: Enrollment by Ethnicity at Alaska Colleges—1990

	% Alaska Natives	% Asian	% Black	% Hispanic	% White	% Foreign	Total
Alaska Bible College	5.4	0.0	1.1	0.0	90.3	3.2	93
Alaska Junior College	15.8	3.2	15.5	4.7	60.8	0.0	342
Alaska Pacific University	8.2	2.2	5.7	3.2	78.2	2.4	1,031
Sheldon Jackson College	27.9	1.0	1.3	1.3	68.5	0.0	308
U of AK Anchorage	5.2	2.8	4.3	2.5	84.0	1.2	18,383
U of AK Fairbanks	15.5	1.8	2.4	1.4	75.5	3.5	7,663
U of AK Southeast	13.1	2.3	1.1	81.3	0.7	0.7	2,973

Source: The Chronicle of Higher Education, March 3, 1993, p. 21.

Native enrollment in post-secondary institutions does appear to be increasing. Native enrollment at the University of Alaska Anchorage is said to have increased 50 percent between 1987 and 1991.

Of those Alaska Native students who do make it to college, according to one long-time Native education administrator, only about half succeed in graduating. What data are available appear to bear this out. According to a University of Alaska Anchorage study, that school's retention of Alaska Natives over a five-semester period averaged 58 percent with retention for specific semesters ranging from a low of 43.8 percent (spring 1989) to a high of 86.5 percent (fall 1988).[61] A lack of standard data and reporting, however, make comprehensive conclusions about Alaska Native retention rates impossible to reach.

According to the UAA study on student retention, of 140 Alaska Natives who enrolled in 1987 for the first time, only eight remained three years later. This 5.7 percent retention rate for Alaska Natives compared to a 10.6 percent retention rate for White students. These rates consider only students who left UAA and do not indicate whether or not they transferred to other schools or returned to UAA later. Overall, the university is said to lose about 60 percent of Native students between their freshman and sophomore years.[62]

Table 3: Ethnicity in Population and College Enrollment in Alaska

Ethnicity	% of Total Population	% of College Enrollment
Alaska Natives/ American Indians	15.6	8.87
Asian/Pacific Islanders	3.6	2.4
Blacks	4.1	3.6
Whites	75.5	81.33
Other and Unknown	1.2	1.56
Hispanics (may be any race)	3.2	2.12

Source: The Chronicle of Higher Education, Almanac, August 26, 1992.

The University of Alaska Fairbanks (UAF) has not conducted a study of Alaska Native drop-outs. It has conducted a study of its Alaska Native graduates for a 10-year period. The study revealed that an increasing number of Alaska Natives have earned degrees at UAF over the last two decades. Most of the increase came, however, between 1989 and 1992.[63]

Of the total of 445 Alaska Natives who received one kind of degree or another at UAF, 107 received associate degrees. Of these two-year degrees, 72 percent were in the General Program. Other majors attracting relatively large numbers of Alaska Native graduates included Human Services Technology (8 percent) and Office Management and Technology (also 8 percent). The remaining Alaska Native graduates at the associate level majored in subjects ranging from Airframe & Powerplant to Science.[64]

Of the total 318 Alaska Natives who received bachelor's degrees at UAF between 1976 and 1992, over 40 percent majored in Education. Other majors attracting relatively large numbers of Alaska Native graduates included Business Administration (8 percent), Psychology (7 percent), and Social Work (5 percent). The remaining graduates at the bachelors level majored in subjects ranging from Accounting (one graduate) to Wildlife Management (two graduates).[65] During the same period, 20 Alaska Natives earned master's degrees at UAF. Of these, 75 percent majored in Education. The other 25 percent majored in subjects ranging from Anthropology to Geology. No Alaska Natives earned doctoral degrees at UAF during the period of the study.[66]

Other branches of the University of Alaska and small colleges in the state have not conducted similar studies. Alaska Junior College, a two-year proprietary institution in Anchorage focusing on career-oriented courses, did review its records for 1990–1993. Out of 96 Alaska Natives enrolled in those years (about 5 percent of the total student population), 50 percent withdrew before graduation. Nineteen percent of the Alaska Native students enrolled during the period graduated, in contrast to 94 percent of the non-Native students enrolled in the same period.[67]

Standard data are also not available for Alaska Native students enrolled in post-secondary schools outside Alaska. Native organizations assisting students financially could provide incidental information for the 1992–1993 school year. The Bristol Bay Native Association reported that it assisted 26 college students attending institutions outside Alaska. Out of the 26, only one dropped out and one transferred back to Alaska. Central Council, Tlingit and Haida Tribes of Alaska, assisted 235 students. Of these, 64 students attended college in Alaska and 171 attended college outside Alaska.

Of all of those students, between 41 percent (fall 1992) and 53 percent (winter 1993) attained honor roll status. Chugachmiut had eight students enrolled outside Alaska. Their grade point averages ranged from 2.35 to 3.09. Kawerak, Inc. (in school year 1991–1992) assisted 61 students at in-state institutions and 25 at out-of-state institutions. None dropped out of school.

Kotzebue IRA assisted three students in attending out-of-state colleges. Their grade points averaged 3.0 or better. Nome Eskimo Community funded six students attending post-secondary institutions outside Alaska and 14 attending post-secondary institutions inside Alaska. The six students had an average grade point average of 2.98. Tanana Chiefs Conference funded 48 college students, whose grade point averages ranged from 1.60 to 3.80.[68]

Why some Alaska Native students have difficulty in college can probably be linked to inadequate preparation in high school and to some of the same conditions that make it difficult for them to succeed in high school. One national study has noted that the overall Native American high school drop-out rate is declining. This is attributed to parental involvement, belief in the relevance of education, community-based curriculum, appropriate teaching styles, caring teachers and administrators, and holistic early intervention programs. The study goes on to suggest that similar qualities would increase Native American successes at the post-secondary level.[69]

III. Findings and Recommendations

A. Principal Findings

1. Skills Necessary for Success

Children are the most important segment of any community, for each community's future lies in its children. To assure that future, the children must be given, through education, the skills that will enable them to succeed in life and the understanding that will continue the community's values. For Alaska Native children, this means that they must receive an integrated education that encompasses two sets of skills and two sets of values.

The first set of skills is that necessary for the children to succeed in traditional Native lifeways. The second set of skills is that necessary for the children to succeed in Western society. The children's education must also integrate Native and Western values so that they are empowered in both cultures. The skills and values are inseparable, for mastery of one cannot be obtained without mastery of the other.

This ideal of an integrated education has not been achieved, or even accepted, in the past. Alaska Native children enter an education system developed by Western culture. In past years the system had eradication of Native culture as one of its objectives. Even after this misguided goal was abandoned, the system still proved unable to meet its own fundamental objective: education of Native children in the skills and values necessary to succeed in Western society.

2. Failure of the Public Education System

This inability of the education system in its current form to meet the needs of Alaska Native children is manifested in many ways. Traditional measures of success in America's public education system include academic achievement, preparation for higher education, readiness to enter the workforce, capacity for leadership, and ability to participate in a self-governing society. Ability to achieve success in these areas is distributed no differently among our children than among non-Native children.

Notwithstanding their innate capacity, too many Alaska Native children consistently score lower than norm groups on standardized tests that are said to measure academic achievement, fail to graduate from high school in acceptable numbers, experience unusual difficulty in moving from high school to college work, do not have the skills potential employers expect, and are ill-equipped to participate in a self-governing society that depends upon a literate and well-informed citizenry.

Despite the success of several innovative local programs, on a statewide basis the public education system now serving Alaska Native children fails to provide an education that will prepare them for life. In too many cases, the education system does not provide our children the education they need to become good citizens, productive adults, and individuals with self-respect and dignity in the communities of their choice.

3. Failure of the Social System

The most thoughtfully designed education system, most up-to-date school facilities, best-trained and carefully selected teachers, brilliantly conceived and executed curricula, and unimpeachable intentions will not, by themselves, significantly improve the educational situation of Alaska Native students. The environments in which many young Alaska Natives find themselves must be rid of alcohol and drug abuse, dysfunctional families, and poverty. Parents and the community must join in the education process if the education system is to do all that it might. Ironically, improved education is part of the solution to these problems and must begin immediately if Alaska Natives are to survive as a distinct culture and with the fulfilling lives to which all Americans are entitled.

4. Needs and Issues

As previously discussed, there are many reasons why the education system as a whole has not adequately served the needs of Alaska Native children. They include economic, health, and social issues as well as differences between Western and Native ways of learning. Some spring from other issues in Alaska Native life being examined by other task forces of the Alaska Natives Commission. To address needs and issues within the purview of the Education Task Force:

- Alaska's education system needs to design model curricula and alternative delivery modes that will prepare Native students to function in Western society while acquiring a clearer understanding of their cultural heritage and traditional lifeways;
- Alaska's education system needs to prepare Native students to be at home in and adapted to rural life as well as urban life;

- Alaska's education system needs to supply teachers knowledgeable of and with respect for Native cultures who are equipped to take advantage of Native ways of learning;
- Alaska's education system needs to accommodate locally created and culturally relevant standards for teachers and students and to assure that teachers and students meet those standards;
- The Native community, including parents and community leaders, needs to achieve a compelling voice in the direction of and widespread ownership of the educational system;
- Replacement of obsolete BIA facilities that never met state codes and standards is critical;
- Facilities built in the future should be designed so that students see the schools as an extension of their community's local culture; and,
- Native arts, fine arts, music (band and chorus) must be included as sources of ongoing recreation.

5. Addressing Needs and Issues

Federally funded supplemental programs should include Native operation of contract programs providing early childhood education as a form of choice and contract programs providing post-secondary education (grade 13). Contract programs providing instruction to administrators, teachers, and students in Native cultural behavior, heritage, and language are needed, as are Regional Education Institutes offering educational services supplemental to those available in village schools. These, too, should be operated by Natives.

Tribally-controlled colleges providing higher education opportunities specifically aimed at nurturing the cultural, social, economic, and political aspirations of Alaska Natives are also necessary and, again, should be Native operated.

B. RECOMMENDATIONS REGARDING ALASKA NATIVE EDUCATION

1. Three-Component K–12 Education System

Continue or take action necessary to create a three-component K–12 education system of Alaska Natives that includes: home community K–12 schooling that is the right of every American child; distance education delivery that effectively redresses the limitations inherent in small rural schools; regional academic and vocational schools that effectively redress the limitations of small rural schools that cannot be overcome by internal improvements and distance education delivery; and vocational schools that adapt curricula to regional and local needs.

2. Total Local Control of Schools
Establish total local control of schools by recasting advisory boards as policy-making boards and increasing Native administrators and teachers through affirmative hiring and alternative certification.

3. Model Curricula for Alaska Native Students
Establish model curricula that meet the needs of Alaska Native students by engaging Native scholars and educators in developing: model K–12 curricula differentiated on a regional basis; model post-secondary programs that will aid Native students in the transition from high school to college or vocational education; and model programs that will aid Native students in becoming proficient in skills necessary to continue the subsistence tradition.

4. Recruitment and Training of Native Professionals
Recruit and train educational staff, including local Native professionals, to meet the special circumstances of Alaska Native students by providing: incentives to Native college students to become teachers; incentives for Native teacher aides to become certified; alternative certification avenues to encourage qualified Native professionals to enter the field of education; alternative certification avenues to establish a role in K–12 education for elders learned in Native culture, traditions, and learning styles; incentives to Native teachers to become school administrators; and instruction in Native culture and language for all teachers and educational administrators certified in Alaska, whether rural or urban.

5. Involvement of Parents and Community
Encourage Native parents and community leaders to become and stay involved with the education of Native children by: establishing ongoing community relations programs that encourage parents to become active participants in the education of their children; making schools places where Native parents feel comfortable and know that their contributions are valued; and encouraging Alaska Native leaders and elders to devote part of their effort to monitoring and improving Native education.

6. Subject Matter Prerequisites
Require a major in a subject matter discipline as a prerequisite for completion of a professional teacher education program at all campuses of the University of Alaska.

7. Teacher Preparation for Village Schools

Require teacher training programs that prepare new teachers and upgrade in-service teachers for assignment in village schools to be standard offerings of the University of Alaska system and routinely available as a means to qualify candidates for teacher certificate endorsements appropriate to a system of certification that distinguishes between competencies necessary to teach in village Alaska and traditional teaching assignments.

8. Distinguishing Qualifications for Teaching in Village Schools

Enact legislation establishing teaching certificates that distinguish between qualifications for teaching in rural schools and qualifications for teaching in metropolitan schools such as qualification in multiple and varied subjects.

9. Teaching Certificates in Nontraditional Fields

Enact legislation establishing limited teaching certificates in fields where baccalaureate degree training is not sufficiently available (such as Native languages) so long as the person to be certificated demonstrates both subject matter expertise and teaching competency.

10. Certification in Native Language and Culture

Allow Alaska Native language, culture, and vocational experts to attain certification as classroom teachers once their competence as teachers has been documented through the State Department of Education.

11. Teacher Tenure Requirements

Amend Sec. 14.20.150(2) of the Alaska Administrative Code to extend years necessary to qualify for teacher tenure to five years, and institute remedies to decrease teacher turnover to enhance student learning and to maintain stability in school programs.

12. Graduation Requirements

Amend minimum state high school graduation requirements to require one credit in Alaska history and culture, and also include environmental education and health education as required curricula.

13. Funding for Curricula Appropriate for Native Students

Enact legislation appropriating specific funding for schools serving Alaska Native children to develop and use linguistically, culturally, and developmentally appropriate curricula, and re-energize the LEARNALASKA Network to provide alternative education in rural Alaska.

14. Indian/Native Education Programs for all Native Students
Amend legislation authorizing Indian/Native education programs to include funding eligibility and accessibility in all areas that includes Alaska Natives.

15. Upgrade and Replacements of Rural Schools
The federal government should appropriate one-time funding of $50 million to $100 million for upgrade or replacement of former Bureau of Indian Affairs schools, and long-term planning for school construction that ensures timely replacement of obsolete plants should be instituted.

ENDNOTES

1   Frank Darnell "Alaska's Dual Federal-State School System: A History and Descriptive Analysis," Ed.D. dissertation, Wayne State University, 1970, microfilm (University Microfilms 71–396), p. 99.
2   Darnell, pp. 99–102.
3   Darnell, pp. 104–105.
4   Darnell, p. 110; p. 112.
5   Darnell, pp. 108–109.
6   Darnell, p. 122.
7   Darnell, pp. 129–130; p. 142.
8   Quoted in Darnell, p. 132.
9   Superintendent of Industrial Training and Boarding School (at Sitka), 1872, quoted in Darnell, p. 131.
10 Darnell, pp. 135–136.
11 Darnell, p. 142, p. 15, p. 152, p. 157.
12 Darnell, p. 171.
13 Darnell, p. 173.
14 Darnell, pp. 174–176.
15 Darnell, pp. 176–177.
16 Quoted in Darnell, p. 183.
17 Darnell, pp. 184–185.
18 Darnell, pp. 193–194.
19 Quoted in Darnell, pp. 196–197.
20 Darnell, p. 198.
21 Damell, pp. 201–202.
22 Darnell, p. 204.
23 Darnell, p. 214.
24 Darnell, pp. 204–205.
25 Darnell, p. 225.
26 Marilou Madden with Brad Pierce and Bob Silverman, "When Money Isn't Enough: Nonfiscal Influences on Student Achievement in Remote Areas of Alaska," copy provided by Dr. Madden, p.3.
27 Madden, et al., p. 5.
28 Madden, et al., p. 10.

29   Judith S. Kleinfeld with G. Williamson McDiarmid and David Hagstrom, *Alaska's Small Rural High Schools: Are They Working?* (Anchorage: Institute of Social and Economic Research, Center for Cross-Cultural Studies, University of Alaska, December 1985), p. 5.

30   Darnell, p. 352.

31   Darnell, p. 352.

32   Alaska Department of Education, Improving School Performance—A Report to the Sixteenth Alaska Legislature, Appendix B, "Extent of the At-Risk Problem," February 1, 1990.

33   Office of Data Management, Alaska Department of Education, Profiles of Alaska's Public School Districts—Fiscal Year 1991 (July 1, 1990—June 30, 1992), p. 11.

34   Testimony of Eileen Norbert, former Director of Native Programs, Nome Schools, before the Alaska Native Commission, Nome, Alaska, September 21, 1992, in records of the Alaska Native Commission.

35   Testimony of Dazee, Executive Director, Bering Strait Economic Council, Inc., before the Alaska Natives Commission at Nome, September 21, 1992, in records of the Alaska Natives Commission.

36   Testimony of Robert Silas, Tanana Chiefs Sub-Regional Village Liaison Officer, before the Alaska Natives Commission at Fairbanks, July 18, 1992, in records of the Alaska Natives Commission.

37   Alaska Department of Education, Appendix B, "Extent of the At-Risk Problem."

38   "Common Characteristics of the Twenty Lowest Achieving School Districts in Alaska," Appendix C, in Alaska Department of Education, Improving School Performance—A Report to the Sixteenth Alaska Legislature, February 1, 1990.

39   Patrick O'Rourke, unpublished Convocation Address, University of Alaska Fairbanks, 1989, quoted in Joint Committee on School Performance, New Directives in School Performance: The Legislature as Advocate and Guarantor—Report of the Joint Committee an School Performance to the Seventeenth Alaska Legislature (Juneau: January 1991), p. 19.

40   Senate Special Committee on School Performance, Fifteenth Alaska Legislature Helping Schools Succeed at Helping All Children Learn (Juneau: Alaska State Legislature, January 1989), p. 22, p. 85.

41   Alaska Department of Education, Office of Data Management, Report on Early Leaver Project Phases I and II 1989 through Fall 1990 (Juneau: Alaska Department of Education, 1991); Karen Swisher et al. American Indian/Alaska Native Dropout Study (Washington, D.C.: National Education Association, 1991), ERIC Document ED 354126, p. 7.

42   Office of Data Management, Alaska Department of Education, Alaska Statewide Early Leaver Report, School Year 1990–91 (Juneau: April 1992), p. 23.

43   Madden. p. 13.

44   AAC 05.040 cited in Kleinfeld, p. 5.

45   Office of Data Management, Alaska Department of Education, Profiles of Alaska's Public School Districts Fiscal Year 1991 (Juneau: Alaska Department of Education, April 1992), pp. 12–121.

46   Office of Data Management, pp. 12–121; p. 123; Fax, "Alaska Native Participation Rates," Division of School Finance, Alaska Department of Education to Alaska Natives Commission, August 20,1993, in files of the Alaska Natives Commission.

47   Kleinfeld et al. p. A-6.

48   Doug Stong. "Facilitating Certification and Professional Development for Small Schools," ERIC Digest: Small Schools, ED 260884, March 1985, p. 4.

48   Joint Committee on School Performance, New Directives in School Performance: The Legislature as Advocate and Guarantor, Executive Summary, Report of the Joint

Committee on School Performance to the Seventeenth Alaska Legislature (Juneau: Alaska State Legislature, January 1991), p. 12.

50   Strong, p. 1.

51   Strong, pp. 2–3.

52   Strong, pp. 1–2.

53   Judith S. Kleinfeld with G. Williamson McDiarmid and William H. Parrett, *Inventive Teaching: the Heart of the Small School* (Fairbanks: College of Rural Education, University of Alaska, 1992), p. xiii.

54   Kleinfeld, et al., *Alaska's Small Rural High Schools*, p. 29.

55   Kleinfeld, et al., *Inventive Teaching*, p. xiv.

56   Alaska Department of Education, Appendix B, "Extent of the At-Risk Problem."

57   Alaska Economic Trends, July 1992, p. 7.

58   Office of Data Management, pp. 12–121.

59   David Whitney, "A Study in Despair. Native American teens 'most devastated' group researched in U.S.", *Anchorage Daily News*, p. A-1, A-10, March 25, 1992.

60   Personal communication, anonymous National Park Service employee, August 24, 1993.

61   University of Alaska Anchorage, Office of Institutional Research, "Student Retention Study Fall 1987 through Spring 1990," March 1991.

62   University of Alaska Anchorage, "Student Retention Study."

63   University of Alaska Fairbanks, Office of Planning, Computing, and Information Systems, "A Comparison of Native and Non-Native Degree Recipients," Institutional Research Series No. 92-6, December 1992.

64   University of Alaska Fairbanks, "A Comparison of Native and Non-Native Degree Recipients."

65   University of Alaska Fairbanks, "A Comparison of Native and Non-Native Degree Recipients."

66   University of Alaska Fairbanks, "A Comparison of Native and Non-Native Degree Recipients."

67   Letters, Margaret Langan, Registrar, Alaska Junior College, April 29, 1993, and May 6, 1993, to Alaska Natives Commission, in files of the Alaska Natives Commission.

68   Letters, Bristol Bay Native Corporation, May 31, 1993; Central Council, Tlingit and Haida Tribes of Alaska, May 11, 1993; Chugachmiut, May 20,1993; Kawerak, Inc., May 7,1993; Kotzebue IRA, May 7, 1993; Nome Eskimo Community, May 7, 1993; Tanana Chiefs Conference, May 5, 1993, to Alaska Natives Commission, in files of the Alaska Natives Commission.

69   Michael D. Pavel, "American Indians and Alaska Natives in Higher Education: Research on Participation and Graduation," ERIC Digest, ED 348197, August 1992, p. 4.

THE STATE OF NATIVE EDUCATION

John C. Sackett

This text was abstracted and edited from John Sackett's keynote address before the Alaska Federation of Natives 1985 Convention in Anchorage, Alaska. John Sackett is a former member of the Alaska State Senate representing Interior Alaska.

Self-respect; their story

IF WITHIN THE CLASSROOM we do not teach our children self-respect, respect for others, how to understand their world and their roles within it, or give them a sense of respect for nature—all that grows and lives upon the land—then we will have failed to educate our children properly.

During the past 18 years that I have served in the state legislature on the finance committee, education has been one of my most important issues and has been my highest priority.

We have won the right to govern our schools. We have created the Regional Educational Attendance Area system that provides greater local control. Over the last 10 years, we have built most of the necessary facilities to provide decent educational opportunities. We have also sought to find the best teachers for our schools.

Yet with the great emphasis placed on education, and the millions upon millions of dollars we have allocated to education, we have failed miserably. Too many of our children have quit school and have turned to alcohol and drugs. Even worse, some have given up. The Alaska Native Health Board reports that suicides among young Natives between the ages of 15 and 24 are increasing and account for the highest rate of suicides for any group.

We have failed in education and one of the main reasons for this dismal failure is that our educational system has missed an important element.

It is not so much what is being taught in the classroom, but rather what isn't being offered. Native students are seriously harmed, and their future prospects for a happy, fulfilling, and rewarding life are greatly diminished.

To identify the problem and implement a solution, we must ask, what does the word *education* mean? What does it mean to educate? We have been conditioned to think that we must educate our people, but yet, we probably don't even know the meaning of this notion.

Many believe that education merely means to go to school, get good grades, graduate from high school, go to college, get a degree, and then to get a good job that pays well. These are common assumptions about education.

Even if we accept these ideas, they are not what we are practicing in most of our schools. We take great pride in our Native students who graduate from college and are able to compete on an equal basis. We can be proud because we know the hard work and the effort that student had to put out to graduate. Statistics from the University of Alaska show that in 1982 only 4 percent of our Native students graduated. The question which needs to be addressed is what about the other 96 percent who don't graduate from college? This statistic does not meet the established goals of the educational system. The evidence is apparent—too many students drop out of high school, turn to alcohol and drugs, and today appear to be choosing suicide at a greater rate than ever before.

Webster's dictionary defines the word *educate*: "To rear, to bring up. To develop a person by fostering the growth of knowledge, wisdom, character, physical health, and general competence."

This definition doesn't say anything about getting good grades, graduating, going to college, or getting a good job with high pay. The definition says that education means to develop a person by fostering the growth of knowledge, wisdom, character, physical health, and general competence.

Our educational system implements only a part of this and ignores the substance. This process is similar to a hunter taking only the hide, but leaving the meat behind. The tragedy is that we are wasting the lives of many of our children.

I believe that changes must be made in our educational system if we are to successfully educate our children.

Students are instructed, lectured, and tested and told to graduate from high school, to go to college, to get a degree, to get a job. While these may be the objectives of some, they are terrifying for many Native students who are often demoralized and who feel hopeless by the time they enter high school. To get a degree and a high-paying job means that Native students must leave their village. They must leave home and family. They must leave a way of life to relocate in larger communities, indeed in another world, in order to achieve the success defined by our schools.

What about the Native student who prefers to stay in the village, who wants to remain a part of our rich culture and build a life among family and friends in the village? If this student does not obtain a college education or get a job with high pay, is this student a failure? The answer is obviously no. Unfortunately, the student who does not choose this path is often left with a sense of failure.

Successful education must foster in the students the ability to think and reason, the ability to understand the world, to appreciate and understand their roles in the world and their relationship with that world.

A successful education must also help generate a sense of competence, a sense of value, and provide contentment, whether one is a corporate attorney in Seattle or a subsistence fisherman along the waters of the Kuskokwim River.

We can fill a young mind with facts and figures; we can teach that young mind to calculate, to read, to write; we can train it to perform surgery, practice law, construct buildings, or operate computers. But, if within the classroom we do not teach our children self-respect, respect for others, how to understand their world and their roles within it, or give them a sense of respect for nature, all that grows and lives upon the land, then we will have failed to educate our children properly. The failure is that these objectives are not the foundation of the educational system of rural Alaska. If we want to meet the challenge of the future, want our children to meet that challenge successfully, and want our culture to survive and adapt, we have no choice but to get involved in the educational process.

One of the potential solutions to our problem is to establish a statewide task force to look for a new public school system. We spend an additional $160 million just in state dollars for our university system. Another $100 million is generated from other sources for our university. We can financially afford to make changes, and morally we can't afford not to make them.

Our cultures have given Alaska its spirit, its mystique, and its magic. We have lived here for thousands of years. If our cultures are to survive, if we are to be responsible to our children and future generations, then we must begin to change our educational system now.

If we want to grow and prosper in spirit and character, we must find a way to reinstill dignity and self-respect in our young people. That is our challenge for the future.

WHY NATIVE EDUCATION?

Dennis Demmert

Keynote speech, Native Educators' Conference, January 31, 1999,
Anchorage, Alaska. Revised, June 2009.

THIRTY YEARS AGO (in 1969), I attended a conference on Native education. Senator Robert Kennedy's recent hearings on Native education publicized problems across Indian country, including Alaska. Forty-two years after Lewis Meriam's report to Congress that services to Native Americans were enormously deficient, and 35 years after Congress passed the Johnson-O'Malley Act to enrich funding for Native education, Senator Kennedy's hearings highlighted the continuing problems. In many schools in Alaska, Native student GPA averages were lower, their drop-out rates higher, and their schooling experiences less satisfactory than those of non-Native students. A counselor reported that in a study he'd done, Native children did as well as non-Native children through grades one, two, and three; and then at grade four, they started to drop behind, and by the time they graduated from high school, they averaged a full grade point lower than non-Native students. On a scale of four, with only three grade points being satisfactory, that's a huge disparity. The early success of those children demonstrated that they had the innate ability to succeed, but as they matured, they fell behind. We heard other accounts of problems of Native children in schools. The tone of that conference was depressing and we were pretty glum about what we were hearing.

Then an anthropologist from the Smithsonian Institution whom we'd invited said, "Hey, it's true that there's a lot to be done yet, but look at how far Native people have come. Formal education has been a part of my culture for many, many generations, and many Native people have had barely more than one generation. It would be unrealistic to think that Native people could move into Western education and immediately be on par with families that have been in the system for hundreds of years. What is truly amazing is how far Native people have come in a short time. Your parents were lucky to get to the fifth grade, and now, literally all Native youth attend high school and many of them go on to college. What you've accomplished in a short time is astounding."

That was what Dr. Sam Stanley said to us in 1969, and that continues to influence the way I think about Native education. The 30 years since then have been truly remarkable. We now have local control of rural schools, which we did not have 30 years ago. We had few Native teachers in our schools then, and now we have countless numbers. We've moved from 1.1 percent of the University of Alaska Fairbanks graduating class in the early 1970s to more than 5 percent in the early 1990s and still climbing. We have doctors, lawyers, corporate managers, engineers, and other professionals with graduate degrees. Our Native corporations are major players in the Alaskan economy and are great supporters of Native education. We've made great progress. But in the larger picture, we still have much to do.

For example, we still have a significant disparity, on average, between Native and non-Native educational achievement. We have high achievers, but we must also work with the next level of students—those who are not the high-achieving self-starters who quickly made incredible strides when support became available through Native foundations. We have young Native people who, with extra help, could also hit those academic benchmarks. We also have young people who may not follow the academic route, but who could use support and training for getting good jobs in the workforce. We also need to break the cycle of social problems that take too many of our youth into social dysfunction. Our Native educational foundations need to analyze the needs of our young people who aren't going on into postsecondary education and get them into the cycle of success. With the help of Native educators, corporations, foundations, and Native families, we can continue to accelerate our movement toward educational and economic parity in the larger American society.

However, we should not mindlessly seek "progress" without asking if there's a price that we're not taking into account. Over the years, I've seen Native people making gains in education, but some gains have been through a displacement process. That is, the more we succeeded in Western education, the less we knew about our old ways. In our old ways,

I would have spent much of my childhood with my maternal uncle, who would have taught me what I needed to know to live a good life in Tlingit society. What happened instead was that compulsory education laws required me to spend the best part of my learning day in a classroom where I was taught English, American history, and American culture. My mind was filled with information from another culture and it would be years before I realized what I missed in my early years.

That realization took seed when I returned to Craig early one spring to work for six weeks. There were no hotels, so I stayed with my maternal uncle, who was delighted to have me. I became something of a captive audience in my off-hours to an uncle who was thrilled to fulfill his traditional role as my teacher. I learned about our clan house in Tuxekan; I learned where our clan lands were; how he made good medicines from plants and seaweed; where he hunted and fished; clan lore, including the clan's story of the giant devilfish; and more. Those six wonderful weeks went by quickly. They made me think about the tradeoffs we were making for Western education.

For example, when I was young, a friend told me that he was going to quit fishing and find work in Ketchikan to support his family. Life was very hard in our early years in the new cash economy and he said that he did not want his children to go through the hardships he had experienced. He was a good worker, and worked his way into a relatively well-paying, stable job. He bought a home and gave his family a good life. He succeeded in taking his children away from the hardships he had experienced.

But his roots were still in the village, and whenever he could, he went back. He took his family so they could learn something about their roots; but it was not a good experience for his children. They were mortified to discover that their grandmother's home had none of the amenities they had in their home. The stores in the village were very small and sold mainly groceries, basic clothing, and fishing gear, so they had no place to hang out. They didn't mix well with the children in the village.

Their father was born into subsistence fishing, so he caught fish to smoke and can. Traditionally, that was family work, but his children did not want to even touch the slimey fish, let alone clean them or prepare them for smoking and canning. Their father worked alone on his fish, but was happy to be putting up fish. His children were city children, and they could comprehend the life and experiences that were so fundamental to his Nativeness. My friend succeeded in giving his children the benefits of Western society, but they lost contact with their culture. I continue to see them from time to time. They are reasonably well educated and are doing well, but they apparently feel no strong ties to their Native roots.

Is this the price we must pay for success in Western education? I think that the answer is "yes," if we pursue success in Western education mindlessly. All it takes is one generation devoid of Native cultural experiences to transform our children into generic human beings. Generic human beings have no meaningful cultural roots. In their comfortable new lives, they can work eight hours at specialized jobs that have no direct connection to gathering food, or building shelter, or directly fulfilling their own needs; they can go home to their own entertainment centers; they can escape from time to time with drugs or alcohol—escapes that all too often capture them; they can accumulate wealth for security in their old age, and they can, indeed, make lives for themselves and their children.

To a degree, of course, we don't have much choice. We're swept along in a social order that compels us to compete with each other for money and to save it for our own needs and our families' needs. We must, of course, do what we can to live the good life in this setting. But for me—I'd rather skip the generic part. There's a profound richness in Native cultures. Our uncles and aunts and Elders can no longer perpetuate cultural knowledge alone. Our schools must incorporate more than token cultural studies into the curriculum. But they won't do it unless we can justify it. So, why Native education in our schools?

Native culture is a part of me, and maybe that's why I want to keep it going. Maybe it's simply a matter of my own ego. Is that reason enough? When Sir Edmund Hillary, the first person to scale Mt. Everest, was asked why he did it, he said, "Because it's there!" That was reason enough for him, but it won't be reason enough for educational decisionmakers. So, what justifies Native education in our schools?

For starters, there's our concern about how poorly too many of our students perform in school. We can take pride in the achievements of our best and brightest students, but when statistical data show that, on average, we're still achieving below the norm, we must focus our efforts on those who are less successful. Many of them have the innate ability, but they may need encouragement, or tutoring, or counseling, or other services not being provided to the degree needed. We want all Native students to do well.

Studies show that Native children respond much more positively to schooling experiences which include cultural knowledge. In elementary and secondary schools, cultural knowledge has been made available through the Indian Education Act programs and the Johnson-O'Malley programs. Those cultural programs have been taught by Native tradition-bearers and they've had a positive impact on the education of Native children. At the University of Alaska, many Native students were very enthusiastic about

Native studies and several credited that for their choices of careers. Cultural studies make their schooling a more meaningful experience. Existing programs are valuable, but they're still largely incidental and elective.

Also, Native cultural studies should not be just for Native students. We've had too many controversies and bitter conflicts that have arisen from a lack of understanding of Native aboriginal rights, and tribal sovereignty. Many Americans, including Native Americans, don't know that Congress, in 1786, acknowledged Indian land ownership and pledged that "their lands and properties shall never be taken from them without their consent . . ." Many Americans do not know that Congress, in 1790, decreed that Indian land could legally be obtained only through federal treaties with Indian tribes. Most of the 2.1 billion acres of land obtained from Indian tribes came through nearly 400 treaties or Indian land settlement acts. The United States made a great array of commitments, tribe by tribe, to Indian people. A complex "special relationship" has evolved between the federal government and American Indian tribes. That relationship is not widely understood. To the uninformed, Native people may appear to receive unwarranted special treatment. To those who know history, the services Native people receive are entirely appropriate and necessary and, in fact, are quite nominal in light of the losses that Native people have experienced. Let's use Native studies in our schools to foster an understanding of the role of Native rights in American history.

There is one more reason I would suggest for the inclusion of Native studies in our schools. Tribal societies have traditions for social relations that are quite different from that of so-called Western society, and those traditions have valuable lessons for all of us. Americans greatly value individual rights and freedom and that has been beneficial in stimulating personal development, creativity, and innovation in our society. Western society benefits from the individual freedom that it so greatly prizes; however, it is not without an enormous downside. There are winners and losers in this hypercompetitive economy we live in. Without going into horror stories, suffice it to say that we have a lot of poverty and social problems in conjunction with our competitive economy. One writer says we've become a "Me first" society and that a sense of social obligation has withered in our competitive society.

Tribal societies, traditionally, were different. Living in environments that could be very harsh meant that potential disaster was forever imminent. One way for tribal members to survive was to work together and help each other as needed. An old woman once told me, "In our old way, we had social security too; but our social security was not a check. Our social security was a community where everybody knew everybody else, and people took care of each other."

Ultimately, the hardest-working, most skilled food gatherers had the most to give and share. My grandfather was such a person, and his message to his sons and sons-in-law was to share what you had with those who, for whatever reason, were less fortunate. Reciprocity was not an issue, but sometimes, anthropologists see behaviors of tribal people through the lenses of their own cultural values and ascribe weird meanings to Native giving and sharing. Somehow, they must satisfy their own logic that self-interest drives behavior. That may be an incipient human instinct, but societies socialize individuals to control instincts and override them with the values of the respective societies. Cooperation was not merely a courtesy nor was it self-serving; it was simply an imperative for community survival. Working together—working for each other—stimulated mutual respect and strong attachments among tribal members. Of course every society has some of both—individuality and cooperativeness—but the difference is a matter of degree. We should not romanticize cooperation in tribal societies—we've had our problems and challenges too—but understanding the ethic of sharing and working together for the common good in Native societies would enrich the education of students in our schools.

I may have tried to cover too much in too little time and perhaps have not provided sufficient grounding for my argument in support of Native education; but in summary, a good Native education program should encourage and support the education of Native students by informing them of their roots; it should go beyond the best and the brightest students and truly promote the education of all Native students; it should promote informed understanding between Native and non-Native people; and it should enlighten all of us on the warmth, the thrill, and the deep personal satisfaction that comes from living together, working together, and helping each other as an interdependent community, much in the tradition of Native societies. A compelling case can be made for Native education, but I have doubts that it will happen without strong support from the Native community. We have a pretty good record of achievement so far. Let's add to it.

Culture and Change for Iñupiat and Yup'ik People of Alaska

<hr>

Edna Ahgeak MacLean

Cultural Heritage of the Alaskan Inuit

THE FORCES OF NATURE determined the lifestyle of the forebearers of the Iñupiat and the Yup'ik, i.e. the Inuit (Eskimo) people of northern and western Alaska. Their ancestors lived along the coast of the Arctic Ocean and the Bering Sea in some of the most severe environmental conditions known to humankind. They survived and flourished by harvesting their food and fuel and the raw materials from which they made clothing and housing and the implements of culture on land and sea. The resourcefulness of those forebearers and the cultural legacy that they have left are a source of pride to their descendants. The latter are determined that the culture they bequeathed will not disappear from the earth.

According to Iñupiaq legend, Inuit migrated from Siberia to Alaska to escape from other warring groups. It is said that a large group of Inuit settled in a place called Utuqqaq, along a river that they also called Utuqqaq (located near Wainwright, in northern Alaska). Warring groups descended upon them periodically and some of the Utuqqaq people, wanting to live in a more peaceful environment, uprooted themselves once more and went further east. They settled in a place called Pinguksragruk (the exact location is unknown to the author). The translation of the Iñupiaq name indicates an area containing protuberances from the ground; there are areas with many pingos, or large mounds formed over the frozen cores of former lakes, such as in the Tuktoyaktuk region of the Mackenzie River Delta in western Canada.) No one knows how long the early Inuit remained in Pinguksragruk. Each time a warring society reached their domain they moved, eventually populating the Arctic seacoast. It is said that this is how the Inuit people reached Greenland (Ahmaogak and Webster, 1968). Modern Greenlanders say that they are descendants of the people of Utuqqaq, so they are told by their tradition bearers, the elders.

The Inuit who migrated northwards and eastwards developed a culture based primarily on whaling, hunting seals and walruses in the coastal areas, and hunting for caribou and fishing in the interior. The wealth of the sea enabled them to establish fairly large, permanent communities centered around Point Barrow (Nuvuk) and Point Hope (Tikiraq) on the North Slope, and at Cape Prince of Wales (Kifigin) on the east coast of the Seward Peninsula.

Activities within the whaling communities were centered in the whaling captains' traditional communal organization called the *qargi* in Iñupiaq. *Uqaluktuat* "life experience stories" and *unipkaat* "legends" were told in the *qargit* (plural form of *qargi*). Here people learned their oral history, songs, and chants. Young boys and men learned to make tools and weapons while they listened to the traditions of their forefathers. The lives of the Inuit revolved around the seasons and the abundance and availability of resources that changed with them. During the dark period from November to January, when the sun does not rise above the horizon, the Iñupiaq people had fun dancing and feasting in the *qargit*. After the joyful activities, the men worked on their hunting weapons and the women sewed new clothing while waiting for the two-star constellation, Aagruuk (the Morning Star), to appear on the horizon in late December. The appearance of Aagruuk indicated that the daylight hours would soon grow longer. After Aagruuk had firmly established itself in the skies, the men began going to their winter hunting areas where they hunted polar bears and seals. In early January the Iñupiaq people cleaned their homes and ice cellars and put new wicks in their seal-oil lamps.

In late January and February, when the days became longer and homes and ice cellars had been cleaned, they donned their new clothing and held competitive games outside. They played games of skill and endurance. There was a keen sense of competition for excellence among men in each *qargit*. Groups went from house to house shouting "Hii! Hii!" It was a celebration of the renewal of light and of life.

In March the whaling captains and their crews began preparing their whaling implements and boats. The old skin of the whaling boat was removed and put outside to dry and be bleached by the sun. The boat frame was prepared to receive a new covering the following month.

Ice cellars were cleaned in early April. In a whaling community the ice cellars had to be cleaned to ensure that the whale which the captain would receive had a clean place to put its *atigi* (parka). The meat and the *maktak* (skin with blubber) of the whale is referred to as the *atigi*, which was given to the whaling captain by the whale. Out on the ice, when the whale was being butchered, the head was removed and returned to the ocean. This allowed the soul or spirit of the whale to return to its home and don a new parka. Much respect was given to the whale, as it is to all of the animals that give themselves to the Inuit people.

During the month of April, too, the whaling captain's wife was busy supervising other women while they sewed on a new skin cover of at least five *ugruk* (bearded seal) skins for the whaling-boat frame. In April smaller Arctic seals gave birth to their young out on the Arctic ice. The female polar bears had already left their winter dens with their cubs the previous month. In the interior it was time to hunt the caribou that migrated north for the summer. The land was awakening. In late April, the whaling crews went out on the ice and put up camp to wait for migrating whales.

In May, the whaling season was at its peak. Many whales migrated along the open leads and under the ice. There was great anticipation and waiting; when a whale was caught, there was joy and excitement. The whole community was one in spirit and there was much jubilation. The seals, with their young, sunned themselves on the ice. Eider ducks began their migration eastward along the Arctic ice. Everything was alive. The ice on the rivers loosened and began to break up. There was no darkness, for the sun never dipped below the horizon.

Many of these traditions are still practiced today. The whaling season usually ends around the first week of June, as the sea ice begins to grow soft and unsafe. Many families go goose hunting in late May and June to gather the newly laid eggs, but hurry back to be part of the whaling celebration called Nalukataq which is still a central part of Iñupiaq culture. Each successful *umialik* (whaling captain) prepares and offers a feast for the entire village, sharing the meat and *maktak* of the whale with all the people. To be a successful *umialik* and to offer a Nalukataq to the village is to occupy the most prestigious position in Iñupiaq society.

In Point Hope the Nalukataq feasting and dancing usually last for three days. In Barrow each feast lasts a day. The celebration takes its name from the traditional activity of tossing people into the air on a blanket made of four bearded seal skins sewn together. Men and women hold the blanket, which has loop handles all around the circumference. A jumper gets on the blanket and allows the people to stretch the blanket tightly and then forcefully propel the person into the air. The people admire the acrobatic feats of the jumpers and laugh good-naturedly at their failures. During this activity and throughout the whole day of feasting, men and women sing songs for the Nalukataq. During Nalukataq everyone receives new boots and parka covers.

After the whaling celebrations in late June, many families go camping. They harvest fish, caribou, and ducks. In Point Hope, it is time to gather eggs from the seabird colonies on cliffs along the coast. The tundra is dotted with families living in tents, enjoying life, and harvesting the bounty of the land and sea that is so freely given during the summer season.

August is the time to dry meat and fish and fill the ice cellars in preparation for the winter to come. Walrus hunting, which began in July, is still in season. At this time the walrus hide and blubber is set aside to ferment into *urraq*, a delicacy that is an acquired taste. The sun begins to dip below the horizon each evening. At this time the caribou shed the velvet from their antlers. The ocean fog rolls in and out and there is mist in the air. It is all very beautiful.

Frost comes in late August and early September. The young eider ducks and other birds begin their migration south. It is the time for fall whaling. The shore ice has long since drifted away, so the whaling boats leave from the shore and wait for the returning bowhead whales to pass. People make nets and snowshoes for use later on in the fall.

The ground, lakes, rivers, and lagoons freeze over and are covered with snow in October. Many people go ice fishing. The caribou are rutting, and it is getting darker. The people who spent summer in tents scattered along the Arctic coast have returned to the villages. Winter is settling in.

After the separation of the summer months the villagers begin socializing again with other village groups. During the latter part of December and early January a social and economic gathering may be held in one of the villages. This gathering is called Kivgiqsuat, the Messenger Feast. The *umialit* (whaling captains) and their crews host these gatherings. An *umialik* and his crew usually spend a few years preparing for Kivgiqsuat. Food is gathered and stored, gifts are made or hunted for, new clothing and numerous other preparations are made for the gathering. During Kivgiqsuat, partners from different villages exchange gifts. The *umialit* show the extent of their wealth and power through Kivgiqsuat, the celebration that brings Iñupiat from different villages together and strengthens their social ties (Spencer, 1959).

The last Messenger Feast on the North Slope of Alaska was held in Wainwright (Alaska) in 1914. Presently the people of Arctic Alaska are revitalizing the tradition of the Messenger Feast. January 1988 saw the first celebration of the Messenger Feast in Barrow in 80 years. True to the spirit of Kivgiqsuat, several pledges were made that were directly related to social and political alliances. Additionally, one village vowed to use the memories of their Elders to enhance the celebration for the following year. This cultural revitalization can only add to the richness of the lives of contemporary Iñupiat.

ORAL LITERATURE THROUGH LEGENDS, ACCOUNTS OF LIFE EXPERIENCES, AND SONGS

Our languages are reflections of our worldviews, which are shaped by the natural and supernatural environment in which we live. Oral literature reflects what is important to us. In the absence of a written record, oral literature contains the history and transfers the wisdom of society.

Much of Iñupiaq and Yup'ik oral literature focuses on the interaction between the natural and supernatural. Iñupiaq oral literature falls into two categories. The *unipkaat* (legends) are accounts of the travels and lives of people at a time when humans could become animals and vice versa, and such transformations are a recurring theme of the *unipkaat*. The main characters of the legends usually have shamanistic powers. *Unipkaat* may contain episodes of *afatkut* (shamans) changing themselves into animals or birds, thus acquiring the attributes (e.g. strength, flight, and even appetite) associated with each animal.

The second category of oral literature consists of stories and life experiences in a more recent setting, called *quliaqtuat* (those that are told). They may also contain episodes of humans becoming animals, but their characters can be identified through genealogies of modern Iñupiat.

The themes of grandparent and grandchild, of the young woman who refuses to marry, of the orphan, and of successful hunters are found throughout Iñupiaq and Yup'ik stories. Legends and life experience stories tell of preferred modes of behavior, the consequences of misbehavior or nonadherence to taboos. They also entertain. The legends are the oral history of the Iñupiat and the Yup'iks. Many of the stories contain songs that were used by the shamans when performing their feats. Shamans were active well into the 20th century.

The following account was given by an old Iñupiaq man in the early 1960s. He observed the activities of at least four shamans in Barrow while a young boy.

> Then in one of the nights Masapiluk and Atuqtuaq, two of the more powerful ones [shamans], with Kuutchiuraq as their third, all went out. We did not know why they went out, leaving Igalaaq behind. They were gone for quite a while; then they began returning one by one. When Kuutchiuraq and Atuqtuaq emerged through the *katak* [inner trapdoor in subterranean sod houses leading into the living area], Igalaaq would call them by name and touch them on the crown of the head. Masapiluk did not return with the two.
>
> Finally Igalaaq said, "Let him do as he pleases." Then he left the *katak* "trapdoor" area and came to sit on the sleeping platform. As we waited expecting him [Masapiluk], all of a sudden from the entrance hallway a polar bear began entering! It was growling! It stayed in the entrance hallway for a while then began coming towards the *katak*. I watched the *katak* intently. As I was watching it, a person's head began emerging. When it surfaced it was carrying pieces of blubber in its mouth! It was also carrying blubber in its arms. It was growling. Igalaaq just watched him. He did not do anything. Finally it entered. After sitting down in the middle of the floor with its legs spread out, it placed all of the blubber it was carrying between its legs and began eating. As I recall, it ate a lot of blubber. Oil was dripping out through the man's labret holes. When he finished he went out. When he began entering again carrying blubber, Igalaaq went down to the *katak* and gave him a good slap on the crown of the head. He disappeared into the entrance hallway and then emerged later without the blubber.
>
> (Ahnatook, circa 1961, from Suvlu Tape collection of Iñupiaq stories, currently being transcribed and translated by the author.)

Sometimes the shamans used their powers to entertain themselves and others.

> One night, they tied Kuutchiuraq up with his head touching his feet and with his hands behind his back. He asked

them to tie twine to him. When the lights were turned out we heard a loon rustling about making its characteristic call, but it was not leaving the house this time! It stayed in the house. We could hear it flying about. After some time had passed, we finally heard it landing. When the lights were lit, lo and behold! All the holes in the house were connected with the twine!

(Ahnatook, circa 1961, from Suvlu Tape collection of Iñupiaq stories currently being transcribed and translated by the author.)

Drum singing and dancing are popular with Iñupiat and Yup'ik people. In the old days there were songs to appease the spirits of nature, call the animals, and heal or do harm to others. Songs that told of individual experiences or group happenings were composed, choreographed, and then sung in front of an audience. This tradition continues. Songs have been composed which tell of someone's first airplane ride, using an outboard motor for the first time, or of someone's visit to another village. More recently, an Iñupiaq dance group from the village of Wainwright, Alaska, traveled to California, and a song and dance routine was created telling of their trip.

Language as a Reflection of the Environment

The concept of interdependence stands out in the structure of the Iñupiaq and Yup'ik languages. Each word has a marker that identifies its relation to the other words in the sentence. There is no set order of words in a sentence just as there is no way of determining what will happen next in nature. Man cannot control nature, but as each event happens, a causal effect occurs which creates special relationships between the components of the happening. The following Iñupiaq statement, *agnam aitchugaa afun suppunmik* (the woman is giving the man a gun) can be said in an additional 11 ways without changing the meaning.

1. *Agnam afun suppunmik aitchugaa.*
2. *Agnam suppunmik aitchugaa afun.*
3. *Suppunmik afun aitchugaa agnam.*
4. *Suppunmik aitchugaa agnam afun.*
5. *Suppunmik agnam afun aitchugaa.*
6. *Aitchugaa agnam afun suppunmik.*
7. *Aitchugaa afun agnam suppunmik.*

8. *Aitchugaa suppunmik agnam afun.*
9. *Afun agnam aitchugaa suppunmik.*
10. *Afun aitchugaa agnam suppunmik.*
11. *Afun suppunmik aitchugaa agnam.*

The word *agnam* (woman) has the marker *m* that identifies it as the subject of the sentence. The word *aitchugaa* (she/he/it gives her/him/it) has the ending *aa* that indicates that it is the verb and that the number and person of the subject is singular and is in the third person, and that the number and person of the object is also singular and is in the third person. The word *afun* (man) has no marker and, since the verb is transitive, is identified as the direct object. The word *suppunmik* (a gun) has a marker *mik* that identifies it as the indirect object.

The Iñupiaq and Yup'ik cultures of today's citizens are very different from those of their grandparents and great-grandparents. In the old days, they lived in sod and snow houses and their main means of transport were the *umiaq* (skin boat), *qayaq* (skin-covered kayak), and *qimmit* (dog teams). Today people live in wooden frame houses and travel in snow-machines, cars, and airplanes. Their great-grandparents depended wholly on the animals of the land and the mammals and fish of the sea for sustenance. Today, although they still use traditional natural resources, people rely heavily on the products and technology of Western culture. The Iñupiaq and Yup'ik cultures have changed drastically and are still changing as more and more non-Iñupiaq or non-Yup'ik tools and materials are used. Instead of bows and arrows or bolas, guns are now used. But although a seal may be killed with a rifle, it is still retrieved with a traditional tool known as a *manaq*.

The vocabularies of the Iñupiaq and Yup'ik languages are constantly changing, reflecting changes in lifestyles. As activities change, so do languages. The Iñupiat have developed new words such as *suppun*, which means "gun." *Suppun* is based on the stem *supi*, which means "to gush out, flow out." Thus the literal translation of *suppun* is "means of gushing out, of flowing out." The gun releases compressed air, hence its Iñupiaq name. The word *suppun* has been added to the language whereas the word *qilumitaun*, or "bola" will soon be forgotten through disuse. On the other hand, the meaning of the word *kangut*, which traditionally means "a herd of animals or a large assemblage of people," has been extended to include the concept of a corporation. A subsidiary of a corporation is then called a *kannuuraq*. The suffix *uraq*, which means "small," is added to create a new word meaning "subsidiary." It was necessary to expand the meaning of the word *kanguq* to include the concept of a corporation following the establishment of 13 regional and more than 200 village corporations under the Alaska Native Claims Settlement Act in 1971. The Iñupiaq and Yup'ik languages are flexible and can easily adapt to encompass new concepts.

Since much of the Iñupiaq and Yup'ik world is covered with snow and ice for long periods of time, and accurate, detailed knowledge of snow and ice is essential to the success and survival of a hunter, the language is rich in terms for different types of snow and ice. A sample is given below (a more complete list may be found in the comprehensive dictionary being prepared by the Alaska Native Language Center, University of Alaska Fairbanks.)

apun	snow
aqilluq	light snow, deep for walking
aqiluqqaq	soft snow
auksalaq	melting snow
auksiqlaq	snow that melts almost instantly
iksiaksraq	snow to be melted for drinking water
kaataq	block of snow which will be used in the construction of a snow house
kaniq	frost which collects indoors
mapsa or *mavsa*	cornice, overhanging snow, an overhanging snowdrift that is ready to fall

People use their language to organize their reality. Iñupiaq and Yup'ik cultures are based on dependence on the land and sea. Hunting, and therefore a nomadic way of life, has persisted. The sea and land that people depend on for their sustenance are almost totally devoid of landmarks. These languages have therefore developed an elaborate set of demonstrative pronouns and adverbs that are used to direct the listener's attention quickly to the nature and location of a particular object. In place of landmarks, words serve as indicators for the location of an object. Each stem gives information about proximity, visibility, or vertical position and implies whether the object is inside or outside, moving or not moving, long or short. For example, Iñupiaq has at least 22 stems that are used to form demonstrative pronouns in eight different cases and demonstrative adverbs in four cases. American English has two demonstrative pronouns, this and that (plural forms these and those), with their respective adverbs here and there.

Language as a Reflection of Perceptions and Intellectual History

An attribute of Iñupiaq culture evident in the language and literature is the fact that the roles of women and men traditionally were not stratified. The type of role undertaken depended on a person's ability and capability. One of the legends told by an outstanding historian, Uqumailaq, runs as follows:

> Once there lived a large number of people and their chief along a river in the interior. Their chief had a daughter. She did not mature slowly. She had a bow and arrow as she grew up. She hunted like a man using the bow and arrow. When she saw a wolf she would stalk it and would eventually kill it with her how and arrow. She did likewise with wolverine. Although she was a woman she was a skillful hunter.
>
> *(Uqumailaq, circa 1961, from Suvlu Tape collection of Iñupiaq stories, currently being transcribed and translated by the author.)*

Woman as hunter is not a common theme in the oral literature, but the presence of such themes indicates that the society of the ancestors was an egalitarian one. In fact, one cheerful little Iñupiaq Elder woman told the author that she had belonged to a whaling crew, and that the only reason she had never struck a whale was because she was so tiny. She laughed and said that she did not have the strength to strike the whale with sufficient force. From the legends and more recent accounts, we learn that men and women had equal status and that a person was limited only by his or her abilities.

The equality of roles for men and women is reflected in the Iñupiaq and Yup'ik languages. The words for woman, *agnaq*, and for man, *afun*, cannot be used to designate humanity. The Iñupiaq and Yup'ik languages have a word *inuk* or *yuk*, respectively, which refers to a human being without specifying gender, and the same word refers to humanity.

The concept of focusing on the whole situation with one or many participants is reflected in the Iñupiaq language. Take for instance the English sentence "there are squirrels" and the Iñupiaq sentence "*siksriqaqtuq*." One is a translation of the other. In English the focus is on the individual squirrels, whereas in Iñupiaq the focus is on the one situation. This focus is clearly shown by the number of the verb. "Are" in English is plural while "*tuq*" in Iñupiaq is singular. The interdependence of actors regardless of number in a given situation is emphasized. An individual does not stand alone.

The Christian religion has been embraced strongly by the Iñupiaq and Yup'ik. This is not difficult to understand because the Iñupiaq and Yup'ik are very spiritual people. Secondly, the Christian concepts of resurrection and a person's ability to perform "miracles," and the story of creation pertaining to a period of darkness and then of light, were already part of the traditional system of beliefs. In Christianity, resurrection occurred in three days, whereas in Iñupiaq tradition resurrection had to occur within four or five days of death, depending on the sex of the person involved.

Although some concepts such as resurrection and the focus on an individual figure who performs miracles are common to both religions, there are some differences with respect to the creation of man. According to the Iñupiat,

> Long before day and night had been created, or the first man made his appearance, there lived an old woman, indeed very old, for the tradition of her having had a beginning, if there ever was such a one, had been lost. We must bear in mind that during the first stage of the world everything remained young and fresh; nothing grew old. The old woman was like a young girl in her appearance and feelings, and being the only inhabitant of the earth, naturally felt very lonesome and wished for a companion. She was one time chewing "pooya" (burnt seal oil residue) when the thought arose in her mind that it would be pleasant to have an image to play with, so, taking her "pooya", she fashioned a man, then by way of ornamentation placed a raven's beak on his forehead. She was delighted with her success in making such a lovely image and upon lying down to sleep placed it near her side. On awakening her joy was great, for the image had come to life and there before her was the first man'. (Driggs, 1905)

Iñupiaq legend tells of the *tulufiksraq*, the Raven-Spirit who is also a man. He is credited with having secured land and light for humanity. According to Iñupiaq legend there was a period of darkness before there was light. This was the time when humans did not age. The Raven-Spirit *tulufiksraq* secured the land and the source of light from an old man and his wife and daughter. Light appeared only after the Raven-Spirit stole the source of light from them. As he was fleeing, the Raven-Spirit dropped the source of light which then exploded and dispersed units of light throughout existence.

This concept is reinforced by the analysis of the Iñupiaq word for sun, *siqiniq*. The stem of *siqiniq* is siqi, which means "to splatter, to splash outwards," and the ending of the word *niq* indicates the result or end product of an activity. So, the Iñupiaq word for sun, *siqiniq*, and the legend of the Raven-Spirit accidentally dropping the source of light which then exploded support the concept of the big-bang theory of the origin of the universe in which the sun is only one of many.

The Iñupiaq word for star, *uvlugiaq*, indicates that light travels from the star, that there is a path that the light from the star takes to arrive on earth. The stem of the Iñupiaq word *uvlugiaq* is *uvluq*, which means "daylight." The suffix *iaq* indicates "a pathway or trajectory" that permits movement from one point to another.

The language and culture of a people are a source of pride and identity, and the oral literature of the ancestors sends messages based on their experiences and their interpretations of these.

CONTACT WITH OTHER CULTURES

The first white men that the Inuit encountered were explorers and whalers who did not always seek to change the lifestyles of the indigenous peoples that they met in their travels. Those explorers who spent lengthy periods of time with the Iñupiat or Yup'ik learned their language in order to communicate with them. However, they introduced diseases such as German measles, syphilis, chicken pox, and influenza that killed many Iñupiat and Yup'ik people. The death toll was particularly high among the Iñupiat because the people lived close to each other along the coast. The Yup'ik were widely scattered along the rivers and were therefore less accessible to the explorers and their diseases. (Vanstone, 1984)

The Russian explorers traded with the Yup'iks who, in turn, traded with the Iñupiat. From the Yup'ik, Iñupiat obtained iron buckets, knives and tobacco. One bucket traded for two wolverine skins. (Ahmaogak and Webster, 1968)

The second wave of white men to reach the Yup'ik and Iñupiat were Christian missionaries. They were different. They were relentless in their self-righteousness, and considered it their divinely inspired obligation to disrupt the social, educational, and religious activities of the Yup'ik and Iñupiat. The first missionaries in northern Alaska were often medical doctors or schoolteachers or both and had to contend with the shamans.

Many early missionaries learned the Iñupiaq or Yup'ik languages in order to translate Christian hymns, scriptures, and the catechism into them. Iñupiaq and Yup'ik could be spoken in churches but not in schools. The language policy for the schools at the turn of the century under the direction of a Presbyterian missionary, Sheldon Jackson, the first Commissioner of Education for Alaska from 1885 to 1908 (Krauss, 1980), is summed up in this quotation from the *North Star* in Sitka (1888):

> The Board of Home Missions has informed us that government contracts for educating Indian pupils provide for the ordinary branches of an English education to be taught, and that no books in any Indian language shall be used, or instruction given in that language to Indian pupils. The letter states that this rule will be strictly enforced in all government Indian schools. The Commissioner of Indian Affairs urges, and very forcibly too, that instruction in their vernacular is not only of no use to them but is detrimental to their speedy education and civilization. It is now two years and more since the use of the Indian dialects was first prohibited in the training school here. All instruction is given in English. Pupils are required to speak and write English exclusively; and the results are tenfold more satisfactory than when they were permitted to converse in unknown tongues.

In 1890, the following edict was issued by the Department of the Interior:

> The children shall be taught in the English language, reading, writing, arithmetic, geography, oral history, physiology, and temperance hygiene. No text-books printed in a foreign language shall be allowed. Special efforts shall be put forth to train the pupils in the use of the English language.

Thus began the destruction of the indigenous languages of Alaska. The Native peoples of Alaska were taught that their languages were not important, their religion was bad, and that they should become like the white man as quickly as possible.

The missionaries had a relatively easy task of assembling followers for their churches in northern Alaska. The diseases brought by the explorers and Yankee whalers wreaked havoc in many families. The Iñupiat had no immunity to such diseases. Consequently many died, including many heads of households. The father and usually the eldest son, although stricken, had to go out and procure food for the family. Even if they fell ill they could not rest and recuperate. Their state would grow worse and they would die. Consequently, the widows and their children had no one to turn to except the white traders who had established themselves along the Arctic coast. That was the origin of the paternalistic relationship between Alaska's First People and the white man.

Although there was some resistance to the changes imposed on them by missionaries, doctors, and teachers, the majority of Iñupiat and Yup'ik followed the rules that were being laid down. On the insistence of teachers and school officials, many Iñupiaq and Yup'ik parents, although not able to communicate effectively in English, began trying to speak English to their children, so that children spoke English at home as well as in school. Educators persuaded the parents that education was essential for their children to succeed in the changing world. But opportunities for education were limited in traditional villages. It was necessary for children to leave their home communities to attend boarding schools in distant parts of Alaska or even the southern states. At this crucial time in their lives, adolescents were removed from their homes, culture, and the traditions of their people. Often a child would leave the community in the fall; a young adult would return in the spring, but without any parental assistance in this most difficult transition of life. At a time when young adults should be learning the skills, tools, and traditions of their culture, they were learning to make napkin holders and aprons in distant government schools.

The late Eben Hopson, the first mayor of the North Slope Borough in northern Alaska, described Alaska's indigenous peoples' experience of the Western educational system.

> Eighty-seven years ago, when we were persuaded to send our children to Western educational institutions, we began to lose control over the education of our youth. Many of our people believed that formal educational systems would help us acquire the scientific knowledge of the Western world. However, it was more than technological knowledge that the educators wished to impart. The educational policy was to attempt to assimilate us into the American mainstream at the expense of our culture. The schools were committed to teaching us to forget our language and Iñupiaq heritage. This outrageous treatment and the exiling of our youth to school in foreign environments were to remain as common practices of the educational system. (Hopson, 1977)

Iñupiaq and Yup'ik Situation Today

The pace of development in the Alaskan north was fast. The changes that have occurred in the lifetimes of our Elders almost defy belief. Most of the time there is no time to react, no time for comprehensive planning. Because change has occurred so suddenly, there are many things that should have changed that have remained the same under a different name. And there are changes that have been so radical and destructive that we have not begun to emerge from their consequences. Western societal systems and norms, however well intentioned, have undermined and displaced the traditional societal systems that supported our people for thousands of years. The disruptive effects of rapid social and cultural change have wreaked havoc on Alaska Native families and communities. This is reflected in a depressing array of social problems including a high suicide rate among young Alaska Natives, a high incidence of alcohol and drug abuse, fetal alcohol syndrome, breakdown of the extended family and clan system, loss of children to the welfare system, loss of language, lack of transmission of cultural knowledge and values, apathy, depression, low academic achievement and high drop-out rate, transitional problems between village and cities, and the dilemma of integrating traditional and nontraditional economic systems (subsistence versus cash-based lifestyle).

When Alaska became a state in 1959, it was allowed to select federal lands within Alaska to aid in its economic development. Alaska Native leaders, seeing that their traditional lands were being claimed by the State of Alaska, began insisting on a settlement of land claims of the Alaska Natives from the United States government. In 1966, the U.S. Secretary of the Interior froze further state land selections, pending resolution of Alaska Native land claims.

The United States government had long known that the North Slope of Alaska has large reserves of oil. The government laid claim to much of northern Alaska as a petroleum reserve, in the name of national defense; however, the shortage of oil in the world market led the U.S. to encourage the oil companies to explore for oil in Alaska. An enormous oilfield was found at Prudhoe Bay in 1968.

The discovery of the Prudhoe Bay oilfield made the North Slope very attractive to the state and federal governments and private industry. Development of the oilfield would interfere directly with traditional uses of the land, so resolution of the Native land claims was necessary. The Alaska Native Claims Settlement Act became law on December 18, 1971, clearing the way for construction of facilities to extract the oil from the ground and market it. This act affected all the Native people of Alaska, not just those in the oil-rich lands of the north.

Oil development has transformed the lives of Alaskan Inuit in a number of ways. The direct influence is surprisingly small. While some Native people are employed in the oil industry, the great majority of workers are migrants from other parts of Alaska or other states. However, the Native Claims Settlement Act, which was passed to allow oil development to proceed, has affected the lives of all Alaska Natives. The Act provides for the establishment of regional and village corporations to manage the land and invest the money given to the Native communities in exchange for the subsurface rights to natural resources on traditional Native lands. Alaska Natives are shareholders in their regional and village corporations. For the first time Alaska Natives are a significant economic force. In addition, a local government, the North Slope Borough, was established in Arctic Alaska, with powers of taxation of property in the oilfields. These revenues support the provision of a wide variety of services to the residents of the Borough, who are mainly Iñupiat. As one example, the North Slope Borough has established and funded a Commission on History, Language, and Culture to support and encourage activities to preserve, foster, and promote the traditional language and culture of the Iñupiat. The Commission was instrumental in revitalizing the Messenger Feast. The North Slope Borough, in cooperation with the State of Alaska, has constructed regional high schools in all the villages of the North Slope, so that it is no longer necessary for young people to leave their homes to obtain secondary education. Since the school curriculum is, to a significant extent, under the control of a Borough School Board, it is responsive to community desires as never before.

ALASKA NATIVE LANGUAGES AND EDUCATION

For 100 years, Alaska's indigenous languages and cultures have faced a steady onslaught of institutional discrimination that called for their eradication and replacement by the English language and cultural norms. The very core of a young child's identity, the language and culture of the parents, was undermined in the schools. Needless to say, this policy has been extremely detrimental to the indigenous groups in Alaska. Attitudes of rejection or ambivalence about the worth of one's language and culture have developed and are, in varying degrees, still prevalent among the adult population. These attitudes have played an important role in the implementation of retention or maintenance programs for Alaska Native languages.

The linguistic and cultural heritage of Alaska Native societies is threatened with extinction. This looming loss is distressing to many members of the Alaska Native community. The situation affects the education of the children who need to feel secure and comfortable in a schooling process in order to reach their academic potential.

Bilingual and bicultural education in Alaska began with the adoption of a bill in 1972 by the Alaska State Legislature declaring that "a school which is attended by at least 15 pupils whose primary language is other than English shall have at least one teacher who is fluent in the native language of the area where the school is located. Written and other educational materials, when language is a factor, shall be presented in the language native to the area" (State of Alaska, Seventh Legislature, Second Session, 1972).

At the same session another piece of legislation was passed directing the University of Alaska to establish an Alaska Native Language Center in order to: "(i) study Native languages of Alaska; (ii) develop literacy materials; (iii) assist in the translation of important documents; (iv) provide for the development and dissemination of Alaska Native literature; and (v) train Alaska Native language speakers to work as teachers and aides in bilingual classrooms."

In 1975, an Alaska State statute was enacted directing all school boards to ". . . provide a bilingual-bicultural education program for each school . . . which is attended by at least 8 pupils of limited English-speaking ability and whose primary language is other than English." The new language in the statute addressed all languages other than English, and thus expanded bilingualism equally to immigrant languages.

The ultimate aim of all bilingual and bicultural programs in Alaska is to promote English language proficiency. Iñupiaq and Yup'ik language and culture programs are seen as contributing to the enhancement of academic achievement which is measured in the English language. Depending on the assessment of the schoolchildren's language proficiency, each district designs a language development program that best meets its needs. In regions where children still speak their Native language, the language of instruction from kindergarten to fourth grade is usually in that language. After fourth grade, instruction in the Native language is usually reduced, for various reasons including shortage of bilingual teachers, lack of curricular materials, and, most importantly, lack of commitment by the community and school to promote the growth and enrichment of the Alaska Native language per se. In the 1987–88 school year, the Alaska Department of Education, through the Office of the Commissioner, and in collaboration with members of the Alaska Native community, initiated a process to establish an Alaska Native

Language Policy for schools in Alaska. The proposed policy acknowledged that Alaska's indigenous languages are unique and essential elements of Alaska's heritage, and thus distinct from immigrant languages. It recognizes that although some children learn their Native language in the home and community, many Alaska Native children do not have the opportunity to learn their heritage languages in this way. The proposed policy further states that schools have a responsibility to teach and use as the medium of instruction the Alaska Native language of the local community to the extent desired by the parents of that community. This is the first attempt by the educational system to establish a process whereby Alaska Natives can make decisions concerning their heritage languages. The revitalization of Alaska Native languages will occur when Alaska Natives celebrate themselves and their heritage, and insist on being active participants in the education of their children in the home, community and schools.

REFERENCES

Ahmaogak and Webster, 1968. [[full cite needed]]

Barnhardt, R., ed. 1977. *Cross-cultural issues in Alaskan education.* Fairbanks: Center for Northern Educational Research, University of Alaska Fairbanks.

Coon, E.D. 1985. *Bilingual-bicultural education in Alaska: Guidelines for conducting programs in elementary and secondary schools.* Alaska State Department of Education.

Darnell, F., ed. 1972. *Education in the North: The First International Conference on Cross-Cultural Education in the Circumpolar Nations.* Fairbanks: University of Alaska and Arctic Institute of North America.

Driggs, J.B. 1905. *Short sketches from Oldest America.* Philadelphia:George W. Jacobs & Co.

Hopson. 1977. [[full cite needed]]

Kisautaq-Leona, O. 1981. *Puiguitkaat. The 1978 Elders' Conference.* Barrow: North Slope Borough Commission on History and Culture.

Kleinfeld, J.S. 1979. *Eskimo School on the Andreafsky: A study of effective bicultural education.* Praeger Studies in Ethnographic Perspectives on American Education. New York: Praeger.

Krauss, M.E. 1980. *Alaska Native languages: Past, present and future.* Alaska Native Language Research Papers, No. 4. Fairbanks: Alaska Native Language Center.

Spencer, R.F. 1959. *The North Alaskan Eskimo: A study in ecology and society.* Washington, DC: Smithsonian Institution Press.

Spolsky, B. 1986. *Language and education in multilingual settings.* San Diego: College Hill Press.

St. Clair, R., and W. Leap. 1982. *Language renewal among American Indian tribes: Issues, problems and prospectus.* National Clearinghouse for Bilingual Education.

Stein, G., ed. 1983. *Education in Alaska's past.* Anchorage: Alaska Historical Society.

VanStone. 1984. [[full cite needed]]

IÑUPIAT ILITQUSIAT

TO SAVE OUR LAND AND OUR PEOPLE

————◆━❊━◆————

John Schaeffer and John D. Christensen

Originally published in 1981
by the Maniilaq Association, Kotzebue, Alaska.

BY NOW MANY INDIVIDUALS have made contributions to the Iñupiaq Spirit movement's message. As it is carried from one village to another the message absorbs the unique flavor and character of participating communities, families. and individuals. All lend a special quality of their own to the Ilitqusiat movement's content.

The movement blends the ideas, dreams, and frustrations of the region's people. The message grows, evolves, and gathers momentum as it travels. Its content is shaped by every village and individual it encounters and confronts.

Regional elders, political and business leaders, young people, villagers, spiritual leaders (notably Friends pastors), and even Nalaugmuit professionals have joined the Spirit movement's ranks. Many voices sing in the Ilitqusiat choir.

John Schaeffer's commanding baritone still leads the chorus. From among the many we have chosen his voice to explain and describe Iñupiaq Ilitqusiat. The language of Ilitqusiat is often and appropriately Iñupiaq, a tongue we are unfortunately not equipped to publish or translate. We regret our inability to offer our readers those portions of the Ilitqusiat message originally delivered in Iñupiaq by leading Ilitqusiat spokesmen like Roland Booth, Robert Newlin, and a number of village residents. Maybe it doesn't matter. Iñupiaq is still primarily a verbal language, spoken and understood by many but read by few. The Ilitqusiat message, particularly in Iñupiaq, has an irresistible power. It will be heard.

The wisdom, concern, and experience of regional elders gave birth to the Ilitqusiat message developed and first articulated by Willie Hensley. The burden of bringing it all back home fell to John Schaeffer. He's traveled from village to village accompanied by Roland Booth, Robert Newlin, Bobby Curtis, Willie Hensley, and, at least initially, Rachael Craig. John Schaeffer—president of the NANA Regional Corporation since its inception, acknowledged leader of his people, and the region's most powerful political figure—has become Ilitqusiat's tireless and committed messenger. He confronts the region's people with some hard, often brutal, truths and alternately proposes an escape from the current social and cultural malaise threatening the Iñupiaq people's very survival. As the apocalyptic grip of convulsive change tightens around Northwest Arctic Alaska, Schaeffer bluntly addresses the current state of despair and offers new hope. From the heart of darkness Schaeffer charts a course leading to a new dawn for the region's Iñupiaq people.

Schaeffer and company travel from one village to the next, a Spirit journey. Its final destination lies beyond the immediate horizon. It represents a return to the ancient spiritual values that have sustained the Iñupiaq people's survival in a harsh and unforgiving land, the values that have made them a good and strong people. It represents a return to the integrity of land and language, the twin elements of Iñupiaq cultural unity. We offer one episode from that journey.

The land: shrouded in snow, caressed by wind, cold, and quiet: seems to go on forever. *Remote* and *isolated* are the terms the casual observer most frequently applies to Northwest Arctic Alaska's villages. Maybe, but not from each other.

The land is honeycombed with winter trails and laced with river valleys, as though the landscape had organized itself into a natural network of regional transportation corridors. The land is not so much a barrier separating regional communities as it is a bond drawing them together.

The Spirit journey is nearing its conclusion. John Schaeffer, Robert Newlin, and Bobby Curtis have grown hoarse, tired, and more than a little road weary during their travels to the region's villages. On the flight to the circuit's final destinations, Buckland and Deering, they seem to be running on commitment, determination, and not much else. Their ranks are thinned. Roland Booth and Willie Hensley, their Ilitqusiat compatriots, were unable to make the Spirit journey's last leg.

Over the plane's steady, monotonous drone Schaeffer nonetheless manages to communicate a genuine sense of excitement and enthusiasm. Obviously pleased with the response in previous villages he honestly looks forward to the next community, the next opportunity to bring the Spirit message to the people.

The meeting opens as all of NANA's village meetings have opened. Schaeffer reviews NANA's corporate progress and current financial status for the community's shareholders. Business, for NANA, has been good, very good in fact. This is hardly surprising. With shrewd and diverse investments embracing everything from a reindeer herd to an oil-drilling rig, NANA is a vigorous, even dynamic, and growing concern. Schaeffer describes the past year as "the best so far. NANA did twice as much business this year as it did in the year before." In fact NANA has done somewhat better than that, $35 million worth of business in 1981 compared to $16 million during 1980. The company, Schaeffer explains, has achieved net earnings of over $1.5 million. Dividends have leaped from 75 cents to $1.25 a share.

"So," Schaeffer shrugs, "we've been doing pretty good . . . with the business anyway. So good in fact it was getting boring, I was thinking about leaving. Why not? NANA seemed to be doing okay and I was offered a lot more money to go and run a company for someone else. It started to sound pretty good to me, make more money, get rich, and see how I could do at running a company where I wouldn't have to worry about some of the things I do here.

"But when I started to think some more about it," Schaeffer continued, "I decided it wasn't enough to take another job just to get rich. Why make more money? Compared with a lot of you I make pretty good money already. I can take care of my family, so what would I do with more money? Spend it? Give it away? So finally I decided to stay.

"Besides when we started looking at some other things, maybe we were doing a good job from a business standpoint, but everything else was lousy. We started to ask ourselves, what's wrong?"

Then he laid it on them.

"One of the problems we've had is we can't get our young people through college anymore. They aren't going after the education they'll need to run our business, not only our business but training to take other jobs; doctors, teachers; that kind of thing.

"We've got things too important to us to sell. In our corporation the land is not for sale.

"We started looking at some statistics because the [NANA] Board wants to spend NANA's money for scholarships so our own shareholders, our young people, can get the kind of training they'll need to take some of these jobs.

"Guess what the statistics tell us. This problem is getting worse, not better. Out of all the kids we send to college only 11 percent finish the first year. That's not very good and it gets worse, less than 2 percent that's two students out of every 100 we send to college, ever graduate. Think about it. Only 2 percent of our young people finish college.

"It costs money to send kids to college. We haven't had to worry about that much up to now because it always used to be that BIA or someone would put up the money, but they've cut those funds back and they'll cut them back more before they're through. So who's going to send these kids to college? NANA's going to have to pick up some of the tab because I know not many of you have $5,000 a year for every kid of yours that decides they want to go to college. So NANA's going to spend money on this.

"I look at this like any other investment. We're going to invest NANA's money in our people because we need these people. If they're trained and they come back to work for us we're going to get our money back because we need trained people.

"Let's take a look at how many college graduates we need. We need about 100 right now. Not just for NANA but 100 jobs around the region at Maniilaq, teachers for the school district and other places like that. Just to start off we need 100 trained professionals.

"When you start to figure out how much that would cost at the rate our students drop out there's no way we can afford to do it. If 98 out of 100 kids drop out before they graduate it's going to turn out to be a pretty poor investment. If I spent NANA's money on that kind of investment you should fire me. With the kind of dropout rate we've got we're never going to make it anyway. We'd have to send 5,000 students to college to get the 100 graduates we need. We don't have that many kids.

"This is one of the areas where we have a problem. We started looking at this. Our kids get just as much of a chance to go. The schools are telling us they might be a little bit shy in some areas like English or math, depending on how good of an education they got in high school. But they're saying they're not that far behind. Besides that, they have special programs for our kids to help them catch up. They have extra courses to help our kids get up to the level everybody else is at. So what's the matter? They're not dumb. They're not any dumber than anyone else and everyone else seems to be going through. There's something else wrong with that but I'll stop here for now.

"We can't get graduates, so what does that mean? That leads me into the next area. Every place I need someone with a degree I'm going to have to hire some Nalaugmuit because there won't be any Iñupiaq for that job. Well maybe a few Iñupiaq but not enough for all the jobs we have.

"Now before I move ahead with jobs, the other thing wrong with this is that when we do get some graduates with degrees we can't trust them to run our company for you because they don't think right. They don't think like an Iñupiaq. They don't look at things like an Iñupiaq. When the few of them that do get through college come back we have to train them over again because they just think like Nalaugmuit and we won't give a Nalaugmuit a chance to run this company because we've got things too important to us to sell, and basically in a business that's what they do. They sell whatever they've got. Everything's for sale.

"Well in our corporation our land is not for sale! We can't have people who think they can sell our land running our company. So our people who go through college, get done and come back thinking like Nalaugmuit, they're no good to us. They're wasted.

"Now let's talk about jobs. Right now NANA has maybe 500 jobs. About one-third, or 150, are held by shareholders. Maybe not by shareholders but by the husband or wife of a shareholder and we count them because they're taking care of a shareholder. That's what we're really concerned about—if our jobs are providing for shareholders and their families. But most of these 150 jobs are held by Iñupiaq. Now the other two-thirds of our jobs are held by other people. mostly Nalaugmuit. We don't even count the few blacks or Puerto Ricans who work for us. As far as we're concerned they're Nalaugmuit, because were concerned about jobs for our people.

"Why aren't more of our shareholders holding those jobs?

"There are a lot of excuses for it like getting our shareholders into the right unions or because a lot of these jobs are far away and it's hard to get our shareholders there. But a lot of it has to do with high turnover because our people won't stay on the job. Sometimes they want to go hunting and fishing and maybe that's all right. I think a lot of our people get that first paycheck, head for the nearest bar or liquor store, and never make it back to the job. That's not all right.

"Our people, a lot of the time, just up and quit. They don't give notice. Our Nalaugmuit managers have a job to do. They need dependable, reliable people, someone they can count on to show up and stay on the job so they hire a Nalaugmuit to replace an Iñupiaq. Pretty soon we haven't got too many of our people working for us.

"One of the things you told us to do was to get jobs for you. Okay, let's say we need 500 jobs. In order to get 500 jobs for our shareholders I've got to create 2,000 jobs. Because of the way things are going 1,500 of those jobs are going to Nalaugmuit in order to get enough jobs for our shareholders. I've got to make our company big enough to have four times as many employees. That's the way it looks on paper.

"That might take care of us for awhile but our people are growing. In five years we'll need twice as many jobs. We'll have to come up with 1,000 jobs if that's what you want me to do. We've got to have 3,000 more jobs for Nalaugmuit in order to get 1,000 more jobs for you. That doesn't make sense, does it? But that's the way things are going with NANA. When you look at it this way we're not doing a very good job. Something's wrong."

"So we started looking. What's the matter? I can make you profits but I can't get your people trained and get them jobs, not enough of them anyway. Something's wrong?"

Our people need the land to live, to survive.

"We can't afford to put those kids through college, not if that many are going to drop out.

"Let's take a look at our shareholders right now. One of the main reasons we got a settlement act and got NANA going was to get the land. When Willie [Hensley] and I and a few of us young rebels got together 15 years ago we weren't trying to form a corporation. That never even occurred to us until later. It was the land we were after. We were pretty young back then but you supported us anyway, at least some people in most of the villages did, because we all knew the land was important to us. We filed a claim for 25 million acres because we knew it was the right thing to do. We ended up with a little less than 2½ million acres, a corporation, and some money. But it was the land we were after because our people need that land to live, to survive. The land is a lot of what we Iñupiaqs are. Everybody understood that in the 1960s, getting the land was important to our survival as a people, as Iñupiaq. So we got the settlement act, started the corporation, and that's where the land went. Two and a half million acres belong to NANA, belong to you.

"Before white people came we didn't look at that land as being owned by anyone. The land belonged to God and everybody could use it. For a long time we resisted the white man's land ownership system but finally when it looked like we were going to lose our land, we used the land ownership system because we had to. We live in America. We may be Iñupiaq, but we're Americans too. And in America land is worth dollars.

"Guess what's happening to our kids. They're being taught that land is worth money. They're being taught that in order to own land you have to have a piece of paper called a deed and that deed is worth money. What does that mean? It means if someone offers you money for your stock you ought to be able to sell it, right? That's what they're teaching our kids and in 1991 that's what's going to happen. Your land is worth money!

"Your kids who are going to own your stock in 10 more years are being taught that stock in a company like ours is worth money. Right now our stock, your 200 shares, are worth maybe $50,000. In 10 years that piece of paper all of your kids are going to have will be worth $100,000. Our land is worth billions. The big corporations aren't going to mind paying a few million for it. Some company from Japan or Europe, some oil company or mining company, will offer our kids $100,000, maybe more, for their shares. What do you think they're going to do? They're going to sell it. Maybe some of you older people won't but your kids will because that's what they're being taught. We're raising our kids to sell us out. Then who's going to own NANA? Whose going to own our land? Not us. Not the Iñupiaq. Some big company will own the land. We're right back to where we were when we thought we were going to lose it.

"When that money from selling the stock, from selling our land is all gone, when all the snowmachines it bought are broken down and all the liquor has been drunk up, guess what you'll have?" A howling wind blows outside, a wind that lays the cold on your face like an iron mask. Schaeffer's harsh verdict is no less chilling.

"You won't have Iñupiaq anymore, just a bunch of poor, hungry people living in their shacks on somebody else's land. You won't even be able to use the land anymore and your children will be scattered to the four winds living in the slums of America's cities.

"You won't even be able to live off the land because it will belong to someone else. They'll be mining or whatever. It will all belong to someone else and it will be all over for our people. We'll be finished."

The land belonged to God. Everybody could use it.

"So what am I doing working my butt off and getting gray-haired for you guys if you're going to sell us out in 1991? Why build a strong, profitable corporation for someone else to come up here and take away from us? That doesn't make much sense either, does it?

"It hasn't been easy for any of us working at NANA. We've been trying to put this together, trying to protect our land, and our kids are being taught that the only thing this corporation is worth is a piece of paper. Come 1991 we'll have worked 20 years for nothing.

"Let me tell you something. For the past eight or nine years Robert [Newlin, NANA board chairman] and I have been bumming around the NANA region. We come around and everybody says, 'Oh no, here come those NANA people again.' Listen, we're all NANA people. We've got to change the way our shareholders feel about NANA, because NANA is more important than just money. We have to change that.

"Take a look at these three problems (college graduates, jobs for shareholders, and land retention). Even though on paper, according to our auditors and accountants, it might look like we're doing great, we're not. We're creating jobs for white people. We're educating our kids to sell us out and if they finish college they go away from us because they start thinking like white people.

"We're educating all of our kids to leave us even if they don't go to college. We're educating them to think like white people so when 1991 comes around they think they're going to make money from their stock. So our land is gone, and when our land is gone what are we? Nothing! So that's my reason for being here tonight. A part of the problem, and only a small part of it, comes from looking at these things from NANA's standpoint.

"We're not doing any good. We're losing. Sure we can still make profits and pay out your lousy $200 dividend every year. But so what? That's not going to amount to anything. We're just making our company a better buy for some big company that wants to buy it in 1991.

"We've got to do something. We didn't work this long and hard just to give it away to somebody else.

"I'm just touching the surface and talking about things that are obvious—things we can look at and put numbers to. That's only a part of what we're talking about here, but it's a start so you know why NANA's involved in this thing. Even from the standpoint of business, the things we want to do—make jobs for our shareholders, get our kids through college, hold on to our land—things aren't working out. We've got a problem. That's where were at.

"When we started out a few years back we went around to the villages and asked you what you wanted. You all wanted phones, TV, electricity, new housing, sewer, and water. We got it for you. We [NANA] can't take credit for all of it. Other organizations worked on your needs, but basically NANA was in the lead.

"We had a study done not too long ago and guess what? Because of all these things you wanted, these things you've got now, you're poorer now than you were 10 years ago. That's what we've done for you, we've made you poorer. Maybe we should start over?"

"We've got other problems. Our suicide rate is the highest in Alaska—10 times the national average. That's the first thing we look at, why our people are actually dying, killing themselves.

"We don't think much about accidental deaths because we know this is rough country. But we have the state's highest rate of accidental death too and a lot of these are really suicides. Maybe someone doesn't have the guts to put a gun to their head, so they go out and crash or get drunk and freeze to death. Our people know enough to take care of themselves. Some of these accidents we've had these past few years, just aren't really accidents. Our people are dying. They're killing themselves.

"Alcohol and drug abuse is getting worse. We don't think much about alcohol abuse. We've had it for years. We all grew up with it. Well now our kids don't even think it's unusual to see their parents drunk. It's getting worse.

"Our families are breaking down. We're not helping with our housing. Families used to live together. They don't anymore. Now the only way you can talk to someone in your family is to call them on the phone. That's what we've done with all our new housing. That's how much help we are.

"We have more violence than we used to, people hurting each other. Our elders and our kids are getting beat up in their homes. We even have a special place for women to run away from their husbands and hide so they don't get beat up, those that have the guts to run away. The rest are still getting beat up. That's how bad things are getting.

"Vandalism, you can't leave anything lying around anymore. It gets stolen or smashed up. That shows us that people don't care about other people's property anymore. Our schools have to hire guards to protect the building from our kids.

"We've got other mental health problems and all the statistics that the experts at Maniilaq and the hospital keep telling us, these problems are getting worse.

"We've got the state and federal government spending millions of dollars on our problems, bringing up all these people to help us, running all these programs and things aren't getting better. They're getting worse.

"What's wrong? How did we get so screwed up? You won't have Iñupiaq anymore, just a bunch of poor people living on somebody else's land."

Sometimes using himself as humorous, or poignant, testimony, Schaeffer reviews the mounting body of evidence. His even gaze seeks out and measures the audience as he draws the grim and inevitable conclusion.

"What all this tell us is, that we're sick. I'm not sick, although I can relate to some of this because I have some of these problems. You're not sick, not as an individual. But we all know somebody else with one or more of these problems.

"We're all sick. As a people we're sick. That's what this means. As a people we're sick. And we're dying. As a people we're dying."

Sometimes he lets the sentence fall with the stark finality of a judge's gavel. On other occasions his voice can scarcely mask the emotional upheaval Schaeffer himself must feel as he says it.

"We're dying!" And his voice seems to collapse under the weight of pain and frustration. Schaeffer's own discovery of the Spirit and his solemn commitment to Iñupiaq Ilitqusiat can be traced to his foreboding awareness of his people's destiny.

"What's missing?" Schaeffer asks. He has not taken a room full of people to the heart of darkness simply to leave them there, reflecting on their shared despair, their cultural suicide.

Schaeffer turns to the coin's other side to speak of Iñupiaq strength and power, power in the darkness.

"After finally listening to what our elders have been trying to tell us all these years and after looking at these things with our board we decided that what's missing is human values or Iñupiaq values. We call them Iñupiaq values simply because we're Iñupiaq and these are our problems we're trying to work on. But they're really, most of them anyway, values that all human beings, all cultures share. We're not the only ones with these problems either. These problems are everywhere and the reason is human values, or Iñupiaq values, aren't being taught. They're not being passed along from one generation to another."

Robert Newlin and Bobby Curtis briefly discuss, define, and illustrate the values that constitute the Iñupiaq people's cultural ethics:

Knowledge of Language
Sharing Respect for Others
Cooperation
Respect for Elders
Love for Children
Hard Work
Knowledge of Family Tree
Avoid Conflict
Respect for Nature
Spirituality
Humor
Family Roles

Hunter Success
Domestic Skills
Humility
Responsibility to Tribe

"You can look at these things," Schaeffer resumes, "and all of you can get different ideas about what these things mean. But it doesn't make any difference because whatever it means to you, if it's good that's all right.

"You're going to see these things everywhere. An Ambler resident suggested that we go to our jade factory, and put these on a plaque for every village. Maybe you won't see them on a jade plaque, but you'll see them all over.

"What's missing is on the inside. There's nothing on the outside that will help us anymore. It has to happen inside of us. We have to get back to our human values, our Iñupiaq values, the things that you learned, or should have learned, as you grew up, the things that make you a good person, responsible to yourself and everybody else."

Your children will be scattered to the four winds.

"We've really been working on things that are not so important, like our business. That's white man's stuff. That's why you've got a half white man running it. We should have been working on these other things, what makes our people tick, what makes them happy, and what makes them do things."

"Why are these values missing? Earlier I asked how we got so screwed up. I'm not blaming anybody. No one's to blame really.

"The first white men who came up here were pretty bad. They were riff-raff, the bottom of the barrel from America. They brought booze and they brought diseases our people weren't ready for. Not only were the first whalers and miners that came up the worst kind of people, but they started living off our food base, killing our whales and caribou.

"Fifty years later when the first good white people came up here, they were the missionaries and they brought something good to our people, the gospel; our people were ready. In those 50 years our population had been reduced by half from disease and starvation. Our people could recognize something good and they wanted what the missionaries had to offer.

"So we gave them our kids and said: Teach them, teach them this new way: because we weren't surviving in the old way anymore."

When our land is gone, what are we?

"The government replaced them with schoolteachers, because they couldn't have these preachers teaching school. But our people couldn't tell the difference. They looked the same, they were doing pretty much the same thing. We asked if they were Christian and they were, just like the missionaries. It even sounds the same, teacher, preacher. So we continued to let them teach our kids. We thought they were teaching them values like they would learn at home or from the missionaries, but they weren't. They just learned reading, writing, and arithmetic, and English. They weren't supposed to speak Iñupiaq in the schools and pretty soon children couldn't even communicate with their parents or elders anymore. They couldn't have learned values if they had wanted to. No one could communicate with each other. We spoke two different languages."

Our land is worth billions. Someone won't mind paying a few million for it.

"That's why the first value is so important. The Iñupiaq language is the only way our older people can tell you about some of these things. They have a hard time telling you about important things in English."

In Kiana Bobby Curtis emphasized this point by pledging, "I want to have a family. I want to have children. But I'm going to make a commitment not to have children until I can speak Iñupiaq to them."

Schaeffer also points out that the critically diminished adult population and the advent of Western society's nuclear family, as opposed to the traditional extended family, also caused a breakdown in the passing of traditional Iñupiaq values from one generation to the next.

"What we have to do," Schaeffer concludes, "is find a way to teach these values to our kids again. No one can do it for us, not NANA, not the school district, not Maniilaq. We have to do this for ourselves. How are you going to do it? That's what I want you, as a village, to start working on and decide tonight.

"Now if you think we're all wrong and you don't think you have any of these problems let us know. We'll go away and never bother you again. But I think you'll agree that you do have these problems and we think this is the answer. And if you agree that you have these problems I'll keep coming back and bothering you until you do something about it. If I can't get you to come to a meeting I'll go to your home. I'm real serious about this and I'm going to become like a preacher to get this across. So what are you going to do?"

And Schaeffer walks away, leaving the floor, and the initiative, to the assembled village residents.

Not everybody likes to hear what Schaeffer has to say. Nearly everyone in the room, however, recognizes the unmistakable sound of the truth in what Schaeffer calls his "pitch."

Come 1991 we'll have worked 20 years for nothing.

One by one they come forward to discuss problems and solutions. The words come with difficulty and when they do come they are often choked with emotion.

By the time the meeting ends the villagers have designed the initial outlines of an Ilitqusiat program for their community.

Committees for elders, women, men, and young people are designated. Programs are proposed. Commitments are made. The Iñupiaq Ilitqusiat program has begun in another village. There is no turning back.

What's missing is on the inside.

The leaders have led. Meetings have been held. Problems and solutions have been discussed. Now the movement's real work begins, in villages, in households, in the hearts and minds of the region's people.

The response to Schaeffer is immediate, spontaneous, and unequivocal. It springs not so much from despair as from the discovery of collective strength and real human and ethnic unity. Men and women prepare to open a new and cleaner page in the history of Northwest Arctic Alaska and restore dignity and pride to the ancient saga of the Iñupiaq people. Iñupiaq Ilitqusiat is an agent of the popular will.

The movement is not building privilege or bureaucracy. It is not a nostalgic return to the past. People are taking their fate into their own hands and realizing the political maturity that grows out of direct action, and immediate involvement.

Every village and group will find its own form, take its own action, and speak its own language. Through the recently established Regional Elder's Council villages will express themselves in harmony. We have taken the first steps to build a stronger and more viable Iñupiaq society.

After hearing all this you can numb your senses with liquor and drugs or go home and watch TV. Look at the deadly love-making and violence on the screen. Is it better than real life? Wake up your mind to learn to live.

When the advertisements come on, walk into the night. Look inward. Peel aside all the external messages and find the message of Iñupiaq Ilitqusiat

Stay awhile in the street. Look at your neighbors passing by and say to yourself: The last word has not been said. Then act. Act with others, not for them. Close the chasm between fate and will. Learn the Iñupiaq values. Teach them. Make Iñupiaq Ilitqusiat happen here and now. It is your own.

Iñupiaq Ilitqusiat draws up a nearly definitive agenda for the forthcoming trial of Iñupiaq identity, for it is clear that a form of civilization is in suspense about its own survival and even its right to survive. Somehow that survival depends on our ability to restore our traditional values and take on our responsibilities to ourselves and to others.

In sharp contrast to a previous decade's struggle for traditional land rights, a struggle which became economic and political, Iñupiaq Ilitqusiat is social and cultural, so that people can become themselves. An entire society is embraced within its scope because Iñupiaq society is implosive: everybody is involved with everybody.

Alaska Native Education

History and Adaptation in the New Millennium

Angayuqaq Oscar Kawagley

Originally published in the *Journal of American Indian Education*,
vol. 39, no. 1 (Fall 1999).

Nature as Metaphysic

FOR THE YUPIAQ PEOPLE, culture, knowing, and living are intricately interrelated. Living in a harsh environment requires a vast array of precise empirical knowledge to survive the many risks due to conditions such as unpredictable weather and marginal food availability. To avoid starvation they must employ a variety of survival strategies, including appropriate storage of foodstuffs that they can fall back on during the time of need. Their food gathering and storage must be efficient as well as effective. If this were not so, how could they possibly hope to survive? To help them achieve this balance, they have developed an outlook of nature as metaphysic.

Not only are humans endowed with consciousness, but so are all things of the environment. The Yupiaq people live in an aware world. Wherever they go they are amongst spirits of their ancestors, as well as those of the animals, plants, hills, winds, lakes, and rivers. Their sense of sacredness

is of a practical nature, not given to abstract deities and theological ratio-
nalization. Pragmatism is the theme of their sacred ways. The *Ellam Yua*,
or Creative Force, is not given the same ultimate stature as the biblical
God. Because nature is their metaphysic, Yupiaq people are concerned
with maintaining harmony in their own environment. The Creative Force
is acknowledged and often given gratitude, though it is the immediacy of
nature that is most important.

The Yupiaq people have many taboos, rituals, and ceremonies to observe and practice that poignantly signify a harmonious ecological orientation. They behave accordingly because of what their culture has taught as
well as an abiding belief in what they and others have experienced first-
hand. There are mysteries of the world that to Yupiaq are unfathomable,
such as the *Ellam Yua*, but these are accepted. Such mysteries keep them
humble and ever mindful of the powers around them.

There were members of the Yupiaq community that transcended all
human levels of knowledge. These were the shamans, the dreamers, and
others who were receptive to nature's voices and intuitively deciphered a
message which was passed on by myth, taboo, ritual, ceremony, or other
forms of extraordinary happening. The shamans were gifted to travel freely
in the unseen world, and they often would return with new songs, taboos,
rituals, or ceremonies to teach. They were skillful with their knives and were
able to reify their remembrances and impressions of the gift from a spirit
with wood, bone, skin, feathers, and stone. These would become sacred
objects to be used in special ceremonies. Amulets were also prescribed by
the shamans to those requesting and willing to trade for them. These often
consisted of animal parts and/or other pieces of earthly creations. Taboos
were often conferred with the amulet or medicine bag, which was usually
worn as a necklace or sewn somewhere on the parka. There are many stories of how they were used when encountering an antagonistic spirit, animal, or another human being. This kind of healing is not new to the Yupiaq
people. The patient's belief in its healing power most likely had a lot to do
with the results.

The Yupiaq are told that if they take from another person's traps, the
person may not know, but the Creative Force will see that people learn of
their deeds and recognize the kind of person they really are. People may try
to change a person's tendency for stealing by joking and embarrassing him
or her in public. However, if there is no change, then he or she might be
shunned by the community. Taking another's life without cause is considered a heinous crime with banishment from the village traditionally being
the justice rendered.

The Yupiaq people were admonished to never do harm to, abuse, or even make fun of animals. Since Yupiaq people live in an aware world, the animals and everything else will always know. Several years ago, there was a news account of several walruses found dead on a beach with only their heads missing. The Fish and Wildlife managers lamented the fact that this was a wanton waste of meat and hides. One old Native man's comment to this was that it was unfortunate that it happened, and that the walruses had not been properly cared for. He concluded by saying that these animals would not be returning to earth. According to him, the misuse, abuse, and disrespect shown the animals would cause the spirits not to return to earth to be born and renew their kind again. From a Yupiaq perspective, this is why certain plants and animals have gone into extinction, and many others are on the endangered species list.

Certain animals represent power, e.g., the bear, wolf, raven, eagle, and beaver. Their commonality is strength and a strong will to live, along with cleanliness and care of self. Each possesses certain characteristics which set them apart from all others: the bear with its strength, the wolf with its social organization, the raven with its ability to remain airborne for great lengths of time, and the eagle with its visual acuity. The oil gland of the beaver is used for amulets, as well as for medicinal purposes. If a person has a shortness of breath, they can chew on a small piece and swallow the juice, thus relieving the stressful feeling. It is also thought to be particularly strong against spirits, so that merely having it in the hand is enough to keep a spirit at bay.

WHEN THE EARTH'S CRUST WAS THIN

Stories and myths abound from Distant Time, when the earth's crust was thin, when it was easy for people and animals to communicate or transform from one to the other. Some tell of animals and birds wearing special parkas with hoods. If they needed to communicate with man, all they needed to do was raise the hood, very much like taking off a mask. Lo and behold, there would be a human face underneath able to communicate in human language. This was an excellent way of learning about animals and how they wanted to be cared for once they gave themselves to the hunter. There is one important difference between human beings and animals. The animals seem to have not been given the knowledge of death. It is only the human who possesses this dubious knowledge. However, the Yupiaq person does not consider death the end, but rather a completion of a cycle that continues. As such, most have no fear of death.

The following story, told by William Oquilluk (1981), an Iñupiaq Eskimo from the Bering Strait area whose ways are very similar to the Yupiaq, provides an illustration of how observations of the characteristics of animals are integrated into the fabric of the Native mythology.

> It is a story of "Two Brothers" living with their mother and father. They are young boys always roaming around their environment. One day the boys are walking amongst the trees when they spot a camp robber nest. The younger boy says to his brother that these birds always steal from the camps and that he will sharpen a stick and kill the young birds. This he does. He climbs the tree and as each bird opens its mouth, he thrusts the stick down their throats killing them. Finally, there is only one left and the older brother forces the younger boy down, thereby saving one bird. Meanwhile, the parents are flying around making frantic noises.
>
> One winter, when the boys are hiking around they spot a rabbit. They give it chase. They get separated and are lost. Many animals help each boy during the year. They are invited to homes very often housing small people. They are housed and fed for a few days. When it is time for them to leave, they are told to go a certain distance before looking back. One time when leaving a home, they looked back and saw a beaver house with two beavers swimming about.
>
> The younger brother ended up in a large community house with many couples living inside. He stayed with them many days. Finally, the eldest man said that he hasn't much time to live, and that the boy will have to leave. The wife tells him how he had killed her children, save one. Because one had been left alive, she would spare his life, but he would have to take the girl as his wife. The little human beings changed to a variety of birds, and left in pairs each singing its own special song. He turned to look at the girl. She had changed to a full-sized human being. They departed and went to their camp which turned out to be quite close by.
>
> The older brother is shown by others the direction to go home. He soon joined the other brother. They grew to

a ripe old age, and eventually the older brother died followed closely by his younger brother. The latter slipped into another world and immediately saw his brother walking toward him. He could see that his brother had a cut on his lip. He noticed that he too had a similar cut. He told his brother that this was his punishment for killing those birds. They pondered the question of where they should go. The older loved the land, while the younger felt at home in the ocean. They decided that they would separate and go to the place of their liking. The older brother became a rabbit, the younger a seal. To this day they are classified together as they both have cleft lips and are brothers!

Mythology is an invaluable pedagogical tool that transcends time. As the storyteller talks, the Yupiaq listeners are thrust into the world of imagination. As the story unfolds, it becomes a part of their present. As you imagine and visualize in the mind's eye, how could you not become a part of it and it a part of you? There is no separation. The story and words contain the epistemological webbing; how is it we got to know these truths? The storyteller's inflections, play on words, and actions give special meaning to the listener. How the participants are to act and interact in the whole are clearly conveyed. To the outsider attempting to understand the meaning of the experience, it may appear to be merely a story, but to the insider it becomes reality leading to a spiritual orientation in accord with nature. This is quality knowledge whose end is happiness and a long life.

The Yupiaq people are admonished not to take themselves too seriously, but to laugh at themselves, with others, and make light of a lot of life's triumphs and tribulations. Joking is a necessary part of life. No matter how serious a ceremony, there will be joking and laughing interspersed between singing, dancing, and moments of silence. Silence is embraced as a time for introspection and collective mindfulness for a greater and better life. Because of this collective mindfulness, the individual man or woman becomes greater as a provider or as a homemaker. And as rational thinking would have it, the whole is always greater than the sum of its parts.

Through the millennia of their existence, the Yupiaq people worked as stewards of their world and maintained a balance between their culture, technology, and the environment around them. Their psychological satisfaction with their nature-mediated technology was on an even plane with their technological attainments. This allowed for nature as their metaphysic.

However, in the last 60 years or more there has appeared an ontological discontinuity. This is the period of time in which they have participated in the destructive acts of misuse, abuse, and disrespect of the ecological processes which produce life in their environment. How did they come about making this destruction of life? What has happened to cause their social organization to disintegrate with concomitant decay of their morality and disillusionment with their way of life?

YUPIAQ LIFEWAYS

Traditionally, men and women had very defined roles. The man was the provider, the one to work with nature in hunting and trapping. It was a solitary effort—solitary in that he did many activities by himself, but in reality he was always accompanied by spirits and in close contact with the animals and earth. His role as provider was to learn as much as possible from his father, extended family members, elders, and others, so as to be a success.

The woman, on the other hand, had to learn womanly duties from her mother, grandmother, and others. This included child rearing, food preparation, garment making, observing taboos having to do with menses and giving childbirth, and mindfully supporting her husband. The man's success as hunter was just as much her responsibility. They made up a team, complemented one another, and were very much equal in standing. The community members' bondedness to each other was mutual, adding to their wholeness and vitality.

When a child was born, the name of a recently deceased person was anointed to the newborn by pouring a little water into the mouth or sometimes sprinkling it onto the head. Thereafter, that was his/her name. The gender was unimportant. The relatives called the baby by that name and the kinship term associated with the person whose name was bestowed on the child. For example, if the deceased person's wife addressed the child, she would address it by name then follow it with "my husband." Thus a "new relative" was made, whether blood related or not.

The traditional houses in which families lived were constructed of sod in a semisubterranean fashion. A high, dry location was chosen, a circular hole dug down three to four feet in depth, and then a framework of driftwood was constructed. Sod was cut and carried to the site and placed on the wood frame with the vegetation-covered side next to the wood. Sometimes grass was placed between to serve as a natural vapor barrier. An opening at the top was covered with a seal or walrus gut canopy. This was removed when a fire was made in the fire pit for cooking or a fire bath. The house was a circular and domed structure with an enclosed entranceway much like the snow igloos of northern Canada.

The structure of the Yupiaq sod house has been likened to the woman's reproductive system. The ceiling's name in the Yupiaq language means "the above covering," a term which is now used to mean "heaven." The skylight is likened to the umbilical cord leading to the *Ellam Yua*, the interior to the womb, and the tunnel-like entrance to the birth canal, or "the way to go out." In the old days, when a person died, he or she was never removed through the entranceway, but through the skylight. The body was lifted and passed through the opening to the place of interment. The act was very symbolic of the spirit's journey to the spiritual land. The body was then placed with knees to the chest and arms around the knees bound together at the wrists—a fetal position, signifying completion of the life cycle and readiness for reincarnation and renewal. The body was then covered with driftwood or rocks, or sometimes with wooden planks, or a canoe or kayak overturned with the body inside.

The *qasegiq*, or community house, was mainly the domain of men and boys entering puberty. This is where much of the storytelling, teaching of arts and crafts, tests of skill and strength, and learning of rituals and ceremonies took place. It was the site of reintegration and renewal of spirit and where balancing occurred. When special ceremonies were conducted, participants from other villages were invited. The whole community and visitors from invited communities all participated and enjoyed the generosity of the host village. They renewed acquaintances and made new friendships, acknowledged the unseen greater powers, paid respects to their ancestors, celebrated the animal spirits, and even made a few marriage arrangements. The ceremonies reaffirmed the truths that the people chose to live by.

Much of men's and women's activities were patterned to the landscape. For those living on the upper riverine systems, the activities were bound to catching and preserving fish and hunting for land animals. Those on the coast hunted sea mammals, fish, and seasonal birds and eggs. The technological tools and implements were made from natural resources most abundant in their location, or were gained in trade from other areas. The materials consisted of wood, bone, stone, and skin, or sometimes nature-refined copper. They may have intuitively known that their technology would be restricted to unrefined natural resources, and that this would conform to their nature-adaptive orientation.

They may have observed themselves and others aging, tools wearing out, rivers getting shallow and changing course, trails where nothing grew, and that death and decay occurred everywhere. When a certain amount of matter and energy are no longer in usable state, some degradation is inevitable. Were they to refine natural resources, they would speed up the entropic process.

A few years ago, there was an old Native man on the Kobuk River speaking about the tundra fires raging about the state. He said that the earth is like a human being; it is aging, its skin is drying and graying. Therefore the fires never burn themselves out, rather they have to have firefighters or heavy rains put them out. He recalled fires years ago that naturally burned themselves out because of lush greenery and moisture. He talked of the earth as a living being, aging, decaying, and perhaps needing to be renewed. The Creative Force has not the patience nor compassion to accept a people that defile and destroy, and will take the shortest route to heal a festering sore.

CONSEQUENCES OF ADAPTATION

The encroachment of Western civilization in the Yupiaq world changed a people that did not seek changing. The Yupiaq people's systems of education, governance, spirituality, economy, being, and behavior were very much in conformity with their philosophy of life and provided for harmonious living. The people were satisfied with the quality of their life and felt that their technology was in accord with it. The culture- and nature-mediated technology was geared to a sustainable level of self-sufficiency.

The people in general were sufficiently content with their lifestyle that they did not readily accept Eurocentric education and religions when the first envoys of the dominant society set foot in their land. Eurocentric knowledge and technological might did not bring the Yupiaq people to compliance—rather it was the incomprehensible diseases that decimated the people. A great number of elders, mothers and fathers, shamans, and children succumbed to these new diseases. Whole villages were wiped out. The missionaries began to open orphanages and schools for the newly dislocated exiles in their own land. A hospital was located on the Kuskokwim River near Akiak and the Moravian Church established a children's home a short distance upriver. The federal Bureau of Education established "contract schools" with religious organizations. Money was paid to these organizations to establish schools and pay for the missionary teachers. The children were taught a new language (English) along with new knowledge and skills to become servants to the newcomers' needs and as laborers for newly established businesses. The Compulsory School Attendance Law was enacted, requiring families to remain in one location for many months of the year, thus ending the Native peoples' practice of moving from place to place according to the seasons and animal migration patterns. The restrictive law initiated a 12-year sentence given all Native children to attend school. Today, that sentence has increased to 13, including kindergarten. This has greatly reduced the freedom of people to be who they are, to learn traditional values, and to live in harmony with their environment. It has meant that the families and children no longer experience the great freedom of earlier times.

The schools do not require that the Yupaiq children learn their own languages and lifeways, but rather they are expected to learn a foreign language and the related humanities and sciences. The majority of teachers are from the outside world and have little or no knowledge of the people with whom they are going to be working. To the original people of the land, these are an immigrant people with a different way of being, thinking, behaving, and doing from the Yupiaq. Few teachers recognize that the indigenous Yupiaq are not like other European ethnic groups, such as the Irish, French, or Italians, who have chosen to leave their homeland. By not teaching the Yupiaq youngsters their own language and way of doing things, the classroom teachers are telling them that their language, knowledge, and skills are of little importance. The students begin to think of themselves as being less than other people. After all, they are expected to learn through a language other than their own, to learn values that are in conflict with their own, and to learn a "better" way of seeing and doing things. They are taught the "American Dream" which, in their case, is largely unattainable, without leaving behind who they are.

The messages from the school, the media, and other manifestations of Eurocentric society present Yupiaq students with an unreal picture of the outside world, as well as a distorted view of their own, which leads to a great deal of confusion for students over who they are and where they fit in the world. This loss of Yupiaq identity leads to guilt and shame at being Yupiaq. The resultant feelings of hurt, grief, and pain are locked in the mind to emerge as depression and apathy, which is further reinforced by the fear of failure in school, by ridicule from non-Natives, and by the loss of their spirituality. There are many contributing factors as to why Native children do not excel in school. I advance the following as a possible variable. I will do this by telling you a Yupiaq story:

> *Aka tamani, ellam kainga mamkitellrani.* In distant time,
> when the earth's crust was thin, is a crane flying around

looking for a likely place to eat. The sky is blue, the sun is shining, the tundra is warming. The crane decides to check out the weather. He begins to fly in a circle. Each time he completes the circle, he gains altitude. He looks at earth from a very high altitude. He then decides to descend and look for food. He flies over a river and sights a skin boat with Yupiat in it slowly paddling down the river. He continues his flight and sees a lake. He flies to it, and finds many kinds of berries. He is very hungry.

He lands on the riverbank. He contemplates going back to the tundra to eat berries, but his mind cannot forget the Yupiat coming down the river. He knows that he could be hunted. He must think of a way to warn him when the people approach. He sits there and thinks. He finally decides that he will use his eyes as sentries. He removes his eyes and puts them on a log. He instructs the eyes by telling them, "Now when you see people coming down the river, you warn me. I will come down and get you and fly off."

After telling them so, he goes back to the tundra and starts to eat berries. Soon he hears his eyes shout, "Crane, crane, there are people coming down the river!" He hurries down, finds his eyes, and plucks them back in the sockets. He looks. There is only a log drifting down the river. The branches must have resembled people. He gets upset and says to his eyes, "Now you be very careful and make sure they are people before you call for me." He goes back to the tundra and eats. Soon, he hears his eyes calling him, "Crane, crane, there is a boat with people in it coming down the river. Come quick!" He hurries down to the log and picks up his eyes and looks. There is only a chunk of tundra drifting down. Tufts of grass move up and down with movements of the clump of tundra.

"Now, look eyes you have made a second mistake. Look very carefully before you call for me. I'm going back to eat some more berries."

Soon afterward, the eyes call, "Crane, crane, people are coming down the river in a boat." This time the crane does not heed the call. He is thinking, "Well, I suppose they see something else that might resemble a boat and people. This time I won't respond." He continues to eat. Soon the eyes call, "Crane, crane, the people are almost upon us. Come quick." He does not answer.

Some time elapses, then he hears the eyes calling from a distance, "Crane, crane, the people have us, and they're taking us down the river."

The crane runs down to the riverbank and finds the log. He feels around, but there are no eyes. He sits down and thinks, "What am I going to do for eyes?" After much thought and consternation at not being able to see, he ambles back to the tundra. A thought occurs to him, "Why not try berries for eyes?" With that he finds blackberries. He plops them into his eye sockets. Lo and behold, he sees, but the world is different shades of black and grey. This can't be, so, he disposes of the blackberries. He finds salmonberries, and tries them. But the world is orange with its color variations and does not look right. So, he gets rid of them. He tries cranberries, but again the world is not the right color. It shows a place of red hues.

Finally, he tries blueberries. This time, the skies are blue, the tundra is green and varied in color, the clouds are white. Whew, these are to be his eyes. And, that is how the crane got BLUE eyes.

This is very mythical and magical. The myth is an analogical way of relating to their environment; it reflects the human mind's response to the world; it has to do with understanding; and it tells them that we humans have the heavy load of intelligence and responsibility to have a beautiful world to inspire them; and it is healing. The Yupiat people accepted this on faith because of the need to know and understand. To them, it made beautiful sense. If these people believe in a worldview that includes a language, an ecosophy, epistemology, and ecopsychology all contingent on Nature, so why should the things of Nature not be understandable and interchangeable. All have a spirit therefore a consciousness, an awareness of the world around them. So, the eyes are able to communicate, perhaps, not verbally but maybe through unsaid words. To the Yupiat, listening not only with the ears but with the mind and heart were essential to become aware of patterns of events that natural laws describe. The sun will rise and descend each day, the earth will continue to revolve around the sun, the spruce seeds will germinate, and so forth. These recurring phenomena will continue to occur in a given way. We accept these on faith that life is science.

Case in point is the crane flying in circles and ascending. The Yupiat knew that the tundra warms under the sun. This becomes visible as one looks out across the tundra on a warm day. One can see a disturbance over the tundra, heat waves rising. They know the scientific principle that hot air rises. This is the principle that the crane is using to get high into the air to look around. Is he not a scientist? Nature is science, science is nature. The Eurocentric scientists tell us that a gene or a combination thereof will produce an eye. After seeing this happen time and again, we accept it on faith. We will never understand the creative design behind the genetic mechanism for producing the eye, just as we will never know what creative forces or what entity started the physical laws into motion to bring about the "big bang." The scientific laws of nature merely explain or describe what physicists, astronomers, astrophysicists, and others have observed. The preconditions leading to this phenomenon have not been seen and are unimaginable. The Yupiat accept that which is unknowable, uncontrollable, and immeasurable.

The Eurocentric scientists tell us many things, such as that there are particles in the atom that are so small that no one will ever be able to see them. They exist only in mathematical statistics. But, we as a people accept these on faith. Do mathematics and physics really exist in Nature, or are they merely constructs of the human rational mind to try to make sense of this world? The important aspect to consider is that the modern creative scientist only deals with the physical and intellectual essences, in other words the outer ecology. In addition, the modern scientist makes theories based on sometimes limited facts, and these theories are made to fit their constructed technocratic societies. They do NOT necessarily fit reality. If these socio-politico-economics and scientific theories do not describe reality, they most certainly will not work in tribal societies because they are transrational. Perceptions can be far removed from what is real, and in Yupiaq thought are incomplete and often erroneous knowledge. This fragmentary approach disassociates them from the whole. In trying to understand the parts to understand the whole, their scientific methods skew their way of looking at things. Their assumptions and expectations muddle their efforts to see things as they really are. The Native creative mythology deals with the whole physical, intellectual, emotional, and spiritual of inner and outer ecologies. The Native person realizes that he/she is a microcosm of the whole, the universe. Therein lies the ultimate difference between the two.

Another problem is that the scientist's own identity remains a mystery. They try to control nature for narrow dehumanizing purposes. They invent antibiotics and weapons of mass destruction. Their lack of self-knowledge leads itself to nature keeping its secrets when we most need to let the book of Nature speak for itself.

The above Yupiaq story is a creative mythology of our ancestors. But is not the physicist who creates the statistics of unseen particles a creative mythologist? Is not the genetic microbiologist who determines what gene(s) cause Alzheimer's a creative mythologist? Is not the microbiologist who creates a clone of a dog not a creative mythologist? This latter thrusts me into the techno-mechanistic world whereby things discovered are rendered into useful tools and gadgets, such as the 747 jet, the snow-machine, outboard motor, cloning living things, antibiotics, fluoride toothpaste, skyscraper buildings, and the plastic raincoat. All are intensive in the use of natural resources and energy. They do not consider that the natural resources and energy sources of Mother Earth are finite, but the ultimate is to gain control over Nature and manipulate it for purposes of humankind. Supposedly, in the Eurocentric eyes, technology will produce more food, energy, and natural resources when they are used up. "Technology is the answer! (But what was the question?)" is a quote from Amory Lovins. Often, the industrial leaders are mainly concerned about financial gains which are driven by greed and ambition. Technological products and inventions are improved means to an often foggy or meaningless end. When a product such as a talking doll, cellular phone, new material for clothing is made, it does not change a small segment of life, but all of life. Psychological and economic changes are impossible to measure, just as bad and evil cannot be quantified. Because of this, technocracy has no conscience.

Mathematics and the disciplines of science have their own languages and areas of expertise. Each are isolated from the other so that there is no understanding of interrelationships and interconnectedness of all phenomena of this universe. In fact, each area of study has its own contrived language that makes disassociation with other disciplines and Nature easy. In these fields of study are an abundance of well-funded research projects generating rampant information and technological devices. But, what do these means lead to? Surely not to abundance of natural resources, natural beauty, and diversity, but, maybe, to natural degradation and poverty and confusion not only of humans but other creatures too. Our education skews our view of reality because of expectations and assumptions it produces as to what it should be.

A YUPIAQ WORLDVIEW

I now delve into the Yupiat ways of knowing and being in harmony with Mother Earth. I have enclosed a diagram of a tetrahedral metaphor of the Yupiaq worldview.

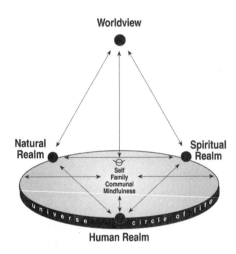

I have drawn a circle representing the universe or circle of life. The circle represents togetherness which has no beginning and no end. On this circle are represented the human, natural, and spiritual worlds. There are two-way arrows between them as well as to the worldview at the apex of the tetrahedron. These two-way arrows depict communications between all these functions to maintain balance. The Yupiat say *Yuluni pitallkertugluni*, "Living a life that feels just right." One has to be in constant communications, with each of the realms to know that one is in balance. If the feeling is that something is wrong then one must be able to check to see what might be the cause for unease or dis-ease. If the feeling of being just right comes instinctively and this feeling permeates your whole being, then you have attained balance. This means that one does not question the other functions intellectually, but that one merges spiritually and emotionally with the others. The circle brings all into one mind. In the Yupiat thought world, everything of Mother Earth possesses a spirit. This spirit is consciousness, an awareness. So the wind, river, rabbit, amoeba, star, lily, and so forth possess a spirit. The human consciousness with its ability to merge into one with all consciousnesses of this world produces the holotropic mind. The holistic mind is given to the nurturance of health, and an environmental ethic.

Thus, if all possess a spirit/soul, then all possess consciousness and the power that it gives to its physical counterpart. It allows the Native person to have the aid of the spirit to do extraordinary feats of righting an unbalanced individual psyche, community disease, or loss of communication with the spiritual and natural world through irreverence toward beings of Nature. Spiritual strength gives its possessor the power to communicate with other beings, adopting aspects of their wisdom or power, and reestablishing links with them when the connection has been lost through negligence or lack of reverence, or by offending either the animal spirits or one of the greater spirits of the natural world. These are not available through Eurocentric scientific research methods but only through the ancient art of shamanism or Nature thought. From this you can see that when we rely on Eurocentric means of research, it is a limiting factor, and this is what our institutions of higher learning espouse and teach. Many areas of social and scientific research teach one way of trying to learn and understand phenomena. Our technological and scientific training imprison the students' minds to its understandings much to the detriment of the learners who enter the mainstream Eurocentric world to become members of progress and development.

The Alaska Native needed to take lives of animals to live. To give honor, respect, dignity, and reciprocation with the animals whose lives were taken, the Native people conceived and put into practice many rituals and ceremonies to communicate with the animal and spiritual beings. These are corroborated through the Alaska Native mythology which are manifestations of fundamental organizing principles that exist within the cosmos, affecting all our lives. It behooves the Alaska Native person to leave something behind such as a piece of dry fish when getting mouse food from the tundra. The mouse food is gathered in the early fall so that the mouse and its family will have opportunity to collect more food for the winter. The seal when caught is given a drink of water so that its spirit will not be thirsty when it travels to the animal spiritual kingdom. This is done to show respect to the animal for having shared and given its life to the hunter. Medicinal plants are gathered respectfully knowing full well their power to heal. It is also to recognize that these were given freely by Nature and that requires that we share these freely. The Alaska Native person is aware that if we do not use these gifts of Nature regularly, mindfully, and respectfully, they will begin to diminish through disuse or misuse. Earth, air, water, fire, and spirit must always be in balance. The elements have an important niche to play in the ecological system. With this concept in mind, it then requires that we carefully examine the lifestyles and technology that are extant in this world. Our lifestyles have become materialistic and given to technological devices and gadgets galore that are not geared to sustainability. Our modern cities with their network of buildings, transportation, communications, and goods and services distribution centers are often destructive and given to conformity. Likewise, the studies of natural resources are given to conformity. They are approached in a fragmentary way whereby an expert in harbor seals does not know what the expert in herring fish is doing. This type of research is geared for measuring and objectifying the species studied for management purposes and not for sustaining Mother Earth.

In the Eurocentric world of science and technology exists many alternative approaches that are nature-friendly and sustainable. They await the time when the global societies evolve from consumerism, materialism, and consumption to ones that are oriented to conservation and regeneration. As Alaska Native people and other indigenous societies, we have much to share with the modern world. I believe it is much more difficult to live in tune with and in concert with Mother Earth than it is to plunder earth, air, fire, water, and spirit using the sciences and their offspring, the technologies, as tools of destruction. Eurocentric mathematics and sciences and the resulting techno-mechanistic inventions impact and change our ways of thinking and present new tools to think with, including the computer and other means of communications. These modern inventions and thinking are inimical to living in nature, with nature, and being of nature. It behooves us as indigenous peoples to learn both ways of knowing and doing, so that we can begin to develop a caring consciousness and a technology that is kind to our being as humans, to the spiritual and the natural. The question now is: How do we counteract the depression, hopelessness, and despair that derive from the unfulfilled promises of the modern world, and what role can schooling and education play in this effort? To address this question, it will be necessary to take a closer look at how traditional education and Eurocentric schooling have fit into the lives of the Yupiaq people.

LEARNING FROM NATURE

It is through direct interaction with the environment that the Yupiaq people learn. What they learn is mediated by their cultural cognitive map. The map consists of those "truths" that have been proven over a long period of time. As the Yupiaq people interact with nature, they carefully observe to find pattern or order where there might otherwise appear to be chaos. The Yupiaq people's empirical knowledge of their environment has to be general and specific at the same time. During their hunting trips into the tundra or on the ocean in the winter, they must have precise knowledge of the snow and ice conditions, so over many years of experience and observation they have classified snow and ice with terms having very specific meanings. For example, there are at least 37 Yupiat terms for ice, having to do with seasons, weather conditions, solar energy transformations, currents, and rapid changes in wind direction and velocity. To the Yupiaq people, it is a matter of survival. This knowledge is passed down from generation to generation by example, by showing, and by telling with stories to reinforce the importance of knowing about the varying conditions. This comprises the rational side of the Yupiaq people.

The rational mind has the ability to see and store many bits of observed information, which can then be mulled over and shared with others for more ideas of what it may mean. This may evolve into a tentative assumption of how and why something is the way it is. Being self-aware of the subconscious and intuition, the Yupiaq people let it play in their minds until a direction or answer evolves. They observe nature's indicators and come to a tentative supposition, followed by testing with further observation of variables that may affect the conclusion. They know that nature is dynamic and they have to change with it. Thus their conduct of life changes with nature. They pass on the truths to the next generation, knowing fully well changes in interpretation will occur, but that certain of their values, such as caring, sharing, cooperation, harmony, and interconnectedness with the created whole of their environment, will continue. This then validates and gives dignity to their existence.

One cannot be conscious of the world without first being aware of oneself. To know who you are, what your place in the world is, and what you are to strive to seek in life is what self-awareness is all about. It is the highest level of human knowledge, to know oneself so intimately that you are not afraid to tell others of life, and to help those that need help with compassion without being dragged down by the troubles of those being helped. Knowledge of oneself is power, and you acquire it by looking into yourself to see what strengths and weaknesses you have. You accomplish this through looking at your own reactions to everyday situations, both good and bad.

To achieve a secure sense of oneself involves meditation, visualization, intuition, and tempering all thoughts and actions with the "heart," which is on a higher plane than knowledge of the mind. "Heart" can best be explained by giving examples: to give freely of oneself to help a person with personal problems; to bring a little bird home with a broken leg and care for it to restore its health; to come upon a moose mired in soft snow and shovel the snow away to free it; to be motivated by kindness and care—these all involve the exercise of heart. You can recognize people with heart by the respect shown them by others through kind words, inclusion in community activities, and acceptance as a stable and common-sensical member of the community.

The Yupiaq's careful and acute observational ability taught them many years ago the presence of a Creative Force. They saw birth and death in the human, and in nature. This Creative Force flowed through everything— the years, months, days, rivers, lightning and thunder, plants, animals, and earth. They were awed by the creative process. They studied, they connected, and nature became their metaphysic. It gave them empirical knowledge. Products of nature extended to them ideas for developing their technology. The spider web provided the idea for the net; the snowshoe hare's feet and tracks, their snowshoes; the mouse's chamber lined with grass, their houses; the moon's phases, their calendar; the Big Dipper and the North Star, their timepiece at night; wind directions, their indicators of weather; flint and slate, their cutlery. Certain plants and herbs gave them their healing powers and they discovered that certain living things were adapted to live in certain areas, while others were able to make physical adjustments through changes in coloration, forming a heavier coat for winter, hibernation, estivation, etc., all under trying conditions. They noticed change across time and conditions, and they recognized that they too would have to change with time and conditions to survive.

It was meaningless for Yupiaq to count, measure, and weigh, for their wisdom transcended the quantification of things to recognize a qualitative level whereby the spiritual, natural, and human worlds were inextricably interconnected. This was accomplished through the Creative Force having endowed all earthly things with spirits, which meant that they would have to deal with all things being alive and aware. Having a Raven as creator of man and woman and everything else ensured that humans would never be superior to the other elements of creation. Each being endowed with a spirit signified that it possessed innate survival skills. It had the will to live, propagate, and care for itself, thus the need to respect everything and to have taboos, rituals, and ceremonies to keep the three realms in balance.

Nature's indicators and voices give much knowledge for making a living, but the intuitive and spiritual knowledge gives wisdom to make a life. Therein lies the strength and tenacity with which the Yupiaq people continue to maintain their identity, despite assaults on the philosophical, epistemological, ontological, economical, and technological fronts. Their template has certainly eroded, but the continuity of their ways to comfort and create harmony persists. As long as the Yupiaq people's spirituality is intact, they will withstand.

A Yupiaq Educational System

If the Yupiaq people are to really exercise the option of educational control it will require that the schools become Yupiaq staffed, Yupiaq administered, and Yupiaq in practice. Outsiders have to realize that outsiders' control, and the resulting forms of curricula and teaching, are not well synchronized to Native consciousness. The Yupiaq people have not been dehumanized to the level that they are unable to devise and implement their own programs to release them from the clutches of poverty and self-degradation. Why should someone from the outside come in with foreign values and forms of consciousness and impose them upon another? The people know their reality far better than anyone else. The Eurocentric models of education and progress have not been able to bring to fruition their promises, so they must acquiesce in their "cognitive imperialism" and allow the Yupiaq people an opportunity to plan and work for their own destiny.

It is for the Yupiaq people to strive for an educational system that recognizes their language and their culture, including their methods of doing science, by which they have learned from their environment and have lived in harmony with it. They do not have to become someone else to become members of the global society—they can continue to be their own people. Yupiaq spiritual values are still applicable today because they are nature-based. Yupiaq consciousness has enabled them to be survivors for many thousands of years up through the 20th century. This survival continues as Yupiaq values, beliefs, practices, and problem-solving strategies are modified and adapted to fit contemporary political, educational, economic, social, and religious institutions. Doing this allows the Yupiaq infrastructure to expand out from the village to encompass institutions such as Native corporations, schools, and churches. The values embedded in these modern institutions are often in conflict with the Yupiaq, so a blending of traditional and modern values becomes necessary.

As Yupiaq people assert greater influence on the educational system, there will begin to emerge a Yupiaq educational philosophy and principles that give cultural and cognitive respect to the Yupiaq learner. Formal schooling can be coupled to the community in such a way that the natural learning that is already taking place in traditional community and camp settings can be validated in the same way as the formal learning which occurs in the school. Students can first learn their language, learn about themselves, learn values of their society, and then begin to branch out to the rest of the world. They may later make a choice as to what they want to do and where to live. Given such a foundation, they can fearlessly enter any world of their choice, secure in their identity, their abilities, and with dignity as human beings.

There is a crying need for healing among the Alaska Native people. One desideratum of this process is the need for Alaska Native people to retain their unique Native identities. This is best done through the use of the Native language because it thrusts them into the thought world of their ancestors and their ways of apprehending and comprehending their world. In the use of the Native language, the students begin to appreciate the richness and complexity of their philosophical and spiritual worldviews. Thus, the need for Native languages to be the foundation upon which the learning rests. The camp learning can take place in all the seasons with the Native elders being the prime movers. The Native language descriptions of traditional activities best convey the relationships between a Native concept and practice. The camps should include not only Native languages and practices but also Eurocentric scientific concepts and practices. All daily activities should be coordinated to effectively and efficiently teach and validate both thought worlds.

These "bridging camps" must not overlook the Eurocentric mathematics and scientific concepts. The students have to have a keen understanding of science and research as many scientific findings corroborate Native observations and also show why Mother Earth is suffering. Many research activities may be for the sake of science, but they do show globally stressed arenas. This makes it necessary that young people learn Eurocentric concepts as well as their own ways of recognizing patterns, symbols, estimation/intuitive measurement, and ways of keen observation of place. The Native students have to realize that our ways of measuring and knowing are identity-building processes. Native students can then pursue careers in mathematics and the sciences buttressed in a worldview that gives them a nurturing disposition to the world.

To make the changes indicated requires a teamwork effort between the elders, parents, younger community members, and tribal leaders. The elders have heard statements made that life in these modern days is much easier. They say that this is true only from the material point of view. It is easy to buy nets, traps, refrigerators, microwaves, snowmachines, outboard motors, and so forth. It is easy for them to get general assistance and other social service monies to buy their needs. But, the elders say that there are hidden costs attached to these material benefits. They are taking part in the exploitation and control of natural resources with a concomitant development of personal avarice and ambition, making them more like the white man. Along with this change is pain and suffering due to conflicts with fellow Yupiaq people. The money will not flow forever, and what will the Yupiaq people do then, if they lose their language, natural knowledge, and their hunting, trapping, and gathering skills. The elders say they are losing the knowledge and skills needed for survival in a fast-changing world.

A YUPIAQ CURRICULUM

The educational process must begin with the consciousness extant in each Yupiaq location. The school should not be compartmentalized into subject areas, but should strive for the care and nurturing of skills such as communication (in their own language and English), decisionmaking (through the use of common sense), analytical and critical thinking, and recognizing that there are many different ways of doing things. Teachers should use the community and environment as sources of instruction and learning. Elders should be included often to share their life experiences and observations. Schools are usually bereft of mnemonics to the communities' Yupiaqness. Artifacts, photos, and posters pertaining to Yupiaq people, values, and admonishments to leading a good and long life should be highly visible. Local and visiting Native leaders should be invited to speak to classes sharing what it took for them to get to their positions.

Although exposure of students to Yupiaq arts and crafts is important, the philosophical, epistemological, and ontological aspects of Yupiaq life should be woven throughout their educational experience. Art is an important avenue for opening new unseen worlds as well as getting to know oneself.

Science and art should be taught together. The Yupiaq technology and its applied science should be incorporated into all science courses. Students should be given opportunities to tinker with gadgets and work on projects for Yupiaq science fairs. At the secondary level, the students should be challenged to try to think of alternative ways of doing things, such as making new tools and making things simpler. For example, they can use complex technology to develop simpler, easy-to-fix, less expensive, more energy-efficient tools made of local materials and adapted to their needs and environment.

Students should be mindful that people are not the only inhabitants of earth, but that we share our environment with "others." All teaching should embrace ecology. What happens to one part of a system ultimately affects the whole. They should be invited to dream and talk about eco-development projects that would enhance the environment rather than detract from it. How might technology help to make the environment more beautiful and productive without artificial means such as chemical fertilizers, hormones, and chromosomal splicing? These modern technological methods try to emulate the Creative Force when we cannot know what the consequences might be.

Organic gardening should be explored using a wood frame with modern plastic covering to grow vegetables and berries. Many fish camps throw away the heads and viscera of the fish being split. A project might include students from different families collecting these and placing them in barrels or drums to make fish fertilizer. The fertilizer can be used to help grow vegetables and berries, with the students rotating responsibilities for the care and maintenance of the plot. Grown vegetables and berries can then be traded for fish, moose meat, and so forth, or put away for special ceremonies in the village. Some might even be used for school lunches.

The students can find out from elders about plants and herbs with medicinal value and begin to cultivate them in the classroom or hot houses. They can explore ways of using the available sunlight during the winter. They can talk about traditional housing technology—what it was made of, how it was constructed, and how it took advantage of the insulating quality of the ground and sod. Modern housing is built with attention to aesthetics, but often is heat inefficient. How might the houses be made better? What materials are available locally? What modern materials might be used as new building material?

Historically, the Eurocentric educational system told the Yupiaq people that their ways of doing and thinking were inferior. The schools took pains to change the Yupiaq cognitive map and introduced them to new kinds of houses, tools, and gadgets. This not only cost the people in terms of their values, traditions, and self-sufficiency, but as a result they became wards of the government—a despondent people dependent on the "good will" of others. Education has made Yupiaq people consumers instead of producers in charge of their own livelihood.

The time has come for the Yupiaq people to pick themselves up and remember the spirituality, common sense, intelligence, creativity, ingenuity, and inventiveness of their ancestors. They must return to an emphasis on "soft technology"—technology that is adapted to culture and environment.

They have been victimized, as have many other people in the world, by the myth of progress and development. Their minds are imprisoned by the modern world, with its syncopating lights and gadgetry that is hypnotic and desirable, but in reality presents a mishmash of images in a shotgun fashion, with little connection to the vagaries of real life. It is time for the Yupiaq to get in rhythm with their own culture. There is no need to forsake all that has been presented by others. Technology and schools have their place, but they must be used with reason and in a sacred way to edify and enhance Yupiaq peoples culture, environment, and the world as a whole.

Reference

Oquilluk, W. 1981. People of Kauwerak. Alaska Methodist University, Anchorage.

PART II

NATIVE PATHWAYS TO EDUCATION

————◆◆✕◆◆————

"Indigenous education, as a medium for both personal development and intellectual empowerment, is critical for the continuance and celebration of Indigenous cultures.**"**

From the *Coolongatta Statement on Indigenous Rights in Education*

SERVING THE PURPOSE OF EDUCATION

Leona Okakok

Originally published in the *Harvard Educational Review,*
vol. 59, no. 4 (November 1989).

ALASKA! TO MANY WHO have never been here, the mere mention of the word brings visions of a vast and barren land, a landscape shaped by the endlessly drifting snow, where the human quest for survival is thwarted at every turn by the malevolent forces of nature. Vast, yes. And though I would not dismiss perceptions of barrenness, cold, and a constant quest for survival, I want to put them in perspective.

When people read about northern Alaska—even excellent material—or come here for a short period of time, they form a perception of our land and people based on experiences having nothing to do with us. For instance, if you come from an area that is rich in varieties of landscape, the flat tundra of the high Arctic—no matter how full of life—may seem barren to you. You will not see all the various signs of life that are obvious to longtime residents of the area. The same applies to the perception of cold. If your mind is focused on the 70° temperatures back home, the spring here will seem cold to you—although it may be even warmer than usual to a seasoned resident.

Many non-Alaskans assume that everyone prefers warm weather. But, though warmth is certainly welcomed and appreciated during appropriate times of the year, for a hunting society in the North it is not the weather of choice during critical overland travel time into hunting areas. Our preference, then, depends more on necessity than sensation. Unusual warmth would concern an Alaskan hunter. An early thaw could severely jeopardize travel to his spring hunting sites, threatening his ability to provide food for his family for the coming year. Travel to hunting sites has to coincide with the migration of certain animals through these areas. If the rivers break up early, travel is hampered, at best, and life-threatening, at worst.

But Native people as well are not immune to applying old perceptions to new experience. My mother-in-law visited my husband and me in California while we were attending school there some years ago. Looking through the backyard window of our apartment, she remarked that someone "ought to cut down this tree back here. It just blocks an otherwise beautiful view." To her, a good view allowed one to see far away without obstruction. She did not realize that, in that part of the world, the tree was a valued part of the view.

We all know that we can go through life convinced that our view of the world is the only valid one. If we are interested in new perceptions, however, we need to catch a glimpse of the world through other eyes. We need to be aware of our own thoughts, as well as the way life is viewed by other people. It is my hope that this article will show you a different way of looking at northern Alaska and at us, the Iñupiat Eskimos who live here.[1]

NORTHERN ALASKA IÑUPIAT ESKIMOS

The Arctic has been home to the Northern Alaska Iñupiat Eskimos for thousands of years. Our history as a people is rich in tradition, passed on through the centuries, generation to generation, by storytellers widely known for their skillful art. These stories and legends both entertain and help us to better understand who we are.[2] Because of the high value we place on the ability to retell these stories and legends accurately, we can better ensure that Iñupiat strengths and values are passed on to each succeeding generation.

Oral history and the art of storytelling, highly developed in a society which used it to pass on subsistence techniques and cultural values, is still practiced today, but the critical element in the process—the audience—has changed. Audiences which used to be composed of young and old listeners now usually include only the elders. Our accelerated entry into the 20th century has brought much confusion. Besides the daily chores critical to life in the Arctic, new and varied concerns, including Western education and religion, vie for the time and interest of the child. Even if children are interested, rarely do they have time to sit quietly, to listen and learn from their elders. The purpose of these long storytelling sessions—that of passing down values and other important elements of our culture—is severely restricted. The elders' role as the teachers and resource regarding contemporary life is no longer a given. Now, excellence in the subsistence way of life does not ensure survival in our modern world. The cash economy, Western civilization, and Christianity—concepts which the elders could not teach when they were introduced—emerged as standards against which others judged our life.

Parents, recognizing the inevitable encroachment of the Western way of life upon Iñupiat land and culture, reluctantly released their young into the hands of schoolteachers, who assured them that this was best for their child. We respected the judgment of these newcomers to the area—teachers and ministers—because they were authorities on the new way of life. They represented the efforts of the United States Bureau of Education, which, through a contractual arrangement with churches, was committed to providing an education to children within what was then the District of Alaska. We did not realize that their objective was to educate our children enough to reject their own culture and to embrace the "more civilized" Western way of life. With this purpose firmly in mind, Western education began for our young.

THE EARLY YEARS

In order to show the disruption caused by the displacement of our own educational system, I will briefly sketch the early development of Western education in our area of Alaska, which began in 1889 when the first school was established in Barrow (it was administered by the Presbyterian Church through a contract with the federal Bureau of Education). This early phase continued until the 1920s, causing changes that affected the whole community: Children were no longer learning the ways of our people at home, and families were severely restricted from taking their children along on extended hunting trips—the children's prime learning experience. Families often had to depend on relatives willing to allow children to remain with them in the village while their parents were on extended hunting leave. Although many elders now gratefully acknowledge their relatives' hospitality back then and recall being treated as children of the household, there was much left to be desired. Certainly there were exceptions, but frequently those who were given the chance to attend school had to continue their basic education—achieving the ability to survive in their world—long after others their age had achieved success as subsistence hunters. The effort to mainstream the Iñupiat children into Western society failed.

The focus of education in the North shifted only after local control was initiated in the mid-1970s. No longer were we, as a people, to be forced to assimilate into Western society. Western education would serve its purpose, but it would be a purpose determined by our own people.

THE DISTRICT

Eben Hopson, the power behind the formation of the North Slope Borough, our Home Rule Government, said in a speech before the local School Board in December 1975:

> Possibly the greatest significance of Home Rule is that it has enabled us to regain control of the education of our children. We must now begin to assess whether or not our school system is truly becoming an Iñupiat school system reflecting Iñupiat educational philosophies, or are we, in fact, only theoretically exercising political control over the educational system that continues to transmit White urban culture. Political control over our schools must include professional control as well in our academic institutions if our academic institutions are to become an Iñupiat School System able to transmit our Iñupiat traditions, values and ideas.[3]

In his speech, Mr. Hopson also reiterated the basic purpose behind the formation of the North Slope Borough School District: stopping the assimilation process which had long been advocated by Bureau of Indian Affairs schools as the only way to "civilize" our people.

In assuming control over our educational system, which began after the establishment of the North Slope Borough School District in the mid-1970s, we, the people of the northern countries, have struggled with the problem of Western content and approaches to education in our schools. While seeking to produce students with scholastic achievements comparable to those of other areas of the United States, the board has also sought ways to bring into our schools certain elements of historical and contemporary Iñupiat Eskimo culture and knowledge of our natural environment. We have found that the attainment of academic skills in our students is directly related to our ability to successfully introduce Iñupiat Eskimo concepts and educational practices into our schools. This paper describes some of our actions in this area. After discussing some important differences between the Iñupiat and Western concepts of education, I will describe some of the modifications to our school system and innovations that we have implemented with some success.

The North Slope Borough School District, established in 1972, is the northernmost school district in the United States and encompasses the northern third of Alaska, an area of approximately 88,000 square miles. The district serves nine schools in eight villages with over 1,500 students, a majority of whom are Iñupiat Eskimo (Northern Alaska Eskimo). The largest of these villages is Barrow, the northernmost community in the United States. Ipalook Elementary School, the largest of the nine schools, is located here, with a school population of 580 children from ECE (Early Childhood Education) through grade six. (Barrow has a separate junior/senior high school.) The smallest of our schools is Cully School in Point Lay, Alaska, with a total pupil population of 46, ECE through 12th grade. Most of the other schools fall somewhere in between Ipalook and Cully.

What draws these nine schools together is a common heritage, language, and the municipal government under which they were established. We decided that local control was the only way to ensure that our values as Iñupiat people were reflected within the school system. Great strides have been made with the formation of the school district and the subsequent redefining of the purpose of education. We had to take a "foreign" system— the Western educational system—and strive to make it work for us. This has not happened without its share of problems, however. The differences between cultures and lifestyles were ignored for far too many years in the hope that what worked for the White population could be made to work for our Native people by mere persistence.

THE ROLE OF LOCAL CULTURE
IN THE LEARNING PROCESS

We, the indigenous people of the United States, have had to overcome many obstacles in order to acquire basic education. One of the main obstacles was language. Not only were we required to learn to read, at the same time we also had to learn the language we were learning to read in. In the late 1930s and early 1940s, in order to help children learn English, teachers visited Iñupiaq parents and instructed them to speak only English to their children. Most parents knew very little, if any, English, so they were effectively being told to sever communication with their children. Parents were willing to comply with this instruction, except that their great love for their children and the necessity to interact with them sustained Iñupiaq in the household, thus keeping alive the foundation of our culture. But severe retardation of our native language did take place in time. Besides ordering that English be spoken at home, teachers punished children for speaking their mother tongue in the classroom. I remember clearly catching myself many times speaking in Iñupiaq during my first few years in school and feeling guilty for doing so. I was rarely caught and, therefore, rarely punished, but others were not so lucky. Many times we'd hear the whack of the ruler either on the head or the palm of the hand of any student caught being "naughty" and speaking in our language.

But we spoke in our own language in order to survive. Imagine learning to say a word in a language you did not know, and having no earthly idea what that word represented. As hard as learning a foreign language was, however, it was easier than absorbing the content of Western education. The worldview of the West, the perspective from which our schoolbooks were written, was totally different from ours. Therefore, understanding what we were learning to read in the English language came very hard. For example, as I was learning to read, one of my earliest realizations was that, in the Western world, grandparents and other relatives are not people you see or visit every day, even when they live nearby in the same town or city. A visit from them is an occasion, a cause for special preparations. This behavior was so foreign to my experience that it took me a long time to understand what I was reading and to realize that extended families are not the norm in the Western world.

In our communities, visiting relatives is a frequent, everyday occurrence, learned in early childhood. Unplanned, spontaneous visits (as opposed to purposeful visits) bond our relationships with relatives and friends. When visiting is unplanned, it does not require a formal invitation; tea or a soft drink is usually served unless it is near mealtime, when visitors will be expected to join in the meal. Other cultural practices, such as the special relationships between grandparents and grandchildren, reinforce these visiting patterns. A high degree of social interaction is the norm in our communities.[4]

During the years my husband and I attended the University of Alaska in Fairbanks, my father's first cousin, an elderly lady, lived right in town, an area where I frequently shopped. When I took my father there for a visit I was soundly scolded for visiting only when I had a purpose—in this instance, taking my father to see her. Although I was living in the same town, I had not nurtured my relationship with my aunt with intermittent, spontaneous visits.

In the Western world privacy is considered such a basic right that I am afraid many find it hard to understand the value of spontaneous visits. It is equally hard for us to understand why anyone would want to have so much privacy that developing nurturing relationships becomes very difficult, if not impossible. This is an example of one area where two very diverse cultures have different but equally valid values; members of both cultures have to strive to acknowledge and to understand each other's differences.

Another example of the proliferation of Western concepts and Western "realities" contained within textbooks is the "fact" that the sun rises in the East and sets in the West. This is included in tests that evaluate the child's understanding of the world around him or her. In the Arctic, however, the sun behaves differently. Depending on the time of year, it can do almost anything, six examples of which are: (1) it doesn't rise at all; (2) it peeks through the horizon for a few minutes; (3) it rises in the South and sets in the South a few minutes later; (4) it rises in the East and sets in the West; (5) it rises in the North and sets in the North almost 24 hours later; or (6) it doesn't set at all. During the whole process of moving from the first instance to the last, so gradual is the sun's movement along the continuum that it is almost imperceptible. You will note that the Western world's "fact" about the sun rising in the East and setting in the West is only one of various northern Alaskan realities. Saying that the sun rises in the East and sets in the West up here would be like saying that a yo-yo with a two-foot string reaches 12 inches. Certainly it does, at some instant, reach the 12-inch point, but there are infinite points along the string that it also reaches, including being fully wound and fully extended.

Because the rising and setting of the sun rarely changes in the rest of the United States, it does seem a useful gauge in determining a child's learning. But for children in the far North, there are too many variables for "the" fact of where the sun rises and sets for it to be useful. For Western students, the direction of shadows or looking in the direction of the rising or setting sun are obvious clues to the time of day. But when these clues were presented in schoolbooks, I was always looking also for clues as to the time of year, which, I later realized, even if they were given, would not have helped at all. Although I am a puzzle fan, I was often understandably stumped by what I later learned was no puzzle at all to Western students.

Those of us who experienced these problems during our schooling realized that we had to find a better way to teach our children. We who work at the grassroots level of education—the locals PTAs, advisory committees, and school boards—are in a unique position to observe schooling in action. We are often the first to know when something works and when it doesn't.

CONTRASTING DEFINITIONS OF EDUCATION

To me, educating a child means equipping him or her with the capability to succeed in the world he or she will live in. In our Iñupiat communities, this means learning not only academics, but also to travel, camp, and harvest wildlife resources in the surrounding land and sea environments. Students must learn about responsibilities to the extended family and elders, as well as about our community and regional governments, institutions, and corporations, and significant issues in the economic and social system.

"Education" and "schooling" have become quite interchangeable in everyday speech. When we talk of a person being educated we usually mean he or she has gone though a series of progressively higher formal systems of learning. Although a person may be an authority on a subject, we don't usually think of him or her as "educated" if he or she is self-taught. Since all of our traditional knowledge and expertise is of this latter type, the concept of "an educated person" has worked against us as a people, creating conflicting attitudes, and weakening older and proven instructional methods and objects of knowledge. Therefore, we, the North Slope Borough School District School Board, have defined "education" as a lifelong process, and "schooling" as our specific responsibility. This is expressed in our Educational Philosophy statement: "Education, a lifelong process, is the sum of learning acquired through interaction with one's environment, family, community members, schools and other institutions and agencies." Within the Home Rule Municipality of the North Slope Borough, "schooling" is the specific, mandated responsibility of the North Slope Borough School District Board of Education.

The Board of Education is committed to providing academic excellence in the "schooling" environment. This commitment to academic excellence shall focus on the learner, recognizing that each student brings to the "schooling" environment his own interests, learning styles, cultural background, and abilities.[5]

We decided that our role is to control the environment of the schooling process: the building, the equipment and materials, the quality of teaching and counseling services—everything about our schools—to ensure that education can take place in the classroom.

Remember that education is also the passing down of a society's values to children. Although I suppose there are people who would disagree, I think teachers pass down values by what they do in certain situations. Showing approval to a child for quickly attempting to answer a question—even wrongly—is valuing a quick answer to questions. At home, this same child may have been taught not to say anything until he or she has observed and observed and observed, and feels certain that his or her answer is correct. At home, the parents value accuracy more highly than a quick answer. They know that accuracy may mean the difference between life and death in the Arctic. In grade school, however, many of us learned that the teacher would "reward" us when we spoke up, whether we were right or wrong. Only by hearing our responses could she determine whether or not learning was taking place. If the answer was correct, she would have the opportunity to praise us. If a wrong answer was given, this gave her the opportunity to correct us.

Education is more than book learning, it is also value learning. To address this issue, we, as a board, have incorporated a cultural component into our new-hire orientation. The bilingual department is an integral part of the orientation, highlighting differences in how our children learn. We hope that awareness lessens the frustration of teaching children who do not respond in ways teachers usually expect.

It is interesting that the root of the English word "educate" is very similar to our Iñupiaq concept of education. It has often been said that to educate means "to draw out" a person's talents as opposed to putting in knowledge or instructions. This is an interesting idea, but it is not quite true in terms of the etymology of the word. According to Webster, "Educate" comes from Latin *educare*, "to educate," which is derived from a specialized use of Latin *educere* (from *e-*, "out," and *ducere*, "to lead") meaning "to assist at the birth of a child."[6]

This old meaning of the English word "educate" is similar to our own Iñupiat Eskimo word *"iñuguq-"*[7]—which literally means "to cause to become a person." It refers to someone who attends to the child in the formative years and helps him or her to become a person. In our Iñupiat Eskimo society, the first few years of a child's life are a time when they are "becoming a person." Anyone who attends to the child during that time of his or her life is said to cause him or her to become a person, *"iñugugaa."*

We Iñupiat believe that a child starts becoming a person at a young age, even while he or she is still a baby. When a baby displays characteristics of individual behavior, such as a calm demeanor or a tendency to temper tantrums, we say "he or she is becoming a person." In our culture, such characteristics are recognized and accommodated from early childhood. As each child shows a proclivity toward a certain activity, it is quickly acknowledged and nurtured. As these children and adults in the community interact, bonds are established that help determine the teacher and the activities which will be made available to that particular child. As education progresses, excellence is pursued naturally.

Parents often stand back and let a child explore and experience things, observing the child's inclinations. If a child shows an aptitude for skills that the parents don't possess, they might arrange for their child to spend time with an expert, or an adult may ask to participate in the education of the child. Thus, many adults in the community have a role in the education of our children.

When you hear the word "educate," you may think more often of the primary Webster definition, which is "to provide with training or knowledge, especially via formal education." In the Western tradition, educating children depends heavily on a system of formal schooling with required attendance until a certain age.

Our concept of education has much in common with the Western concept of "childrearing." It is interesting to us that Eskimo practices of childrearing are commonly regarded as "permissive," in contrast to Western methods. Our perception is that Western child-rearing practices are overly directive and controlling, essentially interfering and intruding in the development of the child. The development of individuality is constrained and childhood is prolonged in Western society.

Though most of the education in our traditional society was not formal, it was serious business. For us, education meant equipping the child with the wherewithal to survive in our world. Because social interaction is a part of survival in the Arctic, this included education in proper social behavior, as well as in equipping the child with the means with which to make a living. As Robert F. Spencer wrote in his description of traditional North Alaskan Eskimo society: "The educative process . . . succeeded in a remarkable way (to produce) an individual capable of living in the cooperative situation demanded by the social and natural environment."[8]

In the traditional Iñupiat Eskimo culture, education was everybody's business. It was okay to admonish, scold, or otherwise correct the behavior of any child, whether or not one was a relative. The success of the child's education depended in large part on how well his or her parents accepted admonishment of their child by other members of their own community. We as a people valued this acceptance highly because we knew that every member of our village was involved in some way with equipping our child for success.

EDUCATING FOR SUCCESS

We need to equip our children for all the choices to be made upon graduation. In the North Slope Borough a majority of our students choose to remain in their villages after graduation. To provide an adequate education for each child, therefore, we need to teach Arctic survival skills, as well as the academic skills needed for success in the Western world.

As stated above, there were problems inherent in the displacement of our traditional educational system with the Western model, which have to be addressed if we hope to make schooling a success for our children. I will now discuss our innovations in several key areas.

TEACHER-STUDENT RATIO

Most survival education took the form of one-to-one learning. A "student" had many teachers, each teaching the child during different parts of the day or year. Young boys were taught hunting skills by their father, uncle, grandfather, or another skilled hunter. Young girls learned from their mother, grandmother, or sister all the various skills needed to run a household, feed the family, and keep them warm.

In the Western education model, on the other hand, groups of students are put in a classroom and taught many skills throughout the year by a single teacher. The one-to-one student-teacher relationship is absent, and the assumption is that a single teacher is proficient in all the skills to be taught to the whole group.

We have addressed this difference in two ways. First, a low student-teacher ratio helps us to better address the needs of individual students. Second, teacher aides hired from within the community provide critical role models for students, since an overwhelming majority of our classroom teachers still have to be brought in from outside our school district.

Although we can never hope to reach the traditional one-to-one ratio through Western classroom teaching, we can recognize the role of other "teachers"—parents, grandparents, community and church members—in the child's life and work with them toward the child's successful learning. We also need to recognize that the hours children spend away from the classroom are as much a part of their education as classroom time. This means teaching them how to use any situation as a learning experience. Excellent teachers recognize and teach this already. These are points we need to keep in mind, as a school board, when planning our educational program.

SKILLS TAUGHT

The traditional education of the Iñupiat people focused not merely on survival but on excellence. Although all children were expected to master the basics of subsistence living, the inclinations exhibited by each child were noted and nurtured. All specialties were needed in order for the culture to survive. A storyteller and philosopher was as integral to the community as a good provider or an excellent seamstress. Once an Iñupiat Eskimo child shows an inclination, such as an interest in archery, storytelling, or sewing, that interest is nurtured by all concerned with his "education." He or she may be apprenticed to a relative or another member of the community who is an expert in that field. Certain other areas of education may be deemphasized so that the child may develop his or her talent.

Some years ago, at a gathering of elders for a regional Elders' Conference, Otis Ahkivgak recalled how he developed his hunting skills to the exclusion of learning other things considered equally important:

> You see, when they would have the "*nalukataq*" (blanket toss) festival I would never pay much attention. I would push along a sled by its stanchions and go hunting down there. That is the reason I don't know the great songs of the "nalukataq" feasts. . . . Although I listened from where the airport is now, when they were singing long and loud I was occupying myself delightfully with the snipes. Although I can try singing them by following my recollection of their singing, I do not know them very well.[9]

Once Western education models were introduced into our culture, the nurturing of individual interests virtually stopped. No matter what the unique interests of the child, all were taught the same subjects, at the same pace, in the classroom.

Although we can no longer deemphasize other subjects a child needs to learn, we can recognize the talent within and use that interest to help the child succeed in other areas. This requires talent and creativity on the part of the teacher. We have excellent, creative teachers, but in order to fully utilize this talent we need to identify policies or regulations that restrict the exercise of their creativity and search for alternatives that fully support teachers.

Another way of attending to the quality of skills taught to the children is through building partnerships within the community. For many years now, departments with the North Slope Borough, such as the Planning, Public Safety, and Health and Social Services departments, have willingly sent employees to classrooms to give talks to students on subjects ranging from secretarial work, to surveying, to management. The children need to see how their studies are applicable to real life: how the command of English is important in secretarial work; the use of calculus in surveying; the role of logic, mathematics, and social skills in management decisions.

PARENT INVOLVEMENT

Another challenge is parent involvement. In our traditional society, once a "teacher" is identified, parents do not interfere. Although they, themselves, may not be experts in whatever is being taught, they have complete faith that the "teacher" will do whatever needs to be done to equip the child with the skills to succeed in our world.

Since Western education was introduced in the Arctic, Western teachers were given the same courtesy previously extended to Native "teachers": they were left to do with the child what they needed to do to educate him or her. After all, the teachers were the experts in the areas being taught, something that they, the parents, knew nothing about. Then, as today, this was often misinterpreted by educators to mean that parents did not care about their child's education, when, in fact, they were doing what they felt was in the best interest of the child.

Parent involvement, or rather the lack of it, is often touted as the problem of educating Native youngsters. What we, as people interested in Native education, need to do, now that we are fully immersed in Western education, is to assure parents that this particular type of education needs parent involvement in order for the child to succeed. Parents will become more involved only when they learn that their knowledge, regardless of the extent of their schooling, is valued and plays an important part in their child's education. Teachers need to reach out to individual parents and to the community. Because school was not a positive experience for some of those who are now parents, going to the school, even for parent-teacher conferences, is often intimidating. We hope that through positive interactions these parents can eventually become not only involved but keenly interested in other aspects of education.

Parent involvement is an important element in another specific area of education in the North: that of passing down the language of our people. As is the case with indigenous languages anywhere in the world, our children are our only hope for the survival of our language. Our cultures, as peoples indigenous to the United States, are unique and to be found nowhere else in the world. Once our languages disappear, we have nowhere else in the world to turn to revive them. Yet there has not been much support for the language preservation programs which Native Americans have been trying to administer. We must make certain that indigenous languages within North America are not allowed to die, and we must employ every humanitarian effort it takes to do so.[10]

CULTURAL IDENTITY

Some of our greatest successes in the schooling process can be attributed to the fact that we take advantage of both the historical and contemporary culture of an area. For example, we invite elders into the classroom to tell stories and teach cultural activities (songs, dances, sewing), because in our society respect for elders is a value taught very early in life, and the classroom has become the place where so much of the child's education transpires. Every year, in the North Slope Borough School District schools, elders go to the schools to teach Eskimo dancing. This is one of the most positive and well-attended programs of the whole year. Eskimo dancing is incorporated into the annual Christmas programs at the schools, along with the usual Christmas songs. The children are very enthusiastic about learning and performing these Native dances.

Iñupiat people have a long tradition of competitive athletic events, which are integral components of gatherings, celebrations, and trade fairs involving many groups from different parts of the Arctic. These unique sports events, which involve skills of agility, strength, and endurance, are fundamental to work and survival in the Arctic environment. In addition to developing skills, sporting events are used to provide lessons about discipline, patience, good humor, cooperation, and sharing: "A different kind of kid gets involved in the Native games than gets involved in basketball or wrestling. It's something Native kids can excel in, receive self-esteem from, that they get in no other way."[11] In the spring, Native high school children from throughout the state compete in Native Youth Olympics. Top finishers receive invitations to compete in the World Eskimo Indian Olympics in Fairbanks later in the summer, and the Arctic Winter Games, an international competition involving Canadian athletes, held every two years.[12]

In 1984, the North Slope Borough School District Board, recognizing that contemporary Iñupiat culture now includes formal institutions, established Student Corporations. This is in response to the rapid growth of public and private institutions and organizations in the last 15 years.[13] Among these institutions are specialized Native corporations that were mandated in the settlement of Native land claims by an act of Congress (Alaska Native Claims Settlement Act of 1971). Corporations are as much a part of everyday life in Arctic communities as subsistence hunting and fishing. Every child, in order to become capable of making life choices, needs to learn the basics of both realms. We, as a board, recognized that Native village and regional corporations needed employees and board members who are knowledgeable in all areas of corporate management. Thus, Student Corporations, established under the Laws of the State of Alaska, were incorporated into our schools. Children learn about how corporations are established, how proxies operate, and how elections and meetings are held. They also learn to evaluate moneymaking projects and, in the process, hone their decision-making skills.

These types of activities within the educational arena serve another, more basic, purpose. After decades of assimilation programs within the educational system that treated local cultures as detriments to the child's education, programs now teach that the culture of the area is not a detriment, but is indeed a valuable tool in the schooling of our children.

BILINGUAL EDUCATION

When bilingual education became a reality in the North, many parents and grandparents were very puzzled—and rightly so—by the about-face in the attitude of school staff in regard to speaking Iñupiaq. Suddenly children were not only allowed to speak Iñupiaq in school but actively encouraged to do so. For many, however, this came too late. Parents who had been punished for speaking their native language in schools were raising their children using only the English language to communicate with them. Iñupiaq in the home was being replaced by a broken Iñupiaq, the English language interspersed with bits and pieces of Iñupiaq. During this time, even bilingual education seemed a contradiction in terms to parents who had been persuaded that Native languages inhibit education.

It has sometimes been painfully hard work on the part of the local bilingual department and others interested in the survival of our language and culture to convince parents and the whole community about the need for language revival. But the efforts are paying off. Our district uses a very effective method, the Total Physical Response (TPR) method, of teaching our language to the children. The TPR method involves the whole learner, not just his or her mind. For instance, the teacher walks as he or she is teaching the world "walk," or portrays the emotions when teaching the words for these emotions. Each new word or sentence we hear a child use tugs at the heart, right in there where we hold memories of the times when we had almost . . . almost . . . lost one of the very abilities that make us uniquely who we are.

ADDRESSING ISSUES

When we talk about educating our children for success we need to examine every facet of schooling to see if it is serving its purpose. Sometimes this requires making some hard decisions. A few years ago we, as a board, reevaluated our philosophy, goals, and policies to make them compatible. After careful research and deliberation we took a bold step. We changed from an individualized learning system to competency-based education. As hard as this decision was, we needed to address the issue of graduates who could not read or write, much less make life choices. We saw that our students were advanced to higher grades not on the basis of skills achieved, but through a process of "social advancement": students were advanced to the next grade even if their skills were not adequate. As a school board, we identified this practice with the way individualized instruction was interpreted and carried out within our district.

Individualized instruction, though very successful in other areas, was never satisfactorily demonstrated within the North Slope. For instance, in some high school classes students were given a book at the beginning of the semester and expected to go as far as possible with it at their own pace. There were no objectives given. The students were only told to read and to do what the text requested they do, with the teacher there as a resource if needed. This was explained to one parent as being individualized instruction. It is instances such as this which alerted us, the board, to problems within our system which needed to be addressed, such as teacher accountability. Recently we instituted a competency-based approach to student advancement because we felt that it was more congruent with our traditional educational practices. In the competency-based approach, skills expected to be mastered by students in a certain grade are identified. The students, then, must demonstrate mastery of competencies before they are promoted to the next grade. This approach is similar to our traditional practices in which elders expected children to master certain competencies before they went on to more difficult tasks.

When the Western economic system became a viable way of life in the North, right along with subsistence, we, as Native people, should have felt an ownership of the educational system that taught our children how to survive in our contemporary world, a world which needs people with academic capabilities. But because it is a Western educational system, we, as parents and local populace, have found it hard to identify with. We tend to view it still as a foreign system that was thrust on us. The move to mastery learning, a type of education which we identify with, has helped us attain ownership of the educational system in our schools. Since we, as a board, have determined that our children cannot survive in our world without also learning the basics of the Western way of life, we have chosen to teach them that way of life, but in the way that has proven to work in educating generation after generation of our children—through mastery learning.

Although competency-based education was widely supported by the parents because of identification with their own teaching style, others had to be convinced that it was in the best interest of our children. The school district, in order to ensure the success of the program, conducted many in-service programs with teachers and parent groups across our district on the elements of competency-based education, including how content is taught, how learning is assessed, long-range plans for curriculum and instruction, identification of competencies in texts and other instructional material, and lesson design. Now in its third year, it has already proven to be a success. We find that our youngest children are ready for advancement because competencies are identified at the beginning of the year, and the teachers know what the child needs to master in order to advance to the next grade.

With changes in our school system in past years happening so often, we also have had to deal with the fact that our educational system was a mishmash of new ideas which, although these were excellent concepts, were never quite synthesized into a coherent unit or system. What happened was that a group of students were taught using one system for a few years, and then were taught using another system. Because of this lack of continuity we have students in the upper grades who need extra help.

We are currently focusing on providing the very best atmosphere for learning for all children, and doing all we can to remedy the problems some of the older children have because of the deficiencies of earlier systems and the lack of continuity. One of the best ways we have found to address this problem is through enhanced guidance and counseling services. Besides providing counselors in each school site, we also provide a district-wide counselor who travels routinely to all schools, providing individual as well as group counseling. She is also available to travel to villages to help in crisis situations as needed. This coming year we are expanding services to give children better access to guidance and counseling, which may help them deal with difficulties for which they may not be well enough equipped.

CONCLUSION

In order to provide the best possible education for our children, we need first to identify the desired "product" of our schooling system and then to provide a system through which to acquire that product.

We, as a board, already know that we want young adults capable of becoming productive, happy citizens in whatever world they choose. We then need to make certain that all aspects of the schooling system, especially the environment, are conducive to the achievement of that goal. Above all, we must make certain that cultural differences in the way we view the goals and objectives of programs are addressed. The way different cultures choose to achieve the same goals and objectives varies greatly. We need to take as much care in choosing the system as we do in defining our goals.

We now have an excellent and effective school system in place, based on research that calls for specifying the school mission, educational expectations, curriculum and instruction, and monitoring time on task, student progress, and home-school relations. Profiles of these characteristics have been done on all of our schools in the district. Therefore, we are not as quick to turn to every current trend in education. We are not, however, hesitant to research new ideas. But we take extra effort to make certain the new ideas are compatible with our philosophy. In this way we assure our children the best education we can give them, as well as provide needed stability in programs and goals. Thus, we can ensure that we are, indeed, serving the purpose of education.

Endnotes

1. "Iñupiat" is the plural form of the name we call ourselves, the singular being "Iñupiaq." "Inuk," the stem, means "a person." The ending "-piaq" means "real," "most common," or "the most prevalent type." Although the plural form is commonly translated as "the real people," a more accurate translation would be "the most common type of people," or "the people we are most familiar with."

    Although either the singular or plural form can stand alone, sometimes—for more clarity—additional nouns are used: If you are talking about one person, you use "Iñupiaq" ("An Iñupiaq (person) came to see me").

    If you are talking about a people, you use "Iñupiat" ("The Iñupiat (people) love to sing"). When the word is coupled with "Eskimo," which is an easily understood (though non-Iñupiaq) word, convention has it take the plural form. Thus we have such sentences as: "She is a fluent Iñupiat Eskimo speaker" or "She is a fluent Iñupiaq speaker." Both are correct.

    The word "Eskimo" is a common term for the circumpolar peoples, who include the Iñupiat as well as other groups. We prefer "Inuit" to "Eskimo," but it is less easily recognized by non-Inuit. If we tried to uncomplicate this for the sake of non-Iñupiaq speakers, the sentence would begin to lose meaning for Iñupiaq-speaking readers. We ask English readers to bear with what seems to be inconsistencies. We are trying, as with everything else, to use a foreign system (English) to get across some Iñupiaq concepts and have it make sense to both groups.

2. For more information on passing down values through traditional stories and legends, see Edna MacLean's keynote speech given at the Alaska Bilingual/Bicultural Conference in 1987, available through the State of Alaska Department of Education and Early Development, 801 West 10th Street, Juneau, AK 99801-1878.

3. Eben Hopson speech, December 1975. On file at the Iñupiat History, Language and Culture Division of the Planning Department, North Slope Borough, P.O. Box 69, Barrow, AK 99723.

4. For more information on Iñupiat extended family relationships, see Rosita Worl and Charles W. Smythe, *Barrow: A Decade of Modernization* (Anchorage: U.S. Department of the Interior, Minerals Management Service, Alaska OCS Region, Socioeconomic Studies Program Technical Report No. 125, 1986); Robert F. Spencer, *The Northern Alaskan Eskimo*, Smithsonian Institution, Bureau of American Ethnology Bulletin 171 (Washington, DC: U.S. Government Printing Office, 1959); or Ernest S. Burch Jr., *Eskimo Kinsmen: Changing Family Relationships in Northwest Alaska*, American Ethnological Society Monograph No. 59 (St. Paul: West, 1975).

5. North Slope Borough School District Policy Manual, Policy AD (Educational Philosophy), Adopted 10/13/76, Revised 8/11/87.

6. *Webster's II New Riverside University Dictionary* (Boston: Houghton Mifflin, 1984), p. 418.

7. Iñupiaq words followed by a hyphen are stems that need at least an ending to make sense. For those interested in more information about the structure of the language, please see the introduction to *Iñupiallu Tan illu Uqalu isa Ila ich, Abridged Iñupiaq and English Dictionary*, compiled by Adna Ahgeak MacLean (Fairbanks: University of Alaska, 1980).

8. Spencer, *The Northern Alaskan Eskimo*, p. 239.

9. Kisautaq (Leona Okakok's Eskimo name), *Puiguikaat (Things You Should Never Forget)*, Proceedings of the 1978 Elders Conference, North Slope Borough, 1981, p. 367.

10. For more information on efforts to preserve Alaska Native languages, contact the Alaska Native Language Center, University of Alaska Fairbanks, Box 757680, Fairbanks, AK 99775.

11. Statement by Reggie Joule, in *Heartbeat: World Eskimo Indian Olympics*, Annabel Lund, writer; Howard Simons, editor; Mark Kelly, photographer; and Clark Mischler, photo editor (Juneau: Fairweather Press, 1986).

12. For more information on these sports, see *Heartbeat*; F. H. Eger, *Eskimo Inuit Games* (Vancouver: X-Press, n.d.).

13. For a description of the recent formation of a profusion of governmental institutions, corporations, boards, and commissions in our areas, see Worl and Smythe, *Barrow: A Decade of Modernization*.

Follow the Lights: Native Ways of Knowing

Bernice Joseph

Keynote peech at the Alaska Federation of Natives Convention
October 20, 2005

I AM HONORED TO BE HERE and would like to thank the Alaska Federation of Natives Board of Directors, staff, and executive director, Julie Kitka, for inviting me to be the keynote for the 2005 Alaska Federation of Natives meeting. I thank my grandparents, mother, and my husband Stewart for providing me with guidance, love, and support.

I wish to address the theme "Follow the Lights: Native Ways of Knowing." I will then discuss the importance of education, maintaining cultural identity, efforts in the development of a curriculum sensitive to our cultures, programs that incorporate indigenous and Western values, and honorary degrees that exemplify what our people know, have to offer, and can do for our youth.

What are Native ways of knowing?

I asked this question of my *ts'ookaal,* my grandmother—what were her thoughts about Native ways of knowing? She asked whether I wanted to know in English or in her Native language. I said, "Gram, you'll have to tell me in your Native language and then translate it. I've taken two semesters of Koyukon, but still have only a limited understanding."

Yoo dona dinaghaneet haghu ghal ts'otl. It was hard for us long time ago.

Grandma's mother, the late Annie Mik'eendootza Ekada, taught her how to set snares, how to cook, but she hardly sewed because she trapped, snared, and was the sole provider for her kids. Grandma Annie lost her husband in 1937, so she provided for her family by herself.

My grandmother Rita learned to sew, crochet, and knit by watching other people. She learned how to make fur skin boots and fish skin boots by watching her mother. When my grandmother's mom was out setting snares and trapping, Grandma would cook, bring in wood, cook for the dogs, and have everything ready for her mother when she got back.

My grandmother spent very little time in the village, as a child. She went home for Christmas and stayed only until the middle of January. During that time she attended the Catholic school in Nulato. She then went back to camp until Easter and stayed in the village for about two weeks to attend school. With this schedule, she completed her Western education up to the fourth grade.

In 1938, Miss Olson, a nurse at the clinic in Nulato, rounded up four girls from the village to work at the hospital that existed in Nulato. The late Ida Agnes, Edna Stickman, Anita Demoski, and my Gram were recruited to help. They attended a basic class for two weeks and soon began delivering babies. My grandmother ended up delivering almost all the babies in Nulato along with the late Esther McGinty. Grandma fondly remembers delivering her late brother Henry's daughter Freda, who later came to be known as "Radar" by her friends and family, at six-mile camp.

Native Ways of Knowing, Grandma continues, to her means to have the utmost respect for her upbringing and the knowledge she has of the land, animals, beliefs, weather, plants, and people around her. She has patience and much love to share with her family and community. Her primary education was at camp where she learned to survive. Her secondary education was to eventually earn her community health aide practitioner's certificate.

I can almost guarantee that if you speak with any Elder today, you will hear them speak of their support of Western education. Most Elders I've spoken to say that it is important to have a Western education to be able to compete in the world we live in today. It's important to understand Western business concepts if you are going to operate a successful business. It's important for our kids to be exposed to Western educational opportunities, BUT not at the expense of our cultures. We are all too familiar with the statistics facing Alaska Natives about educational attainment, suicide, alcohol and drug abuse, and the number of Alaska Natives in prison.

Education is the key to overcoming many of the barriers Alaska Natives face. Yet, it must be an education that is sensitive to Native Ways of

Knowing. Children must be grounded in their cultures and beliefs in order to be successful. Recent studies by indigenous peoples from places such as New Zealand, Canada, and Hawai'i show that students perform at higher levels when they are provided with contextual points of reference that they can relate to in a meaningful way.

As a matter of fact, as we become more global in nature and experience a mixture of different cultures, it becomes more difficult for cultural identity and community to survive. Let me provide an example that was published in the *Harvard Educational Review* in fall 2003. In 1992, a study was done by Keith Osajima documenting the story of a Chinese American student's ambivalence toward and discomfort with issues of racial/ethnic identity that she faced in her daily life. She articulated her position in this way.

> I grew up in a white suburb and my parents are also very Americanized, and spoke mostly English at home, so I don't speak Chinese. I also grew up trying to identify as much as possible with White people and feeling very inadequate because I would never be like them. . . I mean, it's constant conflict with me now. I assume it's going to be for the rest of my life . . . You know either being with White Americans and not feeling I'm like them, or going to the Chinese environment, like Chinatown or something, and not feeling like I fit in there.

This poignant example speaks directly to the question of culture and identity. Imagine how many of our Alaska Native youth must deal with constant uncertainty of their belonging.

Let me take you through a small exercise. Take a moment to imagine your child's classroom. What does your child's classroom look like? What pictures or artwork hang in the school? Are there pictures and objects that the child can relate to? How are the days of the week, months, and years depicted by the teacher? What kinds of literature are the children required to read?

Are there photographs of respected Elders? Do Elders and parents feel comfortable visiting the school? Is there respect for subsistence activities and are students given excused or unexcused absences for hunting, trapping, or other subsistence activities? Are teachers and administrators aware of the subsistence calendar? What type of homework is your student bringing home on a daily or weekly basis? Are students asked to write papers about manatees or moose? Alligators or beluga whales?

My experiences are that most curricula are Western in nature. As a result, students do not see themselves represented in written materials, texts, movies, videos, or literature. From this, it is safe to say that students are learning that it was the Europeans that made history, discovered other lands, shaped the histories of science, the arts, and humanities; and made all the important contributions to the world.

Take, for example, the first things my late great-grandmother Martha Joe learned in school. In her biography, she stated that they had big charts hanging on the wall in school. "The first words I learned were 'c-a-t' and 'r-a-t.' Sometimes it was just like a dream." I wonder if she had ever seen a cat at that point in her life. I believe that this speaks to the need for culturally appropriate curriculum that provides students with a sense of belonging.

There have been great efforts by teacher organizations around the world, nation, and our very own state to change this. There has been work on the K–12 and college-level curriculum. Make no mistake, there is much more work to be done as there continues to be a dominant influence of the Eurocentric mono-logical approach. There have been efforts by organizations like the Association of Interior Native Educators to build curriculum that is based upon cultural activities, identification of animals, land, seasons, and the subsistence round. The Alaska Native Knowledge Network, in partnership with AFN, has been recording and developing curriculum based upon Elders' knowledge and input.

The Effie Kokrine Charter School right here in Fairbanks has been a dream and vision for Alaska Native educators for years. The concept stemmed from the first Education Summit hosted by the First Alaskans Foundation in Anchorage. This charter school opened its doors at the beginning of this academic year. There are many of us that share in the excitement of what they have to offer to Alaska Native students, and non-Native students seeking a new way of learning. This school has over 90 percent Alaska Native teacher hire. They will make a difference for Alaska Native students, so we must support their efforts 100 percent

There has also been recognition through the University of Alaska by honoring Elders for their extensive knowledge through time. Several Alaska Native Elders have been awarded with the prestigious honorary doctorate degree, the highest degree that a university can offer. The first Alaska Native to be honored with an honorary doctorate degree was Dr. Walter Soboleff, a Tlingit. He was awarded the degree in 1968 and was invited back as the UAF commencement speaker in 2003.

The University of Alaska Fairbanks also honored the late Chief Peter John, traditional chief of the Tanana Chiefs region, in 1994. At a summit hosted by UAF Rural Student Services in 1990, Chief Peter John spoke of *Troth Yeddha'*, the hill that UAF now stands on, as an important traditional meeting place for chiefs from the Interior. At the last meeting of the chiefs on *Troth Yeddha'* hill, it was predicted that "people from all over the world will come to this great place of learning." These were the powerful words of our late Chief. He knew that good things would happen on that hill. If you were to visit the "hill" today, you would see people from all over the world coming together to study and learn.

There is important research taking place with scientists working side-by-side with Elders. I asked a colleague of mine about examples from the North Slope. He shared what he termed a "hallmark" case from the 1970s and '80s. The U.S. government estimated a dangerously low population of bowhead whales. The International Whaling Commission was about to rule subsistence whaling off-limits to the Iñupiat people. The whalers of the North Slope knew that there were many more whales than the scientists had estimated, and they showed the scientists that over generations the whales migrated under the ice, not just through open water as the scientists had observed. The North Slope Borough hired their own scientists, and working together with the Iñupiat Elders they developed an internationally respected census method that vindicated the Iñupiat whalers.

There have also been some exciting and successful programs developed at UAF that incorporate Western and indigenous knowledge. The Rural Human Services Certificate Program is built on Alaska Native traditional values. This program developed by the Interior-Aleutians Campus with the work of an advisory council made up of grassroots community people validates respective traditions to facilitate healing through the positive blending of Western concepts with Alaska Native traditional values. The RHS program is thriving and showing continuous improvement since its inception over 10 years ago. RHS counselors and students are working in rural Alaska, achieving the goal of "a counselor in every village."

While there are great things happening, there is much more to do. For Alaska Native people to have their place at the policy-making level and to make sustainable changes, several things must happen. Alaska Natives must be respected for their knowledge. Alaska Native culture must be as revered as the cultures of the Japanese, Chinese, Russians, and other cultural groups from around the world.

We face a huge challenge with the loss of the Alaska Native languages. Until it is as common for students to choose to study their own Alaska Native language in the schools as it is for Spanish, Russian, and French, to name a few, we are a long ways from having equity.

We must work together to build a solid telecommunications infrastructure that will provide our rural residents with quality internet access necessary to diversify their economies and access a quality education.

We must work to "grow our own" policymakers. Our neighbors to the far south of us, the Maori of New Zealand, took bold actions to produce 500 Maori PhDs. Under the leadership and guidance of Dr. Graham H. Smith, a Maori, they embraced an impressive plan to grow their own PhD graduates. Dr. Smith is now working on a similar charge with the First Nations people at the University of British Columbia where they have set a target of 250 First Nations people to earn their PhDs. They will have success because there is commitment by the indigenous people to take a stance and demand that level of commitment by their universities. At UAF, we have begun to develop proposals that will move us toward these types of efforts.

Above all, we must work together to keep rural Alaska a viable place to live. It's going to take our legislators, state and federal government, community leaders, and educators working together to support our communities through municipal funding. It is our collective obligation to support rural communities in order for the whole state to benefit.

In conclusion, I note that the First Alaskans Institute is making great strides towards building Alaska Native policymakers. They are in the process of building a think tank made up of Alaska Native people. It's all about Native minds shaping our future.

Our people have come a long way with only a few decades of Western education, to developing our own curriculum, to be recognized for our traditional knowledge through honorary degrees, and to have our own ways of knowing recognized through institutions such as the Effie Kokrine School to further help us to maintain our sense of who we are as Native people while living in a Western world, but empowered through cultural identity and cultural presence to stand tall and be counted for all of our contributions to education, health, politics, economics, and science. We have done a lot, but we have only just begun.

THE CIRCLE WE CALL COMMUNITY

Miranda Wright

Originally published in *Indigenous Educational Models for Contemporary Practice: In Our Mother's Voice*, edited by Maenette Kape'ahiokalani Padeken Ah Nee-Benham with Joanne Elisabeth Cooper (Mahwah, NJ: Lawrence Erlbaum Associates, 2000)

WHEN I FIRST WORKED WITH THE CONCEPT of community involvement in education, I focused on several elders who were employed as "cultural resources" in their local schools. Discussions with these elders revealed that several were unsure of their contribution to classroom teaching. As one elder stated, "I don't know what they want me down there [at school] for. I don't know how to share my information with them." She had a difficult time trying to plan a meaningful presentation for the students and give them something of value. We started talking about the seasons in our lives and the different things we can do with seasons. It was like the light-bulbs came on for her! She said, "Oh, now I understand. That's what I will do, I will take that circle and I'll put the seasons into it. For example, when we talk about activities on the Yukon River in June, we talk about them differently in our language. The words that we use for the Yukon River and the activities associated with that river are different in June than they are in October." To present her lessons, she incorporated Native language and cultural activities associated with the different seasons of the year.

I went back to the University of Alaska and worked with other Native educators there. We started exploring different models and looking at the cyclical nature of activities and how they progressed from one stage to another throughout the year. We divided the circle into four quadrants representing spring, summer, fall, and winter. The basic premise was to use the four seasons as a vehicle for discussion. The seasons allow for cyclical change: birth, growth, maturity, and reflection, much like the birth of new plants and animals in spring, the growth associated with summer, the maturity or harvest of fall and the reflection and celebration during winter.

The first quadrant was called spring, the time of renewal. In order to capture the essence of our efforts, we decided to refer to our creation legends for an appropriate Native word that would add depth to our model. We discussed several creation legends and found a common thread . . . the presence of a primordial being or spiritual essence. This provided further discussion on the sequence of creation according to traditional legends. Thus, the first quadrant was called *yeege* to reflect the spiritual essence, or visionary phase, found in our creation narratives. This first phase provides a time to explore one's thoughts, to develop a vision for the future, and to establish an introduction, or outline. Moving sun-wise around the circle to the second quadrant, we experience growth during the summer season. Again relying on traditional stories, we learned that land was created before man or animals. Thus, we named the second quadrant *nen* to reflect the formation of the earth. This is a period of growth, a time to develop different programs and/or different skill levels.

Again, moving sun-wise around the circle, we come to the third quadrant, or the period of maturity and harvest. Again referring to the creation legends, we associated this period with the emergence of man or humankind, *Denaa*. As my grandmother would say,

> *Koy* [grandchild] right here is *Denaa*, this is man. Over here are the animals. We used to be one, and we would travel back and forth through each other's worlds. Something happened and we split. This is the real people, this is *Denaa*.

According to our distant time stories, it is during this separation with the animal kingdom that *Denaa* developed knowledge, critical thinking, and language. Consequently, the fall cycle is referred to as *Denaa*. This is the phase where instruction and development of the knowledge base is implemented. The final quadrant, or winter season, is a period of reflection and evaluation, a time to measure the activities of the year and prepare to renew the cycle. This phase is associated with content and accomplishment, and is, therefore, referred to as *Tlee*. The literal translation is head. However, it is also used to specify the head as the fountain of knowledge.

This seasonal model based on our creation stories has worked very well for us. A nice feature of the circular model is the progressive element, or automatic reconnection, associated with the annual renewal or cyclical changes. This model can be superimposed on or in another circle indefinitely to create the different communities within an overarching structure. I've found it to be a wonderful tool to demonstrate the infrastructure within an organization, classroom, family, or community where everyone and everything reconnects. Another analogy that I have used is the blanket toss that is similar to jumping on a trampoline. However, with the blanket toss there are no springs to elevate the individual jumping. Instead, people form a circle around the blanket and pull it taut. Everyone has to pull in unison in order to get the jumper to rise as high as s/he can. If anyone is out of sync, the jumper cannot be elevated any higher. Likewise, as a community we all have to pull together, and when one member of the community leaves, there is a void.

I have always enjoyed the storytelling ability of my people and their ability to apply the events of a story as a lesson for various challenges that people face. The same story may be repeated several times, depending on the current situation. The reason behind the repetition was obviously lost on those who continue to perceive indigenous storytelling as lacking in academic value. Many equate the indigenous style of storytelling with the mentality of a child who must learn by rote memorization. Consequently, these Native stories are often relegated to the folklore section of the library, never to be validated as valuable sources of knowledge.

There are many cultural preservation efforts directed at gathering and recording the stories of our elders. The idea behind many of these efforts is that traditional information will be lost with the passing of the elder. Therefore, it is imperative that we preserve the stories of their life, histories, songs, crafts, and ceremonies. I find it interesting that industry has reaped tremendous financial profits from sales of recorders, audiotapes, and videotapes, so the amateur can build an archive of information that generates another financial investment as we collect (and attempt to understand) the complexities of preserving and archiving information. In discussing this phenomenon, I pose the questions, "What is it that we are preserving?" And, "How long must it be kept in preservation?" I have an image of our cultural heritage locked in a jar with a shelf life stamped on a label, "Use before Nov. 11, 2001."

Some may feel that I am being profane in discussing the knowledge of our Elders in this fashion. I, on the other hand, want to stress the importance of sharing and using the information to perpetuate a living, dynamic culture. What good is the collection of knowledge if it is stored merely for posterity? Our youth are at risk as many struggle with a lack of identity or a sense of false pride. One often hears the phrase "I'm proud to be Indian." When probed further about what it is that makes them proud of their heritage, many are at a loss to express or articulate what it is that makes them proud, whereas others take the noble warrior attitude and become defensive. Yet, their response is indicative of their need for an identity. This example can be taken a level further, to those encouraging us to learn from our elders. However, when probed about what it is they want us to learn from the elders, they too are at a loss to identify or articulate what knowledge they seek. These examples suggest that knowledge of their heritage is so lacking they do not know what questions to ask. Perhaps the Western educational system has had such a dramatic impact on our Native population that our youth do not know how to frame their inquiries from an indigenous perspective. An example that illustrates this is the occurrence at a potlatch hosted by a community to honor the elders who were congregated for their annual conference:

During the period when speeches are made, the Native leaders of this community welcomed the elders and spoke of the honor they felt in hosting such a distinguished group, particularly in light of the fact that most of their Native elders had passed on to their next journey. By hosting the elders' conference they hoped to gain knowledge from the elders in attendance. With that said, an elder from a nearby community rose and asked in traditional Athabascan oratory style, "Where are your young men? Where are your hunters?" He posed these questions as he observed young girls (ages 8–13) serving the elders, a position traditionally reserved for the hunters who provided the game meat and fish for such ceremonies. The speaker went on to explain the purpose of his questions. The same community spokesperson, who previously asked for the elder's assistance and access to cultural knowledge, rose and disputed the elder who offered assistance.

This lack of understanding for the protocol at traditional ceremonies led to my probing further where the balance of understanding could be met. I fear the Western education system has provided at least two generations of students with the tools to evaluate their surroundings through the eyes of Western traditions only. If this is true, our task as Native educational leaders is extremely challenging. Where and how do we provide a mechanism to present a balanced education for our youth to meet the needs of the 21st century, but still be linked to their traditional culture? These are the types of concerns that lead me to focus my direction on the teaching and learning styles of indigenous communities. The task that lies before us is great.

In response to this challenge, I'm currently working with several certified Native teachers who have formed the Association of Interior Native Educators (AINE). This focus group, in collaboration with the Doyon Foundation, where I serve as executive director, is the cornerstone of an initiative called the Academy of Elders, an intensive, two-week summer institute where certified teachers become the students and elders serve as the instructors. Elders from various communities work with teachers to develop curriculum that implements the teaching and learning styles of the indigenous people of the region. The curriculum incorporates stories, hands-on activities, and songs with performance and academic standards established by the state department of education. Additionally, teacher-training components are being developed in conjunction with the University of Alaska to ensure the success of this program. Rather than looking at the differences we have as Native people, we take a global look at the educational needs of our children and youth. Just as each student is an individual, so too do they each learn in their own way. Rather than immediately diagnosing Native American students who experience learning challenges as having attention deficit disorder, more work is needed for educators to understand the cooperative teaching and learning methods common to many indigenous cultures. Educators need to understand the importance of building their lessons on the cultural and social environment of their students and in the community in which they work.

This initiative brings together Native and non-Native educators, school administrators and policy makers, community elders and leaders, and parents and families in active working collaborations. The importance of this work is multifaceted. First, students become the focus of the classroom as teachers incorporate various teaching methods that address the variety of learning styles in the classroom. Second, students are enriched with culturally appropriate activities that teach them about their environment. Third, the family, an essential unit of a community, is integrally involved as a cultural resource to the consortia and to the ultimate education of their children and youth. Finally, the unified effort of this model contributes to the physical and emotional strength of all the communities involved.

Revitalization
of the *Qargi*

———◆•×•◆———

Edna Ahgeak MacLean

Originally presented at the Alaska Anthropological Association
Symposium on "Policy and Planning for Alaskan Languages,"
Fairbanks, Alaska, March 8, 1986.

IN TRADITIONAL IÑUPIAQ COMMUNITIES the *qargi* served as a political, social, ceremonial, and educational institution for the people. Among the Iñupiaq whaling communities along the coast, the *qargi* was an association of the *umialgit* "whaling captains" and their crew members. Other family members, such as the men's wives and children, were not excluded from the *qargi*.

Each community had two or more *qargi*. Each *qargi* had a name and its own club house. Presently, within the North Slope region, only two *qargi* exist. They are the Qanmaktuut and the Unasiksikaat in Tikigaq (Point Hope, Alaska). Historically, there were three *qargi* in Utqiagvik, but they no longer exist.

Membership in a *qargi* provided a sense of belonging, a sense of identity to an Iñupiaq, especially to a man. One could say, *Qanmaktuumiuguruna*, "I am a member of the club Qanmaktuut." Belonging to a *qargi* meant that a man had attained the noblest profession of his society, the profession of a hunter.

There was a keen sense of competition and excellence among men in each of the *qargi*. This was especially evident during the competitive games.

The coming of the missionaries marked the end of these *qargit*, as the activities that took place in the *qargi* were considered pagan rituals and

131

therefore they had to be destroyed. The churches became the meeting centers and the focus of social events, which are now associated with Christian holidays. The missionaries were so relentless in pursuing their task of eradicating pagan rituals and ways that some Iñupiat of today cannot express joy through Iñupiaq dancing and singing. When Western schools replaced the education which young men received in the *qargit*, the learning was no longer relevant to the traditional Iñupiaq way of life.

For the most part, Iñupiaq parents have been isolated from the Western educational system. Traditional roles of parents as teachers of the Iñupiaq way of life were severed when the schools claimed their children. Now these parents are the Elders within our communities. Most of the men have spent their early adult years as subsistence hunters, depending on the land and ocean for their survival. Some parents have taught their skills as hunters and preparers of game to their older sons and daughters, but a large number of younger siblings within these families do not know these traditional skills.

During the 1983 Inuit Circumpolar Conference held in Frobisher Bay, Northwest Territories, Canada, the Inuit Elders gave this message: "Do not forget the Inuit way of Life. There is a great deal of knowledge and skills that the Inuit possess that should be included in the educational process. Do not forget the Inuit Language." The last sentence is especially poignant because of the precarious stance of the Iñupiaq language in Alaska. The Iñupiaq language has suffered greatly and the destruction is almost complete. The loss of the language by the Iñupiaq of Alaska will cut deeply.

There are programs in schools to teach the language, but they are not enough. The effects of the former indoctrination of the parents not to speak Iñupiaq to their children have not been reversed. Even though active indoctrination has ceased, the effects of former efforts remain in an entire generation that accepted this nonsense as if it was the truth. Perhaps more insidious, subtle forms of indoctrination remain. Abstract concepts and skills relating to the "modern" world are discussed only in English. Iñupiaq is reduced to the status of a second or "foreign" language. The whole Iñupiaq community needs to speak Iñupiaq if language revival and maintenance programs are to be effective. The children cannot learn to speak Iñupiaq fluently without the help, understanding, and cooperation of the entire Iñupiaq community.

What is true for the survival of the Iñupiaq language is also true for traditional Iñupiaq skills and customs. We must practice them if they are to be retained as a part of our lives and our heritage.

The Inuit Circumpolar Conference stated in Resolution 83–18 that "there is a need to integrate the traditional Inuit cultural values and the Western cultural values within the educational system . . . that there is a need for more Inuit participation in developing and implementing educational delivery systems and policies . . . that our educational systems are to prepare our children for life based on values and skills from the Inuit culture and the Western culture."

The educational environment of each Iñupiaq community can be altered to make the Iñupiaq feel comfortable about teaching their young people the skills and attitudes of the Iñupiaq way of life. What is needed in each Iñupiaq community is an institution devoted to the teaching of Iñupiaq skills, stories, knowledge of the land and animals, and consequently, of Iñupiaq values and behavior.

The concept of the *qargi*, the community house, should be revitalized. Traditionally the *qargi* was the place where young men went to listen to and learn from the older men. The women did not spend as much time in the *qargi* as the men did, but they were not totally excluded.

The physical layout of the modern-day *qargi* can be as traditional or as modern as the Iñupiaq desire, as long as the people are comfortable in it. Depending on the size of the community, the *qargi* may be a one-room or a multi-room structure, but there should always be a large central room where Iñupiaq dances and competitive games can be held. This large central room can also be used to build boats and sleds or other large items. In addition, it may also be used for community feasts on Thanksgiving and Christmas. As the *qargi* serves as a community center, its educational function will be integrated into the life of the village.

Presently, the Iñupiaq Elders do not have any responsibility for the formal education of the young Iñupiaq. If a community center totally devoted to the teaching of Iñupiaq skills and values were established, Elders and parents would then have the means of teaching the children what they know.

It is possible for the Iñupiaq child of today to be of both the Iñupiaq culture and Western culture. It is possible to establish in each community an educational system in which the students can learn skills that will enable them to function in both cultures. The students can learn to hunt and to work in an office. They can learn to sew parkas and operate computers. They can learn to sing, drum, and dance the Iñupiaq way and also enjoy the dances and songs of the Western culture. They can learn to butcher a seal and make seal oil as well as to bake a cake and marinate steaks. As was expressed at the 1980 Inuit Circumpolar Conference:

> It is not necessary to return to the traditional way of life
> to benefit from the cultural heritage . . . some of the in-
> troduced customs and values have become part of a tra-
> ditional pattern . . . I doubt that we will be able to return
> to the religion of our ancestors. But it is valuable to know
> the wisdom it expressed and the importance it placed on
> deep respect for life, without which the culture of a hunt-
> ing people would remain at a low level.

The Elders in the Iñupiaq communities will be the teachers in the *qa-rgi*. They know the land. They speak the language. They know how to make the tools necessary to hunt each kind of animal. They know how to prepare skins for clothing. They know the songs and the stories of the Iñupiaq.

A certified teacher who can speak Iñupiaq can work side by side with the Elders of each community. Together they can accomplish what needs to be done. The Elders can pass on to the teacher the knowledge they possess and the manner they use to teach the students.

In the course of a day, the certified teacher can work with not just one but with several knowledgeable Iñupiaq. Especially in the larger schools, such as in Kotzebue or Barrow, the class size will have to be reduced when the Elder teaches through demonstration, for instance, how to choose and prepare wood for making a sealing harpoon. The class size must be small enough for the Elder to have individual contact with each student, consis-tent with the traditional Iñupiaq way of teaching. Therefore, several Elders or knowledgeable Iñupiaq will be needed to teach several classes.

Each Elder has his or her individual field of expertise. One may be skilled in making ulus. Another may be expert in skinning foxes. Still an-other may enjoy sewing boots and other articles of clothing. We can expect that the Elders will enjoy passing on the skills of which they are justifiably proud. As many as 10 or more Elders may be teaching in a large *qargi*. Several young people could be helping the certified teacher. While the cer-tified teacher is responsible for several classrooms, the teacher aide stays with the Elder until a lesson or project is finished. In this way the Elder's knowledge will be passed on thoroughly to at least one individual who can then teach it to others.

In the *qargi* the language of instruction and communication will be Iñupiaq, just as in the school the language of instruction and communica-tion is English. Absolutely no English will be allowed in the *qargi*. Students who cannot speak Iñupiaq should remain silent in the *qargi* until they have learned to ask questions in Iñupiaq. Students who can understand but are not able to speak Iñupiaq should be able to take a conversational class in school. As far as possible, the conversational class should reflect what the students need to know to participate in their current *qargi* project. The students in the *qargi* will be evaluated on their oral and manual performance and on their finished products. Iñupiaq literacy (reading and writing) will be taught in the school, not in the *qargi*. All instruction in the *qargi* will be by demonstration, in the traditional way.

The education the students receive in the *qargi* will be coordinated with the education they receive in the school. Before coming to the *qargi* to participate in a project with Iñupiaq elders, a student must complete a preparatory class in the school. For example, if the *qargi* project is to make a whaling harpoon, the students should read about whaling, listen to knowledgeable Iñupiaq talking about the making of whaling harpoons, and learn the Iñupiaq names of the different tools and materials that they will be using in the *qargi* to make their own whaling harpoons. The students may even watch a videotape of someone making whaling harpoons. The preparatory class in the school should enable the students to learn as much as possible from their sessions with the Iñupiaq Elders.

The students can also write compositions for the school about what they have learned or done in the *qargi*. They can put to practical use the mathematical skills they have learned in the school as they build a sled or boat in the *qargi*. The students can apply the Iñupiaq writing skills they have learned in the school as they label items that they are using in the *qargi*. In time, there may even be an Iñupiaq composition class in the school, and an Iñupiaq oral tradition class in the *qargi* so that eventually the students will learn to write and tell stories in Iñupiaq.

The teaching schedule of the *qargi* should not be restricted to a time that coincides with the teaching schedule of the school. The school and the *qargi* should not be competitive institutions; instead, they should complement each other. The *qargi* should open in the afternoon and extend into the evening hours. This scheduling will allow parents to volunteer their time in the evenings. It would be ideal if a mother who is willing to teach how to prepare Iñupiaq foods could teach during the dinner hours and also bring her family to the meal. The *qargi* could announce that the preparation of a certain dish would be taught during a certain week, and women who wanted to teach young girls could volunteer their time for a certain night.

There are many young men and women who are no longer in the schools, but who could learn from the Elder teachers during the evening hours after work. These hours could be a time of communication and learning. There are young men in the villages who need to learn how to make whaling harpoons, and there are young women who need to learn how to make parkas.

Since there are many young parents who do not have the knowledge of the Elders, children and parents may be receiving the same instruction. This is good because parent and child would be working and studying together to learn and to maintain Iñupiaq ways and values.

What are the survival skills that the Iñupiaq youth would be learning from the Elder teacher and from their parents? Here are but a few of the topics that the *qargi* can offer:

1. How to prepare game animals for food and clothing
2. How to make boots, parkas, mittens, and other articles of Iñupiaq clothing
3. How to make hunting weapons such as harpoons, spears, hooks, snares
4. How to set traps or nets for various game
5. How to hunt on the land and on the ocean
6. How to interpret weather signs
7. How to play traditional Iñupiaq endurance games
8. How to sing and dance the Iñupiaq way

There are numerous other topics that could be included in the curriculum of the *qargi*.

The interests of the Iñupiaq-oriented institutions (e.g. Eskimo Whaling Commission, Tagiugmiut Agnat Organization, Qitiktitchirit, Senior Citizens Center, North Slope Borough Commission on History, Language, and Culture, the North Slope Borough School District, North Slope Borough Postsecondary Learning Center, and various dance groups) should be reflected in the activities of the *qargi*. For instance, for courses on Iñupiaq food preparation the *qargi* could buy large quantities of Iñupiaq food from the hunters. Course participants could cook this food to prepare a daily meal for Iñupiaq Elders. In addition, the *qargi* could serve as a lounge and discussion place for the Elders. Various dance groups could come to the *qargi* to practice new songs and dance routines while the classes are in session. It would be great fun for students to work on a class project while listening to live Iñupiaq music and much laughter. Any meetings held in the *qargi* must be in the Iñupiaq language.

The *qargi* should be open all year long. Hunting classes must be included in the cooperative curricula of the *qargi* and the school. Each high school student should participate in at least one hunting/camping expedition. Preparatory classes must be taken prior to each expedition.

University courses can be joint projects with the *qargi*. Practical content in Iñupiaq dancing, art, sports, food preparation, folk medicine, etc. will be taught in the *qargi* while preparatory classes for a session in the *qargi* will be taken in the university learning center.

I hope that the implementation of the *qargi* program will help to re-solve such issues as lack of community participation in education, lack of Iñupiaq teachers, lack of Iñupiaq teaching materials, and therefore lack of Iñupiaq control of the educational system. It is my firm belief that students who develop confidence in their ability to learn traditional skills and values in the *qargi* will become better students in the Western-style school.

Finally, I hope that the revitalization of the *qargi* as the champion of all that is Iñupiaq will lead to the revitalization of the Iñupiaq language and will strengthen the cultural base of each community. I hope that as Iñupiaq Elders and adults learn to use Iñupiaq again as the language of communica-tion and instruction in the *qargi*, this practice will be carried over into other activities of the community.

GROWING UP TO BE TLINGIT

-------◆•◆•◆-------

Dr. Walter Soboleff

Keynote address to the Alaska Native Educators' Conference,
Anchorage, February, 1998

ALASKA NATIVE EDUCATORS' Conference, the Alaska Native Education Association, the Alaska Native Knowledge Network, participants, honored guests, and friends:

The first wave of change in Alaska came via sailing ships from Russia, England, France, Spain, America, and other places over 200 years ago. To these adventurers Alaska must have been a magic picture of overwhelming beauty; the next surprise was to see people in Southeast Alaska coming in canoes to see what this was all about. The ship people had their opinion of the canoe occupants: simple, to be feared, and not their equal. The canoe crew also must have had their own ideas of these newcomers who dared to enter the shores of their home. Little did the hosts know the ships' crew represented a civilization with volumes of printed pages, scholars, buildings of learning, cathedrals, teachers, art, governments, and many other organizations.

Alaska had its style of life amidst the beauty of nature that was their source for every aspect of health and well-being. The early hosts of Alaska, especially in the so-called Panhandle, Southeast Alaska, could not offer the arrivals a printed page itemizing who they are—clans and subdivisions, historical development, clan emblems, language, personal names, geography, ceremonies, dances, songs, art, games, medicines, cosmology, healer, prophet, counselor, spiritually monotheistic—and with a philosophy.

The hosts of Southeast Alaska shores were tolerant and welcomed ships as long as their resources were not plundered. Children were loved and not allowed to run free and had to have an education in customary and traditional manners. This responsibility came from the clan parents—the first teachers—supported by grandparents and kinfolk. The clan residence, *HITT*, was the primary school, a home of four or more families. Other learning places were the river, berry-picking grounds, hunting areas, mountains, bays, ocean, camp sites, rivers, trails, and the community. In other words, the world was their book of knowledge. Each day was a time of learning without sitting at a desk with book, pencil, paper, and a teacher standing before the class taking roll. Daily activities that included lessons using the Native language, observation, and careful listening were a happy experience all day long.

Tlingit education was a pleasant experience for the family and the clan. Unstructured classes continued informally in the four seasons of the year. Basic contents of knowledge included, but were not limited to: physical training (especially for boys), to be economically efficient and sufficient, to be self-determined, respecting self and others, to be spiritually responsive, and to be a continuous learner.

When the United States government and churches opened their schools it was not meant to relieve parents as teachers. Many years ago American educators came up with an idea that the school system should be like three partners at work: parents, pupil, and teacher. This is the winning team.

It was important for parents to be role models as well as devoted to the family. It is pleasing to know how well the clan thought of their greatest resource: their children. The matriarchal society was the school of learning, all joining willingly as volunteer teachers.

Learning was by observing, hearing, and hands-on method. Often grandparents would say, "Come here grandchild, here is a lesson you must remember." An uncle would say, "Nephew, let me show you, this is the way it is done. Now do it right." "Listen, listen, remember what I said," or "Here is the knife, clean that fish like the way you were shown." "Good, good, keep improving." "Listen, listen, remember when you honor yourself, you honor the clan." "Here is a new Tlingit word." "Be a worker, we have no place for lazy people."

In speaking with several Tlingit clan members the general education chart should include, yet not be limited to, the following: legends, history, clan stories and its origin, land ownership, food-gathering areas, art, beading, totemic designs, moccasin-making, tanning skins, ceremonies, songs,

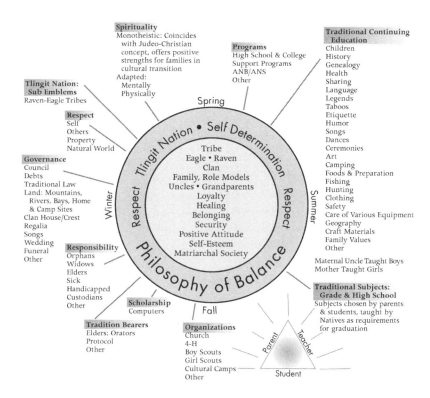

Spirituality
Monotheistic: Coincides with Judeo-Christian concept, offers positive strengths for families in cultural transition
Adapted:
Mentally
Physically

Programs
High School & College Support Programs
ANB/ANS
Other

Traditional Continuing Education
Children
History
Genealogy
Health
Sharing
Language
Legends
Taboos
Etiquette
Humor
Songs
Dances
Ceremonies
Art
Camping
Foods & Preparation
Fishing
Hunting
Clothing
Safety
Care of Various Equipment
Geography
Craft Materials
Family Values
Other

Maternal Uncle Taught Boys
Mother Taught Girls

Tlingit Nation:
Sub Emblems
Raven-Eagle Tribes

Respect
Self
Others
Property
Natural World

Governance
Council
Debts
Traditional Law
Land: Mountains, Rivers, Bays, Home & Camp Sites
Clan House/Crest
Regalia
Songs
Wedding
Funeral
Other

Responsibility
Orphans
Widows
Elders
Sick
Handicapped
Custodians
Other

Tradition Bearers
Elders: Orators
Protocol
Other

Scholarship
Computers

Organizations
Church
4-H
Boy Scouts
Girl Scouts
Cultural Camps
Other

Traditional Subjects:
Grade & High School
Subjects chosen by parents & students, taught by Natives as requirements for graduation

Spring

Winter

Summer

Fall

Tlingit Nation • Self Determination

Respect · Respect

Philosophy of Balance

Tribe
Eagle • Raven
Clan
Family, Role Models
Uncles • Grandparents
Loyalty
Healing
Belonging
Security
Positive Attitude
Self-Esteem
Matriarchal Society

Parent
Teacher
Student

dances, drumming, facial marks for dances or ceremonies, protocol, clan houses, totem carving, family values, and language.

March, April, May	June, July, August	September, October, November
legends	gathering chiton and proper cooking	legends
history	family values	history
clan	salmon fishing	clan family values
family values	canning	deer
preparing hunting and fishing gear	berrying	mountain goat and moose hunting
seal hunting	ferment salmon heads	salmon and meat drying
herring spawn	salmon roe requires expert preparation to avoid botulism (often fatal food poisoning)	ferment salmon heads
olichan drying and rendering oil (the same for seal)		salmon roe ferment
		Coho roe (cheese)

March, April, May	June, July, August	September, October, November
gathering two species of seaweed and cockles	language	making kaxhweich (salmon eggs with crabapple)
language	gathering seagull eggs	post-funeral ceremonies (peer leader well prepared for traditional oration, taught well by clan leaders)
boat safety	wild celery	
boat operation	two species of salmon	hunting and fishing gear repaired and stored for the winter.
boat upkeep	thimbleberry sprouts	
use of navigational aids	soapberries	
weather observation	strawberries	
rules of the road	salmonberries	
Coast Guard boat registration	blueberries	
knowledge of navigational regulations and local geography	red huckleberries	
	thimbleberries	
family teaching other useful lessons such as subsistence time	elderberries	
	highbush cranberries	
repairing or building smokehouse including drying rack and smoke escape	swampberries	
	currants	
	Jacob berries	
learning how to set up camp (usually the summer home).	mountain blueberries	
	and other.	

This schedule of subjects may be considered as a starting point for local consideration and revised as needed. The planning should determine subjects required for graduation and fulfill expectations for a special certificate noting this achievement. As a constant reminder, an authorized listing of the subjects should be known by the student and teachers at all times and progress noted including a passing mark and date.

In general, there is a proper method of handling and preparing foods plus the art of cooking which are all an important part of Native life and learned from the teachers. There is also the important lessons of personal hygiene taught in the men's department and the women's department. Anything that would harm the physical body is not permitted.

The maternal uncle was strict and stern in teaching his future leaders. In turn, the nephew would enhance his uncle's position of leadership. Matriarchal strength and wisdom was a source of quality vital to students' success. Native education included the basics for successful participation in a complex society undergirded with a philosophy of balance—this flows well in art forms, orations, and various ceremonies. The Chilkat blanket is an example of balance. Imagine a center line and note how one half matches the other half; similarly an oration responded to by an oration from the opposite tribe and/or clan. Native education as shared in a traditional manner gave necessary strength to the society. Finally, family values was an aid for strength of character (see values listed below). *E. Goahyuxhghwon*: "Have courage and no defeat."

In promoting Native education, traditional knowledge helped our ancestors live through the ice age, wind, rain, cold, famine, cold sleeping places, not much clothing, bare feet, and a lot of willpower. Through Native education, may we once again get some of these powerful lessons taught at home and in the school classroom. We are all Native teachers by example and should volunteer our time to educate our youth in the subjects as outlined in the chart.

Native subjects or courses required for grade and high school promotion should be considered by Native educators, parents, and Elders, together with the school board. Including Native subjects is an excellent way to involve the family, relatives, and community. Imagine a mother, father, uncle, grandparent, and other traditional leaders together in an educational venture.

Several of the Native subjects are seasonal and should not detract from the regular school year attendance; to do a special course or project, allowance should be made and not abused. The instructor should have the liberty of how to grade. The Native teachers, customary and traditional, will add quality to the program and should be honored accordingly.

Yes, yes, this combination with the present school system is a long overdue "winning team."

Cultural Values Identified by Tlingit Elders

(reprinted with permission of Dr. Walter Soboleff)

- Be obedient; the wise never test a rule.
- Respect Elders, parents, property, and the world of nature. Also respect yourself so that others may respect you.
- Be considerate and patient.

- Be careful of how you speak, for words can be either pleasing or like a club. Traditionally, when you speak, those listening can imagine seeing your clan or family line.
- Your food comes from the land and sea. To abuse either may diminish its generosity. Use what is needed.
- Pride in family, clan, and traditions is found in love, loyalty, and generosity.
- Share burdens and support each other.
- Trespass not on others' rights, or offer royalty and/or restitution.
- Parents and relatives are responsible for the family education of children—men teaching boys and women teaching girls.
- Care and good health are important for success of the person and clan.
- Take not the property of others; an error reflects on the family and clan.
- Living is better in peace, including humor.
- Through famine, ice age, sickness, war, and other obstacles, unity and self-determination are essential to survival.
- Good conduct is encouraged to please the spirit we believe is near.

PART III

HONORING INDIGENOUS KNOWLEDGE

———◆◆◆———

❝Indigenous peoples have the right to be Indigenous. They cannot exist as images and reflections of a non-Indigenous society.**❞**

From the Coolongatta Statement on Indigenous Rights in Education

INDIGENOUS WAYS OF KNOWING

IMPLICATIONS FOR PARTICIPATORY RESEARCH AND COMMUNITY

Patricia A. L. Cochran, Catherine A. Marshall, Carmen Garcia-Downing, Elizabeth Kendall, Doris Cook, Laurie McCubbin, and Reva Mariah S. Gover

Originally published in *American Journal of Public Health*, vol. 98, no. 1 (January 2008): pp. 22–27

RESEARCHERS HAVE A RESPONSIBILITY to cause no harm, but research has been a source of distress for indigenous people because of inappropriate methods and practices. The way researchers acquire knowledge in indigenous communities may be as critical for eliminating health disparities as the actual knowledge that is gained about a particular health problem. Researchers working with indigenous communities must continue to resolve conflict between the values of the academic setting and those of the community. It is important to consider the ways of knowing that exist in indigenous communities when developing research methods. Challenges to research partnerships include how to distribute the benefits of the research findings when academic or external needs contrast with the need to protect indigenous knowledge.

According to an Alaska Native saying, "Researchers are like mosquitoes; they suck your blood and leave." This saying reflects the fact that an extensive body of health-related research has been conducted about indigenous populations around the world, but appears to have had little impact on their overall wellbeing. (1–6) To improve this situation, it is important to ask why so much research has produced so few solutions.

Why are researchers viewed with skepticism by many indigenous peoples? Participatory research has often been proposed as a solution to this skepticism because it engages participants in the research process at all stages. Participatory research has been described as a "collective self-reflective enquiry undertaken by participants in social situations in order to improve . . . their own social practices" (Kemmis and Taggart 1988:5). Thus, participatory research simultaneously contributes to basic knowledge in social science and social action in everyday life. Although a full discussion of participatory research cannot be presented here, even this model of research, as it is typically practiced, does not prevent the risk that indigenous ways of knowing are marginalized by the scientific and academic community (Caldwell et al., 2005; Smith, 1999; Rigney, 1999; Cook, 2006; Arbour and Cook, 2006; CCPH, 2006; Kendall, et al., in press). Participatory researchers need to consider the power that indigenous methods can bring to research design and to the entire research process.

We first provide a brief overview of the problems associated with research partnerships in the past to provide a context for the concerns we raise. We then describe some examples of successful research partnerships and developments in participatory research. We provide specific examples of indigenous ways of knowing that have educated us regarding the possibilities of research design. Finally, we discuss one of the continuing challenges for participatory research: how the benefits of research can be managed and distributed fairly.

THE NEED FOR PARTICIPATORY RESEARCH

Recent progress has been made through the incorporation of participatory research procedures in indigenous communities (Cook, 2006; Marshall, 2001). However, it is important to consider and understand the reasons indigenous people might object to the idea of partnerships with researchers—why communities are wary or apprehensive at times even when the proposed research will address an important health issue (Kolb et al., 2006). Historically, research conducted on indigenous people has been inappropriate because it has often served to advance the "politics of colonial control" (Caldwell et al., 2005; Dodson, 1994). For instance, in the early years of colonization in Australia, research was preoccupied with "classifying and labeling" in an attempt to "manage" Aboriginal people (Dodson, 1994). Although unethical research that carries risks to the health and welfare of indigenous participants has generally ceased, this early approach to research led to significant distrust of researchers (Caldwell et al., 2005). Unfortunately, some types of inappropriate research practices have continued, largely through the use of culturally insensitive research designs and methodologies that fail to match the needs, customs, and standards of indigenous people and communities (Cook, 2006; Kolb et al., 2006; Arbour and Cook, 2006; CCPH, 2006; Kendall et al., in press; Schnarch, 2004). Researchers have a responsibility to cause no harm, but even well-intentioned research has been a source of distress for indigenous people because of its implications, methods (Caldwell et al., 2005), and lack of responsiveness to the community and its concerns (Kolb et al., 2006).

The most significant impact of insensitive research is the perpetuation of the myth that indigenous people represent a "problem" to be solved and that they are passive "objects" that require assistance from external experts. (Smith, 1999). Too often, health research documents significant issues and problems using inappropriate methods of identifying those problems, with a resulting overstatement of the negative aspects of these communities. It is no surprise that individuals and communities feel stigmatized when this research is published. No community wants to have the reputation of having the most alcoholics or the most people with mental disorders.

One example of the type of violations of trust perpetrated by researchers in indigenous communities is the recent Havasupai medical genetics case in Arizona (Shafer, 2004). In the Havasupai study, blood was collected by researchers under the guise of an investigation into the genetics of diabetes. It is understood that because diabetes was a major concern to the Havasupai tribe, they granted approval for years of ongoing blood collection. Issues of informed consent provide essential context for considering this case and the subsequent violation of tribal trust. The blood samples, understood to be collected in order to determine genetic precursors of diabetes, were used in a series of additional studies to examine the genetics of schizophrenia, among other topics. Blood samples were distributed nationally to other researchers and used in tribally unauthorized research, resulting in the advance of academic careers through, for instance, dissertations and scholarly publications. For the Havasupai, however, their trust in researchers—who had been invited to assist in the process of redressing the epidemic and debilitating impact of diabetes on an American Indian community—was broken.

A similar example involves the Canadian Nuu-chah-nulth people, whose blood was ostensibly drawn for health research on arthritis and was used instead to establish ancestry (Arbour and Cook, 2006). This deception has led to intense suspicion of research among the Nuu-chah-nulth people and a reluctance to engage in further research, even when it may be beneficial.

It is not surprising, given these examples, that the indigenous experience of research has been predominantly negative, both in terms of its processes and outcomes. Experiences such as these have compounded the negative attitude of indigenous peoples toward research and have reduced their willingness to participate in the research process.

RESEARCH PARTNERSHIPS AND INDIGENOUS WAYS OF KNOWING

It is clear from these examples of inappropriate indigenous research that how we go about acquiring knowledge in indigenous communities is just as critical for the elimination of health disparities—if not more so—as the actual knowledge that is gained about a particular health problem. An important negative impact of inappropriate research methods, no matter how laudable the intent of the researchers, is that they can reduce the validity and reliability of research findings (Marshall et al., 2003), thus minimizing the utility of the conclusions and wasting the time of participants.

According to Maori researcher Linda Tuhiwai Smith (1999), academic knowledge is organized according to disciplines and fields of knowledge that are grounded in Western "ways of knowing" and are therefore inherently culturally insensitive. Western research simply interprets indigenous knowledge from a Western framework, effectively distorting reality. In Australia, indigenous researchers have claimed that Western research has

> led to a continuing oppression and subordination of Indigenous Australians in every facet of Australian society to the point that there is no where that we can stand that is free of racism (Rigney, 1999:113).

Too frequently, the definition of what constitutes acceptable research design rests with academic researchers, for whom methods that do not conform to the "gold standard" of experimental design can be considered questionable in terms of rigor and value. To solve this problem from a statistical perspective, practitioners and researchers have recommended strategies such as oversampling and pooling of data (Murray, 2003; Marshall and

Largo, 1999). Although we support these recommendations, remedies also need to be sought at the level of conceptualization and research design. Researchers must begin to expose the underlying assumptions of Western research and the ways in which this research maintains oppression (Stone, 2002).

Researchers in health and human services have recently been advised to give greater consideration to the influence of culture on their science (Mays et al., 1996). As Gergen et al. have written,

> To what degree and with what effects is psychological science itself a cultural manifestation? . . . It is immediately apparent that the science is largely a byproduct of the Western cultural tradition at a particular time in its historical development. Suppositions about the nature of knowledge, the character of objectivity, the place of value in the knowledge generating process, and the nature of linguistic representation, for example all carry the stamp of a unique cultural tradition (1996:497).

From various fields of study, challenges are now arising as to how science is defined and the nature of science itself as a "cultural manifestation." Du Bois, for example, initiated her exploration of science by stating that "Science is *not* "value-free"; it cannot be. Science is made by scientists, and both we and our science-making are shaped by our culture (1983:105).

Indeed, as Harding has argued, those who refuse to question the way science is practiced are avoiding the "scrutiny that science recommends for all other regularities of . . . life" (1986:56).

Given the negative impact of inappropriate research with indigenous communities, there is an urgent need for an ethical research approach based on consultation, strong community participation, and methods that acknowledge indigenous ways of knowing (cook, 2006; CCPH, 2006; Kendall et al., in press). Ensuring that the research used by researchers who work in indigenous communities is both culturally appropriate and rigorous in design is essential for (1) obtaining new knowledge and understanding in regard to health disparities and (2) evaluating interventions to eliminate these disparities. To date, much of the nonindigenous response to calls for appropriate indigenous research has been at the level of process and methodology. The participation of indigenous people has often been mere token inclusion. Further, one might assume that in applying qualitative methods, researchers will address cultural insensitivity by using methods of data collection that are in line with traditional cultures. However, questions about appropriate research methods and indigenous communities go beyond the "quantitative versus qualitative" debate and focus on the root issue of how we go about knowing.

As Bernal (1998) indicated, there is a distinction between methodology and epistemology that has not always been recognized. Epistemology is the understanding of knowledge that one adopts and the philosophy with which research is approached. This issue cannot be disentangled from history or from the social position one holds within society as a result of that history. Knowledge reflects the values and interests of those who generate it, and it is these values that then determine the methods that are used and the conclusions that are drawn. These values and worldviews can lead majority cultures to disregard knowledge that is gained through another set of values and worldviews.

A long-standing and favorite example is exemplified by the Inuit whalers, who detect the presence of whales by listening for the sound of their breathing (Barreiro, 1992). In contrast to this method, the "scientific count" conducted by the International Whaling Commission included only those whales that could be seen passing from the edge of the ice. Although the Inuit methods had been criticized as being inaccurate because their counts did not match those of the International Whaling Commission, their estimates of whale numbers, based on listening to the whales' breathing, "were verified by successive aerial surveys (Barreiro, 1992:28). Another good example is found in the navigational expertise of the Native Hawaiian ocean voyagers, who had perfected knowledge about sailing long before Europeans had done so (Kamehama Schools, n.d.). Native Hawaiian voyagers collected knowledge from swell patterns; currents; moon phases; surface water quality; bird migration; star, planet, and sun positions; and cloud shapes. Multiple examples exist in which indigenous knowledge and the use of indigenous ways of knowing within a specific context have produced more extensive understanding than might be obtained through Western knowledge and scientific methods.

The health sector might also benefit from better understanding and appreciation of indigenous ways of knowing. Working in partnership with individuals who have indigenous knowledge, skills, and abilities in the area of health might help us to minimize rates of chronic conditions or disabilities and to ensure equitable access to appropriate health and rehabilitation services.

The Alaska Native Science Commission (ANSC), which serves as a model for promoting participatory research and the use of indigenous knowledge, was created to bring together research and science in partnership with Native communities and to serve as a clearinghouse, information base, and archive of research involving Alaska Native communities (ANSCa). The genesis of the ANSC was the Arctic Contamination Conference held in Anchorage in 1993, where a position paper was prepared that stated the desire of the Alaska Native community to become actively involved in scientific research, to become aware and informed of science investigating Native lives and environment, and to ensure that when science is performed in Alaska, it is with the knowledge, cooperation, and understanding of the Native community (ANSCb).

Importantly, the ANSC is concerned with addressing factors related to chronic illness, which can result in disability. In one example of participatory research conducted by the ANSC, residents became alarmed by high rates of cancer in their region and perceived a relationship between these rates and the presence of local military sites. They found that people's diets increasingly included store-bought foods, soft drinks or soda water, and improperly stored canned and frozen foods. It seemed that, over the same time period, more people were dying from stomach cancer, ulcers, and other cancers (ANSCc).

Although the community could not make causal attributions, this knowledge provided them with the capacity to take action. They were awarded grant funding to engage in research about food sampling, preservation, storage, and nutritional benefits and to clean up some of the military sites. The project clearly demonstrates how beneficial collaborative research can be for the people who are the focus of the research. The principles and practices of the ANSC highlight how researchers can no longer expect indigenous communities to be "compliant" with university-based research efforts and should be aware of the concerns, rights, and research protocols established by communities.

Another example of a participatory model that builds on indigenous knowledge is found in the work of the Canadian Institutes of Health Research (CIHR). One of the 13 founding institutes of the CIHR, the Institute of Aboriginal Peoples' Health (IAPH), is dedicated to leading an advanced research agenda in Canadian aboriginal health. The profile of the IAPH includes support and promotion of health research that has a positive impact on the mental, physical, emotional, and spiritual health of aboriginal people at all life stages. The IAPH is the only national aboriginal or indigenous health institute in the world that is devoted to the advancement of holistic and multidisciplinary health research for indigenous people. Canada decided in 2000 to establish such an institute not only because of its own domestic health disparities but also because of the

United Nations' call for improvements in the health of indigenous peoples. In the long term, CIHR-funded health research is expected to improve the health of Canadian aboriginal people through the active participation and involvement of aboriginal communities in setting their own research agenda and through the development of research guidelines that ensure culturally competent research that is protective of the health, safety, and human rights of aboriginal people.

Australia has recently moved one step closer to the ideal situation in which indigenous knowledge and participation are integral to the conduct of indigenous research. In the most recent revision of the National Health and Medical Research Council's guidelines for the conduct of indigenous research (NHMRC, 2003). researchers are required to submit only research proposals that are ethically defensible against an indigenous value base rather than against Western research ethics. The document clearly outlines six values that have been generated by Australian aboriginal and Torres Strait Islander communities: (1) spirit and integrity, (2) reciprocity, (3) respect, (4) equality, (5) survival and protection, and (6) responsibility. Thus, depending on the views of the particular community, it may be critical that indigenous ways of knowing are fully integrated into the research design and that the research is both participatory and beneficial to the community.

DECIDING WHO BENEFITS FROM INDIGENOUS KNOWLEDGE

Partnerships between academic researchers and indigenous communities must be clear regarding what, and for whom, the expected benefits are to be. For the academic researcher, there are university requirements for faculty retention or promotion; these requirements usually include professional presentations, grant proposals, books, and articles. For many who work in indigenous communities, there is the sense of contributing to the social good, community well-being, and social justice through their research. Yet there is also the conflicting sense that knowledge that has been uncovered, revealed, or shared must be protected and that the different purposes and values of community research participants must be both acknowledged and accommodated to the extent possible (Marshall, 1994).

A key issue that continues to damage the concept of research in the minds of many indigenous people is the area of intellectual and cultural property rights. Who gets credit for the knowledge that is gained from research conducted in indigenous communities? A full body of research and scholarly activity is being devoted to issues of indigenous cultural and intellectual property rights; we can but touch on this important topic here. For this discussion, however, it is important to understand that knowledge gained from indigenous communities is both local and specific to a given research effort, but it is also global in terms of history and potential impact.

Who "owns" the knowledge and has the right to patents or copyrights? What is the responsibility of researchers to advise indigenous people about how to protect the knowledge they have—knowledge that might benefit the larger community? A useful example comes from a Mixe local coordinator of a research project in Oaxaca, Mexico. In a published report, he revealed knowledge about a local herbal remedy for prevention of kidney stones. He stated:

> There are some herbs, for example . . . I've been in a wheelchair for 17 years and, thanks be to God, I don't have any kidney problems—no stones, no infections and that's entirely due to the herbs. As you can see, if we think about what we have at hand, it can really serve us well. Because otherwise we'd always be thinking about antibiotics, about operations for gall stones (Marshall et al., 1998).

Murray was later contacted by researchers who wanted to further explore the herbs in question. She stated that there would be a need to discuss intellectual and indigenous property rights with the Mixe owners of the knowledge. The researchers were never heard from again. However, an American Indian colleague who visited the Mixe community also recommended that the medicinal herbs should be further investigated so that people with spinal cord injuries and secondary conditions associated with kidney problems could benefit from them. Beyond those whose health might directly benefit from the herbs, it is unclear who would benefit from further investigation and who would hold the rights to the knowledge.

In another example, an Australian aboriginal woman advised us that her community knew through "bush medicine" how to cure cervical cancer. Who should and could benefit from this knowledge? If the knowledge became the property of research facilities, including those associated with universities, the benefit would most likely accrue to pharmaceutical companies via patents and profits; however, others in need might also benefit. What about the women in Appalachia, where cervical cancer is epidemic? Or should that particular aboriginal community that holds the knowledge be the only ones to benefit? How should their discovery be adequately recognized and protected without preventing the widespread use of a beneficial health product? This challenge is not insignificant, and the extent to which it can be resolved may influence the willingness of both indigenous communities and nonindigenous researchers to engage in partnership research in the future.

CONCLUSIONS AND RECOMMENDATIONS

Some would say that indigenous communities have been "researched to death," that researchers only take and give back nothing; there is good justification for this perception. Ultimately, those of us who serve as researchers with indigenous communities must resolve the conflict—or at least our sense of conflict—between the values of the academic setting and those of the community. We must continue to participate in conversations and seek guidance on how to deal with individual instances of intellectual and cultural property rights, indigenous rights, and academic or professional responsibilities. We need to continue to explore our understanding of knowledge, what constitutes valuable knowledge, and how it is gathered and how it is shared.

Acceptance of indigenous ways of knowing by nonindigenous researchers will bring with it time-consuming and fundamental changes in research methods. A major challenge to researchers who wish to work in indigenous communities is the collaborative identification of research methods, inclusive of indigenous ways of knowing, that lead to sustainable, efficacious services that redress health disparities among indigenous people without violating their rights.

There are no easy solutions to the challenges raised in this essay. We have reported on the efforts of work groups, symposia, summits, and institutes that are attempting to address these issues. We know that the work of local institutional review boards and community research groups produces a wealth of unpublished but critical conversations that tackle these same concerns. In the spirit of sharing what has influenced us after decades of conducting participatory research in indigenous communities, we offer the following recommendations as topics in need of further attention by those engaged in participatory research activities.

1. Academic researchers, and the institutions that sustain them, may have to relinquish their hold on the role of "principal investigator" to facilitate truly collaborative research, seeing themselves primarily in a service role, accepting community direction

regarding priorities for research, considering indigenous ways of knowing in research methods, and sharing or giving up entirely—depending on community needs and desires—the dissemination of research findings (including where, how, and if research results are published, as well as who speaks for the research team in a standard 10-minute conference presentation).

2. Research sponsors must require participatory research procedures in indigenous communities and support such work through the funding of community-based positions that enable communities to be engaged in a discussion of research methods at the design table.

3. Participatory researchers in indigenous communities need to look globally for a range of useful operational models and practices; for instance, Australia, Canada, and New Zealand have been actively addressing culturally appropriate research design in indigenous communities over the last few decades.

4. Research sponsors who value participatory research—and, in particular, community-based participatory research—must understand that the Western-style empiricism to which they are accustomed may not be the research method of choice in indigenous communities. Research sponsors will need to view as valid—and support through funding—participatory research that uses alternative ways of knowing as a foundation.

5. Using indigenous ways of knowing in research methods is different from using or benefiting from indigenous or cultural knowledge per se. Nonetheless, the use of indigenous ways of knowing to better understand a topic—to make an impact on eliminating health disparities, for instance—may lead to the exposure of indigenous knowledge and the challenges we have raised in this essay.

6. Participatory research in indigenous communities may also involve capacity-building, which will require additional funding. Asking local community members and indigenous service providers in indigenous communities to serve on a research design development committee means removing them from their substantive roles and services. Researchers are typically funded to carry out participatory research; community participants in participatory research are typically not funded—the funding stream may need to be shared more equitably. Even though there are examples of capacity-building in participatory research (T.E.

Downing, University of Arizona, unpublished data, 1995), the question remains, whose capacity needs to be built if indigenous ways of knowing are to be incorporated into the research design?

Finding ways to maintain trust, increase institutional support, and redefine partnership roles—but continue moving forward in participatory research—is a challenge we embrace, and we encourage others with interest in indigenous communities to accept it.

REFERENCES

Alaska Native Science Commission (ANSC). A partnership approach, http://www.nativescience.org (accessed September 19, 2007).
———. ANSC origins, http:// www.nativescience.org/html/origins.html (accessed June 24, 2004).
———. The Traditional Knowledge & Contaminants Project, ANSC & Institute of Social and Economic Research, UAA, Alaska traditional knowledge and native foods database, http:// www.nativeknowledge.org (accessed June 24, 2004).
Arbour, L., and D. Cook. 2006. DNA on loan: Issues to consider when carrying out genetic research with Aboriginal families and communities. *Community Genet.* 9:153–160.
Bernal, D.D. 1998. Using a Chicana feminist epistemology in educational research. *Harvard Educ Rev.* 68:555–582.
Barreiro, J. 1992. The search for lessons. *Akwe:kon J.* 9:18–39.
Caldwell, J.Y., J.D. Davis, B. Du Bois, et al. 2005. Culturally competent research with American Indians and Alaska Natives: Findings and recommendations of the first symposium of the work group on American Indian Research and Program Evaluation Methodology. *Am Indian Alsk Native Ment Health Res.* 12:1–21.
Community-Campus Partnerships for Health (CCPH), University of Washington. 2006. Achieving the promise of authentic community–higher education partnerships: A community partner summit executive summary, http://depts.washington.edu/ccph/pdf_files/ FINALCPS_Executive_Summary.pdf (accessed September 19, 2007).
Cook, D. 2006. The importance of ethically sound health research to improvements in aboriginal health. Paper presented at Forum 10: Combating Disease and Promoting Health, Global Forum for Health Research; October 29–November 2, 2006, Cairo, Egypt. Available at http://www.globalforumhealth.org/filesupld/ forum10/F10_final-documents/papers/ Cook_Doris.pdf (accessed September 19, 2007).
Dodson, M. 1994. *The Wentworth Lecture—The end in the beginning.* Australian Aboriginal Studies No. 1. Canberra, Australia: Aboriginal Studies Press.
Du Bois, B. 1983. Passionate scholarship: Notes on values, knowing and method in feminist social science. In *Theories of women's studies,* ed. G. Bowles and R.D. Klein, 105–116. Boston: Routledge and Kegan Paul.
Gergen, K.J., A. Gulerce, A. Lock, and G. Misra. 1996. Psychological science in cultural context. *Am Psychol.* 51:496–503.
Harding, S. 1986. *The Science question in feminism.* Ithaca, NY: Cornell University Press.
Kamehama Schools. n.d. Policy analysis and system evaluation, http://www.ksbe.edu/pase (accessed June 24, 2004).
Kemmis, S., and R. McTaggart. 1998. *The action research planner,* 3rd ed. Geelong, Australia: Deakin University Press.

Kolb, B., A.M. Wallace, D. Hill, and M. Royce. 2006. Disparities in cancer care among racial and ethnic minorities. *Oncology* 20:1256–1261.

Kendall, E., C. Marshall, T. Catalano, L. Barnett. In press. The spaces between: Partnerships between women researchers and indigenous women with disabilities. *Disabil Rehabil.*

Marshall, C.A. 1994. Researcher as advocate: An "outsider" perspective regarding research involving American Indians with disabilities. In *Insights and outlooks: Current trends in disability studies*, ed. E. Makas and L. Schlesinger, 271–277. Portland, ME: Society for Disability Studies & The Edmund S. Muskie Institute of Public Affairs.

———. 2001. Cultural factors in conducting research and ethical responsibilities in serving American Indians with disabilities. In *Rehabilitation and American Indians with disabilities: A handbook for administrators, practitioners, and researchers*, ed. C.A. Marshal, 165–175. Athens, GA: Elliott & Fitzpatrick Inc.

Marshall, C.A., G.S. Gotto, and J.A. Bernal Alcántara. 1998. *Vecinos y Rehabilitation (Phase III): Assessing the needs and resources of indigenous people with disabilities in the Sierra Mixe. Final Report.* Flagstaff: Northern Arizona University.

Marshall, C.A., and H.R. Largo, Jr. 1999. Disability and rehabilitation: A context for understanding the American Indian experience. *Lancet* 354:758–760.

Marshall, C.A., P. Leung, S.R. Johnson, and H. Busby. 2003. Ethical practice and cultural factors in rehabilitation. *Rehab Ed.* 17:55–65.

Mays, V.M., J. Rubin, M. Sabourin, and L. Walker. 1996. Moving toward a global psychology: Changing theories and practice to meet the needs of a changing world. *Am Psychol.* 51:485–487.

Murray, L.R. 2003. Sick and tired of being sick and tired: scientific evidence, methods, and research implications for racial and ethnic disparities in occupational health. *Am J Public Health.* 93: 221–226.

National Health and Medical Research Council (NHMRC). 1991. Guidelines on Ethical Matters in Aboriginal and Torres Strait Islander Research. Approved by the 111th Session, Brisbane, Australia, June 1991. Available at http://www. nhmrc.gov.au/ethics/human/ ahec/ history/_files/e11.pdf (accessed September 20, 2007).

———. 2003. Values and ethics: guidelines for ethical conduct in Aboriginal and Torres Strait Islander health research. 148th session, June 5, 2003. Available at http:// www.nhmrc.gov.au/ethics/human/conduct/guidelines/_files/   e52.pdf   (accessed September 20, 2007).

Rigney, L.I. 1999. Internationalization of an indigenous anticolonial cultural critique of research methodologies: A guide to indigenist research methodology and its principles. *Wicazo Sa Rev.* 14: 109–121.

Schnarch, B. 2004. *Ownership, Control, Access, and Possession (OCAP) or self-determination applied to research: A critical analysis of contemporary First Nations research and some options for First Nations communities.* Ottawa, Ontario: First Nations Centre, National Aboriginal Health Organization.

Shafer, M. 2004. Havasupai blood samples misused. *Indian Country Today,* http://indiancountry. com/content.cfm?id=1078833203 (accessed September 19, 2007).

Smith, L.T. 1999. *Decolonizing methodologies: Research and indigenous peoples.* London: Zed Books Ltd.

Stone, J.B. 2002. Focus on cultural issues in research: Developing and implementing Native American postcolonial participatory action research. In *Work Group on American Indian Research and Program Evaluation Methodology (AIRPEM), Symposium on Research and Evaluation Methodology: Lifespan Issues Related to American Indians/Alaska Natives with Disabilities*, ed. J.D. Davis, J.S. Erickson, S.R. Johnson, C.A. Marshall, P. Running Wolf, and R.L. Santiago, 98–121. Flagstaff: Northern Arizona University. Available at http://www.wili.org/docs/ AIRPEM_Monograph.pdf (accessed September 16, 2007).

Alaska Native Traditional Knowledge and Ways of Knowing

Carl Hild, Editor

Workshop sponsored by the Rural Alaska Community Action Program,
Inc. and the Indigenous People's Council for Marine Mammals
September 13–14 1994, Anchorage, Alaska

Day One: The Opening

The opening prayer by Dr. Walter Soboleff thanked the Creator for the fine day that had been provided for the gathering and asked that all the participants be appreciative. He asked for divine guidance during the workshop and that the participants work together for the common good of everyone. He gave thanks to a larger Spirit than his own and asked for help for all. This became the theme of the next two days. He was able to provide the summary in his opening prayer, but the rest of the participants would only learn that as the days unwound.

Larry Merculieff called the meeting to order and turned it over to Jeanine Kennedy, executive director of the Rural Alaska Community Action Program, for an opening statement. She spoke of her new grandson and how happy she was of the child's birth that day. From this point on, the theme of interest in future generations also became an integral part of the meeting.

The connections that had been clearly placed before the group within the first minutes were those linked to a larger Spirit, to the Creation, to all people, and to future generations. This connectedness provided insight as to the scale of the concerns, but also created problems as the English language does not reflect such associations well.

THE IMPORTANCE OF TRADITIONAL KNOWLEDGE AND WAYS OF KNOWING

Larry Merculieff began his presentation on the importance of traditional knowledge and ways of knowing by drawing a circle. It was a circle with several wavy lines running from the edge to its center. This is the world. The lines are the paths of individuals. The center is the Creator.

He talked of indigenous peoples from around the world. There is a belief that the time is coming near when the four sacred colors of peoples will come together. They will share their ancient traditions and wisdom for the benefit of all. In order to deal with the growing global monoculture of Western European/American influence, it is important to keep the diversity of indigenous cultures. It is time to reestablish the links to the Elders and restrengthen the Alaska Native cultures. Cultural diversity increases the chances of human survival, quality of life, and proper stewardship.

He proceeded to discuss this view of the world and contrast the Alaska Native perspective to that of the Western European viewpoint. He drew a straight line and commented that the Western worldview is linear, quite different from the Alaska Native perception. He stated that recent agreements with the dominant culture have placed briefcases in the hands of Alaska Natives. Perhaps it is time to go back to the traditional packsacks.

He then went on to describe some of the different tendencies between Western and Alaska Native worldviews:

Western	Native
Linear	Circular
Talks a great deal	Listens
Decides with numbers	Decides with issues
Thrives on details, specialized	Looks for large picture, wholistic
Looks at parts of whole	Looks at connections between parts
Void of spirit	Filled with spirit
Objective	Subjective

Control the environment	Live with all of Creation, adapt to environment
Goes to extremes	Lives in balance
Uses male structures	Uses female structures

Mr. Merculieff went into more detail on this final point. He stated that male structures include the following characteristics:

Top-down decision making	Do not compromise
Do not use intuition	Seek control
Do not use feelings	Do not listen
Aggressive	Competitive
Physical	Violent

Stemming from all of these basic philosophical differences, the relationships within families and communities are in conflict. A real concern is also how the Western society treats its Elders. They are removed and placed in institutions away from home, family, and community. This lack of respect is repeated when Western scientists come into the communities and rarely involve the Elders except to interview them.

Alaska Native young people are seeing this lack of respect of the Elders at many levels. They then believe that they too do not need to listen to the old people. The young people are preoccupied with things of the youth-focused Western culture and are not paying attention to their own culture. They are asleep within their own culture and are referred to sometimes as "dreamers." It is time to provide a wake-up call to the young people. It is time to reestablish the rightful position of the Elders. It is time to refocus on Alaska Native cultures and the wisdom they hold.

The Western culture promotes the idea of an age of independence. At the age of 18 or 21 a person is considered an adult and goes away from his or her family. This goes against the Alaska Native cultures in that an individual is always part of a family and that network of relationships offers protection. It is not unlike the network of linkages between the various parts of Creation that provide for continued life for all. No one part is independent of the rest.

There is confusion within the governance of the community. There are Village Councils, Traditional Councils, local and regional governments, and state and federal governments all determining what goes on in a community. There need to be cooperative working relationships between all levels. Joint meetings could offer an opportunity to foster agreements and unified programs.

Leaders need to go to a healing camp. Too many have lost touch with their cultures and themselves. Many of our leaders are spread so thin that all they have time to do is go from one meeting to the next. This means they have little time to focus on the people and doing what the people want. Leaders as a result are reacting to all the things coming in from the outside instead of being proactive. There needs to be an effort to have all groups working for the betterment of Alaska Natives. Traditional means of dealing with the environment offer a chance to seek common themes for cooperation. This effort should be based on trust and respect of all the participants.

There were questions raised:

- How to get groups to work together?
- How to reinvolve the Elders so they again would be in a position of respect?
- How to protect the traditional knowledge?
- How to involve people in the preservation of Alaska Native cultures?
- How best to influence outside decision makers who are not of an Alaska Native culture?
- How do the international principles that have been generated on sustainable development apply on behalf of Alaska Natives?
- How to become less influenced by Western culture?
- How to assure self-determination?

ELDERS' PERSPECTIVE ON ALASKA NATIVE TRADITIONAL KNOWLEDGE

Dr. Soboleff presented information about the Elders' perspective on traditional knowledge. There were no libraries or computers in the past. The important things that needed to be passed down were in the stories and songs that everyone heard. Everything was in the mind and each person was responsible for learning the lessons of previous generations. The traditional style of learning was watching, listening, feeling. Young people learned from adults as well as from the animals and the environment. In order for this exchange to take place there needs to be a time and place for Elders to express themselves.

Children were taught to listen to people they respect, but to learn you must respect yourself first. People will not listen to a drunkard or a person who is careless about themselves. People will listen to Elders who have been successful in their life and who are sought for counsel. However, those Elders will not be boastful or proud and so it is the responsibility of the young to seek out the information of their ancestors.

In contrast to the circle drawn before, Dr. Soboleff drew a square box. This is the family. This is the treasure box of culture. Many things are hitting this box but it must be protected. If the family and community break, then the box of culture breaks.

In the past young people were assigned to help their Elders. They learned from them. This does not happen today and so there is a need to record the wisdom of the Elders so that it can be passed along. When people take care of themselves they protect the family and their culture. There is a great need to protect the Alaska Native languages, as the words are so important to the holding of culture. It was said that half of a culture is gone when the language is lost. As the workshop continued this lack of correct words became more and more evident.

Traditional knowledge took on many aspects during the following discussion.

It is a goal for cultural survival. Elders must become active teachers of the children. Young children can learn language and should be bilingual. There is not enough sharing of this information at home normally. It is good to use it at hunting or fish camp, but it must be used more.

It is wisdom. It is passing what has been learned by previous generations on to future generations. Groups around the state should list their basic beliefs and have them posted everywhere around the community as constant reminders for behavior.

It is for others. The lack of information among Russian Inuit is sad. For 70 years they have been denied their culture. The Alaskan Inuit may now be able to share and reintroduce aspects of their culture which have been lost. It may even be for the "White tribe" as they need to learn many of the lessons of being in harmony with Creation.

It is Native education. It is the embodiment of community standards which are based on family values. It provides young people with the inner strength to deal with the world, and often are the only lessons offered to live in the real world. Formal Western schooling provides many facts but does not teach values.

It is life values. Throughout the world as the population increases there will be an ever-growing demand for better understanding so that everyone will be able to enjoy life. The "White tribe" has not done well at managing aspects of the riches of Creation. They are now looking to the indigenous cultures of the world for new approaches and processes in order to lessen the impact.

When the group began to discuss the obstacles to the use of traditional knowledge, the language being used suddenly became inadequate. There is a general lack of respect by the Western cultures for anything that is not written. This places the oral traditions of Alaska Native cultures in a position of not being recognized nor respected for the wealth of information they contain. Even when the values and subtleties of these traditions are defined in English they lose much of their full cultural basis. The richness of the words of Alaska Native languages needs to be passed on to future generations without interpretation through English.

Alaska Natives may need to start their own institutions to establish the requirements for the collection, utilization, and stewardship of the ancient lessons. The true value of traditional knowledge is not just in its recording. It has a spiritual component which is critical to its application. Traditional knowledge must be lived to be known, used, and passed on to future generations.

Traditional knowledge cannot be picked up by watching a videotape or hearing it once. It is a process. Children need to hear it over and over. They need to be presented with new parts of it when they are ready to learn. Giving it to them too early or too late will not allow it to be used with understanding. Understanding a child's ability to learn and practice aspects of the culture is key to passing along traditional knowledge. Elders have taken a lifetime to learn this information, and they need a lifetime to share it.

Elders need to be with young people. The communication between generations was not a problem in the past. The home, family, and community structures allowed for active and regular exchanges. The Western culture has introduced many of the problems of a generation gap separating children from their Elders. Perhaps the youth can be encouraged to go to their Elders to collect the information. Have the students tape-record the stories and help in their homes. The Elders are like rare books which hold great information but need to be cared for so their wisdom continues to be available.

There was a brief mention of concerns about the preservation and misuse of traditional knowledge. How to collect it becomes a growing issue of not knowing what has already been gathered, and where it is. Once on tape where does it go and who knows what is on which tape? Some materials have been recorded on outdated technology and now cannot be recovered. How to protect the information from exploitative individuals who then put their own name on it? How to assure that the information gathered is not then used to establish regulations that hurt Alaska Native cultures? These are important topics but the co-chairs were aware that further discussion on these matters would take the group away from the next section to address, "subsistence."

DAY TWO: SUBSISTENCE

There immediately was a problem. The word "subsistence" is not an Alaska Native word. It does not really mean the same thing to the people who write the laws that it means to those who practice it. There was the additional concern that even by talking about it that it then loses part of its value. Subsistence is not just taking food from the local environment. This one word cannot be used to define the Alaska Native way of living.

Eric Smith, attorney for RurAL CAP, was asked to define subsistence. He spoke of "customary and traditional usage." But clearly subsistence is more than the amount of protein that is put on the table to keep Alaska Natives alive.

"To define subsistence would be to define ourselves." "We cannot define our culture in terms of another language." "We need to learn terms and use them to our advantage." "Subsistence provides for life and is a physical example of thanks."

The participants spoke many Alaska Native languages' but the one common language to all was English. It was suggested by Dolly Garza that perhaps the group should define what they mean by subsistence in words or short phrases in English, and then identify one Alaska Native term that conveys the larger definition that can be used and incorporated into daily expressions by Natives and non-Natives.

It was pointed out that there is a legal definition of subsistence. There may be confusion if there is a new word. If there is an Alaska Native understanding that subsistence does not represent what they want it to mean then it must be changed, and if that means changing the laws then that can be done. However, there will be no change unless there is a new concept and a new word.

It was agreed that this group could not generate that new word or agree to use just one definition for all Alaska Native cultures. It was also agreed that the concerns of those present were clear and that they should actively work to put down what their perception of subsistence is for their culture. It was then decided that a letter would be written to the Alaska Federation of Natives requesting that the Elders and Youth Conference consider the problem faced by this group. A list was then prepared of what "subsistence" means.

The participation was broad. The note takers were scrambling to keep ahead of comments. The list grew rapidly and in ever-expanding circles. It was very clear that the word and concept in the legal documents fell far short of the Alaska Native perception of this activity. A full list of the definitions is included in the attached letter to AFN.

After an intense period of discussion a break was called. Upon returning from the rest it was clear that the group had broken into small groups on its own. Some clarified the words and suggestions. Others discussed the application of the list. Still others began to search for common themes and then find Alaska Native terms to reflect what was being said.

The definition was more than a word, more than an activity, more than a process. They offered phrases covering the mind, body, and spirit. They addressed the relationship of all things and the need to respect and live in balance with Creation. They portrayed love, survival, generosity, growth, and the cycles of life. They focused on the connections between father and mother, parent and child, Elder and youth, grandparents and future generations. They focused on the continued success of the individual, the family, the community, the region, the culture, and all of humanity.

The words were tried. Phrases changed. If "wordsmithing" is appropriate, this group was forging new materials in the fiery passion of what is the blast furnace of Alaska Native culture. As the group hammered out the meanings they more closely realized the need to take this message to the Elders. The group felt that it could not determine the words adequately, but knew they now had to go back to the Elders for this wisdom.

As language was being drafted for the letter to AFN words continued to be modified. It was made clear by Frank Charles that the letter should not say "our mind, body, spirit, and the other Creation," but become inclusive and be "and the Creation." He also pointed out that what has changed in the relationship with the Elders is not to be focused on the Western influences, but from "our own turning away." Language was adjusted to "the role of the Elders and the respect shown them by ourselves has diminished." The group was taking ownership of their influence by the Western culture and their desire to learn again from the Elders.

WHAT DO WE WANT?

The original request to fund this workshop was entitled "Cultural Interface: Principles, Policies, and Protocols." Larry Merculieff turned the focus to what is it that the group would like. If there were principles for the collection and utilization of traditional knowledge, what would they be?

It was mentioned that the Association of Village Council Presidents has developed a local policy for the approval of all research in their communities. They have stated they will define the research and wherever possible do it themselves.

It was also mentioned that the Alaska Federation of Natives had passed a policy on principles for conducting research in Alaska. A copy of that policy was obtained and provided to all the participants.

The group then put forward some of the issues that they felt needed to be part of any statement of principles or policy on traditional knowledge.

- Research should be defined by the community.
- We will not participate in research that violates our ethics, values, or spirituality.
- We are equal, and we will only participate in programs, projects, or initiatives that treat us as equals.
- Our way of life changes over time. We adapt to these changes through the way we do things such as responsible change in light of new technology. Such change in a living culture should be allowed and requirements that mandate use of outdated technology such as paddles and harpoons are not appropriate.
- The Alaska Native cultures and ways of life are the foundation for self-regulation.
- Adequate funds must be provided to Alaska Natives to exercise co-management and to engage in our own research.

WHERE DO WE GO?

Larry Merculieff opened the last session with two comments. The first was about the strength of Alaska Native cultures. "Our young people are dying because we do not have this." The cultures must be preserved in order to save lives. He then reflected on wisdom passed to him from an Elder. "In the past we would live life and think about the mystery of death. Now we do not live and think about the mystery of life."

The word "resource" is Western and defines a thing. It is a thing that is used for profit. It is a thing to be taken. The person best able to take it becomes wealthy. It is not alive. This concept is opposed to the Alaska Native way of looking at Creation. Again the group was struck by the inappropriateness of the English word.

"Resource management," the Alaska Department of Fish and Game, and sports hunting are examples of taking away the respect that Alaska Native cultures have held for all parts of Creation. Western culture believes in dominating nature, that the spirit of animals is not impacted by tagging and radio tracking operations, and that killing animals can be done for fun and trophies. This is not the belief of Alaska Natives.

The group generated a list of concepts that belong to what they perceive to be a "resource." Again it was agreed that the Elders should be asked to talk about this issue and provide some guidance on what words to use and how to portray the connections between Alaska Natives and the environment which sustains them.

The Elders are the historians, the treasured books that contain knowledge, understanding, and wisdom. They are educators, guides, and decisionmakers. Alaska Natives need to clarify a more active way to involve the Elders. It is the Elders who should be contacted first in a community and asked for consent and approval before any traditional knowledge is shared. It is their wisdom that will provide direction for the utilization and stewardship of Alaska Native understanding of the world.

Rather than sending Elders away from their homes, families, and communities they should be brought back. An Elders Council could be formed to provide direction to all Alaska Natives. When the Elders are sent away Alaska Native cultures are being sent away.

The group then prepared the language for their request to the Elders that will be sent through the Alaska Federation of Natives for the Elders and Youth Conference to be held in mid-October 1994. With this final work of putting ideas on paper, Larry Merculieff called once again on Dr. Soboleff to lead the group in prayer.

SUMMARY

Dr. Soboleff opened the meeting with a prayer. He also closed the meeting with a prayer. He had set the tone for the meeting from his first words. He was respectful, thankful, and asked for help. The participants of this workshop over two days were respectful, thankful, and are now asking for help.

There was a great deal of remembering going on at the workshop. People recounted stories and lessons they had learned as children. The accounts echoed the love and respect that was held for those who have gone before and who learned hard lessons to pass on to their children's children.

The sense of the discussion was one of thanks for having learned the ways of Alaska Native culture. Thanks for the bounty of the Creation. Thanks for the happiness and spiritual strength that such involvement brings. Thanks for life.

The call for help was deep. The workshop had allowed these individuals to voice the heaviness in their hearts. They could see that what they learned was not being made available to the youth of today. They were stating that something is very wrong. Their conclusion was that they had lost touch with their Elders. The ownership was on their shoulders and they now knew that an effort would have to be made by themselves to mend those relations.

Dr. Soboleff closed the meeting with appreciation. Appreciation for the fine day, appreciation for the good meeting, appreciation for everyone's energies and thoughts, appreciation for a renewed effort to listen more closely to the old lessons.

Letter of request sent to the Alaska Federation of Natives for the Elders and Youth Conference

To the Alaska Federation of Natives and the participants of the Elders and Youth Conference:

We, the participants of the Alaska Native Traditional Knowledge and Ways of Knowing Workshop which was held on September 13 and 14, 1994 at the Rural Alaska Community Action Program offices, hosted by the Indigenous People's Council for Marine Mammals, and supported by the Bureau of Indian Affairs, agreed to the following.

Many of our Elders need help which they may not be getting, particularly help in terms of sharing our traditional foods. This has occurred because our level of use of traditional ways regarding family and family values has changed. Many of us are institutionalizing our Elders by placing them in care facilities away from their homes, families, and communities. The role of the Elders and the respect shown them by ourselves has diminished in many communities.

We respectfully request that you provide us with guidance to be able to restore the treasure box of traditional culture, which is the family unit, which has always been our first school. We request that this be discussed at your meeting and that it be addressed in terms of steps we need to take to restore the proper role and respect of Elders amongst our peoples.

Within our discussion we have been frustrated by our inability to communicate the breadth of our beliefs. We humbly request your assistance in finding a word or short phrase that better describes our traditional way of life. This word or phrase would be used by the Alaska Native community instead of the word "subsistence." The use of the word "subsistence" has become one of limited perception and perhaps has negative connotation in the taking of food from the local environment, and does not adequately reflect the true sense of its cultural basis.

We are including a list of words and phrases that all describe parts of our way of life not encompassed by the word "subsistence." We hope that you can find an indigenous word or phrase. Such a word or phrase could then be presented to the AFN convention for adoption.

Way of life
Unity, circle of interaction, survival
Recreation
Camaraderie, comradeship, companionship,
and community
Spirituality
Sense of pride
Sense of well-being
Source of nutrition
Sense of accomplishment
Sense of family strength
Self-determination
Holistic
Connectedness
Interdependence
Traditional continuity from time immemorial to today
Sharing
Culture
Respect for all it brings
Conservation and stewardship
System for young people to learn

Enjoying land inheritance
Embodiment of beliefs, practices, and customs since
time immemorial
Protection of land
Basic international Human Right to maintain one's
lifestyle
Cultural heritage
Connection between old and young
Source of family unity
Source of security
Source of song, dance, and storytelling
Our way of government and laws
Our birthright
Process of moving young into inheritance (rite of
passage)
Barter, sharing, exchange, and trading for family, com-
munity, regional, and inter-regional
Source of learning values
Way to get specific knowledge about Creation
Process of transmitting values
Process and system which reflects the interconnected-
ness of everything and how it affects our culture, consid-
ering seasons and special times traditionally set aside for
hunting, fishing, berrypicking, etc.
Celebration of life, liberty, and happiness
Adaptability and versatility
Sustainability and balance, living in peace and harmony
with all Creation
A wholesome way of life
It is a wholesome way of life, guided by customs and
traditions given to us from the beginning of time of our
people. It is the very roots of our existence.

Our group identified some words as a first attempt.

Aleut	*toomin on gre ta son*	Those things that keep us alive.
Tlingit	*sh xha da yuk da utk*	Working for the things that will be in and around your mouth.
	ha koos tee ee	Our way of life.
Gwich'in	*t'eediraa'in*	Striving to live off the land.

Iñupiaq	*inuuniaqtaut*	Striving to live as a people.
	inuuniagniqput	The way we live as a people.
Yup'ik	*anguussaak*	Concept for survival
	yuungnaqsaraq	Our way of being
Siberian Yup'ik	*key yaq tak tak*	Way of life

We also discussed the word "resource." It has become a reference to a thing and no longer holds the respect of making use of a living part of Creation. Again we attempted to describe in English what we knew was a much larger definition of "resource."

- Food
- Sustenance
- Clothing
- Spirit
- Peace of mind
- Therapy
- Our home
- Gifts from the Creator
- Harvest
- Security
- Our being we are one with the land and sea
- Creation, which is wise and teaches its relatives that all should be respected
- All is equal

Everything is alive and breathing, made by the Creator and is to be respected and treated as such. If we do not treat those Creations properly and with respect, the abuse will affect our mind, body, and spirit, as well as all Creation.

It is clear that we struggled with the limits of English in portraying our understanding of the relationships we have with Creation and the importance of that connectedness with our way of life. Our efforts to find better words were limited. However, these are only starting points from which your larger and more knowledgeable group can go forward.

We thank you for your consideration of this request. We will offer whatever assistance we can during the AFN meetings for a better understanding of this aspect of our cultures.

Sincerely, (for all the participants of the workshop)

Larry Merculieff, Co-Chair
Dr. Walter Soboleff, Co-Chair

Special thanks to the Bureau of Indian Affairs.

Aleut/Alutiiq Region

Cultural and Intellectual Property Rights

Gordon L. Pullar

Keynote Address to the Alaska Native Educators' Conference
February 1, 2000, Anchorage, Alaska

My thanks to Lolly Carpluk and other conference organizers for inviting me to be here tonight. And my special thanks to Teri Schneider for her kind introduction.

On a sad day such as today I don't think I could launch into a speech before offering my sincere respect to the memory of Morris Thompson, who we all lost yesterday. I had the honor of serving with Morrie on the AFN (Alaska Federation of Natives) board for several years and he was always someone I looked up to and learned from. He was a strong leader, a successful manager, and a dedicated advocate for Native people. Above all, however, he was a genuinely kind and caring person. We all owe him a debt of gratitude. We'll miss him.

Being asked to speak here tonight takes me back a few years ago when my friend Harold Napoleon asked me to speak at the AFN Youth/Elders Conference that he was coordinating. I did my presentation and it seemed to go okay and as I stepped down from the podium I saw that Harold was waiting for me with a smile on his face. "You weren't as boring as everyone said you were going to be," he said. So having reached that lofty plateau once, I hope to do it again tonight and not be as boring as everyone said I was going to be.

I will begin with a disclaimer. That disclaimer is that I'm not an expert. I don't believe in experts. In fact, a sure way for someone to draw my suspicion and distrust is to claim to be an expert or to brag that he or she knows "all there is to know" about any topic. I am, however, a lifelong student. I try to observe, listen, and learn. And as any good student will tell you, "the more you learn the more you realize you don't know." So the topic tonight is one I hope to continue to learn more about, that I am trying to learn about, and one that I'm sure many of you have more knowledge about than I do. But you're not going to escape that easily. I have developed some thoughts that I will share with you.

Over the past few years we often hear the terms "intellectual property rights" and "cultural property rights" with only some vague notion of what they might mean. However, the meanings are often different from person to person and country to country. And the meanings become even more diverse among indigenous peoples.

Intellectual property is a common term within the American mainstream culture. We have all heard of and, to some degree or another, are familiar with patents, copyrights, and trademarks. All of these things are usually associated with litigation and long court battles. There seems to be no end to what people will dispute when it comes to these concepts. Just this week, for example, television personality Rosie O'Donnell was in the news for filing litigation against a Portland, Oregon, radio station for using the name "Rosie" in its ads. The name was being used in the context of Portland being known as the City of Roses.

The concept of cultural property rights among indigenous peoples has different connotations than the charge of the misuse of Rosie's name implies. Cultural property rights may refer to one's inner identity. It is about ancestors and ways of doing, saying, and knowing things. It is about culture and everyone on earth is entitled to a culture. It is about the past, the present, and the future. It is about life.

Over the past couple decades, there have been some issues of cultural property rights that have emerged in my home area of Kodiak Island that I have been involved with. One was the issue of the repatriation of human remains. Skeletons representing over a thousand people were taken from Kodiak Island during the 1930s and stored in the Smithsonian Institution. The reason given for not returning them was that they were the property of, that is they belonged to, all the people of the United States. It was a sad scenario when the remains of ancestors were considered "property." In fact, in one letter from the Smithsonian, it was stated that the remains could not be returned because the Smithsonian had a responsibility to care for them on behalf of all American citizens, not just "discrete interest groups." They were returned and reburied in the fall of 1991 but only after considerable legal wrangling and an act of Congress. It is difficult even now to think of those ancestral remains as property. The government identified them as property, but Native people cannot usually make that kind of connection. They just know they have a responsibility to return the remains of their ancestors to their intended resting places. In virtually all documents advocating for cultural property rights, the issue of repatriation of human remains is mentioned. But sometimes the meaning of the word "property" is different from one culture to another.

But it is not just lawyers and government bureaucrats that invoke legalese into such a sacred concept as a people's cultural heritage. Indigenous peoples, as well, tend to think of these property rights in a legal sense. But in today's world there is no choice. We often have to resort to the legal and political arenas to preserve and protect our birthrights. In the arena of international law and indigenous rights there are a few instruments that have made cases for indigenous cultural property rights in one form or another. For example, the International Labour Organization Convention Number 169, Article 2 (b), stated the following (passed in 1989):

> Governments shall have the responsibility for developing, with the participation of the peoples concerned, coordinated and systematic action to protect the rights of these peoples and to guarantee respect for their integrity. Such action shall include measures for promoting the full realization of the social, economic and cultural rights of these peoples with respect for their social and cultural identity, their customs and traditions and their institutions.

The United Nations Draft Declaration on the Rights of Indigenous Peoples which passed out of the UN Working Group on Indigenous Populations in 1994 and is now working its way through the UN hierarchy (formally adopted by the UN General Assembly in September, 2007) says in part:

UN Draft, Article 8:
"Indigenous peoples have the collective and individual right to maintain and develop their distinct identities and characteristics, including the right to identify themselves as indigenous and be recognized as such."

UN Draft, Article 12:

"Indigenous peoples have the right to practice and revitalize their cultural traditions and customs. This includes the right to maintain, protect and develop the past, present and future manifestations of their cultures, such as archaeological and historical sites, artifacts, designs, ceremonies, technologies and visual and performing arts and literature, as well as the right to the restitution of cultural, intellectual, religious and spiritual property taken without their free and informed consent or in violation of their laws, traditions and customs."

UN Draft, Article 13:

"Indigenous peoples have the right to manifest, practice, develop and teach their spiritual and religious traditions, customs and ceremonies; the right to maintain, protect and have access in privacy to their religious and cultural sites; the right to the use and control of ceremonial objects; and the right to the repatriation of human remains."

UN Draft, Article 14:

"Indigenous peoples have the right to revitalize, use, develop and transmit to future generations their histories, languages, oral traditions, philosophies, writing systems and literatures and to designate and retain their own names for communities, places and persons."

UN Draft, Article 24:

"Indigenous people have the right to their traditional medicines and health practices, including the right to the protection of vital medicinal plants, animals and minerals."

UN Draft, Article 29:

"Indigenous peoples are entitled to the recognition of the full ownership, control and protection of their cultural and intellectual property. They have the right to special measures to control, develop and protect their sciences, technologies and cultural manifestations, including human and other genetic resources, seeds, medicines, knowledge of the properties of fauna and flora, oral traditions, literatures, designs and visual and performing arts."

I know that many of you are familiar with the Mataatua Declaration on Cultural and Intellectual Property Rights of Indigenous Peoples adopted by indigenous people in New Zealand in 1993. One recommendation in this declaration that I see as crucial is that indigenous people should define for themselves their own intellectual and cultural property.

How do we "define for ourselves"? And what are cultural property rights to us? How should we exercise those rights? As the Nike slogan goes, "Just do it!"

I believe, for example, that we should not allow outsiders to define who we are. This has been going on for 200 years in Alaska and has caused considerable confusion. In my area of Kodiak Island, the Russian fur traders that arrived in the late 18th century called the Sugpiat the indigenous people living there (Aleuts) just as they had done to the Unangan in the Aleutian Islands. They did this because of the similarities they observed between both the Unangan of the Aleutian Islands and the Sugpiat of Kodiak Island to a coastal indigenous group on the Kamchatka Peninsula.

The people on Kodiak began using this term in their own language, the result being the word "Alutiiq." The name Alutiiq has had a revival and has grown in popularity in recent years, mostly as a way for the Sugpiat to distinguish themselves from the Aleuts of the Aleutian Island who have a different culture and language. But Alutiiq is a good term because a conscious decision was made by the people to use it.

As if things weren't complicated enough, enter the anthropologists who decided to call the Sugpiat "Pacific Eskimo" or even "Pacific Yup'ik" because of the close linguistic similarities with Yup'ik people. While virtually no Alutiiqs use this term, anthropologists insisted for quite a number of years that they were correct.

I don't believe there is anything wrong with people from Kodiak Island calling themselves Aleuts and, because it has been in use for so many generations, it may not be likely that a return will be made to Sugpiat. But it should be the responsibility of the people to learn the history of these terms so they can make an informed choice. But whatever terms are used they are, to me, cultural property. As cultural property, there are responsibilities and duties attached. Learning those responsibilities and duties is where we find ourselves today. There are a number of important and exciting projects going on today that are directly addressing and defining those responsibilities and duties.

Dr. Erica-Irene Daes, the Chairperson-Rapporteur of the United Nations Working Group on Indigenous Populations, said in 1995 to the 47th session for the Commission on Human Rights, Sub-Commission on Prevention of Discrimination and Protection of Minorities: "To be effective, the protection of indigenous peoples' heritage should be based broadly on the principle of self-determination, which includes the right and the duty of indigenous peoples to develop their own cultures, knowledge systems and forms of social organization."

I would like to emphasize some parts of Madame Daes' statement. She said, "the right and the duty of indigenous peoples to develop their own cultures, knowledge systems and forms of social organization." She made it a point to mention the principle of self-determination which is crucial to all we do as Alaska Native people and communities. Without exercising self-determination, Native peoples cannot exercise their rights or their duties and cannot define for themselves what their cultural and intellectual property is. But before we can make such definitions we must search for the questions. As Thurber said, "It is better to know some of the questions than all of the answers." Thank you very much and I hope I wasn't as boring as everyone said I was going to be.

Copies of some of the documents referred to by Dr. Pullar can be viewed on the Alaska Native Knowledge Network website at http://ankn.uaf.edu/rights.html.

Western Society's Linear Systems and Aboriginal Cultures

The Need for Two-Way Exchange for the Sake of Survival

————⬦⬥⬦————

Larry Merculieff

Presented at the Conference on Hunting and Gathering Societies
May 30, 1990, Fairbanks, Alaska

GOOD AFTERNOON. I am truly glad to have this opportunity to meet and talk with you about issues affecting the sciences, aboriginal peoples, and people throughout the world.

For those of you who don't know me, I am an Aleut, one of three distinct aboriginal peoples in Alaska. I was born and raised on the Pribilof Islands, a group of tiny islands in the middle of the Bering Sea. My people have lived in the same region of Alaska for almost ten thousand years. Although I have been certified by the State of Alaska as an expert on Aleut history and culture, I am not a scientist by Western standards, so please bear with me and look not to the scientific construct of what I am about to say as much as to the concepts I wish to convey. These concepts deal with the linear systems of Western society, the cyclical systems of many aboriginal societies, and the challenges both pose to communication and transfer of knowledge which is essential to maximizing the probabilities of human survival.

About five years ago I attended the World Conservation Strategy Conference in Ottawa. Among the delegates from throughout the world were representatives of aboriginal groups from Africa, Australia, North and South America, the South Pacific, and Europe. The World Conservation Strategy, adopted by 134 nation-states, is a blueprint for protection of the environment and sustainable economic development. The Strategy was of interest to the indigenous peoples' representatives, not so much for what it included as for what it did not include: the knowledge and experience the indigenous peoples can contribute to the goals of the World Conservation Strategy. This omission gave the representatives a focus for action, so they caucused. During the caucus, each representative, in turn, gave a description of the basic thrust of their cultural systems and the issues they faced. Much to our amazement, we found a substantial degree of commonality. Differences existed only by degrees, but not in substance. This commonality formed the basis for a global coalition of aboriginal or indigenous peoples for the purpose of amending a folio of the World Conservation Strategy. The amendment would formally recognize that linkages with aboriginal peoples who have had sustained contact with their immediate environment for many generations is important to the ultimate success of the strategy.

I was astonished that the original document, born of some of the best minds in the world concerned about environment and development, did not already incorporate the policy of linkage with aboriginal people. Since I was privileged to have had a very traditional Aleut upbringing, I am keenly aware of the depth of knowledge and experience about the environment inherent in my own cultural system. It did not occur to me that we would need to convince the intellectual powers behind this influential document of the utility of such knowledge and experience. But that is exactly what had to be done, and after five years of effort, the United Nations will consider our amendment to the WCS folio.

This experience caused me to reevaluate my life's experiences with regard to how, when, and if institutions deal with aboriginal peoples. I already knew of prejudices, misperceptions, misconceptions, ethnocentricity, and racism as obstacles to recognition of a people's value. Some of that may have been at play here, but there was something else involved in this instance. I did not begin to put my finger on what it was until I realized there was a definite pattern in the breakdown of communication between aboriginal peoples and the well-intentioned, well-meaning mainstream individuals in positions of power, authority, or professional standing in Westernized institutions throughout the world. I will attempt to explain what is behind this breakdown in communications. I realize I have just made a statement that implies use of a sweeping generality, but I put it in these terms to highlight something to which we all should be alerted.

I can best communicate what I mean by recounting something that happened in a remote village in Alaska where scientists, land and resource managers, and seven tribal Chiefs met last year to discuss subsistence. The seven tribal Chiefs represented people in villages highly dependent upon hunting and trapping for survival.

The Chiefs invited state wildlife management officials and their field biologists to make a presentation and to engage in discussions. One of the state representatives gave a 45-minute presentation on how they were going to conduct a field reconnaissance on moose, to determine the health of the local populations. The individual gave a good description of the state's methodology, and indicated that the reason this particular study was important was that the current bull-to-female ratios and overall numbers of moose indicated that the population was at a critical threshold of sustainability. Further negative changes might jeopardize the health of the moose population. The state game official completed his presentation and asked for questions.

The lead spokesperson for the traditional governing group did not ask any questions except in a rhetorical sense as he gave a 45-minute dissertation. He said that people in all surrounding villages had noticed a distinct drop in marshland water levels. He noted that the food sources for moose in the marshlands were adversely affected. He asked if anyone from the State had counted the number of beaver in these areas or the number of dams these beavers had built. He noted that at least 20 small tributaries to the Yukon River were dammed. He commented that State Fish and Game may propose to cut villagers' subsistence take of moose as their answer to the problem, but that no studies were planned on beaver. The leader said, "It seems to me you should listen to us and find ways to work together." The State game official responded that they should go to their regional game advisory board, which would consider this information and, if they choose, give recommendations to the State Board of Game which had the ultimate decision-making power. Both sides of this dialogue left the meeting feeling that they never connected—and they didn't connect. The scientist had a script to follow of proper scientific procedure. His job was to collect limited field data on moose only. The Native groups provided information that went beyond the training of the field scientist and the scope of his field assignment. The Native groups fully understood that the final decision-making body—the State Board of Game—had a mandate to scientifically manage the state's wildlife populations and habitat. This mandate requires that heavy weight be given to scientific field data and minimizes the importance of what appears to be anecdotal information. Result: the Native voice was never heard.

I choose to recount this exchange because it is a microcosm of how cross-cultural communication breaks down when people do not understand that each comes from a different worldview, a different frame of reference which leads people to different conclusions because they use different facts on the same issue. I have witnessed this breakdown time and time again around the world. The cost of such breakdowns is dramatic in human terms: massive institutional failures in attempting to help indigenous peoples in education, economic development, law enforcement, governmental structures, social services, environmental concerns, and resource and wildlife management.

In this microcosmic example, the two worldviews could be described as cyclical on the one hand and linear on the other. The scientist is indoctrinated in the linear construct, as is most of Westernized society. Think about it: in the educational system, we begin with kindergarten, first grade, second grade, and progress to college and graduate school until we end up as a doctoral candidate. It is inherent in this linear progression that anything in the beginning of the line is inferior to anything at the end of that line; i.e. a PhD is superior to a master's, is superior to a four-year college degree, etc. In technology development, we developed the sun dial, then the pendulum clock, then pocket watches, to wristwatches to digital watches to computerized watches. Again, anything at the beginning of the technological line is inferior and more than likely discarded for the most current gadget. In science, the linear progression evolved into scientific specialization and continued refinement of the scientific methodology from its origins of the simple use of logic, common sense, and visual observations. Each of these linear constructs, whatever their origins, influences what we choose to observe in Westernized societies.

Contrast this with the people who live their lives by the seasons and in response to their immediate environment. Theirs is a world in which the interdependence of man, animal, plants, water, and earth—the total picture—is always immediate, always present. And the total picture—every day, every season, every year—is seen as a circle. Everything in their lives is connected: the marshland to the beaver, the beaver dams to altered conditions, the new conditions to the moose herd, the moose herd to the marshland. Each affects the other. And it is this intimate knowledge of the environment (all of the curves in the circle) that has allowed these people to survive for hundreds of generations.

In his presentation, the Chief described a specific sequence of events his people had observed that demonstrated their worldview of connectedness, details which the specialized scientist could not factor into his equation. The scientist's job was to make methodical aerial transects of an area and count the number of male and female moose in each transect and record the data. This scientific data carries more weight in management forums than the empirical evidence presented by the Natives—evidence which is often considered anecdotal in the scientific community. What is overlooked by dismissing such information is that the Native comes from a community of people who have had sustained contact with their immediate environment for thousands of years and who through a cultural information system, have passed on their visual observations, knowledge, and experience. In this context, the Native information is anything but anecdotal. It comes from an individual with an invaluable storehouse of information and knowledge about the environment that is irreplaceable and nonreplicable. This knowledge tells the person, for example, that environments are in a constant state of flux. By the time the scientist formulates data with adequate time series to make the information useful, the model may be outdated. In addition, the knowledge tells the person that periodic chaos accompanies the symmetry in nature and that scientific models have yet to become sophisticated enough to incorporate the predictability of such chaos and its effect on the symmetry. As such, Native people respect intelligent visual observations more than scientific models. They have to—their lives and their children's lives literally depend on it.

If individuals in decision-making positions would acknowledge information passed on by Native peoples, it could save them time, money, and effort. I was reminded of this when I read a story about a scientific study that was conducted by the University of California. Hundreds of thousands of dollars were spent to send researchers down in a submarine to make visual observations of halibut to determine if they ever fed above the ocean floor. Ever since I was a child, I knew halibut did feed off the ocean floor because of what I was taught and what I observed. Frequently we would catch halibut after pulling our subsistence fishing line halfway off the sea bottom, so we knew that the fish were mobile and would follow prey a great distance off the sea bottom. We even found shallow diving birds in halibut stomachs and we caught halibut that were feeding above substantially elevated underwater terrain. The halibut's coloring alone should have told the researchers something, as the fish are black on top and white on the bottom to better camouflage them from predators. If halibut only stayed on the bottom of the sea they would be entirely black since predators looking down towards the bottom would see a dark environment. When one looks up from the bottom, it is lighter, explaining why halibut are lighter on their bottom to protect them when swimming off the sea floor. We could have saved the scientists money or, better yet, they could have paid us for the information.

In the true story I have recounted about the tribal Chiefs and the situation with the World Conservation Strategy, it occurs to me that decision-makers indoctrinated in the linear systems of Westernized societies regard many aboriginal groups as primitive and their knowledge base as inferior because they have not progressed according to linear principles. It is no wonder that aboriginal groups feel they are simply engaging in powerless politics; that their voices and their knowledge of the environment are falling on deaf ears.

The actual end result of these kinds of dynamics is what we are witnessing today: the creation of a monoculture—one dominant culture which subsumes the other and tells the other, in no uncertain terms, that they must conform to the linear worldview if they want to be heard. For the cyclically based aboriginal cultures, this message heralds their inevitable destruction if they acquiesce. Some say that this is progress. Let's examine that.

We have all heard about the animal rights movement. This movement is born of the linear systems. People who subscribe to animal rights believe that humans have now evolved to the point that we are the only animal capable of making moral choices. Therefore, it is incumbent upon us, they say, to recognize that it is immoral and inhumane to kill animals or to allow them to suffer at our hands. Societies that kill animals are brutal and primitive. This line of thinking has made tremendous inroads around the world and it threatens every culture that uses biological resources as part of their economic activity.

The animal rights movement was the primary factor in destroying the traditional way of life in my home in the Pribilofs. My people harvested fur seals on a sustainable basis for 200 years on two tiny islands that are currently home to a million fur seals, three million birds, and 700 Aleuts. During those two centuries and for the millennium before, Aleuts worked with their own environmental ethics, and all life on the Pribilofs thrived, including the fur seals. But beginning in 1976, the fur seal population began to decline. The animal rights coalition blamed our taking of 16,000 nonbreeding male seals (from the population of one million) as the cause of the decline. Our people said they noticed some bird species and sea lions also declining and said that these declines were probably connected. But the animal rights groups, in true linear thinking, ignored these observations and simply focused on the seals. With a well-funded campaign aimed at stirring up the emotions of the public, the animal rights groups succeeded in stopping the seal harvest five years ago and, in the process, destroyed our only economic base. To replace it, we are developing a regional bottom-fish port which will bring in thousands of transients and massive development. This new economy may do more to destroy habitat and disrupt the wildlife than anything in the islands' history, and it has the capacity to accomplish this within a single generation.

I find it supremely ironic that, today in Alaska, scientists and others are beginning to notice with alarm the decline of all the species observed by my people and are scurrying to find answers. If any of these species becomes endangered, it could shut down all major fisheries in the state. U.S. law requires elimination of any human activity that results in disruptive contact with endangered species.

Historically, my people were the stewards of the Pribilof Islands, living close to land and sea, using the resources wisely, and adjusting the take of animals according to their knowledge and experience. That is now disappearing quickly as the need to earn hard cash to survive outweighs the need to be concerned about the environment. Termination of the seal harvest in the Pribilofs has severed the economic and cultural link between the people and the seals. It was this economic and cultural link that ensured a truly symbiotic and functional relationship between man and animal. It was this linkage that provided the human incentive to be stewards. People who have not had sustained interaction with their immediate environment over generations have difficulty understanding a vital principle underlying successful aboriginal cultures: these cultures are banks of extensive, invaluable knowledge and experience about how to sustain ecosystems, but they exist by virtue of the economics of survival.

The U.S. Congress took action against this seal harvest based upon a large public outcry against what was viewed as a brutal, archaic practice. Now, Aleuts can kill seals for subsistence, but we cannot use any part for any commercial purpose. The law even allows us to kill seals at sea if we use a traditional craft manned by no more than five people with no firearms, but harpoons are allowed. No engines, we must use oars. This was the Congressional version of traditional seal hunting practice; no one thought about how ridiculously cumbersome this at-sea method is when we can find seals on land by the hundreds of thousands. Meanwhile, the seal herd continues to decline along with the sea lions and certain bird populations. All of these are being studied individually as single, disconnected species. This, despite the fact that all of these animals have a common food base. And, the renewable, biodegradable products (sealskin garments) are no longer available. Instead, they are replaced with nonbiodegradeable, non-renewable, petroleum-based synthetics.

It's nice to anthropologically glamorize aboriginal cultures, to insist that such cultures help preserve wildlife by stagnating their hunting technologies, and to promulgate laws that totally eliminate economic incentives. Sadly, this philosophy, intended to somehow protect wildlife, leads to greater destruction of wildlife; it most certainly ensures that people living in some of the most pristine and delicate wilderness areas of the world lose what is at the root of all successful cultures: the ability to grow and adapt as required to survive, and to seek out and enhance strategies for economic survival appropriate to their location. Show me a culture without these two elements and I will show you a people that is dead or dying.

To digress again, this new law, dictating how Aleuts are to deal with seals, replaces traditional laws. In this instance, and indeed in all such instances, wildlife and habitat are or were protected because the aboriginal people had the power to decide for themselves what to incorporate into their culture, language, and laws. By so doing, protection of wildlife and habitat became synonymous with ensuring the survival of cultures. Again, the picture comes full circle. The primary difference between such aboriginal laws and laws in the present-day legal context is that aboriginal laws have been intricately woven into everyday life and living. Enforcement is done by social pressure to conform to societal norms, not by threat of punitive actions. The approach of interjecting outside authority based upon noncyclical constructs very quietly, but with great force, erodes the utility of incorporating management of wildlife and habitat into culture and everyday living. In effect, this destroys ways of living that are successful models of as much harmony with nature as humans are capable of achieving. Can we accept this as a price of progress?

Everyone is struggling to find scientific models that work in managing ecosystems because we are disrupting them on a massive scale. We are disrupting them because humans, unlike most life on earth, have no niche. Without a niche, we stumble into and disrupt natural systems all around us. The fact is, cultural systems which have, as a paradigm, intimate interaction with the environment, are the closest humankind will come to having a niche. I suggest that the humane, morally proper, and most efficient laws must complement, supplement, and enhance rational local systems already in place seeking to do the same thing.

Alaska is experiencing similar situations to the rest of the world in terms of its successes (or more appropriately, its failures) in dealing with issues directly affecting aboriginal peoples. In Alaska, the vast majority of villages are not economically self-sufficient and, indeed, have become increasingly dependent upon government transfer payments, government grants, and government jobs, despite the untold millions upon millions of dollars poured into rural economic development. Most young Native people score in the 20- to 30-percentile level in national standardized academic achievement tests. Over 30 percent of these students fail to complete high school when they leave their villages to attend urban schools. Alaska Natives represent between 12 to 15 percent of the statewide population, but approximately 25 percent of all persons arrested, 25 percent of all persons convicted of felonies, and 34 percent of all persons incarcerated. Suicide rates, alcohol abuse, fetal alcohol syndrome are all far above national norms. They are at crisis levels. Given all of this, there is, in the Native community, a growing sense of disenfranchisement and distrust of Western institutions with a consequent growth of legal and civil confrontations. I submit to you that Alaska is not atypical of what is happening to indigenous groups around the world (outside of malnutrition, starvation, and overt violation of human rights). I further submit to you that part of these failures can be attributed to the lack of understanding of the differences in worldviews and the role the lack of understanding plays in the success or failure of everything we do to provide solutions to human survival. These are not just failures that hurt a particular group of people. They are forcing a singular worldview, a monoculture if you will, which could spell the destruction of humankind on earth.

The United Nations is beginning to recognize the value of indigenous knowledge and so are some scientists. They are beginning to understand that cultural diversity and bio-economic diversity may be just as essential as genetic diversity in achieving accommodation with the environment in a way that enhances the chances for human survival. The fact of the matter is that cultural and bio-economic diversity are rapidly disappearing. Aboriginal peoples in the South Pacific, South America, North America, Africa, India, and the circumpolar North are all experiencing the same challenges to their cultural viability. They are only different by degrees, but the principles undermining their cultures are virtually identical. These principles include the subtle or overt destruction of intimate links with their immediate environments, causing replacement with inappropriate economic activities that are based on a singular worldview. The result of this destruction is environmental degradation, destruction of habitat and wildlife, development of mega-economic development projects, and irreplaceable loss of invaluable knowledge and experience. As professionals involved with hunting and gathering societies, I believe it is incumbent upon all of you to try to understand what is happening. We must all become vocal advocates for cultural and bio-economic diversity if we hope to prevent the extinction of homo sapiens.

Thank you for your attention.

Aspects of Silence: When Do Traditions Begin?

Miranda Wright

THE QUESTION "WHEN DO TRADITIONS BEGIN?" will be explored in terms of the verbal silence maintained by the Koyukon Athabascans as they incorporated and/or adapted Western forms of expression into their everyday lives. The focus will be the oral traditions and cultural practices which have endured in Koyukon burials. This particular group of Athabascans has been studied numerous times by various researchers, many of them affiliated with the Catholic Church. Because of this, I am not surprised to find much of the data regarding "symbolic representations" remained embedded in the self-imposed silence of my people—a deep silence often expressed by the phrase "That's just our way."

As an Athabascan woman raised under the community standards of the Kaiyuh people, I accepted the response "It's just our way" as an appropriate answer to complex questions. This was true, particularly if the question required a lengthy response, such as a story or revelation through oral tradition. Often the situation was not appropriate for such discourse, so the answer "It's just our way" served two purposes: (1) it served as a polite reminder that the time is inappropriate for full disclosure, and (2) it left the door open for future discussion.

The learning process of the Koyukon is not one that is forced or imposed upon individuals; rather it is nurtured by the curiosity and advancement of the individual. A self-motivated person will constantly pursue answers through demonstrated attempts to emulate their role models and mentors. The instructors are aware of this process, although it may not be articulated by them.

I experienced this process of instruction or transmission of cultural knowledge through much of my life. Therefore, I was deeply moved by the response I received to an inquiry I made as I prepared my second brother for his final journey. As I viewed by brother for the final time, I observed how he was dressed in contemporary clothes: his favorite navy corduroy Levi's and baseball jacket. Yet on his feet and hands he wore traditional moose-hide footwear and gloves. His contemporary sport shoes were placed in the casket, and a rosary or prayer beads symbolic of the Catholic Church was entwined in his hands. I asked why our people are buried with traditional footwear and moose-hide gloves. I was enlightened with the oral tradition the Elders shared with me. This tradition tells of the Koyukon belief in an afterlife; of a middle world, an upper world, and a lower world; of separate worlds for those who died a sudden death and those who died a normal death; of a special world for medicine people, and another for dogs; of the great journey taken from the realm we live in, to the middle world, and finally to an outer world or the ultimate destination; of a path one travels on this journey mired with challenges, obstacles, and mountains which are tempting, slippery, icy, as well as frightening; of how successful completion requires great balance, agility, stamina, and belief; of how the relatives who remain on earth can assist the deceased on their journey through the clothes they are buried in, the songs which are composed for them, and through the communal feasts and give-away ceremonies. All this information is embodied in the silent response "That's just our way."

In referring back to the previous example, many of my people are reluctant to discuss the meaning of the footwear and the gloves for fear that a Christian funeral and/or burial would be denied. The presence of the prayer beads or rosary entwined in the moose-hide-glove-clad hands insures that the deceased is given every opportunity for a successful journey to the afterlife, just as a Christian funeral and burial complements the communal feast and give-away ceremony. The composed songs which eulogize the deceased are comparable to the hymns and prayers offered in a Christian service.

Once I had a firm understanding of the significance of these practices, it became apparent why my people refer to their burial customs as "that's just our way." By their own standards, knowledge is not forced on an individual, it is nurtured through a self-motivated process developed at an individual rate. Emulation or acceptance of a practice generally indicates a working understanding of traditional customs. The persistent similarities between the pageantry and ritual of the Catholic mass and teachings with those of traditional ceremonies and practices were enough to indicate that the Catholics had similar beliefs, they just expressed them differently. Moreover, their method of transmitting knowledge was more judgmental and demanding. Therefore, it was less confrontational to remain silent about the integration of traditional belief with Christian forms of expression. As one Native elder put it, "I see lot of similarities with our way and the Bible. Both of them are good. For myself, I need both ways."

Armed with all this insight, I continued to probe the "aspects of silence" maintained by the Koyukon in my study area. I expanded my inquiry to the physical structures found in graveyards and cemeteries. Archival research confirmed many of the changes in burial structures that the Koyukon mention in their oral accounts of various events. One constant was present throughout these changes. The spruce tree is always represented at the burial site in some form. In very early accounts, the soft ground at the base of the tree made for easy digging. Often one only had to peel the moss cover back to expose dry ground. Most often, however, the corpse was bound in a fetal position and propped at the base of a spruce tree. The corpse was then entombed in a conical-shaped structure formed with other trees, limbs, and brush.

Infants wrapped in fur or buckskin were tied to a limb higher in the tree, in similar fashion to the disposition of the placenta. Others, particularly the medicine people, were sepulchered in a box which was elevated on a platform secured to four spruce posts. However, as with the Koyukon belief in several worlds or outer dimensions, their burial practices also varied according to the circumstances surrounding death. In some cases cremations were conducted, with the ashes gathered into a birch-bark container and tied to the limb of a spruce tree, eventually to return to nature. While the particulars of these circumstances are difficult to uncover, accounts are documented in both oral tradition as well as in the work of Zagoskin (Michael 1967), Dall (1898), Whymper (1871), Nelson (1899), Cantwell (1902), Stoney (1900), Jacobson (1977), Schwatka (1900), Hrdlicka (1930), De Laguna (1947), McQuesten (1952) and Jetté (1908).

During my youth, I never questioned the changes in these burial structures. I was keenly aware of the older section of the cemetery, having seen several older structures collapse and eventually slide down the hillside during the spring thaw. Exposed skeletal remains were offered a quiet prayer and covered over with dirt. The spirit houses had a door with windows that faced the east. Personal goods were often placed in these dwellings, particularly china or enamel cups. Some had brass kettles while others had a mirror attached to the spirit pole. In some instances, a canoe or hunting spear was still visible. These items represented the individuality of the deceased person and served as an announcement or introduction to people on the other side. A canoe or spear might indicate the individual was a good hunter or provider. Western trade goods might indicate that this was a very friendly person who maintained harmony with strangers. Being a part of the Baby Boomer era, I naturally assumed that the American flag flying over some graves represented those men who were veterans of World War II. I saw the spirit poles as a natural place to fly the flag.

One day I came across a photo of the Nulato cemetery taken in 1910. Flying over the spirit houses and attached to the spirit poles were American flags. I reiterate the date 1910 because of my earlier statement in which I indicated the American flag was probably flown over the graves of World War II veterans. If you recall your history, World War I had not even occurred by 1910; Alaska did not become a territory of the United States until 1912. In fact, Alaska Natives and American Indians were not considered citizens of the United States until 1924. This image raised many questions in my research. In addition to the flags, the crosses were painted with black-and-white designs with many symbols, colors, stripes, numbers, and shapes. Once again I was off to Nulato loaded with questions. What did these flags mean?

The people of Nulato seemed almost amused at my ignorance as they offered comments such as "Of course flags were flown over the graves before the war. There was a military station in the early days and flags were readily available." When queried about a potential connection to the American government they responded, "Of course not, our people were not concerned with those people in that way. It's the colors and the design of the flag that was important. The animal carvings and animal pelts which formerly adorned the spirit poles were gradually replaced by white cloth supplied by the people of the other language, then by the red-and-white striped cloth with the stars".

The colors black, red, and white were all represented in the photo. I was reminded that during our most important winter ceremony, Heeyo, or stickdance, the spruce pole was traditionally painted with red, white, and black bands. The hitting sticks used during the sacred songs were also painted in this fashion. The black design was traditionally made with ashes or coals. This was also used to paint a warrior's face for protection during battle; it was sprinkled around dwellings, windows, and doors to ward off evil spirits; and it was used in other ways as a means of protection. Red paint was obtained from ocher and was also used as war paint to instill the power of life. Many implements such as snowshoes were also painted with red ocher for strength and stamina. White, a neutral color between the other two, maintained harmony and balance.

These answers stimulated more questions. If the flags do not represent American patriotism, what do the other structures in the graveyard really mean to the Koyukon people? Are the crosses really representative of Christianity? How about those picket fences? What do they mean? Finally the big picture came into view. There was a wonderful tall spruce pole next to the old community hall which was painted with white and black bands. This pole stood approximately 60 feet high. On the very top was anchored a set of caribou antlers. My paternal great-grandfather was said to have erected this to symbolize his membership in the Caribou Clan. As a tyke growing up in the village, I again assumed this was a flagpole. I reasoned that it had stripes like a flag; therefore it must be a flagpole! When Grandma tried explaining the significance of her father's accomplishment, I found myself lost in the abstract concepts she tried to explain to me in Koyukon. While I understand the Koyukon language, I am not a fluent speaker. Therefore, I would pose my questions to Grandma in English. She in turn could not explain those abstract Koyukon concepts to me in her limited knowledge of the English language. In frustration she would end my lessons. She would later pick up the discussion in another context to instill some understanding of the concept to me. Grandma passed on in 1993, prior to my acknowledging an understanding of her teachings. However, the groundwork she laid paid off when I began to delve into the cosmology of the Koyukon. As I picked up bits and pieces of information from different sources, the image became clearer and I began to appreciate the self-imposed silence of my people. If I, a member of the society, could not understand the symbolic meanings embedded in our traditions, how could we expect people from another language to understand or even care? The Koyukon people were very aware that the dominant society was making a concerted effort to impose their values and beliefs on those they came in contact with. The stories that were shared with the people of another language were not told properly. Often they were referred to as children's tales or dismissed as folklore. There was a break in communications. The Koyukon chose to express their traditional customs privately.

I had reached these conclusions shortly after my experiences with Grandma. Therefore, I became very focused on gaining a deeper understanding and appreciation for those aspects of silence maintained by my people. I wanted to become a professional voice to validate the beliefs and values of the Koyukon people. As my research progressed I developed a deeper understanding of the cosmology which governs the Koyukon and of the holistic approach which binds and maintains harmony in our society. This balance is maintained in all aspects of Koyukon life, including the tripartite clan system which tells of Noltseen, the clan associated with things of the earth, minerals, rocks, and animals that den; of Medzeyh Te Hut'aan, the clan associated with things from the above (the caribou with antlers which reach to the sky represents this clan); and of Tonee dze Ghel tseel le, or middle clan associated with wood and water, or as Eliade (1958) puts it, the "Axis Munde," the link between the upper and lower clans.

This connection, harmony, and unity are found in the burial structures of the Koyukon from the very early days when the flexed corpse was placed in the soil at the base of the spruce tree enshrouded in a conical shelter, to the day of the spirit houses with spruce poles decorated with animal figures and animal pelts, to today with the picket fence and cross. While the triangular roof pieces of the spirit houses are no longer visible, the three arms of the cross remind us of those connections. When the dead are interned, they are placed with their head to the west, so that they will face the east, the proper direction for a new beginning.

References

Cantwell, J.C. 1902. Report of the operations of the U.S. Revenue steamer Nunivak on the Yukon River Station, Alaska, 1899–1901. Senate Document 155-2. Washington, DC: Government Printing Office.

Dall, William H. 1898. *The Yukon Territory, explorations in 1866–1868.* New York: Downey & Co.

De Laguna, Frederica. 1947. *The prehistory of Northern North America as seen from the Yukon.* Wisconsin: The Society for American Archaeology, No. 3.

Eliade, Mircea. 1958. *Rites and symbols of initiation.* New York: Harper Torchbooks.

Hrdlicka, Ales. 1930. *Explorations and field-work of the Smithsonian Institution in 1929.* Washington, DC: Smithsonian Institution, publication 3060.

Jacobson, Johan Adrian. 1977. *Alaskan voyage 1881–1883.* Chicago: The University of Chicago Press.

Jette, J. 1911. *On the Superstitions of the Tena Indians.* Anthropos, Vol. 6, p. 257–268

McQuesten, Leroy N. 1952. *Recollections of Leroy N. McQuesten of life in the Yukon 1871–1885.* Anchorage: Alaska Historical Society.

Michael, Henry N., ed. 1967. *Lieutenant Zagoskin's travels in Russian America, 1842–1844.* Toronto: University of Toronto Press.

Osgood, Cornelius. 1958. *Ingalik social culture.* New Haven: Yale University Press.

Schwatka, Frederick. 1900. *Along Alaska's great river.* Chicago: George M. Hill Company.

Stoney, George M. 1900. *Naval explorations in Alaska.* Annapolis: U.S. Naval Institute.

Van Stone, James. 1899. *E.W. Nelson's notes on Indians of the Yukon and Innoko Rivers Alaska.* Chicago: Fieldiana, Anthropology 70.

Whymper, Frederick. 1871. *Travel and adventure in the Territory of Alaska.* New York: Harper & Brothers, Publishers.

Culture, Chaos, and Complexity

Catalysts for Change in Indigenous Education

———◆◆✕◆◆———

Ray Barnhardt and
Angayuqaq Oscar Kawagley

Originally published in B. Despres (ed.), *Systems Thinkers in Action:*
A Field Guide for Effective Change Leadership in Education
(New York: Rowan & Littlefield Education, 2006)

THE PRINCIPLES OF SELF-ORGANIZATION associated with the study of complex adaptive systems are being brought to bear on education in rural Alaska through the educational reform strategy of the Alaska Rural Systemic Initiative (AKRSI). Indigenous education in Alaska provides a fertile testing ground for the emerging sciences of chaos and complexity. These newly established sciences have derived from the study of complex physical (e.g., weather), biological (e.g., animal behavior), and economic (e.g., the stock market) systems whose dynamics exhibit adaptive patterns of self-organization under conditions which on the surface appear chaotic (Gleick, 1987; Waldrop, 1994; Sahtouris, 2000; Gribbin, 2004).

The constructs, principles, and theories emerging under the banners of chaos and complexity have also been extended to the study of human social systems (Epstein and Axtell, 1996; Shulman, 1997), and to the management of formal organizations as complex adaptive systems (Wheatley, 1992; Battram, 2001). It is the latter applications of complexity theory that are being brought to bear on education in rural Alaska through the AKRSI educational reform strategy.

The AKRSI was established in 1994, bringing together more than 50 stakeholder organizations involved in education in rural Alaska. The institutional home base and support structure for the AKRSI was provided through the Alaska Federation of Natives in cooperation with the University of Alaska, and with funding from the National Science Foundation and the Annenberg Rural Challenge (now Rural School and Community Trust). Statewide leadership for the AKRSI was provided by a director based at the Alaska Federation of Natives and two co-directors (the authors) employed by the University of Alaska Fairbanks. In addition, a regional coordinator was employed in each of the five major cultural regions of Alaska. As such, the AKRSI was the first major statewide educational endeavor initiated by and implemented under Alaska Native leadership and control.

The purpose of the AKRSI was to implement a set of initiatives that systematically documented the indigenous knowledge systems of Alaska Native peoples and developed pedagogical practices that appropriately integrated indigenous knowledge and ways of knowing into all aspects of the education system. In practical terms, the most important intended outcome was an increased recognition of the complementary nature of Native and Western knowledge, so both can be more effectively utilized as a founda-

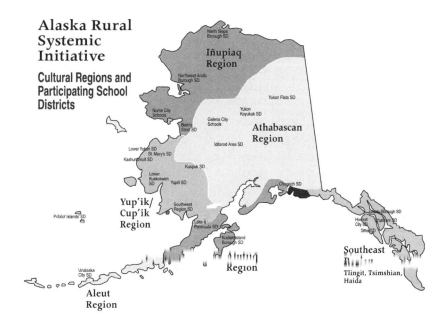

different elevations. Behind these variables, however, there are patterns, such as prevailing winds or predictable cycles of weather phenomena, that can be discerned through long observation. Over time, Native people have observed that the weather's dynamic is not unlike fractals, where the part of a part is part of another part which is a part of still another part, and so on. For indigenous people there is a recognition that many unseen forces are in action in the elements of the universe, and that very little is naturally linear, or occurs in a two-dimensional grid or a three-dimensional cube. They are familiar with the notions of irregularities and anomalies of form and force (i.e., chaos). Through long observation they have become specialists in understanding the interconnectedness and holism of all things in the universe (Kawagley, 1995).

The sciences of chaos and complexity and the study of nonlinear, dynamic systems have helped Western scientists to also recognize order in phenomena that were previously considered chaotic and random (Eglash, 2002). These patterns reveal new sets of relationships that point to the essential balances and diversity that help nature to thrive. Indigenous people have long recognized these interdependencies and strive for harmony with all of life. Western scientists have constructed the holographic image, which lends itself to the Native concept of everything being connected. Just as the whole contains each part of the image, so too does each part contain the makeup of the whole. The relationship of each part to everything else must be understood to produce the whole image (Wilber, 1985).

With fractal geometry, holographic images, and the sciences of chaos and complexity, the Western thought-world has begun to focus more attention on relationships, as its proponents recognize the interconnectedness in all elements of the world around us (Capra, 1996). Thus there is a growing appreciation of the complementarity and symbiosis that exists between what were previously considered two disparate and irreconcilable systems of thought (Barnhardt and Kawagley, 1999).

Among the qualities that are often identified as inherent strengths of indigenous knowledge systems are those that have been described as the focal constructs in the study of the dynamics of complex adaptive systems: "Complexity theory is about identity, relationships, communication, mutual interactions" (Stamps, 1997:36). These are qualities that focus on the processes of interaction between the parts of a system, rather than the parts in isolation, and it is to those interactive processes that the AKRSI reform strategy is directed. In so doing, however, attention must extend beyond the relationships of the parts within an indigenous knowledge system and take into account the relationships between the system as a whole and the other external systems with which it interacts, the most critical and pervasive being the formal education systems which now impact the lives of every Native child, family, and community in Alaska.

THE FORMAL EDUCATION SYSTEM

Formal education is still an evolving, emergent system that is far from equilibrium in rural Alaska, thus leaving it vulnerable and malleable in response to a well-crafted strategy of systemic reform. The advantage of working with systems that are operating "at the edge of chaos" is that they are more receptive and susceptible to innovation and change as they seek equilibrium and order in their functioning (Waldrop, 1994). Such is the case for many of the educational systems in rural Alaska, for historical as well as unique contextual reasons. From the time of the arrival of the Russian fur traders in the late 1700s up to the early 1900s, the relationship between most of the Native people of Alaska and education in the form of schooling (which was reserved primarily for the immigrant population at that time) may be characterized as two mutually independent systems with little if any contact, as illustrated by the following diagram:

Prior to the epidemics that wiped out over 60 percent of the Alaska Native population in the early part of the 20th century, most Native people continued to live a traditional self-sufficient lifestyle with only limited contact with fur traders and missionaries (Napoleon, 1991). The oldest of the Native Elders today grew up in that traditional cultural environment and still retain the deep knowledge and high language that they acquired during their early childhood years. They are also the first generation to have experienced significant exposure to schooling, many of them having been orphaned as a result of the epidemics. Schooling, however, was strictly a one-way process at that time, mostly in distant boarding schools with the main purpose being to assimilate Native people into Western society, as practiced by the missionaries and schoolteachers (who were often one and the same). Given the total disregard and often condescending attitude toward the indigenous knowledge and belief systems in the Native communities, the relationship between the two systems was limited to a one-way flow of communication and interaction up through the 1950s, and thus can be characterized as follows:

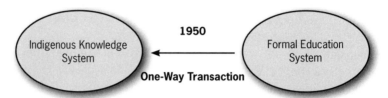

By the early 1960s, elementary schools had been established in most Native communities, and by the late 1970s, a class-action lawsuit had forced the state to develop high school programs in the villages throughout rural Alaska. At the same time (in 1976), the federal- and state-operated education systems were dismantled and in their place over 20 new school districts were created to operate the schools in rural communities. That placed the rural school systems serving Native communities under local control for the first time, and concurrently a new system of secondary education was established that students could access in their home community. These two steps, along with the development of bilingual and bicultural education programs under state and federal funding and the influx of a limited number of Native teachers, opened the doors for the beginning of two-way interaction between the schools and the Native communities they served, as illustrated by the following diagram depicting rural education by 1995 (when the AKRSI was initiated):

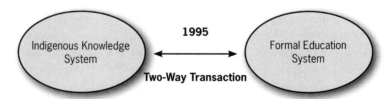

Despite the structural and political reforms that took place in the 1970s and '80s, rural schools have continued to produce a dismal performance record by most any measure, and Native communities continue to experience significant social, cultural, and educational problems, with most indicators placing communities and schools in rural Alaska at the bottom of the scale nationally. While there has been some limited representation of local cultural elements in the schools (e.g., basket making, sled building, songs and dances), it has been at a fairly superficial level with only token consideration given to the significance of those elements as integral parts of a larger complex adaptive cultural system that continues to imbue people's lives with purpose and meaning outside the school setting. While there is some minimum level of interaction between the two systems, functionally they remain worlds apart, with the professional staff overwhelmingly non-Native (95 percent statewide) and with a turnover rate averaging 30–40 percent annually.

With these considerations in mind, the Alaska Rural Systemic Initiative has sought to serve as a catalyst to promulgate reforms focusing on increasing the level of interconnectivity and synergism between the formal education systems and the indigenous knowledge systems of the communities in which they are situated. In so doing, the AKRSI seeks to bring the two systems together in a manner that promotes a symbiotic relationship such that the two previously separate systems join to form a more comprehensive holistic system that can better serve all students, not just Alaska Natives, while at the same time preserving the essential integrity of each component of the larger overlapping system. The new interconnected, interdependent, integrated system we are seeking to achieve may be depicted as follows:

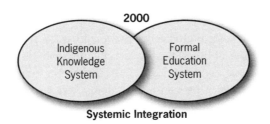

2000

Indigenous
Knowledge
System

Formal
Education
System

Systemic Integration

Forging an Emergent System of Education for Rural Alaska

In May 1994 the Alaska Natives Commission, a federal/state task force that had been established two years earlier to conduct a comprehensive review of programs and policies impacting Native people, released a report articulating the need for all future efforts addressing Alaska Native issues to be initiated and implemented from within the Native community (Alaska Natives Commission, 1994). The long history of failure of external efforts to manage the lives and needs of Native people made it clear that outside interventions were not the solution to the problems, and that Native communities themselves would have to shoulder a major share of the responsibility for carving out a new future. At the same time, existing government policies and programs would need to relinquish control and provide latitude and support for Native people to address the issues in their own way, including the opportunity to learn from their mistakes. It is this two-pronged approach that is at the heart of the AKRSI educational reform strategy—Native community initiative coupled with a supportive, adaptive, collaborative education system.

Manuel Gomez, in his analysis of the notion of systemic change in education, has indicated that "Educational reform is essentially a cultural transformation process that requires organizational learning to occur: changing teachers is necessary, but not sufficient. Changing the organizational culture of the school or district is also necessary" (1997:06). This statement applies to both the formal education system and the indigenous knowledge systems in rural Alaska. The culture of the education system as reflected in rural schools must undergo radical change, with the main catalyst being standards- and place-based curriculum grounded in the local culture. In addition, the indigenous knowledge systems need to be documented, articulated, and validated, again with the main catalyst being place-based curriculum grounded in the local culture.

The standards referred to here, however, are not just the usual subject-matter standards established by the state, but also include a set of "cultural standards" that have been developed by Alaska Native educators and elders to provide explicit guidelines for how students, teachers, schools, and communities can integrate the local culture and environment into the formal education process so that students are able to achieve cultural well-being as a result of their schooling experience (Assembly of Native Educators, 1998). The focus of these cultural standards is on shifting the emphasis in education from teaching about culture to teaching through the local culture as a foundation for all learning, including the usual subject matter.

If educational advocates are to abide by the principles of complexity theory and seek to foster the emergent properties of self-organization that can produce the systemic integration indicated above, then it is essential that they work through and within the existing systems. The challenge is to identify the units of change that will produce the most results with the least effort. In the terms of complexity theory, that means targeting the elements of the system that serve as the "attractors" around which the emergent order of the system can coalesce (Peck and Carr, 1997). Once these critical agents of change have been appropriately identified, a "gentle nudge" in the right places can produce powerful changes throughout the system (Jones, 1994).

The key agents of change around which the AKRSI educational reform strategy has been constructed are the Alaska Native educators working in the formal education system coupled with the Native Elders who are the culture-bearers for the indigenous knowledge system, along with the Native-initiated cultural standards adopted by the Alaska Department of Education. Together, these agents of change constitute a considerable set of "attractors" that are serving to reconstitute the way people think about and do education in rural schools throughout Alaska. The role of the Alaska Rural Systemic Initiative has been to guide these agents through an on-going array of locally generated, self-organizing activities that produce the "organizational learning" needed to move toward a new form of emergent and convergent system of education for rural Alaska (Marshall, 1996). The overall configuration of this emergent system may be characterized as two interdependent though previously separate systems being nudged together through a series of initiatives maintained by a larger system of which they are constituent parts, as illustrated in the following diagram:

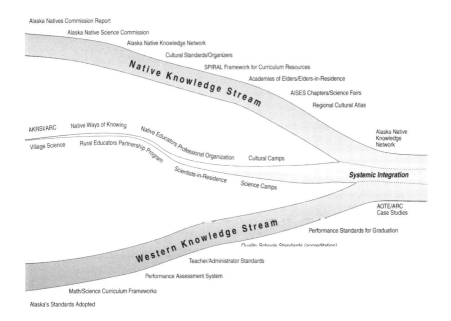

The components of the emergent system representing the indigenous knowledge subsystem and the formal education subsystem are depicted here as they appear 10 years into the systemic reform initiative. Over a period of 10 years, the two subsystems have been brought in contact with one another with an increasing level of two-way interaction occurring daily that is slowly building the interconnectivity and integration of functions that is the goal of the reform strategy. Each of the initiatives in the field surrounding the two subsystems serve as a catalyst to energize the "attractors" within the subsystems in ways that reinforce the efforts of the agents of change identified previously.

For example, the Alaska Native Knowledge Network assembles and provides easy access to curriculum resources that support the work underway on behalf of both the indigenous knowledge system and the formal education system. In addition, the ANKN newsletter, *Sharing Our Pathways*, provides an avenue for ongoing communication between all elements of the constituent systems. Concurrently, the AKRSI has been collaborating with the Alaska Department of Education and school districts in bringing Native educators from the margins to the center of educational decision making to shape policy development in ways that take into consideration the cultural context in which students acquire and demonstrate their knowledge, using the cultural standards as a guide.

CULTURAL INTERVENTION STRATEGIES

As the AKRSI component emphases are shifted from one region to the next, continuity is provided through the efforts and guidance of an AKRSI regional coordinator in each cultural region, who insures that the activities from each initiative are adapted to the cultural makeup of their respective region. Along with the regional adaptation of each of the initiatives, there are also a series of cross-cutting themes that integrate the initiatives within and across regions each year. While the regional initiatives focus on particular domains of activity through which specialized resources are brought to bear in each region each year (culturally aligned curriculum, indigenous science knowledge base, etc.), the following themes cut across all initiatives and regions each year:

1. Documenting cultural/scientific knowledge
2. Indigenous teaching practices
3. Standards/culturally based curriculum
4. Teacher support systems
5. Culturally appropriate assessment practices

As schools adopt the emphasis that these initiatives bring to engaging students in the study of culture, community, and place, they are engaged in common endeavors that unite them, at the same time that they are concentrating on particular initiatives in ways that are especially adapted to the indigenous knowledge base in their respective cultural region. Each set of initiatives and themes have built on each other from year to year and region to region through a series of statewide events that bring participants together from across the regions. These include working groups around various curriculum themes, academies of elders, statewide conferences, the AKRSI staff meetings, and the Alaska Native Knowledge Network. Following is a brief description of some of the key AKRSI-sponsored initiatives to illustrate the kind of activities that have been implemented, as they relate to the overall educational reform strategy outlined above.

Alaska Native Knowledge Network

A bimonthly newsletter, website and a culturally based curriculum resources database have been established to disseminate the information and materials that have been developed and accumulated throughout Alaska (http://www.ankn.uaf.edu).

S.P.I.R.A.L. Curriculum Framework
The ANKN curriculum clearinghouse has been identifying and cataloging curriculum resources applicable to teaching activities revolving around 12 broad cultural themes organized on a chart that provides a "Spiral Pathway for Integrating Rural Alaska Learning." The themes that make up the S.P.I.R.A.L. framework are family, language/communication, cultural expression, tribe/community, health/wellness, living in place, outdoor survival, subsistence, ANCSA, applied technology, energy/ecology, and exploring horizons. These themes have also been used to formulate whole new curriculum frameworks that have been implemented in several schools and districts. The curriculum resources associated with each of these themes can be accessed through the ANKN website.

Cultural Documentation/Atlas
Students in rural schools are interviewing Elders in their communities and researching available documents related to the indigenous knowledge systems associated with their place, and then assembling the information they have gathered into a multimedia format for publication as a "cultural atlas."

These initiatives have focused on themes such as weather prediction, edible and medicinal plants, geographic place-names, flora and fauna, moon and tides, celestial navigation, fisheries, subsistence practices, food preservation, outdoor survival, and the aurora.

Native Educator Associations

Associations of Native educators have been formed in each cultural region to provide an avenue for sustaining the initiatives that are being implemented in the schools by the AKRSI. The regional associations sponsor curriculum development work, organize academies of Elders, and host regional and statewide conferences as vehicles for disseminating the information that is accumulated. In addition, a statewide Alaska Native Education Association has been formed to represent the regional associations at a statewide level.

Native Ways of Knowing

Each cultural region has been engaged in an effort to distill core teaching/learning practices from the traditional forms of cultural transmission and to develop pedagogical practices in the schools that incorporate these practices (e.g., learning by doing/experiential learning, guided practice, detailed observation, intuitive analysis, cooperative/group learning, listening skills, and trial and error).

Academies of Elders

Native educators have been meeting with Native Elders around a local theme and a deliberative process through which the Elders share their traditional knowledge and the Native educators seek ways to apply that knowledge to teaching various components of the curriculum. The teachers then field test the curriculum ideas they have developed, bring that experience back to the Elders for verification, and then prepare a final set of curriculum units that are pulled together and shared with other educators.

Cultural Standards

Alaska Native educators have developed a set of "Alaska Standards for Culturally Responsive Schools" that provide explicit guidelines for how students, teachers, curriculum, schools, and communities can integrate the local culture and environment into the formal education process so that students are able to achieve cultural well-being as a result of their schooling experience. In addition, a series of six additional sets of "guidelines" have been prepared around various issues to offer more explicit guidance in defining what educators and communities need to know and be able to do to effectively implement the cultural standards.

VILLAGE SCIENCE CURRICULUM APPLICATIONS

Several volumes of village-oriented science and math curriculum resources, including a "Handbook for Culturally Responsive Science Curriculum" (Stephens, 2000), have been developed in collaboration with rural teachers for use in schools throughout Alaska. They serve as a supplement to existing curriculum materials to provide teachers with ideas on how to relate the teaching of basic science and math concepts to the surrounding environment.

All tasks associated with implementing the various initiatives outlined above were subcontracted out to the appropriate state or regional entities with responsibility and/or expertise in the respective action area. In this way, the expertise for implementing the various initiatives is cultivated within the respective regions, and the capacity to carry on the activities beyond the life of AKRSI is embedded in the schools and communities for which they are intended. Responsibility for the statewide support system (newsletter, website, curriculum resources, etc.) for the regional initiatives has been taken up by the University of Alaska Fairbanks, and the regional Native educator associations have taken on the task of sustaining the impact of the initiatives within and between regions.

Together, these initiatives constitute the work of the Alaska Rural Systemic Initiative and are intended to generate a strengthened complex adaptive system of education for rural Alaska that can effectively integrate the strengths of the two constituent emergent systems. The exact form this new integrated system will take remains to be seen as its properties emerge from the work that is underway. Accepting the open-endedness and unpredictability associated with complexity theory, and relying on the emergent properties associated with the adage "think globally, act locally," we are confident that we will know where we are going when we get there. It is the actions associated with "thinking systemically, acting categorically" that have guided us along the way, so we continue to move in the direction established by the AKRSI educational reform strategy outlined above.

IMPACT OF THE SCHOOL REFORM STRATEGY

The Alaska Rural Systemic Initiative has completed its 10-year cycle with a full complement of ongoing rural school reform initiatives in place stimulating a reconstruction of the role and substance of schooling in rural Alaska. The educational reform strategy we chose—to foster interconnectivity and symbiosis between the formal education system and the indigenous communities being served in rural Alaska based on current concepts, principles, and theories associated with the study of complex adaptive systems—has produced an increase in student achievement scores, a decrease in the dropout rate, an increase in the number of rural students attending college, and an increase in the number of Native students choosing to pursue studies in fields of science, math, and engineering.

The beneficial academic effects of putting students in touch with their own physical environment and cultural traditions through guided experiences have not gone unnoticed by school districts and other Native organizations around the state. One AKRSI school district has urged all of its schools to start the school year with a minimum of one week in a camp setting, combining cultural and academic learning with parents, Elders, and teachers all serving in instructional roles. One school in the district has built in to their program a series of camp experiences for the middle school students, with a well-crafted curriculum addressing the state content standards as well as the cultural standards. Given the accountability demands of No Child Left Behind, a central question throughout all these educational innovations has been, what impact do they have on student academic achievement?

With the advent of the state standards-based benchmark tests and the High School Graduation Qualifying Exam in 2000, we now have four years of data on student performance in the 8th- and 10th-grade math exams, from which we can make comparisons between AKRSI-affiliated schools and non-AKRSI schools for those two grade levels (AKRSI, 2005). Opposite are two graphs showing the percentage of students performing at the "advanced" or "proficient" levels on those exams.

The most notable features of these data are the significant increases in AKRSI student performance for both grade levels each year between 2000 and 2003. However, while the eighth-grade AKRSI students showed significant progress in closing the achievement gap with their non-AKRSI counterparts from 20 to 17 percentage points, the 10th-grade students in both groups showed a substantial gain from 2000 to 2003, leaving the achievement gap largely intact at that grade level.

In addition to the state benchmark data, we also have norm-referenced test results for ninth-grade students who have been taking the Terra Nova/CAT-6 since 2002.

Eighth Grade Mathematics Benchmarks 2000–2003
% Rural Students as Advanced/Proficient

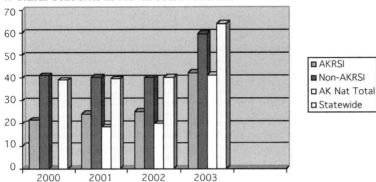

Tenth Grade Mathematics HSGQE 2000–2003
% Rural Students as Advanced/Proficient

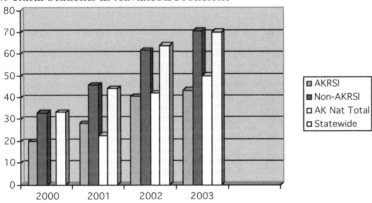

Ninth Grade Mathematics Terra Nova/CAT-6 2002–2004
% Rural Students Scoring in Third and Fourth Quartiles

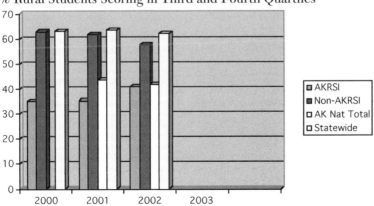

Though the differentials for each group between 2002 and 2004 remain small, the AKRSI students do show a slight increase in performance, while the non-AKRSI students reflect a small decrease in their performance over the two years.

The consistent improvement in academic performance of students in AKRSI-affiliated schools over each of the past four years leads us to conclude that the cumulative effect of utilizing the school reform strategies outlined above to increase the connections between what students experience in school and what they experience outside school appears to have a significant impact on their academic performance.

The AKRSI initiatives outlined above have demonstrated the viability of introducing strategically placed innovations that can serve as "attractors" around which a new, self-organizing, more integrated educational system can emerge, which in turn shows signs of producing the quality of learning opportunities that have eluded schools in Native communities for over a century. The substantial realignments already evident in the increased interest and involvement of Native people in education in rural communities throughout Alaska point to the applicability of complexity theory in shaping reform in educational systems.

While the National Science Foundation funding of the Alaska RSI initiative has been the catalyst for the core reform strategy as it applied to the areas of math and science, we have been fortunate to acquire substantial supplementary funding from the Annenberg Rural Challenge and other sources to implement comparable initiatives in the areas of social studies, fine arts, and language arts. All of these funds combined provide an opportunity to address the issues facing schools in Native communities throughout rural Alaska in a truly comprehensive and systemic fashion.

As a means to help document the process of systemic reform in rural schools, we joined in a project that resulted in seven comprehensive case studies of educational practices and reform efforts in nine rural communities/schools in Alaska. The case studies are funded through the Northwest Regional Educational Laboratory by a field-initiated grant from the National Institute for At-Risk Youth under the U.S. Department of Education. Since all of the communities were in school districts associated with the Alaska Rural Systemic Initiative, we were able to obtain a good cross-section of in-depth data on the impact of the AKRSI reform effort over a period three years (Kushman and Barnhardt, 1999).

We are mindful of the responsibilities associated with taking on longstanding, intractable problems that have plagued schools in indigenous settings throughout the world for most of this century, and we have made an effort to be cautious about raising community expectations beyond what we can realistically expect to accomplish. Our experience is such that we are confident in the route we chose to initiate substantive reform in rural schools serving Alaska's Native communities, and while we expected to encounter plenty of problems and challenges along the way, we were able to capitalize on a broadly supportive climate to introduce changes that over time will not only benefit rural schools serving Native students, but will be instructive for all schools and all students. We are grateful for the opportunity to explore these ideas and find ways to strengthen and renew the educational systems serving people and communities throughout our society.

References

Alaska Natives Commission. 1994. *Alaska Natives Commission: Final Report.* Anchorage: Alaska Federation of Natives.

Alaska Rural Systemic Initiative. 2005. *Final Report.* Fairbanks: Alaska Native Knowledge Network.

Assembly of Native Educators. 1998. *Alaska Standards for Culturally Responsive Schools.* Fairbanks: Alaska Native Knowledge Network.

Barnhardt, R., and O. Kawagley. 1999. Education indigenous to place: Western science meets indigenous reality. In *Ecological education in action*, ed. G. Smith and D. Williams. New York: SUNY Press.

Battram, A. 2001. *Navigating complexity: The essential guide to complexity theory in business and management.* Dover, NH: Industrial Society Business Books Network.

Capra, F. 1996. *The web of life: A new scientific understanding of living systems.* New York: Doubleday.

Eglash, R. 2002. Computation, complexity and coding in Native American knowledge systems. In *Changing the faces of mathematics: Perspectives on indigenous people of North America*, ed. J.E. Hankes and G.R. Fast, 251–262. Reston, VA: National Council of Teachers of Mathematics.

Epstein, J., and R. Axtell. 1996. *Growing artificial societies.* Cambridge, MA: MIT Press.

Gleick, J. 1987. *Chaos: Making a new science.* New York: Penguin.

Gomez, M. 1997. *Science and mathematics for all.* Washington, DC: National Science Foundation.

Gribbin, J. 2004. *Deep simplicity: Chaos, complexity and the emergence of life.* New York: Penguin Books.

Helander-Renvall, E. 2005. *Composite report on status and trends regarding the knowledge, innovations and practices of indigenous and local communities: Arctic region.* Geneva, Switzerland: United Nations Environment Programme.

Jones, R. 1994. Chaos theory. *Executive Educator* (October):20–23.

Kawagley, O. 1995. *A Yupiaq world view: A pathway to ecology and spirit.* Prospect Heights, IL: Waveland Press.

Kushman, J., and R. Barnhardt, R. 1999. *Study of Alaska rural systemic reform.* Portland, OR: Northwest Regional Educational Laboratory.

Marshall, S.P. 1996. Chaos, complexity and flocking behavior: Metaphors for learning. *Wingspread Journal* 18(3):13–15.

Napoleon, H. 1991. *Yuuyaraq: The way of the human being.* Fairbanks: Center for Cross-Cultural Studies, University of Alaska Fairbanks.

Peck, K., and A.A. Carr. 1997. Restoring public confidence in schools through systems thinking. *International Journal of Educational Reform* 6(3):316–323.

Sahtouris, E. 2000. The indigenous way. In *EarthDance: Living systems in evolution,* 323–343. New York: iUniverse Press.

Shulman, H. 1997. *Living at the edge of chaos: Complex systems in culture and psyche.* Wilmette, IL: Daimon/Chiron Publications.

Stamps, D. 1997. The self organizing system. *Training* (April): 30–36.

Stephens, S. 2000. *Handbook for culturally responsive science curriculum.* Fairbanks: Alaska Native Knowledge Network.

Waldrop, M.M. 1994. *Complexity: The emerging science at the edge of chaos.* New York: Doubleday.

Wheatley, M.J. 1992. *Leadership and the new science: Learning about organizations from an orderly universe.* San Francisco: Berrett-Koehler Publishers.

Wilber, K., ed. 1985. *The holographic paradigm and other paradoxes: Exploring the leading edge of science.* Boston: New Science Library.

PART IV

CULTURALLY RESPONSIVE CURRICULUM

———◆◈◆———

66To be Indigenous is both a privilege and a birthright. It is therefore the responsibility of all Indigenous peoples to ensure that their respective cultures, philosophies and ideologies remain strong and continue to grow.99

From the *Coolongatta Statement on Indigenous Rights in Education*

The Indigenous Worldview of Yupiaq Culture

Its Scientific Nature and Relevance to the Practice and Teaching of Science

———◆►◄◆———

Angayuqaq Oscar Kawagley, Delena Norris-Tull,
and Roger Norris-Tull

Originally published in *Journal of Research in Science Teaching,*
vol. 35, no. 2 (1998): 133–144, © John Wiley & Sons, Inc.

IS SCIENCE AN INVENTION of European thought, or have legitimate scientific bodies of knowledge and scientific ways of thinking emerged separately in other cultures? Can indigenous knowledge systems contribute to contemporary science teaching? Here we describe evidence from the Yupiaq culture in southwestern Alaska which demonstrates a body of scientific knowledge and epistemology that differs from that of Western science. We contend that drawing from Yupiaq culture, knowledge, and epistemology can provide not only a more culturally relevant frame of reference for teaching science concepts to Yupiaq students, but also a potentially valuable context for more effectively addressing many of the recommendations of U.S. science education reform initiatives.

"The science accounted for in this book is largely part of a tradition of thought that happened to develop in Europe during the past 500 years—a tradition to which people from all cultures contribute today" (Rutherford and Ahlgren, 1990:136). As this quote from *Science for All Americans* implies, Western science has become the prototype for what counts as science today, and other ways of thinking and doing science have been largely discounted by the Euro-American scientific and educational communities. With its emphasis on controlled experimentation, replicability, and alleged objectivity, science as practiced in laboratories and as traditionally taught in U.S. schools does differ from the practice and thinking found in many indigenous cultures, but does that mean that what occurs in other cultures is not truly science? Our experience with Yupiaq culture in southwestern Alaska leads us to believe that such indigenous groups practice science in ways that have similarities to—and important and useful differences from—Western science, and that the worldview underpinning this indigenous vision of science has valuable implications for science instruction.

Scientific hypotheses and knowledge acquisition generally have their roots in observations and insights about the natural world. Nevertheless, scientists and educators today often present textbook/laboratory science as the true science. Such a narrow view of science not only diminishes the legitimacy of knowledge derived through generations of naturalistic observation and insight, it simultaneously devalues those cultures which traditionally rely heavily on naturalistic observation and insight. In addition, contemporary science classes commonly portray science as a discrete body of knowledge distinctly separated from most other subject areas and as a body of knowledge discovered by European and Euro-American scientists. This characterization makes science an activity foreign to the way of thinking of cultures in which science is interwoven within most aspects of daily life.

Philosophers of science generally acknowledge the elusiveness of a definition of the nature of science, and in particular tend to disagree with common characterizations of the nature of science depicted in recent science education literature (Alters, 1997). Nevertheless, in our conversations with science educators and scientists in the United States, we have been confronted with the assumption that the nature of science is clearly defined. Lee (1997) pointed out that statements in *Science for All Americans* (Rutherford and Ahlgren, 1990) and *National Science Education Standards* (National Research Council, 1996) demonstrate that these important reform documents both promote a Western scientific cultural tradition. We agree with Lee that the tendency to define science strictly from the viewpoint of Western culture has serious and detrimental ramifications for students from non-Western cultures and languages, and we add that a Eurocentric view of science places unnecessary limitations on the development of scientific literacy for all students.

We contend that no single origin for science exists: that science has a plurality of origins and a plurality of practices. In this position statement, we support that belief with examples of scientific knowledge and ways of thinking about the world from one indigenous culture, that of the Yupiaq people of southwestern Alaska. As with many other indigenous groups, the worldview of the Yupiaq people has enabled them to survive for thousands of years. We contend that knowledge embedded in that worldview is scientific in nature, and that it remains relevant to today's world.

Throughout this article, we will refer to the term "worldview" as a means of conceptualizing the principles and beliefs—including the epistemological and ontological underpinnings of those beliefs—which people have acquired to make sense of the world around them. Our usage is intended to be consistent with *Webster's New World Dictionary of American English* (Neufeld and Guralnik, 1991), which defines "worldview" as "a comprehensive, especially personal, philosophy or conception of the world and of human life." As perceived by the authors of this article, the concept of worldview is also closely related to the definitions of culture and cognitive map (Berger, Berger, and Kellner, 1974).

Alaska Native Culture and Education

The majority of residents in rural Alaska are Alaska Natives who live in villages with small populations (25–1,000 people/village). With some 20 Alaska Native languages spoken in the state, many school students speak an indigenous language as a first language. Many families in rural Alaska maintain a lifestyle that is largely dependent on subsistence hunting and fishing. Wild foods (salmon, caribou, moose, and numerous wild berries and herbs) form a major portion of their food supply, and many rural residents rely on commercial fishing in the summer months as their main financial support.

The Yupiaq (also known as Yup'ik) culture is one of several Alaska Native cultures known to Westerners as Eskimo (a term which has too often been used pejoratively). Members of the Yupiaq culture reside in southwestern Alaska on an area of land larger than many individual states in the contiguous 48 states. There are no roads connecting these villages, which are isolated by hundreds of miles from access to the highway systems that connect cities such as Anchorage to the contiguous states. Despite their isolation from the rest of the nation, rural villages have been affected greatly by modern Western culture. Televisions and telephones have become common. While dogsleds still are used recreationally, snowmachines have become the more common mode of transportation in winter, and four-wheelers and power boats have become common in the summer.

Teachers and administrators in rural Alaska schools are mostly Euro-American and short-term, many staying in a village only one or two years (with a few staying for less than a week). While the villages themselves strongly reflect their particular Alaska Native culture, Euro-American culture dominates the school and the curriculum. In the recent past, Alaska Native students were forbidden to speak their native language in the schools. Indeed, eradication of Alaska Native culture was an early goal of Alaskan educational systems (Alaska Natives Commission, 1993). The activism of Alaska Natives and of groups such as the Alaska Federation of Natives has gradually brought change.

The Alaska Natives Commission (1993) produced a report addressing the educational problems and needs of Alaska Natives. Twenty-one percent of Alaska's K–12 students are Alaska Natives. However, "twenty-two of Alaska's 54 school districts have student populations of 75 percent or more Alaska Natives. . . . In some school districts up to 30 percent of Native children in elementary school are below grade level" (p. 14). In 20 school districts (19 of which had 60 percent to 98 percent Alaska Native students), students scored "on average below the 22nd percentile in either reading, mathematics, or language arts at the 4th, 6th, or 8th grade" (p. 15), and "only about 67 percent of Alaska Native students complete high school" (p. 17). Alaska Natives who do complete high school score dramatically lower (about 40 percent lower) than Caucasian Alaskans on the American College Test (ACT). Among the various factors contributing to student failure, the report cites poverty and the cultural and linguistic differences between students and school personnel.

As a result of Alaska Native activism, many rural school districts today offer instruction in the local language and culture (Alaska Natives Commission, 1993). For example, in Manokotak, Alaska, children are taught in Yup'ik from kindergarten to third grade. In Chefornak, Alaska, Alaska Native teacher aides conduct weekly classes on local traditional music and dance. Nonetheless, less than 4 percent of Alaskan teachers are Alaska Natives. Small rural schools must rely on Alaska Native volunteers and Alaska Native teacher aides for specialized instruction in local language and culture. Thus, most of the instruction is from the viewpoint of the Euro-American teacher, and there remains a wide gap between the culture of the child at home and the culture of the child in school.

Alaska Native Contributions to Science and Technology

Alaska Native scientific knowledge has largely been ignored by Euro-American scientists. However, in recent years knowledge from indigenous Alaskan cultures has contributed to several scientific studies. For example, the knowledge of local villages was used in an environmental impact study conducted in the Alaskan tundra. Indigenous elders' knowledge of bowhead whale behavior was used to correct an inaccurate count of bowhead whale population in the North Slope region (Bingham, 1997). In southwest Alaska, a group of scientists participating in a public hearing provided data demonstrating that beluga whales did not feed on salmon. A group of local Alaska Natives (mainly Yupiaqs) persuaded the scientists to visit a nearby beach where they opened the stomach of a recently harvested beluga. When several large salmon spilled out, one of the elders was reported to have said, "How'd those get in there then?" (R.S. Nelson, personal communication, 1996).

In the past few years, several educational studies of the traditional knowledge and practices of Yupiaq people have been conducted in southwestern Alaska. The Ciulistet group, an organization of Yupiaq teachers, has conducted ongoing studies of Yupiaq mathematics and science in an effort to bring that knowledge directly into classrooms in Bristol Bay villages (Lipka, 1994a, 1994b). Two of the authors (A.O.K. and R.N.-T.) have participated in a number of the research meetings held by the Ciulistet teachers/researchers.

Kawagley (1995) conducted an ethnographic study of Yupiaq knowledge and ways of knowing and doing science in Akiak, a small village of 385 people near Bethel, Alaska. Kawagley is the first Yupiaq to receive a PhD. He received permission of the Tribal Council of the Yupiit Nation and the Yupiit School District to conduct observations and interviews in Akiak. He visited classrooms, reviewed school curricula, and interviewed local teachers and villagers. Having grown up in the region, Kawagley views himself as a participant-observer.

Each of these studies relied heavily on interviews with village elders and on the lifelong experiences of the Yupiaq researchers. Interviews with elders, respected for their wisdom and knowledge, reveal a rich body of indigenous knowledge and well-defined ways of viewing the world. In the meetings of the Ciulistet teachers, the elders have often been invited to demonstrate their knowledge through stories and through physical demonstrations of skills. For example, elders have taught the younger teachers and schoolchildren how to make river fish traps and how to prepare and sew caribou skins for clothing items.

Much of Yupiaq scientific knowledge is manifested most clearly in their technology. One may argue that technology is not science. However, technology does not spring from a void. To invent technological devices, scientific observations and experimentation must be conducted. Yupiaq inventions, which include the kayak, river fish traps, and a wide range of hunting and fishing gear, represent technology that could not have been developed without extensive scientific study of the flow of currents in rivers, the ebb and flow of tides in bays, and the feeding, resting, and migratory habits of fish, mammals, and birds.

For example, each item of fishing gear is typically developed to capture a particular species of fish in a particular type of water (in a river, under ice, on the shore of the bay, or in the open ocean). To make the appropriate traps and nets, the fisherman has to have significant scientific knowledge of the behaviors of each species of fish, tidal patterns, and the patterns of flow of water in rivers. In remote villages, most food is still retrieved from the wild. Therefore, all young men must have extensive knowledge of migration patterns, mating habits, and feeding behaviors of wildlife (including seals, walrus, several species of whales, moose, caribou, ptarmigan, and many species of waterfowl).

Yupiaq women gather wild foods and preserve and prepare foods from animals, which are harvested mostly by the men. The women know when and where to collect wild berries, which provide a crucial source of vitamins. They typically have extensive knowledge of local wild plants, including a wide variety of edible and medicinal ones. They know when and where to gather grasses for basket-making. Many still know how to prepare clothing, including shoes, coats, and raingear, from skins of caribou, moose, seals, and even salmon. Most know how to prepare and preserve fish, moose, and caribou for long-term storage.

Tepa, or "stink heads," is a Yupiaq delicacy. King salmon heads are buried, wrapped in grasses. The fermented heads are eaten. To be safely prepared, the fish must be stored in the right type of soil at the right temperature. This was a relatively safe food to eat until the introduction of plastic bags. Fish stored underground in plastic bags are more likely to develop botulism than fish stored in grasses. It was soon discovered that the traditional method of preparing the "stink heads" was safer than the modern way.

Yupiaq people have extensive knowledge of navigation on open seas and rivers, and over snow-covered tundra. They have their own terminology for constellations and have an understanding of the seasonal positioning of the constellations. They have developed a large body of knowledge about climatic and seasonal changes—knowledge about temperature changes, the behavior of ice and snow, the meaning of different cloud formations, the significance of changes in wind direction and speed, and knowledge of air pressure. This knowledge has been crucial to survival and was essential for the development of the technological devices used in the past (many of which are still used today) for hunting and fishing.

In his book *The Demon-haunted World*, Carl Sagan (1996) remarked on the discovery of quinine by pre-modern people in the Amazon.

> They must have tried every tree and every plant—roots, stems, bark, leaves—tried chewing on them, mashing them up, making an infusion. This constitutes a massive set of scientific experiments continuing over generations—experiments that moreover could not be duplicated today for reasons of medical ethics. Think of how many bark infusions from other trees must have been useless, or made the patient retch or even die. In such a case, the healer chalks these potential medicines off the list, and moves on to the next. (p. 251)

Likewise, Yupiaq traditional knowledge reflects an understanding of the natural world based on a "massive set of scientific experiments continuing over generations." Yupiaq scientific knowledge is based on thorough longitudinal studies and observations of the natural surroundings. Traditionally, knowledge was passed down from the elders to the youth through storytelling. Until very recently, the Yupiaq language was not written down. Thus, all important knowledge was preserved by oral traditions which were crucial to survival. The preservation of the next generation depended on an efficient method of learning that previous generations had already discovered (such as knowledge of seasonal and long-range weather patterns, salmon migration patterns, and knowledge and skills about river ice and sea ice formation and movement).

Besides through oral tradition, knowledge and skills are handed down in other ways as well. Fishing, hunting, and food gathering and preparation practices are passed on to children by working with, observing, and mimicking their parents, grandparents, and older siblings. Typically, the person teaching the skill will say very little. The learner is expected to observe closely and mimic what is being done. It is quite common for children to become quite skillful with a variety of tools, including sharp knives, at an early age. To translate Yupiaq teaching and learning into current educational jargon, one could state that teaching strongly emphasizes modeling and guided practice, and that cooperative learning, peer tutoring, and hands-on learning are essential strategies.

Yupiaq Worldvew

In addition to a body of knowledge about the natural and physical world, Yupiaq ways of thinking about the world reflect a worldview distinct from the Western way of thinking. In Yupiaq culture, science is not separated from daily life. Their science is interspersed with art, storytelling, hunting, and craftsmanship.

In contrast to the idea that science is a body of knowledge discovered by scientists working in their laboratories, Kawagley (1995) found that Yupiaq villagers see themselves as the producers of knowledge. In their daily lives, these men and women are the observers of their environment. There are no special gatekeepers of knowledge. The elders of the community are the repositories of traditional knowledge and they see it as their responsibility to educate the younger members. However, Western culture has interfered with the traditional teaching and learning mode. Suppression of the Alaska Native language and culture has resulted in a generation of youth many of whom cannot communicate with the elders in their own communities (Alaska Natives Commission, 1993). Schoolteachers have in many cases replaced the elders as the transmitters of knowledge.

The Yupiaq people have difficulty with many Western concepts and the words to describe or define them. Western words come from a worldview that is objectivistic and techno-mechanistic, as opposed to the Yupiaq worldview which is ecological and spiritual. Thus the concepts and word-thoughts (and metaphors) of the Yupiaq people are often ineffable because they are based on feelings of connectedness and relationships. Therein lies the Yupiaq problem with words such as "science" and "mathematics" and the various scientific and mathematical disciplines and their concomitant terms and concepts. These all are strange and foreign to the Yupiaq people. Kawagley (1995) asked a group of Yupiaq elders to define "mathematics" and "science."

The elders' discussion of the definition of mathematics focused on the Yupiaq word *Cuqtaariyaraq*, "the process of measuring." The other definitions that were considered reflect further abstractions of their thinking processes as applied to one who uses mathematics. These included "someone who is astute and perceptive"; "an expert evaluator"; "an expert assessor"; "someone who evaluates something, mentally assessing the feasibility and coming pretty close to the estimate"; "becoming good at calculating"; "becoming good at visualizing." Finally, they agreed that the best Yupiaq definition of mathematics would be "the process of measuring and estimating in time and space (p. 57).

No Yupiaq word exists for "science." When asked to define science, the elders defined it as:

> "Trying to know"; "trying to understand"; "trying to grasp the origin"; "trying to find the source"; "the process of understanding"; "way to try and understand through process of elimination"; "a process that is the science of life"; and "a process of seeing and predicting the future." (pp. 57–58)

Western scientific knowledge has become so specialized that it is often difficult to take the whole organism of the whole system into account. Western culture segregates science from other realms of knowledge and even subdivides science into various categories, so that a scientist specializing in one field may well lack a basic understanding of other scientific and nonscientific fields. For Yupiaqs, scientific knowledge is not segregated from other aspects of daily life and it is not subdivided into different fields of science. To design a fish trap, for example, one must know how the river behaves, how the salmon behave, and how the split willow of which the trap is made behaves (i.e., one must have an understanding of physics, biology, and engineering).

While the Yupiaq people we have interviewed value observation highly, they do not consider direct observation as the only way of attaining knowledge about the universe. Spiritual understanding is another way of obtaining knowledge—observing one's inner spirit, as well as one's outer environment, contributes to the whole range of Yupiaq knowledge.

Kawagley (1995) noted that Yupiaq people view the world as being composed of five elements: earth, air, fire, water, and spirit. Aristotle spoke of the four elements: earth, air, fire, and water. However, spirit has been missing from Western science. The incorporation of spirit in the Yupiaq worldview resulted in an awareness of the interdependence of humanity with the environment, a reverence for and a sense of responsibility for protecting the environment.

The elders Kawagley interviewed commented that

> This is what our ancestors have said . . . they've said not
> to pollute the land. They've said that if we're not careful
> with our refuse, some animals, though they were plenti-
> ful once, will no longer be around. They were actually
> foreseeing their future when they told us that. That's the
> science of life. We have to take care of our tundra in order
> to have plenty and have abundant wildlife. (p. 58)

In the past, before the introduction of Western materials and ways of doing things, Yupiaq people practiced what may be thought of as *soft technology* (Lovins, 1977). This low-impact technology involved the making of tools and preparation of shelters, clothing, and food with as little harm to the natural and supernatural worlds as possible. The shamans were the intermediaries between the spiritual and natural worlds. They informed the people of what was appropriate or not in their dealing with the earth. The use of natural materials made all objects ultimately recyclable. The people took extensive precautions to protect the lives of the animals and plants they depended upon for their existence.

Kawagley found that Yupiaq people are involved in the human effort to develop a worldview consonant with themselves, nature, and the spiritual world. Such reverence for nature has been largely missing from Western cultural interactions with the environment. Einstein (1956) stated, "The ancients knew something that we seem to have forgotten. All means prove but a blunt instrument, if they have not behind them a living spirit" (p. 24).

In Western culture today, science, philosophy, and metaphysics are treated as separate areas of study; yet, historically this division was not so apparent. Western scientific and philosophical thinking has often turned to questions about the nature of existence and of God. Even in modern physics, such great thinkers as Einstein and Hawking have not found it necessary to separate questions about God from questions about the behavior of the universe. Yet, many Western scientists and science educators today treat science and spirit as separate and unrelated entities.

In Western science, the closest to Yupiaq science can be seen in the study of ecology, which incorporates biological, chemical, and physical systems (earth, air, fire, and water). However, even many ecologists have ignored the fifth element, spirit. Lack of attention to the fifth element has resulted in a science that ignores the interaction and needs of societies and cultures within ecosystems. Only recently has ecological study begun to seriously consider and incorporate human social needs and concerns about changes in ecosystems.

CONCLUSIONS

As depicted by science education professors in the United States and by documents such as *Science for All Americans* (Rutherford and Ahlgren, 1990) and *National Science Education Standards* (National Research Council, 1996), the nature of science is seen as clearly defined and based on a Western tradition. We believe that the nature of science is not clearly defined or clearly definable, but rather that it is largely dependent on the cultural tradition of the practitioner of science.

We believe that there is no one way to do or think about science. Science is not strictly European in origin. Modern scientific knowledge is a blend of the observations and insights of many different cultures. Besides the large body of scientific knowledge that came out of the Chinese, Greek, Egyptian, and Arabic cultures, a significant amount of modern scientific knowledge originated in the knowledge of indigenous cultures. For example, about 121 modern prescription drugs were derived from plants. Western researchers would not have known which plants to test for healing properties without the knowledge supplied by traditional healers (Abelson, 1990).

Yupiaq science is a science based on observation of the natural world coupled with direct experimentation in the natural setting. The science conducted in Western laboratories is largely a way of doing science that is Western in origin and is in some crucial ways distinct from the way that science is and has been done in indigenous cultures. Western science tends to be impersonal, formal, and elitist (only certain college-educated individuals are granted the status of *scientist*). Indigenous science is informal and nonelitist. Western science promotes a mechanistic view of the universe. Indigenous science incorporates spirit.

There is a large body of science that exists in Yupiaq culture—but it is a science that is rapidly disappearing as the language is disappearing. Recent publicity has altered us to concerns about the loss of knowledge of plant medicines in the Amazon rain forests as the Amazon tribes disappear (Jackson, 1989). However, we know very little about what we are losing as the cultures and languages of indigenous Alaskans disappear.

IMPLICATIONS FOR CURRICULUM DEVELOPMENT AND PEDAGOGY

Not enough has been written that provides specific examples of methods for making science and mathematics education truly accessible to *all* students, even students in a remote Alaskan village of 300 people. The National Science Teachers Association now has several books that will be of value to teachers, such as *Science for All Cultures* (Carey, 1993). The Northwest Regional Educational Laboratory has just produced a good attempt in its *Science and Mathematics for All Students* (1997). However, even this booklet lumps all minorities into one category ("students of color") and unwittingly implies that this amorphous group of students all share the same challenges in mathematics and science achievement.

Rodriguez (1997) criticized the *National Science Education Standards* (National Research Council, 1996) for what he refers to as a "discourse of invisibility" with regard to women and minorities. He criticized the National Research Council for not taking a strong stand in providing guidelines for how to promote the scientific literacy of all students. The science education community must take the lead in addressing the needs of those students for whom research has demonstrated that science and mathematics instruction as traditionally practiced in American schools has failed. Those students include a disproportionate number of females and a disproportionate number of Latin American, African American, Native American, and Alaska Native students.

What is the best way to teach science in Yupiaq classrooms? Many elders in Yupiaq villages want their young people to learn the traditional knowledge and skills that enabled their ancestors to survive in the past, not just because it is a part of their heritage but because that knowledge is still relevant to life in the villages today. They also want their young people to learn scientific knowledge and skills of the world outside the village—because the elders understand that that knowledge is also relevant to the lives of their children. The elders understand that the Yupiaq view of the world is different from the view of the world as seen through the eyes of the Euro-American teachers in their schools. They want their children to understand both worldviews—because they see both as crucial to the survival of their youth.

However, science instruction as it has been traditionally delivered has not been effective. Science curriculum as it has historically appeared in rural Alaska has been based on textbooks which, for example, have assumed that grasshoppers, turtles, cows, and sidewalks were a part of every child's daily life. Many rural Alaskan students have seen none of these. In contrast, most rural Alaskan students have many experiences with nature that urban and suburban students lack, experiences (such as hunting caribou and seals) which school textbooks and standardized tests never include in the examples.

Science historically has presented Yupiaq students with a bewildering, largely irrelevant body of information in a different science subject each year. Science has been taught through reading textbooks (as opposed to the oral method more familiar in local cultures) and listening to lectures that incorporate many unfamiliar terms. It has been graded competitively (in a culture that values cooperation). Students are required to memorize an enormous amount of unrelated abstract information with no clear use in real life, Because Western methods of teaching science often run counter to the students' own cultural experiences, Yupiaq students have been disenfranchised not only by *what* is taught but also by *how* it is taught.

We believe that one way, and possibly the most effective way, to improve learning in Yupiaq classrooms is to infuse indigenous knowledge and worldview in the curriculum. To effectively incorporate Yupiaq culture into classroom content and practice requires some fundamental changes in the way students, teachers, and schools function. Designing instructional materials and practices which acknowledge and respect Yupiaq society represents much more than just movement away from an outdated view of science and science teaching, however. It also represents significant progress *toward* the goals, outcomes, and recommendations of recent science education reform documents, documents such as *National Science Educational Standards* (National Research Council, 1996) and *Science for All Americans* (Rutherford and Ahlgren, 1990), as well as being congruent with emerging understandings of the teaching and learning process.

It is interesting to note that although these science reform documents pay little attention to the educational needs of specific minority groups and female students, the changes in curriculum and pedagogy recommended in these documents in many cases closely correspond to the changes necessary to incorporate Yupiaq knowledge, worldview, and culture into the classroom.

A Yupiaq worldview, like recent science reform documents, invokes a more holistic view of science, minimizing the artificial distinctions among concrete subjects in science while emphasizing the interconnectedness and interdependence of all dimensions of nature and human activity. The Yupiaq heritage can bring to the classroom a multidisciplinary, multidirectional, and multisensory learning style, with the total environment, natural and artificial, as the learning laboratory.

For example, one of the authors observed the following science lesson conducted by an Alaska Native student teacher with a group of six students in grades three through seven. The student teacher asked the children to design an experiment. The children decided they wanted to know what type of substance would work best to remove hair from caribou hides. They came up with a variety of solutions to test, including laundry soap and caribou brains (one student remembered that she had seen someone use caribou brains in preparing hides). One student's father, who was watching the lesson, walked out to his shed and brought back the head of a caribou he had recently killed. He sawed it open so the children could extract the brain. The teacher and a village elder present assisted the children in gathering the materials they needed for the experiment but they did not give the children any suggestions about how to carry out the experiment. The children soaked the caribou hide in plain water, in water with laundry soap, and in water with caribou brains. They soaked the hides for 24 hours. Then they tried to scrape the hair off the hides using a traditional knife. The teacher and the elder (a grandmother with much experience in preparing caribou hides) continued to watch without giving advice. The hair did not come off the hides. Finally, the children spontaneously asked the grandmother what they could do differently. The grandmother then explained that when she prepares caribou hides she soaks them in the river for many days. She also told them that the brain is used for tanning the hides, not removing fur.

In this lesson, the children combined knowledge from their own culture with experimental techniques they learned from the Western culture. They naturally pursued a hands-on discovery experience. The adults (including a variety of extended family members) provided a nonjudgmental facilitative learning environment that allowed the children the freedom to learn on their own by experimentation. The children pursued ideas from their peers until they exhausted their options, at which point they sought the wisdom of the experience of their elders.

This is but one example of ways in which indigenous culture can be incorporated into a science class. Ecological themes can provide another natural way to combine the rich Yupiaq heritage with Western knowledge. Oral legends about the land or the animals, as told by the elders, can be included in the lessons. These legends often include morals about the importance of conservation, including respect for the land and for wildlife. Incorporating elders into the life of schools helps to restore in children respect for these rare, valuable human resources. Naturalistic observations, so much a part of the Yupiaq way of life, are also an important part of what ecological researchers do. Children can develop their observational skills with the modeling and assistance of local community members, while also learning the quantitative techniques so highly valued in Western scientific traditions.

The spiritual or mystical element of Yupiaq understanding can manifest itself throughout the curriculum not as religious instruction, but as such things as reverence for the natural world, acknowledgment of humanity's dependence on and responsibility to our ecosystem, and appreciation of the mysteries of the universe. Learning to respect the spirit of the river that flows by the village is infinitely more relevant to the life of the child in rural Alaska than drawing a picture of an atom that appears in the textbook. It may also be a more precise metaphor. The fine arts can be incorporated into the science lesson in a variety of ways: for example, through the use of traditional dance (such as dances related to certain hunting or fishing traditions) and through artwork (such as carvings that depict wildlife or dance masks that represent spirits of animals).

What emerges from incorporating indigenous worldview, knowledge, and culture into Alaskan schools is a curriculum which can integrate the natural sciences with social sciences, language arts, fine arts, and mathematics in a way which the learner can recognize as having legitimate meaning in daily life.

A classroom reflecting Yupiaq culture looks and feels much like the village outside the classroom door. Groups of individuals of various ages, from young children to the elders of the community, are engaged in hands-on activities, working together to complete meaningful tasks or to solve concrete, multifaceted problems relevant o their daily lives. The natural environmental setting is a common tool for learning. Both Yupiaq and English are spoken, as each has its own contribution to the learning; and as Kawagley (1995) stated, "We should make use of the Yupiaq language because it is a tool of the spirit and therefore the voice of the culture" (p. 116). Everyone has an opportunity to express opinions if they wish, and decisions are arrived at by consensus.

In the Yup'ik village and in the classroom that might reflect it, assessments are authentic. In the village, one's skill as a hunter is based on factors such as the number of caribou harvested in a day, not the accuracy with which one shoots at paper bull's eyes; assessing a student's understanding of basic hydrodynamics might be based on the student's examination of the river to predict the best channel for a loaded skiff, not the student's responses on a multiple-choice test. Evaluations are prescriptive and on-going; rather than, "You received a C- on your hydrodynamics project," a teacher might say, "You nicked your propeller a little when you tried that channel. Look at the way the river comes off that cutbank and try to figure out where the least amount of gravel got deposited." If a student does not yet grasp a particular skill, the student might be given further modeling of the skill and then be given another opportunity to attempt it on his or her own. The student continues practicing and further modeling is provided until the skill is mastered.

Where feasible, the elders are actively involved in telling the stories and demonstrating the crafts and practices of the Yupiaq heritage. Teachers and community members work together to assist students in strengthening their identification with their own culture while simultaneously learning to use the tools and knowledge of Western science as a force that can help them maintain self-reliance and self-sufficiency.

Pedagogy that thus draws from indigenous knowledge, worldview, and culture can provide students with not only a locally relevant science education, but also in many ways with the kind of learning environment and experiences recommended for students everywhere.

REFERENCES

Abelson, P.H. 1990. Medicine from plants. *Science* 247:513.

Alaska Natives Commission. 1993. *Report of the education task force.* Anchorage.

Alters, B.J. 1997. Whose nature of science? *Journal of Research in Science Teaching* 34:39–55.

American Association for the Advancement of Science. 1993. *Project 2061: Benchmarks for science literacy.* New York: Oxford University Press.

Berger, P., B. Berger, and H. Kellner. 1974. *The homeless mind: Modernization and consciousness.* New York: Vintage.

Bingham, C. 1997. NAFWS meeting encourages balance between traditional knowledge and Western science. *Bristol Bay Times*, April 17, p. A10.

Carey, S.J., ed. 1993. *Science for all cultures.* Arlington, VA: National Science Teachers Association.

Einstein, A. 1956. *Out of my later years.* Secaucus, NJ: Citadel Press.

Jackson, D.D. 1989. Searching for medicinal wealth in Amazonia. *Smithsonian* 19(11): 95–102.

Kawagley, A.O. 1995. *A Yupiaq world view—a pathway to ecology and spirit.* Prospect Heights, IL: Waveland Press.

Lee, O. 1997. Scientific literacy for all: What is it, and how can we achieve it? *Journal of Research in Science Teaching* 34:219–222.

Lipka, J. 1994a. Culturally negotiated schooling: Toward a Yup'ik mathematics. *Journal of American Indian Education* 33(3):14–30.

———. 1994b. Schools failing minority teachers: Problems and suggestions. *Educational Foundations* 8(2):57–80.

Lovins, A.B. 1977. *Soft energy paths.* New York: Harper & Row.

National Research Council. 1996. *National science education standards.* Washington, DC: National Academy Press.

Neufeld, V., and D.B. Guralnik, eds. 1991. *Webster's new world dictionary of American English,* 3rd Collegiate ed. New York: Prentice Hall.

Northwest Regional Educational Laboratory. 1977. *Science and mathematics for all students.* Portland, OR.

Rodriguez, A.J. 1997. The dangerous discourse of invisibility: A critique of the National Research Council's National Science Education Standards. *Journal of Research in Science Teaching* 34:19–37.

Rutherford, F.J., and A. Ahlgren. 1990. *Science for all Americans.* New York: Oxford University Press.

Sagan, C. 1996. *The demon-haunted world.* New York: Ballantine.

THEIR SILENCE
ABOUT US

WHY WE NEED AN ALASKA NATIVE CURRICULUM

Paul Ongtooguk

IN 1981, I BEGAN MY CAREER as a teacher in rural Alaska—a circumstance that no doubt would have surprised my high school teachers and counselors. I am Iñupiat, and when I attended high school in Northwest Alaska in the early 1970s, teachers and counselors gave me little attention and no encouragement about my future. As was true for many other Alaska Natives at that time, school officials never mentioned college as a possibility for me and even discouraged me when I broached the subject myself.

The curriculum at my high school in Nome was virtually silent about us, our society, and the many issues and challenges we faced as a people caught between two worlds. In fact, educational policy since the turn of the century had been to suppress Native culture and "assimilate" us into the broader society. Everything that was required—everything that had status—in the curriculum was centered on white people and was remarkably like what might have been found anywhere in the U.S.

Many things have changed for the better since my days as a student. Native communities now have some control over their schools, Native cultures are no longer suppressed, and Native students are encouraged to go on to college. But aside from a few Native studies programs, the standard curriculum in Alaska's rural schools is much the same as it has always been. I'm not suggesting that Native students should bypass American history or other subjects taught throughout the U.S. I am saying that Native students also need a curriculum that teaches them about themselves.

The Native Studies Curriculum Development Project is creating such Native curricula. Native educators and school districts are developing curricula to help Native students not only understand their own histories but also see their cultures as very much alive and capable of grappling with contemporary problems. My own experiences in the school system—as both student and teacher—shed light on why we need such curricula.

As recently as the mid-1970s, the teachers and counselors at my high school in Nome had quite different expectations about the future of white students and of Alaska Native students. In a certain sense, they didn't need to worry much about the future of Native students. At that time, close to half the students from Native villages dropped out well before graduating. And suicide rates among male Native students—like myself—were 10 times higher than among white students. In my own school, students who had died were initially given their own pages in the yearbook, but when so many died that the yearbook was becoming a virtual obituary column, the policy was dropped.

But even for Native students who made it to high school graduation, teachers and counselors generally assumed that we were all best suited for vocational-technical programs—programs that trained us to be secretaries, carpenters, heavy-equipment operators—rather than for college. The only direct counseling I received was to take the military vocational aptitude test, or to become a truck driver. Still, despite the denigration of Alaska Native societies in school, I began to see through the veil of silence about our history and culture. I learned, in places other than school, that we were a courageous and ingenious people who had made a rich life under sometimes inhospitable conditions.

And I was one of the fortunate few Alaska Natives from my generation who went on to college and graduated. I think I succeeded because I had two things that most Native students didn't. I had parents whose love of books gave me the grounding I needed, and I had a friend who believed I could succeed when I wasn't sure myself.

While studying to become a social studies and history teacher at the University of Washington, I discovered the Pacific Northwest collection at the Suzzallo Library. I was amazed to find thousands of volumes written by European and American explorers, linguists, anthropologists, educators, missionaries, and adventurers about the history, culture, and life patterns of Alaska Natives. Until then, I had not realized how much of our history had been written, how much of our lives had been described, and how important we—as a people—were to the rest of the world.

But as I became acquainted with the literature, I was also surprised at what was not included: Alaska Native perspectives about the gold miners, the commercial fisheries, the sale of Alaska, and other critical aspects of Alaskan history. In fact, the perspective of Alaska Natives, particularly during the contact period of modern times, was almost entirely absent.

I became determined to find ways of giving Native students an informed perspective about the circumstances of Iñupiat history and the issues Native people face today. By the early 1980s, when I came back to Northwest Alaska to teach, the recently created Native school board in my district had required that an Iñupiat studies course be added to the curriculum. I was assigned to teach that course, and at first I was puzzled because my Native students often spoke of the Iñupiat in the third person—as "them" rather than "us." Then I realized that all the previous teachers had been non-Natives, and that the students had adopted the teachers' perspective of Natives as "others." One of my first goals became to have my students say "we" and "our" when they talked about Iñupiat—a shift in language that would indicate an implicit change in perspective.

The curriculum guide for the course, prepared primarily by white teachers and administrators, was mostly a "how to" guide for traditional Native crafts like ivory carving, basket making, and skin sewing. The issues important to our people were almost entirely overlooked: there was no coherent picture of continuity, conflict, and transformation by which to understand the Iñupiat community, the region, and the challenges Iñupiat students faced. I radically reorganized the curriculum, shifting the emphasis from arts and crafts to readings, discussions, and investigations about Iñupiat culture and history—from the Iñupiat perspective as well as other perspectives.

The course I modified is still taught in Northwest Alaska. It is a step in the right direction, but it is not enough. As an Alaska Native educator, I want broad Native studies curricula that incorporate an informed Native perspective. I do not want to see curricula that are parodies of who we are or that portray our cultures as things of the past.

In recent years we have begun to break the silence about us in the schools. We ask that the next generation of Alaska Native students be able to attend schools where our history and our societies are included in lessons about people, history, and the world. We believe the Native Studies Curriculum Development Project will help us reach that goal.

EDUCATION AND
THE SUBSISTENCE WAY
OF LIFE

Art Davidson and Harold Napoleon

Originally published as a chapter in
Does One Way of Life Have to Die So Another Can Live?
(Bethel, Alaska: Yupiktak Bista, 1974)

The Yukon-Kuskokwim Region is considered the most "backward" in Alaska and as such stands a chance of preserving its culture through the educational system. It is our intent that by incorporating the study and practice of our culture in our schools we can save this culture from which we come. It is our conviction that the Yupik way of life can be saved and only our young can save it.

—Harold Napoleon, 1974

WHAT KIND OF EDUCATION will prepare our children for the uncertain future that lies ahead? How can education give them the options to strike their own balance in living on a combined subsistence and cash economy? How can we prepare our children to meet the unpredictable and difficult circumstances of the rapidly changing world?

We did not always have these problems of the meaning and purpose and approach to education. Before the erection of school houses and the introduction of professional teachers to whom Western civilization entrusts the minds of their children, education was growing up in a village. Education was done in the home with the father, mother, grandmother, grandfather, brother and sister, uncles, aunts, cousins, and friends. Education was also given by the weather, the sea, the fish, the animals, and the land. Children at a very early age came to terms with the elements. We did not have to worry about relating education to life, because learning came naturally as a part of living. Education was the process of living from the land, of subsisting, of surviving.

The coming of Western civilization broke this unity of education and living. Suddenly survival depended upon knowing a new language, new skills, and new ways of relating to people and the world. Today we have entrusted the minds of our young to professional teachers who seemingly know all there is to know. They are teaching a child how to read, write, repair a car, weld two pipes together. But they are not teaching the child the most important thing. Who he is: an Eskimo or Indian with a history full of folklore, music, great men, medicine, a philosophy, complete with poets; in short, there was a civilization, a culture which survived the harshest of environments for thousands of years. Now this culture and the subsistence way of life are being swept away by books, patents, money, and corporations.

It is not our intent to wage war on Western civilization. We merely want to come to terms with it—on our own grounds. We do not dislike Western civilization or the White Man. We simply treasure our young and our culture. It is our belief that both can live together side-by-side, but not necessarily eating out of the same bowl. We can share potlatches and Christmas together.

Most parents see school as a necessary and vital thing if their children are going to share and take part in the Western way of life. If we are to control our own lives and run our own affairs we must each know the ways of the dominant culture. And we must have well-educated leaders who can look after the interests of the Yupik people. But the shortcomings of the present educational system have to be recognized.

When formal education began in this region in 1886 with the first Moravian mission, people began giving up some of the mobility of the subsistence pattern of living. In order to be near the school, they had to forgo some traveling to hunting and fishing camps. But even though people have become well settled in villages all of which have schools, the achievement rate for Native children has remained far below the national average. In 1960 the average educational achievement level in this region was only 2.6 years. By 1970, the average had risen to 4.6 years.

Underlying the high dropout rate and absenteeism among students is the fact that school is an alien atmosphere for the children. Well over 90 percent of the Native students in this region enter school speaking Yupik Eskimo which is spoken within the family as well as throughout the entire community life. Their lives become ordered by the ringing of bells and the calling of roll. They begin learning about buses, cows and chickens, Thanksgiving, baseball, and spaceships; all of which may be interesting, but are nevertheless foreign to the village. Parents within this region have stated over and over again that acculturation and adjustment to Western society is not and cannot be a goal of education. However, a student's adjustment to the school environment demands acculturation which in turn represents a loss of traditional values and increased isolation from his own culture.

Look at the children at the age of five or six when they begin going to school to learn their ABCs from the adventures of Dick and Jane and their sense of history from the lives of George Washington, Franklin Roosevelt, and Richard Nixon. The young children cannot identify with this way of living and these people. And so, as they are being prepared to go out into the world, they begin to lose a sense of their own identity, their own place and person.

This process of alienation continues and even accelerates when the children reach high school age. To attend high school they are usually away from their home most of the year. Their courses are designed to prepare them to go on to college and then on to various careers and professions. They are oriented toward finding the best-paying jobs. Their lives become organized to the clock, the working day instead of the routines of living in a village.

Although the modern education system can give the children many skills that will be valuable, the process is usually very hard on them. During the time the children are away at school, learning more and more of the skills that it will take for them to live in the cities and become leaders in that world, they are learning less and less about their people and themselves. When they come back educated they are no longer the same children that we once saw leave for school. Some of them return home after so many years and are strangers to their own people. But much worse, they are strangers to themselves.

It has always been difficult for parents to send their children from their village to go to school. Their sadness has been balanced by the belief that this was necessary for their children's future, so they could make their way in a changing world. Now many of these parents are realizing that the education system has a great weakness that is leaving many children unprepared to live either in the village world or the outside world. It doesn't develop and strengthen a child's own self-image and confidence. His education doesn't help him know who he is or where he came from. His education leaves him stranded somewhere between the village way of life of his parents and the white way of life he has been taught in school. He is between two worlds, not really belonging to either.

EDUCATION AND SURVIVAL

Our young people are often not prepared in practical ways to live in either world. Their high school programs supposedly lead to careers and professions, but all too often the young people cannot find jobs. Employment in the region is scarce, with many skilled jobs going to white people who gained experience outside the region. Some young people migrate to the cities where there are more opportunities, only to find they are not prepared for the competition of the wage-earning marketplace.

Likewise, the young people are often not prepared to live in the bush. During their student years they have not been learning all the skills necessary to subsist off the land. One result of their studies has been that many have not had the opportunities to learn how to hunt, fish, prepare food, and make clothing. If subsistence skills are lost, there could be tragic consequences to the Yupik people who have by nature been self-sufficient. People have survived in this region only because they have known how to draw food, clothing, and shelter from the land. In this time we are living now, people are tempted to depend upon money. If a person has one skill that can earn him money, he can go to the store and buy food, buy clothing, buy plywood and two-by-fours to build a house. But there is great danger in this. Inflation is driving up the costs of everything so that one must work more for less. We have also seen that there are sometimes shortages of store-bought things. Sometimes one cannot find the food one needs at the store. Sometimes clothing, fuel, building materials, and other things are not available. If a person knows only how to live from the store, he will be lost if one day the things in the store cost too much or are simply not available. But if the person also knows how to live from the land he will survive.

Until recently only a few radical economists and environmentalists dared suggest that there are limits to growth and wealth, that there could be a world economic crisis. But recently we have heard the President of the United States warn that a recession or depression might come. We hear world leaders warn that the world's economic system may collapse, that there may be widespread famine. But it is not hard to imagine our difficulties if such an economic disaster comes. If storebought supplies become scarce across the nation, our region will probably be one of the first places in which they disappear altogether. If there is nothing in the stores, money will be worthless.

And if money is worthless, the cash-earning skills we have been taught will be worthless. The people who will survive will be the ones who have the skills to live from the land.

As a people and as individuals we must consider very carefully how our education can make us dependent upon the Western economic system, the future of which is unstable at best. If our children are educated just like other children in Anchorage, and Des Moines, Iowa, they will grow to be just as dependent upon the Western economic system. Our children could come to be just as vulnerable as anyone to the fluctuations of the stock market and the whims of Arab oil dealers. But if the education our children receive helps them retain some of the subsistence skills and self-sufficiency of their ancestors, they will carry into the uncertain future tools which may make the difference between surviving and perishing in difficult times.

Subsisting and surviving require different skills in different places. The knowledge one needs to survive in Harlem is different than the knowledge one needs to survive in midwestern farm country. Men living in the jungles of Brazil must know certain things to live in their environment; men living in the highlands of Nepal must know other things. The Yukon-Kuskokwim Delta is a very demanding environment which can seem hostile to those who do not know its ways, but which can provide life to those who know how to live with the land. Education of children in this region should equip them to live with the land.

Even if there is never an economic collapse, subsistence skills and knowledge of the land and waters will be invaluable. Such knowledge will permit Yupik people to live a fuller, richer life. And it will help them use, protect, and manage subsistence resources in the context of the modern world. As long as subsistence resources continue to be the resource base of this region, knowing how to use them and care for them will continue to be extremely important.

Just as important to the subsistence way of living as the skills of hunting and fishing, sewing, and preserving foods are the ways of cooperating and working together. As elaborate as the modern classroom may be, it is still not equipped to really teach children the ways of sharing and helping others that have in the past been learned in the home and village. In fact, the competitive atmosphere of modern schools in many ways works at cross-purposes to the cooperative atmosphere of traditional Eskimo education. This conflict is so fundamental that Pat Locke, a Sioux Indian wise in the ways of both Native and Western education, once said that all the differences between the two processes of education stem from the fact that the purpose of Western education is for the individual to find ways to excel and promote himself, his career, his life; whereas, the purpose of Native education has always been for the individual to find ways to serve his family, be a useful part of his community, to work for and with his people.

In our region, in our past, sharing and cooperation have not been just social niceties. They have been ways of survival. If everyone were just looking out for himself, the Yupik culture would have vanished long ago. It has been through sharing and helping each other that people have survived. Children learned these ways naturally as they grew up in the village. It is a great event when a boy gets his first seal, not just because he has proven himself a hunter but because he has something to share with others. His first seal is divided among people in the village, first to the older people who can no longer get seals themselves.

Frank Nokozak has related how he learned the ways of sharing and helping others: (John Paul Jones interpreting):

> You know what the older people used to do for him? They would share their things with the people who did not have them. He did this for the people who did not have . . . When the people come to his place, he gives them food. People go to his home to ask for dried fish. He gives dry fish to those people because they need it. He said he wouldn't be like that if it wasn't for his dad who used to tell him to always be kind and give to the people who do not have. His dad used to tell him to be that way because you only live once. The people are born in one time and die. He repeated that it was his dad that taught him always to be kind and share. (Testimony, D02 Land Hearings, Federal-State Land Use Planning Commission, 1973)

The classrooms can neither teach the skills nor impart the values and character which link the children to the subsistence way of life of their culture.

BUILDING A NEW WAY OF EDUCATION

The process of young people losing their identity and not being prepared to cope with life is costing us many young people each year. And each year our young people seem a little less self-sufficient, a little less able to live from the land. These problems have been growing since our first contact with whalers, traders, and missionaries. How can they be dealt with? We do not have ready-made solutions. But we do have a starting point and a direction in which to head. To make education more meaningful for our children we must start with our people in the villages and proceed to develop an educational process that combines the learning of ABC's and algebra with our traditional values, skills, and ways of living and learning.

To begin developing this type of learning process, Yupiktak Bista started in the spring of 1974 a Cultural Heritage Program in which students at the Bethel and St. Mary's high schools returned to villages for two weeks. During this period, older people in the village taught the students their own history and traditional skills. A live-in learning experience was chosen over a "Native studies" course because such courses set students up as observers much the same way a bird-watcher studies a bird or an anthropologist studies a culture. If the student is just a watcher, he remains inactive when he should be an active participant and he can actually become further disassociated from himself and his culture. Only by "living" his own culture will a student come to appreciate, understand, and be a part of it.

In describing the Cultural Heritage Program to some students, Peter Atchak, who helped get the program started, once said:

> When you get to a village the older people will tell you stories about how things were a long time ago. The women will teach the girls how to be women. And the men will teach the boys how to be men.

So it was that students went out to villages, often not their home villages, to live with foster parents who could teach them traditional ways. As the following comments by the students reveal, it was quite an experience for them. A boy who went to Hooper Bay said:

> Activities I participated in were the Eskimo dance and telling stories to the old people (testing my skills, whether I knew or not the stories they told me; they let me do the talking the day after they talk). What I made during the cultural heritage program was the spear, the spear handle, fish hook spear, fish hook spear handle, ivory ring, a model seal out of soap stone, a parka, water boots out of seal skin, and information about how to make sleds, boats, and drawings of the old. The new skills I learned were to balance on top of the wavy sea in a kayak, and throw a

spear without tipping over and a lot about hunting in the sea with just the kayak.

Man, it was all right! Because they were open to me as well as to my friends who went down to Hooper Bay. I would like to go back to a village where I stayed. And I was just getting dreaming with the old people. They brought me to their world. They let me feel I was old when I got out of their stories.

Another boy summed up his experiences in Toksook Bay by saying:

All of these projects were of an advantage to me, cause I have never really gotten into Eskimo culture. Now I have a brief meaning of how survival takes place, what skills were needed to become a man, and how to make things to live off of.

Staff of the Kuskokwim Health Corporation said:

Especially noteworthy to us has been the reaction of the students and dormitory parents to the First Cultural Heritage Program. At a time when Bethel was experiencing some pre-breakup behavior the high school students returned enthusiastic and in a positive frame of mind. Therefore, we would encourage the continuation of such a stimulating program with many desirable mental health consequences.

The high school nurse was another person who noticed a change in attitude and outlook on life. Peggy McMahon said:

In working with the high school students as their nurse, I have been able to observe their behavior and attitudes throughout the school year. As always, the first semester of school started out with high enthusiasm in both teachers and students. However, there seemed to be a real let-down in spirit after the Christmas vacation. Class attendance seemed to drop and I found many more students in my clinic with vague physical complaints and emotional problems. It seemed that many students were using the excuse of going to the nurse's clinic, but just wanted to talk to someone about their restlessness with school and desire to go home. More than the usual number of students seemed to be down during the months of January, February, and March. I think the introduction of the First Cultural Heritage Program at this time was valuable. It came at the end of the third quarter when spirits were especially low. I know that I was having difficulty dealing with the negative and demanding attitudes and behavior of many of the students during February and March. The Cultural Heritage Program seemed to give everyone a chance to learn different things and in a different setting than the school building. The first week after the Program I found that the students seemed happier, less demanding and better able to cope with some of their problems than they were before the two-week program.

Some of the strongest reactions to the Cultural Heritage Program came from the parents and old people who had worked with the students. Hilma Shavings from Mekoryuk said she felt this approach to education was

very important for our children, since a lot of our children are losing their own culture. I feel this program is a little bit of a beginning for our kids to see how their ancestors live to survive in this land that white man would call harsh country. I feel this should be an ongoing program because even my own kids don't know how we have lived. They haven't seen the houses we used to live in. My own girl, that's going to Junior College, doesn't know how to sew how we do . . . I think this cultural heritage program will help the students. You never know what they might run into during their lifetime. At least, in case they run into some hardships they'll know how to make their own things. If it's a girl, make their own clothes and sewing and things like that. If it were a man, at least he will know how to survive if he was out on the tundra. You'll never know with all these traveling by snowmachines, airplanes, outboard motors, if you'll get to your destination. At least they should know how to survive without having to depend on these conveniences all the time.

Also emphasizing the importance of knowing traditional skills was Andrew Brown of Mountain. Village:

This program was one of the best things that ever happened in this area. The things our forefathers used to do is too good of a thing to let it phase out. Who knows when the things the students learn might be the ones for survival in case of emergency or anything that will cut us off from the outside world. It could be for a short time or for a long period. Our land can still provide us clothing and food. Our young people should learn how to tackle with these things. Our culture is phasing out. Right now is the time to revive it back.

In Chevak, David Friday said:

I've been home for a long time and I was home during the time the St. Mary's students and Bethel Regional High School students were at home and most of the people participated with the Cultural Heritage Program. Because of what's been happening some of these people haven't been doing these things. Then all of a sudden this Cultural Heritage Program came to the people. It made an impression on me that these people are learning that their culture is cool. I think this Cultural Heritage Program helped the people out in the villages too. Some of them dug up cultures from the past to teach these children. They are the type of people, I think, that are caught between two cultures. They don't know what to do or how to make a living because they are confused. I think with this program, it helped find themselves in a situation where some of these people weren't really too certain of who they really are, their real selves, where they'd be satisfied and happy about it . . . There was a comment from an old man who said, "I don't want to pass this life unless I pass my knowledge to another younger person." I think this Cultural Heritage Program has opened that door to many of our people.

The Cultural Heritage Program is not meant to turn back the clock, to prepare young people to live just as their ancestors did. Its purpose is to begin building a new educational process which will be based on our way of life. The value of passing on traditional ways is not because it is a way to turn from the present world, but because it simply offers young people the best hope of making their way into a troubled and uncertain future. Knowing the ways of their Yupik ancestors offers young people the invaluable qualities of self-confidence, self-reliance, and the ability to live from the land should they choose to or should this become necessary for survival.

Modern education reflects the ways that Western civilization appears to have lost its way and no longer makes any sense. But we are now tied to this dominant culture. We must know its ways; we must have the necessary tools to cope with its problems and make use of its opportunities. So it is, that to find ourselves as individuals and as a people and make our way into the future, we will need the knowledge and ways of learning of our heritage and also the skills and knowledge of Western civilization.

How can a new process of education that draws from both cultures be created? What policy and institutional changes must be made? How will new curriculum, methods, and teachers be introduced? These are not easily answered questions.

The difficulties of bringing about change in the entrenched educational system are many, but our experience with programs like the Cultural Heritage live-in has shown us that they are not impossible to overcome. And the basis for change toward an educational process combining two cultures must be an appreciation and acceptance of multicultural equality. In education, multiracial equality recognizes that Native students are still Native people. Many of them may prefer to speak the language of their people and to live in villages as hunters, fishermen, wives, and mothers, rather than enter the competitive and materialistic life of the cities. Their education should prepare them for this way of life. It should not, as the present system does, cut off this option. And all of our children, even those who go on to college and professions beyond our region, need to know their roots in the subsistence way of life of the Delta in order to know themselves. So it is that the education of all our young people must include learning some of the old ways and learning how to subsist on the Delta today.

Multicultural equality implies that parents and grandparents should be involved in the educational process, as teachers, advisors, counselors, administrators, and school board members. A man or woman who has lived in a village all their life and perhaps has never gone to high school may nevertheless have more meaningful ideas about high school education on the Delta than a professor armed with degrees and years of experience.

The wisdom of our old people should be respected at least as much as the knowledge of the schoolteacher. Each finds within himself a balance between the elements of these two heritages and ways of life. Education should help keep options open for young people to live different kinds of lifestyles. The classrooms should not close the doors on the subsistence way of life that has been a good way of life for the Yupik people for thousands of years.

Alaska's Cultures

Building a Context for Stories and Traditions

Paul Ongtooguk

THE HUMAN HISTORY OF ALASKA begins many thousands of years ago. The oral traditions, legends, and stories about the early era of human existence in Alaska are rich, varied, and sometimes surprising.

Books written by researchers, texts written by visitors, and photographs describe the dress, food, crafts, and tools used in the lives of the many original peoples of Alaska. But this essay is a description of a few of the underlying beliefs of many Native peoples. It can provide a context to better understand traditional times.

Alaska Native societies had much in common, even though they differed in languages, clothing, dance, social organization, political structures, and foods. The physical nature of Alaska required a community approach to creating a life and society on this land. Extended families and hunting partners were vital to survival. Extended communities were made up of several families.

Legends, oral traditions, and stories give us a glimpse into how important it was in traditional Alaska Native societies to learn to share with others, to work hard, and to value wisdom. In the old times, Alaska Native cultures say that humans were closer to animals, and better able to understand their animal wisdom, humor, and sometimes dangerous personalities. From these creatures humans could learn how animal and human natures shared.

Some creatures have not been described by modern science, such as huge eagles and 10-legged polar bears. But some Alaska Native groups connect mammoth tusks and other remains of prehistoric creatures to the past and their understanding of the natural world. It is easy upon first hearing or reading these stories, legends, and oral traditions to dismiss them as superstition. Much is also lost when a story is translated from its original language.

It is a very different experience when stories and legends are encountered closer to their original context. The home place for a story might be a room with several Elders after they have been served first in a community meal of local foods. Some of the foods may be from large animals and common plants. Other foods are less common and are served not only for calories of energy but for the vitamins and minerals they provide. They too were part of the traditional Native diet long before they were described by modern science. Some foods are simply eaten as rare treats. Mountain goat, Dall sheep, certain bird and fish eggs, the roots of certain plants, the smaller parts of certain sea mammals, the taste of plants as flavoring in hot drinks, or the marrow from the bone of creatures are served at certain times and in certain places.

Sometimes the Elders are wearing clothes or holding ceremonial objects that represent the unique wealth of the waters and lands around the communities. They might have rare items brought in by trade with neighboring tribes. Clothes might include the tails of weasels or the fur of certain mountain rodents, sheep, or goats. These pieces were not easy to gather nor to create, as part of elaborately designed and sewn pieces.

In many places and among many Alaska Native people the time of stories might have included several traditional social and specific story dances. These dances were, and still are, a part of the inheritance of families, houses or clans, communities, or as part of the legacy of a region. The instruments used, tone and form of singing, structures, and themes varied by peoples and cultures. The roles of children, women, men, the time of year, and the event shaped why a certain dance was performed and by whom.

Imagining such gatherings will help you better understand the stories, legends, oral traditions, and lifestyles of Alaska Native people. The stories are not only about something out there and separate from you, but can be about something that is a part of you too.

PART V

STRENGTHENING NATIVE LANGUAGES

——◆◆✕◆◆——

&&The survival and revival of Indigenous languages is imperative for the protection, transmission, maintenance and preservation of Indigenous knowledge, cultural values, and wisdom.&&

From the *Coolongatta Statement on Indigenous Rights in Education*

I WILL SPEAK AGAIN!

Cecilia R. Martz

Presented at the 15th Annual Alaska Anthropological Association Meeting, Fairbanks, March 25–26, 1988

FEW LANGUAGE PROGRAMS have been successful in overcoming the suppression of Native languages that took place in the schools over the past 80 years. I remember my own personal experiences of being punished when I spoke my own language, Cup'ik, in the school. When I first went to school at the prime age of four, I did not have knowledge of even one English word in my whole vocabulary. Yet, without any English instruction, I was required to say a full English sentence. The teacher was an Eskimo woman who taught all grades. She called me up one day after school to tell me I needed to say one English sentence every day like the other students. So I learned one sentence that caused me to rush home every day after school so I would not get beaten up by my sister. That one sentence was, "My sister always chews tobacco." I used that sentence for several months because I knew no other English.

After being expelled from school for being too young, I re-enrolled at age seven. I had my former teacher for one year and after that 99 percent of my teachers were Caucasians. During my third grade, I was sent to St. Mary's Mission as a boarding student. My knowledge of Cup'ik was extensive by that time. I knew all my prayers, songs, dances, stories, rules and regulations of living, Cup'ik social context words, everyday living words, and I could count up to 999. I could read and write Cup'ik using the old Catholic missionary orthography.

When I arrived at St. Mary's Mission, I was told I had to go to confession in English, write letters home in English, speak English to the authorities in and out of school hours, and learn my religion in English. The only times I could relax and use my own language were during the free periods when I was with friends, when I was thinking my own thoughts, and when I was dreaming during sleep. My Cup'ik language level stayed about the same with some loss. As I advanced through the grades, my own language suffered. I started forgetting. The only radical thing I did was to start writing letters in Cup'ik to my dad.

After high school I went away to college and spoke English for nine months straight. My language suffered the most then.

Now after having worked for about 10 years in education, and having seen and explored different language programs, my determination to maintain language learning in the village is stronger than ever.

While teaching conversational Yup'ik to nonspeakers at a community college, we found a language learning method called Total Physical Response. This is the method we have found to be closest to learning a language naturally.

Example: When our baby was still in diapers, I would tell him to "*Qurrailitameng aqvaten.*" He was barely one year old. He would amble off and get a diaper. I would say, "*Quyana!*" when he handed it to me. Then I would say, "*Inarriuten,*" and he would lie down to be changed. While changing him, I would be saying things like "*uugun aug'arluku,*" "*yuutuku,*" "*assilriamen cimirluku,*" and "*tauga.*" Afterwards I would say to him, "*trash-aamun egglukuku*" and he would throw it away. The little child understood everything I said and followed my directions, but he could not say any of the words I was using. Right now he can say them fairly well. By the time he was three years old, he had heard those words five times a day, seven days a week, 52 weeks a year for three years. He'd heard them at least 21,840 times. He also heard other words, sentences, phrases, and exclamations in everyday life 21,840 times. In most cases, he would have an action attached to the words and most of the time the action was a command given to him by someone else.

This is an example of learning a language through the Total Physical Response method, in which there is more retention of the language being taught.

In a village like my hometown of Chevak, where the Cup'ik speakers are still abundant, but are nonetheless losing ground, a TPR method of language instruction is the most effective way to retain the language. Kindergarten through third grade should use the TPR method of teaching a language, with the difficulty of the lessons increasing with higher grades.

In the fourth to sixth grades, a maintenance program that focuses on oral language skills should be established. Looking back at my Cup'ik experience, I recall one very successful method. While we were growing up, we learned songs, games, and sayings associated with inorganic and organic objects in our everyday lives. We learned these from older children. These were also taught to us in context by older people. There are hundreds of these songs, rhymes, games, and sayings that can be collected, sequenced, and made into lesson plans by appropriate people.

Examples include:

- Jumping rope and singing in time to *"Luugumaa ayaagumaa tartumayaqumaa . . ."*
- Hand games such as *"Cuuki, cuuki amaqucuk talliqucuk—kaq!"*
- Sayings such as *"Qaqaqaqa unuaqu quuniryunilkuvet mayuariua irniaten kaugtuaryarturciqanka,"* when a certain bird is heard overhead
- Finger play such as *"Qiliqiliaraqa, qiliqa, qaquqa, tengayuka, kuluka"*

Another method to use is miniature family dolls. These miniature dolls include a set of parents, two or more children, a set of grandparents, and household items. These doll sets were only used after the arrival of the first snow geese in the spring. As I grew up I learned about kinship structure and terms, life and death, visiting procedures, interactional patterns, subsistence activities, animals and food preparation, seasonal activities, and much more through countless hours of play with these dolls. Using this method, a group of students could develop their own soap operas with these dolls all the while reinforcing the complex network of social and cultural values that are an essential part of any language. They could only be used for a short period right before the end of the school year in the spring after the first snow geese arrived, but children would be encouraged to take them home and play during the summer until the first snowfall required that they be put away.

During the winter, when miniature dolls are forbidden, a *qucgutaq* method could be used in the classrooms. Snow or sand could be brought into the classes and this method used on different occasions depending on the lessons. The process is different from the miniature dolls, but the learning content is the same. These students would also be involved in simple drama, theater, and dance using the stories, legends, and songs that are so abundant in Cup'ik culture.

Written words could be introduced without the students realizing it. Not only are we teaching oral skills, but many other skills that the students are not aware of learning. To me, that is the best form of learning because it results in longer memory retention and it is not forced or mandatory like math and English. All of the above focuses on developing and maintaining oral skills in the language.

For the seventh and eighth grades, a more sophisticated and difficult program would be introduced including reading and writing. An adult literacy program can be linked with this group. Since both the students and the adults would be starting at the same level, they could help each other, with the adults having a more extensive vocabulary and experience to add to that of the students. Since these students are a bit more sophisticated, they could also have Cup'ik speech contests. There are some Cup'ik stories that have been passed down through the ages unchanged, even to the exactness of inflections and pauses. After learning these stories, the students will have to say them exactly the way the stories were told many years ago. The judges would be some Elders in the village.

These students would also get translating and interpreting training which would include actual translating where appropriate, such as during church services. The students would know when they graduate to more difficult assignments that they are on their way to becoming fluent speakers.

Such a program cannot be expected to succeed simply by placing a Cup'ik speaker as a teacher, however. Prospective teachers should be carefully screened and complete a comprehensive TPR method training program before actually beginning to teach. Also further training should be provided for maintenance in line with the rate of difficulty of the lessons. Additionally, these teachers need to be carefully instructed in using cultural materials in the classroom.

Kass'aqs talk about evaluation for any program. For the K–3 program the evaluation is already built in. If a student does not follow through with the TPR commands, he/she has not mastered the lesson.

For the 4–6 program, the ability to verbalize the many sayings, games, stories, roles in theater, dances, and songs would be the basis for their evaluation.

For the higher grades, the speeches, the writing, and memory would be the evaluative measures.

It is my belief that without community involvement, language programs will not succeed. It is imperative that adults be involved in such a way that they come to realize there are benefits for them that go beyond the monetary one resulting from their work as "resource persons."

Language programs will not succeed if the community, school, churches, and other service agencies do not consider them important. The community as a whole has to decide what is important. The language programs, if they take place in the school, will need knowledgeable people as supervisors and as board members, not just because the programs mandate it, but because they, as educators and as community members, consider it important. The community needs to know what is happening to other languages as well as what is happening in their own village with their own language.

One very important key to making language programs succeed is the person hired to carry out the wishes of the community. That person has to organize the program components in such a way that they become visible and necessary, because if a program's end results are not needed, it is already headed for failure. The person who is selected to carry out the program has to have certain qualifications. He/she has to know the status of Alaska Native languages in general, read and write in his/her own language, and have deep fluency and grammatical knowledge of his/her own language. This person should have teaching skills in his/her own culture as well as teaching skills in the *kass'aq* world, knowledge of specific content areas and skills in curriculum development, both in the *kass'aq* and in his/her own cultural ways. I could go on and on about the qualifications. Perhaps most important of all, that person must have an oversupply of energy, hope, and vision.

I can see a flourishing language in my village and other villages in the next five to ten years if instructional programs such as those I have described were to come into existence.

LANGUAGE TEACHING RESOURCES

Asher, J. 1982 Learning another language through actions. *The Complete Teacher's Guidebook*. Sky Oaks Productions, Inc.

Fitzhugh, W., and S. Kaplan. 1982 *Inua, the spirit world of the Bering Sea Eskimos*. Washington, D.C.: Smithsonian Inst. Press.

Krasher, S. 1983 *The natural approach*. West Hayward, CA: The Alemany Press.

Krauss, M. 1980 *Alaska Native languages: Past, present, and future*. Fairbanks: University of Alaska.

Mather, E. 1985 "*Cauyarnariuq*", Bethel: LKSD.

Stevick, E. 1980 *Teaching languages, A way and ways*. Rawley, MA: Newberry House Publishers.

COLLABORATION IN EDUCATION

Ayaprun Loddie Jones

Keynote speech, Alaska Native Education Council Conference,
Anchorage, October 9, 1998

My PARENTS WERE MY FIRST TEACHERS and they made me very knowledgeable of my Yup'ik culture. They collaborated in my educational upbringing, each one knowing their specific roles. My father was the head of the household, sheltering, feeding, and loving all the 13 children in the family. My mother's role was to raise the family, take care of Dad's catch, and model what a mother should be. They taught us in our first language, Yup'ik. Together they taught us, using the traditional methods where our mother talked to us every morning about what to do and what not to do. She used the traditional discipline method, but never raised her voice and my father never intruded, but gave his support.

What are the discipline policies in the schools doing to our children? Those of us who were raised by our elderly parents know that the Western schools are doing the opposite of what our parents did. Our children don't show a lot of respect anymore, one reason being that the working mothers have turned them over to be raised by a line-up of babysitters.

To follow up on the roles my parents had, I'll tell a story about the time that my family and I came back from a long, tiring day of berry-picking. Just before we had dinner, my mother said, *"Kitak tauna neqliurru,"* meaning "Get your husband's plate ready." Without thinking I responded, *"Atam ellminek piyumauq,"* "Oh, he gets his own food!" My mother got up and said, *"Takumni pingaituq,"* "Not while I'm around," and she gave a plate of food to my husband. My husband said, "See!" and he looked like he had just made the winning touchdown of a Super Bowl game! In this day and age, most women have jobs and their roles seem to be reversed.

For my teacher preparation I was trained in a field-based teacher preparation program called the Alaska Rural Teacher Training Corp. There are a lot of professionals, principals, etc. from the other culture who gave me the confidence and belief that I can be a good teacher and who believed in me. They also helped raise my self-esteem and helped me seek to improve myself.

We, the Native speakers, were trained in the Western school system. Why can't there be collaboration and have the teachers be trained in our culture and language? When the missionaries had to reach and convert their Native followers, a lot of them learned our languages.

We have to have pride in what was given to us by our parents. Every year we are losing our most precious and important resources—our Elders. What a fine gift it would be to give the gift of our Native tongue back through our Yup'ik-speaking young people. I feel proud to be involved in the Yup'ik Immersion Program. At least this community knows the importance of retaining our language and culture.

In this day and age there are too many controversial issues facing our lives, both in our communities and in our schools. We must get self-esteem and pride back into our children, or else we'll keep losing them to drugs, alcohol and finally suicide. Let's work together and aim for one goal—the happiness of our young people.

I will end the speech with the following story.

> There were two people who had bought a new outboard motor and were out hunting. All of a sudden the outboard motor fell into the water because it wasn't securely fastened to the boat. The two waited a while, hopeful that more hunters would pass by and help them, but no one came by. Finally one of them said, "I'm going down to check on the motor," so he took off his clothes and dove under. After a while the second person was wondering why his partner never surfaced and finally looked down, where he saw his partner trying to start the motor under water. He hollered down to him, "Hey, why don't you choke it first?"

No matter how much we seem to be drowning in our jobs as educators, let's work for the well-being, success, and future of our children!

Evolution of the Yup'ik Language

Oscar F. Alexie and Gerald S. Domnick

Paper Presented at the 13th Annual Meeting of the Alaska
Anthropological Association, March 7–8, 1986, Fairbanks, Alaska

VERY LITTLE ABOUT OUR cultures remains constant. We are ceaselessly adapting to an ever-changing physical and social environment. The flexibility of cultures is demonstrated by the many forms in which they are found throughout the world—as diverse as the physical environments in which they are found. Indeed, it is the relative ability of a culture to adapt to new challenges that is often used to judge its health and vitality. A culture that cannot readily adapt to new demands that are placed on it is usually doomed to extinction.

As a major part of culture, language shares many of its characteristics. In order to survive and prosper, a language must be able to readily adapt to new objects and concepts that its users create or ones that they adopt from other languages/cultures. A language that cannot or is not allowed to serve the communication needs of its users will die. Adaptation occurs by either creating brand-new words (often by employing material already present in the language) or by borrowing and/or modifying another culture's word for the concept to fit into the new language. Borrowed words are often adapted, both phonologically and in meaning, to the point where they are unrecognizable to a speaker from the contributing language. Despite this introduction of "foreign" material, the language almost always retains its own unique identity. The English Language, despite the massive amounts of borrowed words, has remained solidly English in character.

Central Yup'ik (hereafter referred to as "Yup'ik"), along with other Alaska Native languages, has been no exception to this process and has been resilient in adapting to the multitude of new objects and concepts introduced by other cultures, and by Western culture, specifically, over the past 200 years. Yup'ik people have borrowed words traceable to Iñupiaq, Aleut, Chukchi, Athapascan, Russian, English, Saami, and other languages (Jacobson, 1984). Until recently, this borrowing apparently occurred, as is usually the case with all languages, without disturbing the basic nature of Yup'ik.

The first major and lasting contact with Western European culture came with the advent of the Russians in the 18th century. As a result of this contact, and with the introduction of many new material goods, as well as Christianity, Yup'ik acquired about 190 borrowed words from the Russian language (Michael, 1967).

Initially, the presence of the Americans had about the same effect on the language and culture of the Yup'ik people as did the Russians. Missionaries came, albeit of different sects, and material goods continued to be introduced. The language continued to successfully adapt to new influences as it always had. However, changes were soon to occur that would eventually have more severe impacts on the language. The American legal, governmental, and educational systems were extended over the Yup'ik lands to an extent that had never occurred under Russian influence. The Yup'ik people found themselves compelled to follow the dictates of these institutions and to participate in their proceedings. Beginning in the latter half of the 19th century and continuing throughout the 20th century up to the present, Western civilization experienced an industrial and technological revolution that generated huge numbers of new implements and other material goods, many of which were quickly embraced by the Yup'ik people. The advancement of Western science brought improvements in medicine that also found their way to Southwest Alaska. Each of these influxes brought with it a whole array of new terminology that was specific to that subject area. Hundreds, if not thousands, of new concepts and tools that had no word equivalent in Yup'ik began to be introduced into use in Southwest Alaska. On top of this came a huge influx of immigrants into Alaska, especially after the 1960s.

The effect of all this on language usage in Southwest Alaska is worthy of further examination. In the Russian period, there were relatively few Russians in Southwest Alaska at any one time. They were always a small minority of the population. Interactions with Native people were largely confined to trading posts and rarely went beyond trade and missionary work.

Thus, there was never any reason for most people to learn Russian. Only certain people, often creoles or those otherwise more heavily involved with trade, would be relied on as interpreters by both parties involved (Eastman, 1983). In reality, it was probably more pressing for the Russians to learn Yup'ik, the language of the people on whom they relied for their economic livelihood and even survival. For most Yup'ik people, it was sufficient to absorb a few words for new items received through trade, such as coffee, tea, flour. Yup'ik was still the language most suited for life in that area.

This situation remained for the early American period also. Many early missionaries learned to speak Yup'ik as a matter of necessity. By the mid-20th century, many of these conditions had changed. The newcomers to the area no longer depended so heavily on the Native people for existence. The situation reversed itself as people adopted new technologies and became involved in the institutions of Alaska and of the United States. English began to become more and more the "language of survival." This, along with a policy of Native language suppression practiced by the government, undoubtedly dealt the language a serious blow and affected its ability to adapt to new concepts.

Since time immemorial, Yup'ik had easily adapted to new concepts, but during the middle of the 20th century and continuing up to the present day, another trend has made itself evident. As time progresses, a larger and larger percentage of Yup'iks are becoming functional in English. As new items are introduced into the culture, occurrences of new "Yup'ik" words being created seem to be more and more rare. There is a definite lag in the development of new terms. Witness the word "*icarcuun*" (literally, device for writing). The term was initially used for referring to pens and pencils—an application that worked quite well. Later came along the typewriter and the same word was applied to it. Later yet came the electronic typewriter and now there are computer word processors. There are no specific terms for each of these instruments. They are all called an *igarcuun* in Yup'ik, or the English word is used. New terms are sometimes created but they often vary from region to region, village to village, or even person to person. This leads to confusion and frustration when trying to use them. The usual solution is that a term such as "preliminary hearing" ends up having to be described at length or, more commonly, the English word is simply inserted intact into the Yup'ik sentence. Borrowed words are no longer adapted into Yup'ik, but are absorbed intact. These "solutions" are unacceptable to many Yup'ik people for several reasons:

1. Having to interpret one English term using a lengthy Yup'ik explanation is a tremendous burden for interpreters in a courtroom,

hospital, or other serious situation and often results in mistranslation and misunderstanding.

2. Simply inserting an English word into a Yup'ik sentence often still leaves the Yup'ik-dominant speaker in the dark as to what the word means. (A comparable situation would be how understandable the sentence "He became *'cumilnguq'* when I told him" would be to the average American.) There are still a large number of people who are monolingual in Yup'ik. There are a multitude of others whose dominant language is Yup'ik and whose command of English is extremely limited, especially in technical areas. For these people, inserting English words does nothing to facilitate understanding.

3. As cultural pride increases, many Yup'iks grow concerned by the ever-increasing amount of these wholly imported English words in everyday Yup'ik language speech, accompanied by a decrease in the amount of Yup'ik words. This, as time goes by, makes speaking Yup'ik less and less practical in everyday life.

The situation that is faced by Yup'ik people is not a unique one. There are scores of languages that find themselves faced with a similar dilemma. Relatively few languages in the world have totally adapted themselves to the scientific and bureaucratic world. With a growing awareness of the field of language planning, peoples of the world have also come to realize that it is not necessary to wait for language change to occur naturally. Many nations have full-time commissions/academies whose sole function is language cultivation (Eastman, 1983). The Native peoples of Alaska are witnesses to the fact that deliberate policies can be created and implemented to affect language use, having direct experience with the policy of language eradication that was all too successfully carried out.

One tool that can be used for lexical modernization is the "word conference." In a nutshell, the word conference is a gathering of several speakers of the language, representing various locales, to deliberately and conscientiously come up with clear, concise terms in the target language for items that do not already exist in it. The Yup'ik Language Center of Kuskokwim Campus was first introduced to the idea when attempting to set up a program to train interpreters and translators for courtroom, hospital, and government situations—a need long recognized in the area. The challenge that immediately reared its head was that of finding Yup'ik words that could be used for the many technical terms in these fields. We came in contact with the Department of Information of the Northwest Territories in Canada. At that time, they had a functioning interpreter/translator corps which was staffed by well-trained interpreters/translators. They willingly offered us any advice and materials that they had to help us set up our own program. They too were facing the dilemma of lexical modernization, but they felt that they were adequately dealing with the problem on a continuous basis with the use of word conferences. After a series of demonstrations, we quickly decided to adopt the method and modify it to our specific needs.

We recognized that the use of the word conference allowed for public input from the Yup'ik people and gave an inroad to legitimacy. Legitimacy of the terms in the eyes of the people was something that was always in the back of our minds during the entire process. YLC staff could just as easily and much more cheaply have sat down and created perfectly acceptable terms ourselves. Using this route, however, would probably cause people to not accept and use the terms, perhaps resenting someone else trying to tell them what kind of word to use for what.

Another difficulty partially addressed by the use of word conferences was that caused by dialect differences. Central Yup'ik has several distinct dialects whose users have strong feelings of pride toward their own particular dialect and, in many, a very natural feeling that their particular manner of speech is perhaps a little better or "more normal" than others. Keeping in mind that intense feelings of dialectal competition could end up being very destructive to language cultivation, we made great effort to make sure that all of the major dialects were represented. Reducing dialect competition would help in limiting the amount of terms finally arrived at. We felt that it was important to have one term/phrase that everyone would recognize and accept. The fewer words that everyone was using for a particular object or concept, the better chance there would be of having them accepted. It would also make it easier for interpreters if they didn't have to stop to consider which one of many words to use in a serious interpreting situation. As it turned out, it was not as difficult of a problem to solve as we had expected. It was brought out and unanimously agreed upon by conference participants that it was better to accept a new Yup'ik word from another dialect than to gain another new English word.

There were several other decisions made that affected how the conference was to be put together and run. Again, for legitimacy reasons, we also decided to rotate the villages every so often from which the representatives came. This would insure the widest amount of participation. Those villages not directly participating in a particular conference would receive a copy of the terms decided upon and would have an opportunity for comment. Associating the whole process with a known and respected institution like the college also gave inroads into acceptance. On recommendation from a

YLC staff member, we attempted to recruit Elders or middle-aged people with an extra-good command of the language. He suggested that these people would be aware of many older descriptive terms and usages not currently in everyday use and that many of these would more accurately describe the concepts we were working with. This later proved to be true.

Good material preparation for the conferences proved to be an absolute necessity. Staff attended public meetings, court sessions, and medical-related meetings and made note of commonly used terms that might present problems when being translated into Yup'ik. They then met with professionals from those fields to make sure that the proper contextual meaning for each word was understood (a local lawyer, for example, volunteered to help us with legal terms). During these meetings, the professionals also contributed other words that were missing from our list that they felt should be included and helped us prioritize the list that we had already gathered.

The conferences themselves lasted for three full days. The process was very straightforward. A word was given to the group and thoroughly explained, in Yup'ik, using examples and illustrations where applicable. This was done until both staff and participants were satisfied that the English term was fully understood by all. At that point, people would begin to propose words and phrases that they felt captured the essence of the English terms. After a list was constructed, each proposed word was scrutinized by the group to determine which one of them came closest to capturing the essence of the English term. The words were made as short and concise as possible. After the conference, the people returned home to their respective villages and solicited feedback from their neighbors. People were shown the words and asked about the clearness of their meanings. Some participants presented the list to the city councils for comment at public meetings. Adjustments were made as necessary. Villages that did not have participants at a particular meeting had lists sent to them by way of mail.

The lists were compiled and made available to the public. We particularly directed them towards the local radio and television stations who could use them in Yup'ik-language news broadcasts, as well as hospital and agency staff who are active in the interpreting fields. Kuskokwim Community College could also use them as material in an interpreter/translator training program.

Many of the terms developed are completely self-evident when they are first heard. Others are not. One conference participant made an observation on how well the legal terms developed were understood by the average villagers he had shown them to. He commented that those who had some experience in the court system easily understood the new terms, but those who had no such experience had a slightly more difficult time. At any rate, the terms were infinitely more understandable than the corresponding English terms were.

This reaction is both understandable and logical. In English, the first time people hear the word "modem" (an electronic device for communicating with microcomputers over telephone lines), it is probable that most people, unless they were involved directly with the technology, had no idea what the word meant. However, after hearing it explained once or twice and perhaps having contact with one, the word began to spread and come into more common use until it was fairly widely recognized. No doubt the same process occurs with new words like automobile, photocopy, silicon chip, missile. Some of the words need to be explained the first few times that they are used, but continued exposure to the terms make them more widely recognizable and encourages their use.

The word conference is not the only tool that can bring about language cultivation or, in the end, preservation. There are too many factors involved for this to be true. However, we have found it to be a very powerful and useful tool that can be utilized by many languages that are struggling with modernization.

References

Eastman, Carol M. 1983. *Language planning: An Introduction*. San Francisco: Chandler & Sharp Publishers, Inc.

Jacobson, Steven A., compiler. 1984. *Yup'ik Eskimo dictionary*. Fairbanks: University of Alaska, Alaska Native Language Center.

Michael, Henry N., ed. 1967. *Lieutenant Zagoskin's travels in Russian America 1842–1844*. Toronto: University of Toronto Press.

MEDIATING ATHABASCAN ORAL TRADITIONS

—◆※◆—

Beth Leonard

Originally published in the *International Journal of Multicultural Education*, vol. 10, no. 2 (2008) (http://ijme-journal.org/index.php/ijme/index).

INTRODUCTION

I AM DEG HIT'AN ATHABASCAN from Shageluk, Alaska. In my current role as assistant professor with the University of Alaska Fairbanks School of Education I teach "Alaska Native Education," a semester-long (15-week) senior-level core course in the Elementary Education Program. Although UAF has one of the higher percentages of Alaska Native/Native American students in the U.S. (16 percent), the majority of my students are not Alaska Native or Native American. Some of these students may choose to teach in an Alaska Native community in rural Alaska, or will have Alaska Native students in their urban classrooms. For both Native and non-Native students, knowledge of Alaska Native educational paradigms and worldviews is critical for understanding why Western educational systems have impacted Alaska Native peoples, and how these systems continue to influence Alaska Native education today. Also, with the current emphasis on pedagogy-of-place educational models, it is vital for students to understand the challenges of presenting complex cultural materials in appropriate and respectful ways.

In this article, I describe how I use three versions of one Deg Hit'an Athabascan narrative in my course to build students' understandings of Alaska Native worldviews and educational processes. I begin by presenting contextual information related to the author and the Deg Hit'an cultural area. I then provide a paraphrased version of the narrative followed by an explanation of how I attempt to mediate by providing additional contextual information through visual sources and explanations of two of the narrative titles. I conclude with comments on the importance of developing cross-cultural understandings of Alaska Native worldviews and broadening concepts of education and educational processes.

INDIGENOUS EDUCATION: DEFINITIONS AND PROCESSES

> There is a shared body of understanding among many Indigenous people that education is really about helping an individual find his or her face, which means finding out who you are, where you come from, and your unique character ... Indigenous education is, in its truest form, about learning relationships in context. (Cajete, 2000a:183)

Topic areas in the "Alaska Native Education" course include examining the history of Western education for Alaska Natives and Native Americans, Alaska Native values and principles, and contemporary issues in indigenous education. I begin the course with an overview of Alaska Native/Native American educational contexts and worldviews, using readings by Vine Deloria, Jr. (Deloria and Wildcat, 2001), Jeanne Eder (Reyhner and Eder, 2004), Esther Ilutsik (1999), Oscar Kawagley (Kawagley and Barnhardt, 1999), and Paul Ongtooguk (2000). My primary goal for this topic area is to help students understand the complexity of oral traditions and their connections to traditional educational processes within Alaska Native contexts.

After examining how Western and Alaska Native educational systems differ in content, pedagogies, values, and goals, the students and I discuss the continuing roles of oral traditions within educational processes for Alaska Natives. According to Cajete (1994), the current educational system continues to disregard the fact that "myths, legends, and folk tales have been cornerstones of teaching in every culture" (p. 116). In the process of facilitating students' understandings of oral traditions and their connections to traditional educational processes we begin to explore the worldviews of the Deg Hit'an and other Alaska Native people. As Cajete states in the quote at the beginning of this section, these worldviews guide educational processes that involve developing and maintaining relationships that extend far beyond social realms.

To help illustrate Deg Hit'an Athabascan worldviews and educational processes, my students read a traditional creation narrative by the late Deg Hit'an elder Belle Deacon (1987c) entitled "The Old Man Who Came Down From Above the Second Layer of This World." Students also view a videotape of Deacon (1976) telling another version of the same narrative titled "The First Man and Woman." Prior to recording these English-language versions, however, Deacon (1987b) recorded a version in Deg Xinag (the language of the Deg Hit'an) that she titled *Nij'oqay Ni'idaxin* translated as "The Man and Wife." The Deg Xinag version is also translated into English; however, many of the cultural concepts and worldviews, or "thick description" as described by Geertz (1973), remain concealed in the translated version as well as the English-language versions where Deacon attempts to mediate for non–Deg Hit'an audiences. This mediation is evident in the three titles of Deacon's narrative listed below:

Table 1: *Three Titles of Deacon's Narrative*

1.	*Nij'qay Ni'idaxin*: The Man and Wife
2.	The Old Man Who Came Down From Above the Second Layer of This World
3.	The First Man and Woman

The first two narrative titles are examined in more detail in subsequent sections. In the next section, I will present a brief description of the narrative and storytelling contexts. These contexts are extremely difficult to provide solely via narrative descriptions, and may come across as one-dimensional for those not familiar with the complexity of Alaskan land scapes and cultures.

CONTEXTS OF ORAL TRADITIONS: CHALLENGES OF TRANSLATION AND INTERPRETATION

In my research with Deg Hit'an narratives, I find that traditional narratives of Alaska Native people, as translated, often fail to articulate the relational and educational paradigms within Alaska Native cultures. Examination and explanation of these "deep structures" as referenced above is necessary to understanding Alaska Native methods of education and worldviews. As Lomawaima and McCarty (2006) note, "translation is never a mechanical process of matching word to word. Translation is an intellectual and aesthetic challenge to reconcile unique concepts, transverse divergent ways of categorizing experiences, and illuminate the unfamiliar" (p. 104). In facilitating students' understandings of the cultural paradigms of the narrative "The Old Man Who Came Down From the Second Layer of This World, I present aspects of the Deg Xinag version, *Nij'oqay Ni'idaxin*, "The Man and Wife." This examination of both the English and Deg Xinag versions helps illustrate some of the worldviews and cultural paradigms that may not be apparent to an audience not familiar with Athabascan cultures nor fluent in the Deg Xinag language.

To help broaden the context of Deacon's narratives, students read the introduction to "Engithidong Xugixudhoy: Their Stories of Long Ago" (Deacon, 1987a), the volume containing the referenced narrative. This introduction includes a short biography of Deacon's family and a statement by Deacon that highlights the importance of listening, remembering, and individually reflecting on these narratives as part of the learning process: "*Yixudz vighoyen'uxdhij. Agide yidong xinag yitojchijdi dina'ididine' yidong. . .* You should think about everything. Then you'll get the old wisdom that was told to us in the past" (Deacon, 1987a:3–4). In this statement, Deacon uses the term *yidong xinag* to refer to "the old wisdom". The word *xinag*, originally referred to earlier in this document as "language", takes on additional meanings when combined with the word *yidong* or "long ago"; that is, "the old language," "the language of our ancestors," and notably, "the old wisdom." One could argue that speakers may also use the term *xinag* to refer to the vast stores of knowledge used to educate succeeding generations via the power of breath in oral traditions.[1]

In addition to what the students read prior to viewing the videotape, I also show photographs of the Deg Hit'an area via a PowerPoint presentation and explain my connections to the Deacon family. These value systems that acknowledge and honor relationships and connections, as Cajete notes above, remain an integral part of educational paradigms for Alaska Native and other indigenous peoples. Pre-service teachers, especially those who are considering teaching positions in Alaska Native communities, should have at least an elementary understanding of Alaska Native value systems, cultural connections, and relationships in order to effectively communicate with students and their families.

All of the narratives in Deacon's book were recorded in her home in Grayling, Alaska, an Athabascan community on the Yukon River in interior Alaska. The recordings also capture household sounds including knocking as visitors come by, Deacon's little dog barking, her husband John talking, and the kitchen clock ticking. My parents and I visited the home of John and Belle Deacon on many occasions, so listening to these recordings is like a trip back in time to those visits in the late 1960s and early 1970s. These background noises do not distract from the story, but instead add to the context and overall appeal of the audio versions, effectively bringing the past into the present for those of us who knew John and Belle Deacon.

The Deg Hit'an area includes the villages of Anvik, Grayling, Holy Cross, and Shageluk. Grayling is located within the Holikachuk language area (Krauss, 1982), however, several Deg Xinag speakers reside there as well. The Deg Hit'an area is the westernmost cultural area within the Athabascan region that stretches from Holy Cross, Alaska, to Hudson Bay in Canada as illustrated by the Alaska Native Peoples and Languages Map (Krauss, 1982) below:

Figure 1. Alaska Native Peoples and Languages Map.

Anvik, Grayling, and Holy Cross are located on the lower-middle Yukon, while Shageluk is on the Innoko River, a Yukon River tributary. Holy Cross is considered part of the Deg Hit'an area but borders the Yup'ik area and is currently a mixed Athabascan-Yup'ik community. Many Grayling residents are originally from Holikachuk, an Innoko River village above Shageluk that was abandoned in 1963. It should be noted that during the pre-European contact period, and for some time post-contact, most residents did not live year-round in one location, but rather moved among summer, winter, and spring camps located on the Innoko or Yukon River. I use the following photos of the Innoko River and Shageluk in my PowerPoint presentation so students have some concept of the physical landscape within this region.

The following is an extremely condensed, paraphrased version of Deacon's narrative; both the audiotaped and videotaped versions are quite long at over 40 minutes in length.

NARRATIVE SUMMARY OF "NIJ'OQAY NI'IDAXIN: THE MAN AND WIFE" (DEACON, 1987B)

Deacon begins her narrative by identifying a couple living by themselves at the mouth of a side stream or slough. The man spends a lot of time trapping, while the wife stays at home chopping wood, sewing, and cooking for her husband. The wife always makes "ice cream" for her husband and after he eats he specifically asks for this dish. As the man continues to go out

Figure 2. Innoko River below Shageluk, Alaska.

hunting and trapping for days at a time his wife begins to feel lonesome. This cycle of the same activities goes on for a number of years, with the wife regularly mixing ice cream for her husband. One day during the fall season she does not feel well and does not make the ice cream for him. The man urges his wife to make the ice cream as he does not get full without it and he sleeps well after eating ice cream. His wife then goes outside for snow to make ice cream and does not return. The man searches for her and finds the bowl and spoon she had taken with her, but finds no tracks beyond the water hole. He mourns for her during the subsequent fall and winter, becoming thin and weak and thinking that he will die.

At midwinter an old man, whom the husband later learns is Raven, visits him and tells the husband that his wife was stolen by a giant and taken to "a land deep down in the water" (p. 15). Raven tells the man that he will not be able to get his wife back without his (Raven's) help. After the man has eaten and rested, they begin work cutting down a large spruce tree with a stone axe. They then limb the tree and cut the top off, making it about "twelve arm spans long" (p. 19). The spruce is then carved into the shape of a pike, with the insides and mouth hollowed out. After the pike is complete, they tie a rope to it and drag it to the water hole. Raven tells the man to chop a hole in the water hole big enough to accommodate the

Figure 3. Shageluk, Alaska.

fish, and fetch other items for his journey. These items include birch punk, a clay lamp to provide light for the man while inside the fish, and weasel skins to provide a disguise once he reaches the underwater village. Raven then "blew with his hands and made medicine with a song" (p. 24). He then hits the fish on the back and it sinks to the bottom of the river, producing a humming noise that shook the man.

Upon reaching the underwater village the man leaves the fish and finds himself in the underwater village with a "big kashim and many winter houses" (p. 25). The man rescues his wife from this underwater village and he and his wife return to their home. Upon their return, Raven is waiting for them and washes the pike's head and teeth with a rag. Raven then instructs the fish to "stay in a place where there are lakes, where no one will go," and "For people who step there on the ice of the lake, you will shake your little tail" indicating "someone's impending death." The fish then "goes to the bottom," however they (man and wife) "don't know where" (p. 31).

Upon their return the wife begins to make ice cream, and she and her husband dress in new clothes. The wife plans to give Raven the ice cream and some cooked game. Raven tells the man and wife, "I am Raven from the upperworld. I don't eat this food. I live only on food that is placed in the fire" (p. 31), and that he will stay with them one more night, leaving at the first light of the next morning. Raven then instructs them to build a fire and burn first the food, then the bedding he used while staying with the man and wife, and lastly the new clothes. Raven then "floated upward" and "disappeared behind the clouds up in the other world" (p. 33). Deacon ends the story with "*Idixunili'on'*," literally, "That is as far as the story goes" (p. 33).

MEDIATING ORAL TRADITIONS IN THE CLASSROOM CONTEXTS

In presenting these narrative versions, there are usually a number of terms and concepts unfamiliar to non-Native students; these may include "Raven", "ice cream", "pike", "weasel", "punk", and "kashim". In the PowerPoint presentation referenced earlier, I include photos of the great northern pike, weasel or ermine, punk (a fungal growth often burned as a mosquito repellant), a modern version of Grayling's "kashim" or community hall, and the Shageluk mask dancers performing the "Crow (Raven) Dance." Students understand that the creation of the pike is a central theme within the narrative. However, because of the limitations of the translated versions, students need additional contextual information to understand the connections between the Deg Hit'an people and the pike; these connections began with the creation of the pike and extend into the present.

For the Deg Hit'an people, pike or "jackfish" are an important part of the traditional subsistence[2] cycle as they are abundant in the region and can be harvested year-round from lakes, side streams, and rivers. Pike are an ancient, aggressive, predatory fish, and can grow up to six feet in length and 50 pounds in weight (Nelson, 1983:72–73). Pike is usually served boiled, roasted or fried; the meat can also be used to make *vanhgiq* or "ice cream",

a significant food staple and a central theme within Deacon's narrative. Deacon refers to several types of ice cream in her narratives, including those made with fish, caribou, or moose fat, or snow. Pike is one of the fish used to make fish ice cream, as the meat flakes well and is readily available at most times of the year, although other white fish are used as well. The process of making fish ice cream or *vanhgiq* is extremely time-intensive. *Vanhgiq* is made by combining fat (fish oil, or more recently, hydrogenated vegetable oil) with the boiled meat of the fish. After the fish is boiled, the skin is removed and the meat deboned. The liquid is then squeezed out of the fish meat by hand until it becomes dry and pow-

Figure 4: Great Northern Pike[3].

dery. The fish meat and fat are combined and whipped using one hand until light and fluffy. During this process, people who may be in the house must remain quiet as the ice cream is mixed. Sugar, berries, and sometimes milk or a sweetened cream mixture are then added to finish the dish. Blueberries, lowbush cranberries, crowberries, and/or salmonberries seem to be the most popular fruit to add to the ice cream currently. Today the Deg Hit'an people continue to serve *vanhgiq* in large quantities at potlatches, mask dances, funerals, and memorial feasts. The connections among the pike, *vanhgiq*, and funeral feasts are further reinforced in the subsequent section that discusses the Deg Hit'an universe.

As one of the main characters, "Raven" also warrants further explanation. The Deg Xinag term for "Raven," literally means "your (plural) grandfather" or "you guys' grandfather." These connections are further emphasized in the "Man and Wife" version as Raven calls the husband and wife "*sitthey*," literally, "my grandchildren." In the Deg Hit'an culture and other

Alaska Native cultures, Raven (or "Crow") plays a central role as a creator; also a "trickster" or character who initiates change. In this narrative, Raven creates and animates the pike, but also functions as an educator to help the husband and wife understand their place in the world and the proper protocols for dealing with "Raven" and those who reside in other "levels" of the Deg Hit'an universe. These levels and protocols are explained in a subsequent section as I examine the narrative titles.

Finally, I address the term "kashim" as both a physical building and educational construct. Traditionally, men of the community lived in the kashim, so this building was, in essence, one of the educational centers for the younger men and boys in the community. This building was part of the place-based educational system where young people learned the necessary skills in order to survive and flourish in this area. The kashim was also used for various ceremonies including the mask dances, funeral and memorial feasts; today these ceremonies are still held in the kashim so this place continues to function as a community educational center.

In the next two sections, I briefly examine two of the narrative titles: *Nij'oqay Ni'idaxin* and "The Old Man Who Came Down From Above the Second Layer of This World."

NIJ'OQAY NI'IDAXIN: THE MAN AND WIFE

As stated previously, the term *nij'oqay ni'idaxin* is translated as "the man and wife." A morphological[4] examination of this title reveals the reflexive prefix *nij-*, meaning "with each other" used to mark vital, reciprocal social relationships. The affix *-'o* is a contracted form of the stem for "wife," that is, *-'ot* (unpossessed form), and the final segment *-qay* indicates "multiple persons" or can stand alone as the word for "village." Other reflexive terms from the Deg Xinag Noun Dictionary are listed below:

Table 2: Deg Xinag Reflexive Kinship Terms

Deg Xinag	English Translation	Comments
Nijngonhye	Mother and Child	*ngonh* – "your mother"
Nijto'ye	Father and Son	*-to* – unpossessed stem for "father"
Nijq'uye	Aunt and Niece	*-q'u* – unpossessed stem for "aunt" (mother's sister)
Nijqing'qay	Husband and Wife	*-qing'* – unpossessed stem for "husband"

In his analysis of similar Koyukon[5] narratives, Thompson (1990) observes that many of these:

begin with the phrase *"Neejkkun kkaa jedo"* 'A man and wife were living together'. . . In such forms, the older or most important member of the pair is the only one explicitly stated. . . If a story begins with this phrase, one can assume that the couple will be broken up by either abduction or infidelity. (pp. 100–101)

The Koyukon term used in this example, *"neejkkun kkaa"* (cognate to the Deg Xinag term *nijqing'qay* above), indicates that the husband or man is the "older or more important member of the pair." Deacon's use of the term *"nij'oqay"* in her title puts the emphasis on the woman or wife, indicating her importance in this creation story.

However, the meaning of *ni'idaxin* is not explained in the translation. In examining the morphology of the word, the prefix *ni-* may refer to something specific in the environment. The areal prefix *xi-* indicates something within the wider environment. Athabascanist James Kari (2007) notes the verb theme *-dax* in this example means "plural events occur," or "experience plural events." The final portion of the word *-in* can be translated as "those who" are in a position or constant state.

Table 3: *Nij'oqay Ni'idaxin: Morphological Analysis*

Deg Xinag	English Translation	Morphological Analysis
Nij'oqay	The Man and Wife	*nij* – reciprocal prefix *'o* – contracted form of kinship term "wife" *qay* – plural P. (person)
Ni'idaxin		*ni* – *'idax* –plural events occur, experience plural events *in* – "those who" (are in a position or constant state)

The previous analysis illustrates the kinds of complex cultural information that remain veiled at the conclusion of the original translation process. These concepts are also not obvious from the English translations. This example illustrates the structural aspects of the language that emphasize the reciprocal relationship between the man and his wife, and their connections to a specific place through time.[6]

THE OLD MAN WHO CAME DOWN FROM ABOVE THE SECOND LAYER OF THIS WORLD

As noted in previous sections, my students read Deacon's English version of the narrative "The Old Man Who Came Down From Above the Second Layer of This World." Deacon's use of the word "man" in her English title and text differs from the translation of the Deg Xinag version. In the translated Deg Xinag title "The Man and Wife," the term "man" is used to identify the husband in a reciprocal relationship with his wife as noted above. Also, in the Deg Xinag version, Deacon uses the term *Yixgitsity* or "Raven" to refer to the character who comes to aid the husband. In her English version, Deacon does not use the term "Raven" at all, rather, she refers to Raven's character as the "Man" or "Old Man" throughout the narrative.

To explain what Deacon means by "the second layer of this world," in the next section I refer to sources by Cornelius Osgood, a Yale anthropologist who completed an extensive ethnography of the Deg Hit'an.

FOUR LEVELS OF THE DEG HIT'AN UNIVERSE

Osgood's (1959:103–106) discussion of Deg Hit'an spiritual beliefs includes a section titled "The Universe and Determinate Things" in which he talks about the concept of a four-level universe. The first level is "the apparent world of normal living things." According to Osgood, the *yeg*, or "spirits that have departed from their partner bodies," inhabit the other levels, however the shaman's *yeg* can continue to exist on the first level.

Most departed spirits reside on the second level known as "Raven living" which is slightly below the surface of the apparent world. Osgood reiterates a story of how this level was created by Raven during the time when "the animals and man still spoke a common language" and people did not die as they do today; as Osgood describes it, "actually, there was no place to go." Raven married "a fine-looking young woman," but later became captivated with her mother and sought to find a way to live with her. Raven then began digging a hole, "finally coming out on a bank of a faraway river," a project that took two years. After building two summer houses on two adjacent points of land, he then returned to his village and "hoped that his mother-in-law would become sick" as "the world was already too crowded with people." His mother-in-law did sicken, and stopped eating. Raven then led her into the tunnel he had made and they spent four nights on this journey.

The third level is called "up on top of the sky;" Osgood describes this as "a good place but little is actually known about it." This level has "a very large lake with very large fish in it" and accommodates the *yeg* of people "who have frozen to death, who have been killed in war or murdered, who have died in childbirth, or who have committed suicide (except for those who drown themselves)."

The fourth level and lowest level is called "fish trail" and holds *yeg* of people "who have drowned, either accidentally or by intention. . . There they have a village which is neighboring to the several villages occupied by different species of salmon." The *yeg* that inhabit this level can go up "through a hole in order to visit their friends in Raven's living."

Funeral and memorial ceremonies held today still reflect the values and protocols taught by Raven in this narrative. Funerals or potlatches for the dead last four days, also noted by Osgood (1958:275) in his ethnography. Prior to sealing the casket, four candles are placed in each corner of the casket to provide light during the four-night journey to the afterlife. The following quote by the late Hannah Maillelle of Grayling, Alaska, describes "last rites" of stamping the feet four times, observed prior to the closing and nailing of the coffin lid:

> At a funeral people stamp their feet four times the last thing when the coffin is still open, before they close it. They lift the person's spirit up so they don't bury the spirit with them. It's a spirit sending. There's always somebody there by the coffin that's supposed to be lifting the spirit up. You just tell the person *"Diggi ts'in'!,"* "up" in Native. If you don't do that they hang around all the time. But if you do that they go up. (Maillelle, 2002)

The husband and wife are highly proficient in a number of subsistence skills, however are still learning about their place or level wherein they appear to be the only humans. The relationship they develop with Raven or the Old Man over the course of time teaches them the importance of reciprocal gifting (through burning) of food and clothing to Raven and others who inhabit the other levels. In "The Old Man Who Came Down From Above the Second Layer of This World," the Old Man (Raven) states:

> But all that food which you put away for me—ice cream, things—you make big fire on the bank tomorrow morning. You burn the FOOD first. Then you put my bundle, my blanket, and BURN it up. And those boots, parky, mittens, cap, everything, bundle it up and burn it too. And it'll come down to ashes. And then you'll see me get out of sight. And it will be, when I get back to my place up there, it will be there just brand new; I'll put it on. (Deacon, 1987c:40)

The ongoing nature of social relationships and obligations to those who have died and journeyed to another level continue to be recognized today, highlighting the resilience of these beliefs and practices despite opposition by missionaries and educators. Relatives of the deceased burn selected pieces of clothing prior to the burial, and burn small portions of food at each of the community meals during the four-day funeral ceremony.

CONCLUSION

In addition to the narrative titles explained in this paper, there are a number of other connections within this narrative that my students and I examine during the course topic area on "traditional education." In a forthcoming publication, the *Alaska Native Reader* (Leonard, 2009), I discuss some of these aspects including an overview of Athabascan narrative genres, epistemological and ontological aspects of the "pike," definitions of "subsistence," and values inherent in Athabascan subsistence practices. My experiences with Deacon's narratives in many ways parallel those of my students who are not familiar with Deg Hit'an culture. Because I am not fluent in the Deg Xinag language, this limits my understanding of Deacon's narratives, although I grew up surrounded by the culture of the Deg Hit'an people. Many of the practices described by Osgood and other anthropologists remain central in Deg Hit'an communities, despite opposition by early missionaries and educators as noted previously. Currently, however, education about these beliefs and practices varies among families and communities within this area.

In his book *Keeping Slug Woman Alive*, Pomo/Miwok scholar Greg Sarris (1993) discusses Bateson's notions of "culture contact" (p. 43), that is cultures come into contact cross-culturally but also interculturally as well. My research is in many respects a cross-cultural, intercultural, and somewhat decontextualized endeavor considering my background; a background that resulted in my initial experience with oral traditions in written formats, then secondarily through listening to audio recordings. I am careful not to classify myself as an "expert" on the Deg Hit'an culture as I am a cultural insider in some ways, however in other ways I remain a cultural outsider, as noted above.

Stories, or mythology, according to Cajete (2000b) "are alternative ways of understanding relationships, creation, and the creative process itself . . . how humans obtain knowledge, how they learn responsibility for such knowledge, and then how knowledge is applied in the proper context"

(p. 44). These mythologies contain "expressions of a worldview in coded form" (p. 62). Through examining Deacon's narratives in English and Deg Xinag, my students begin to understand the complexities of oral narratives in translation, respect worldviews that emphasize connections that extend well into and far beyond social realms, and reconstruct narrow concepts of education and educational processes. For teachers who serve Alaska Native students, knowledge of the contexts of education (both historical and contemporary), worldviews, and value systems remains vital to establishing and maintaining respectful communication with students, their families, and communities.

References

Bielawski, E. 1990. Cross-cultural epistemology: Cultural readaptation through the pursuit of knowledge. Paper presented at the 7th Inuit Studies Conference, University of Alaska Fairbanks.

———. 1996. Inuit indigenous knowledge and science in the arctic. In *Naked science: Anthropological inquiry into boundaries, power, and knowledge*, ed. L. Nader, 216–227. New York: Routledge.

Cajete, G. 2000a. Indigenous knowledge: The Pueblo metaphor of indigenous education. In *Reclaiming indigenous voice and vision*, ed. M. Battiste, 181–191. Vancouver, BC: UBC Press.

———. 2000b. *Native science: Natural laws of interdependence.* Santa Fe, NM: Clear Light Publishers.

Deacon, B. 1976. The first man and woman. *The Anchorage Historical and Fine Arts Museum Exhibit and Lecture Series—Athabascans: Strangers of the North.* Videotape. Anchorage: University of Alaska Media Services; Alaska Native Cultural Heritage and Information Bank.

Deacon, B. 1987a. *Engithidong xugixudhoy: Their stories of long ago.* Fairbanks: Alaska Native Language Center.

———. 1987b. Ni\'oqay ni'idaxin: The man and wife. In *Engithidong xugixudhoy: Their stories of long ago*, 5–40. Fairbanks: Alaska Native Language Center.

———. 1987c. The old man who came down from above the second layer of this world. In *Engithidong xugixudhoy: Their stories of long ago*, 34–40. Fairbanks: Alaska Native Language Center.

Deloria, Jr., Vine. 1994. *God is red: A native view of religion,* 2nd ed. Golden, CO: Fulcrum Publishing.

Deloria, Jr., Vine, and D.R. Wildcat. 2001. *Power and place: Indian education in America.* Golden, CO: Fulcrum Resources.

Geertz, C. 1973. *The interpretation of cultures.* New York: HarperCollins Publishers.

Ilutsik, E. 1999. Traditional Yup'ik knowledge: Lessons for all of us. *Sharing Our Pathways: A newsletter of the Alaska Rural Systemic Initiative* 4(4):1, 8–11.

Johnson, M. 1992. *Lore: Capturing traditional environmental knowledge.* Hay River, Northwest Territories: Dene Cultural Institute.

Kari, J. 2007. Comments for Beth Leonard (personal communication). Fairbanks, AK.

Kawagley, A.O. 1995. *A Yupiaq worldview: A pathway to ecology and spirit.* Prospect Heights, IL: Waveland Press, Inc.

Kawagley, A.O., and R. Barnhardt. 1999. Education indigenous to place: Western science meets Native reality. In *Ecological education in action: On weaving education, culture, and the environment*, ed. G. A. Smith and D. R. Williams, 117–140. New York: State University of New York Press.

Kawagley, A.O., D.Norris-Tull, and R.A. Norris-Tull. 1998. The indigenous worldview of Yupiaq culture: Its scientific nature and relevance to the practice and teaching of science. *Journal of Research in Science Teaching* 35(2):133–144.

Knudtson, P., and D. Suzuki. 1992. *Wisdom of the elders*. Toronto: Stoddart Publishing.

Krauss, M., cartographer. 1982. *Map: Native peoples and languages of Alaska*.

Krupa, D.J., ed. 1996. *The gospel according to Peter John*. Fairbanks: Alaska Native Knowledge Network.

Leonard, Beth. 2009. Deg Xinag oral traditions. In *Alaska Native reader*, ed. Maria Shiáa Tiáa Williams. Durham: Duke University Press.

Lomawaima, K.T., and T.L. McCarty. 2006. *To remain an Indian: Lessons in democracy from a century of Native American education*. New York: Teachers College Press.

Maillelle, H. 2002. Gan tr'idighine': What we said (2/26/02). *Deg Xiqi Xinatr'iditlghusr: Conversational Deg Xinag*, http://www.alaskool.org/language/Athabaskan/Deg_ Xinag/ClassSpring2002/summary_02_26_02.htm (accessed June 28, 2006).

Momaday, N.S. 1997. *The man made of words*. New York: St. Martin's Press.

Nelson, R.K. 1983. *Make prayers to the raven: A Koyukon view of the northern forest*. Chicago: University of Chicago Press.

Ongtooguk, P. 2000. Aspects of traditional Iñupiat education. *Sharing Our Pathways* 5(4):8–12.

Osgood, C. 1958. *Ingalik social culture*, vol. 53. New Haven, CT: Yale University Press.

———. 1959. *Ingalik mental culture*, vol. 56. New Haven, CT: Department of Anthropology, Yale University.

Reyhner, J., and J. Eder. 2004. *American Indian education: A history*. Norman: University of Oklahoma Press.

Ridington, R. 1990. *Little bit know something*. Iowa City: University of Iowa Press.

Sarris, G. 1993. *Keeping slug woman alive: A holistic approach to American Indian texts*. Berkeley: University of California Press.

Thompson, C. 1990. *K'etetaalkaanee: The one who paddled among the people and the animals: An analytical companion volume*, 4th ed. Fairbanks: Alaska Native Language Center.

Wright, M. H. 1995. The last great Indian war (Nulato 1851). Unpublished M.A. thesis, Department of Anthropology, University of Alaska Fairbanks.

Zepeda, O. 1995. The continuum of literacy in American Indian communities. *Bilingual Research Journal* 19(1):5–15.

ENDNOTES

1   See sources by John (Krupa, 1996), Momaday (1997), and Zepeda (1995) that provide examples of the power of breath within spoken or oral language.

2   "Subsistence" is a term widely used, and for the most part narrowly understood, especially in contemporary political contexts when referring to the hunting and fishing practices and rights of indigenous peoples. For most of Alaska's non-indigenous residents, non-Native politicians in particular, the terms "subsistence" or "subsistence lifestyle" are rarely explored or understood beyond superficial levels. Shallowly defined, subsistence seems to indicate a general knowledge of how to live off the land or "subsist" on what the land has to offer in terms of hunting, fishing, and trapping. For

indigenous peoples, these limited definitions disconnect practices, or lived experiences from spiritual dimensions. For more detailed explanations of subsistence worldviews, see publications by Yup'ik scholar Oscar Kawagley (1995; , 1998), Koyukon cultural anthropologist Miranda Wright (1995), Vine Deloria, Jr. (1994), Ellen Bielawski (1990; , 1996), Robin Ridington (1990), Richard Nelson (1983), Martha Johnson (1992), and Peter Knudtson and David Suzuki (1992).

3   Public domain photo from U.S. Fish & Wildlife Service website: http://images.fws.gov/default.cfm?fuseaction=records.display&CFID=357997&CFTOKEN=93245000&id=5 C7EA00D%2D1143%2D3066%2D4085A76079B10CC3

4   Students accepted into the elementary education program are required to take "Language, Linguistics, and Education," a linguistics course geared toward educators versus linguistics majors. By the time students enroll in "Alaska Native Education" during their junior or senior year, most have completed this course and are familiar with terms used in linguistics such as morphology, phonology, syntax, semantics, semiotics, affixes, etc.

5   The Deg Hit'an and Koyukon Athabascan cultural regions share many similar beliefs and practices.

6   It should be noted that Kari and Deacon did discuss titles to each narrative prior to publication and Deacon chose the English title "The Man and Wife." Kari's (2007) translation of the term *nij'oqay ni'idaxin* is "the man and wife are living, spending their lives."

PART VI

EDUCATION FOR SELF-DETERMINATION

———◆·×·◆———

"We, the Indigenous peoples of the world, assert our inherent right to self-determination in all matters. Self-determination is about making informed choices and decisions and creating appropriate structures for the transmission of culture, knowledge and wisdom for the benefit of each of our respective cultures. Education for our communities and each individual is central to the preservation of our cultures and for the development of the skills and expertise we need in order to be a vital part of the twenty-first century."

From the *Coolongatta Statement on Indigenous Rights in Education*

THE CRY OF THE LOON

MYSTERIOUS, MOURNFUL, REMEMBERING PLACE

Angayuqaq Oscar Kawagley

Originally presented at the Bilingual Multicultural
Education Equity Conference, 1999, Anchorage, Alaska

WAQAA, GREETINGS TO EACH AND EVERYONE OF YOU. Some of you may well be asking, why have I chosen the *tunutellek* as my subject for this occasion? The Yupiaq name means "that which is packing something." Indeed, the loon is carrying a heavy burden.

Wherever the loon exists, there are Native people, and you will have many loon stories that are mystical and magical in their content. Among them is the story of the blind boy who is made to see by the loon diving into the water with the boy on its back. This is repeated three times. In each dive and emergence, the boy could see a little clearer, and on its third emergence, the boy could see clearly. The loon helped the boy to see, and likewise, it can help us to understand ourselves and see our connection to Mother Earth today.

Listen to the call of the loon. Its call is God-given through nature. It is its own language and understood by others of its kind and other creatures. Only we, with our ability to think and rationalize, do not understand, because we listen only with the mind, not with mind and heart well sprinkled with intuition. To some the call is eerie, as if some bad thing is about to happen. Maybe an *alangguk*, an apparition of some kind is about to appear. It conjures up many thoughts that are not based on "what is" but on "what if." This is the fear that most of us face as a Native people, especially when thinking about changing education. "What if" the educators, legislators, and powers that be do not believe that this could be done? But regardless, we must take those steps necessary to change education so that it takes into consideration, in fact makes, an educational system based on our own tribal worldviews. When thought of in that context, then it includes our Native languages, ways of generating knowledge, research, ways of making things, and ways for using them respectfully.

Our Native languages come from the land. They are derived from the land. It is the language of the land that makes our Native people live in harmony with Nature. According to the Muskogee Cree, Bear Heart, harmony is a tolerance, a forgiving, a blending. This is what our Native languages allow us to do. Our Native words come from the creatures and things of Mother Earth naming themselves, defining themselves through action words—that's reality! Nature is our teacher. Information and rationality are a small segment of knowing and learning. In the use of our Native languages, we come to live life intimately because we are enmeshed in it rather than looking at it from a distance through a microscope or telescope. It then behooves that we relearn our languages and learn to live close to nature to regain our health as a Native people. When we have that vision and goal, and work toward it, then we will have harmony; we will have tolerance; we will forgive; and we will again blend into our world. We will be using our five senses and intuition to learn about our place. The loon never lost its spiritual vision. It has a love for life, its environment, and its creator. Its education was from Mother Earth for the heart, for it to become creative and to know how to live in its community, its habitat.

The loon still gets messages from its unconscious with new thoughts or solutions to problems. We, as human beings, have cluttered up our conscious minds with information and rational thinking, so that our world of dreams is no longer sought through meditation, vision questing, fasting, and looking deep into the silence within us for direction. Not only have we become socio-politico-economic dependents, but we depend on outside sources to take care of our problems, whether it's individual, family, or community. You see, the loon looks into its inner ecology knowing that no one else can do that for it. It knows that it is incumbent upon itself to look out for its own interests. In order for us to receive guidance and direction for our lives, we must relearn what the loon does naturally. We must look into ourselves where power and strength lie and tap into it to begin to address our own problems.

Another strength of the loon is that it teaches and nurtures its young to live as a loon. It does not require that someone else do the educating. The loon develops the loon worldview of its young closely connected to others and its place. As it migrates from place to place, it remembers and appreciates the diversity and beauty of Nature. It nurtures its offspring to become independent, yet knowing its dependence on the abundance of Nature to succor its needs. It teaches its young to "do unto others as you would have them do unto you." This is true love; this is unconditional love that we need in this world. A love for self, a love for others, and a love for place, giving one a sense of responsibility to take care of oneself, to care for others and the environment that one lives in. The loon's cry is remembering a place that was harmonious, full of the beauty and diversity that Nature so loves. This is heart talk! This is science—knowing place.

Very much like our Native people, the loon's life is not all roses and peace. The loon has a few problems, such as taking off. It is very much like the Wright brothers in their early experiments at becoming airborne. The little homemade engine revs up, but has just enough power for it to barely get off the water. Just as the underpowered plane, the loon frantically flaps its wings and seemingly runs across the water's surface. Once in a while, the loon will crash onto the tundra, but it crawls back into the lake somehow and tries again. We, as a Native people, are testing our wings and power! If we find that some of our ideas do not work, we need to go back and try again, maybe with a different approach and tools. We must not be overly ambitious by overplaying our knowledge and abilities, but recognize our limitations as human beings. We must do that which we know we can succeed at first, and then progress to more difficult tasks. If we fail, we must NEVER GIVE UP!

The sad fact about this precious bird, the loon, is that it is losing ground in its efforts to survive. Our Canadian friends look upon it with great respect—so much so that it is on their one- and two-dollar coins. They are called the "loonie" and "twoonie." It is a known fact that the loon's numbers are growing smaller at a fast rate across the North. There is a problem that is so ominous and insidious that it is overwhelming the loon. It is not of its own making. It is human-made pollution consisting of chemical, biological, nuclear, and noise which is destroying its habitat. It is we humans who are destroying its habitat and, unfortunately, as we destroy its habitat we are destroying ourselves in the process.

The loon may well ask, "What was the question that makes technology the answer in the first place? Who asked it and when?" Technology is the product of human rationality, though it is inherently neutral, until it is put to use for some human purpose. Take for example, the computer. Some think it has the capacity to solve many of our problems. It is speedy and answers questions with facts the human has fed into it. However, I say use it sparingly, as a tool. Too often, it encourages individualism to the point of isolationism. The excessive user wants to be alone with a mindless machine. If you feed it garbage, you get garbage in return. It takes away clear thinking, problem-solving skills and above all, removes common sense.

Modern technology lends weight to a society that is inclined to take and take from the natural environment, to make things without giving back. It wants to cut into Mother Earth to remove its natural resources. It entices people to want more of its products. In so doing, indigenous people, creatures, plants, and landforms become the victims of Eurocentric concepts of progress and development. They are merely removed as detritus and, in the process, we destroy a people and their place. The loon's mournful cry is in recognition of this needless destruction that is taking place by "bigger and better" technological machines of devastation.

The mournful cry of the loon is much aware of its dwindling food sources, the inability of some of its eggs to hatch, and its members succumbing to poisons and new diseases. It recognizes that to not have children, to not have family, to not have a community, is to be scattered, to be falling apart. Many of our Native families are falling apart. I recognize that there are healthy Native families in the villages. But I would say that these healthy families are too often surrounded by and witness to a holocaust of pain and misery. Our villages are, in essence, communities in name only. They are often not working together for the common good as in the old days. The unhealthy and dysfunctional families have youngsters seven, eight, or nine years old who are raising and taking care of their younger siblings. Why should I worry about these young children acting as parents? Because these youngsters are missing an important aspect of their young lives—that of being a child! A child to be loved by parents, to be nurtured and taken care of by parents, to play as a child, to talk as a child, to imagine as a child. Oh, the yearning of the child just to be a child! Many children miss this growing-up phase.

As if this was not enough, we allow video games, movies, and television to become the babysitters while we go out and party, play bingo, gamble, and do things that make us sicker. While the children are viewing and doing these things, they are seeing killing, cheating, lying, men beating women and children, all kinds of sex, adult language, and many other undesirable aspects of life. The mournful cry of the loon is reminding us of the time when there were secrets from children, things that were not to be known by them until they were considered ready. Today, there are no secrets in the modern media. Go out on the playground, a school party, or anywhere youngsters are gathered. Listen to their language! You will hear a lot of foul language. The language that the youngsters use is an indicator of how bad the situation has become. There is no respect for the parents, teachers, Elders, and most certainly of other young people. We see children having children, children killing children, children killing Elders, children committing suicide, children dropping out of school, children without hope—sad children. What a sad state for us to be in!

These states of affairs contribute to the loss of childhood. We must gain control of what the children learn, see, and do. We do this by regaining control of our own lives. We control this by turning off the television during dinnertime so that heart talk can take place. Heart talk is kind, gentle talk that makes one want to be polite to everyone and everything around them. This talk allows members to know each other, what their likes and dislikes are, to know of problems they are having with friends, siblings, and school. It allows the family to find out what they would like to see change in the home and why. This is where a family that loves and talks together becomes stronger because they know each other, love, and care for one another. This is family.

The loon does not blame anyone even though its environment is rife with problems and pollution is beyond its control. Its mournful call reminds us that we, as humans, must do our part to regenerate and reciprocate with Nature. We, the Native people, must quit blaming others for our problems. When we blame others, we are saying that someone else should take care of the problem and deal with our feelings about the situation. We don't like what has been happening in the schools, so we blame the state, district, and teachers. We are saying to them, "take care of the problem," and "take care of my hurt and confused feelings about my own education. Please, heal me." Why should we continue to do this? Why should we continue to say how confused and mixed up we are by the new civilization that has come to our villages?

Now we have frame houses that are poorly insulated, built on stilts, and expensive to maintain. But we are "educated," because we no longer live in sod houses. We have snowmobiles instead of dog teams that can often save our lives. We have flush toilets with Lysol cleaners that empty into an unhealthy lagoon, thereby making it unnecessary for us to go outdoors in all kinds of weather, whereby Nature can take care of natural wastes in a natural way. But, we are educated. We have antibiotics and hormone-laced hamburgers instead of smoked dry fish which is more healthy. We use toilet paper which kills trees instead of sphagnum moss which prevents rash and the spread of germs. But, we are educated! So well educated as to think our Native languages and cultures are no longer useful. This is what the loon is mourning. Why have we, the Native people, given up so easily? Giving up has been a very costly venture to us as a Native people. But, we are educated.

The loon's standards of life and making a living are impeccable, thus allowing it to live successfully for many thousands of years. Its basic standard is respect—a respect for the Greater Being, spirits, others' rights to live a life that fits their needs, and a respect for the environment. It is taught aspects of its place by its parents using all five senses. The young are taught how to play; taught the ritual of swimming, diving, and making its call; taught how to select a nesting place; taught the art of making a nest; taught to appreciate the life forms within its place and taught to live a life that is interacting with all that is around it. It knows that it is a loon and always will remember that. Yes, its standards are simple and intertwined, leading to a life that is full of meaning and direction.

For those of us who are indigenous or Native people, we must resurrect our ways of recognizing and paying homage to the Ellam Yua spirits and Nature. When we regain our spirituality, we will again learn to laugh from our hearts and play because "those who know how to play can easily leap over the adversaries of life. And one who knows how to sing and laugh never brews mischief" (an Iglulik proverb). When we awake at dawn and look at the sun rising and life begins to stir again, this is mysterious. The loon is telling us of this mystery of life—its mysterious connection to us. This is sacred. When we begin to understand this, we will begin to change our relationship to our environment. We will begin to experience a need for a new existence. I am happy to state that among the Alaska Native people, the Yupiat have striven for and are heading for a new existence! We have many Yupiat Elders and others who have become teachers for all of us, and all point to the same direction—a new consciousness for life. A new consciousness that is vibrantly traditional, full of truth, beauty, health, happiness, and love. These five attributes of life provide the foundation for the answers to the question that each and every one of us will ask ourselves as to the type of life that we want to pursue. As we put this into practice, we will become the model of existence for now and in the future.

In this contemporary world of chaos, we can create our own reality. We can re-create ourselves as we want to be. We have the power within us to do this. We have three things that will help us to do this. First, we have our past through myths, stories, rituals, and ceremonies. We can draw from them that which will help us reconstruct, and dispense with those that will not be of help to us in our efforts.

Secondly, we have our imagination and ability to see what we would like to be in the future. What will we look like? What will we live in? How will we make our living? What kinds of things will we possess? How will we recognize the spiritual?

Lastly, we have our rational, thinking minds that react to things around us and thus enable us to connect with things as they are now. We know what we are, know what others think of us, know how we try to make a living, know how the federal and state governments work against us, and know how we react to negative as well as positive things that happen to us. Knowing these time and thought spirals can help us to reconstruct our reality and ourselves.

It is time that we make songs about alcohol and drugs, telling of their power over us, telling us it is now time for us to give up and be released from their use, and give up or relinquish our emotional ties to these destructive elements. If we merely release these from our lives, we will return to it. So it is absolutely necessary that we give up our emotional ties to it, i.e., I do it because it makes me feel good and allows me to talk and mix with people. This is an emotional tie that will get you back to it.

The loon reminds us that its standards for life are high, and so should ours be. In looking at the federal and state educational standards, I get confused as to the real meaning of them. Perhaps it's the fragmented and convoluted approach by fields of study that make this so. It does not show me a need for a change in education. There is an old Chinese saying that goes something like this: When there is someone pointing at the moon, only the idiot looks at the finger! These Eurocentric standards require that we look at the content of the various fields of study. They tell us what our students are purportedly to know at the end of secondary school. Content, thus information accumulation, and processing, seems to be of overriding importance. As I've said before, information and rationality are a very small part of learning. But those alone fail to give direction and wholeness to the standards. This is not to say that they are useless, but they can be if left alone.

The needed additional ingredients are the Alaska Standards for Culturally Responsive Schools. These say to me that there needs to be a change in the whole of education, not only schooling. Schooling is that which happens in the structure called the school. Education is that which happens within and outside the family, school, and community. The latter is all-inclusive. In reading and thinking about the standards, I get the distinct feeling that there is a need to change the way that we teach, the things that we teach about, the materials we use, how we measure growth and development, and where things are taught. The cultural standards behoove us to make sure that something is done to accommodate the Native thought-worlds and worldviews. The loon would desire this for its survival and ours. We are now on that pathway.

In conclusion, the cry of the loon is encouraging us to balance our physical, emotional, intellectual, and spiritual selves to begin to live lives that feel just right, walking peacefully and expressing it to others in our own Native languages. *Piurciqukut Yuluta pitallketuluta*—"we will become people living a life that feels just right." *Quyana!*

WHO CONTROLS ALASKA NATIVE EDUCATION?

Paul Ongtooguk

Alaska Native Education Summit,
sponsored by the First Alaskans Institute
November 30, 2001, Anchorage, Alaska

WELL, I HAD BETTER KNOW SOMETHING about pedagogues, right? Here's what I know about them. Originally, they were Greek slaves who were charged with providing the education of the ruling class. That's what they were doing, and it always struck me that only in the Western system could they come up with the idea of somebody who was enslaved to liberate the minds of others.

I'm happy to be here. All of us, we're Alaska Natives. We've come from thousands of miles, representing hundreds of communities and a dozen cultures, to rededicate ourselves to the transformation of Alaska Native education. We have had success in the education of Alaska Natives for thousands of years. We have learned about the spiritual, social, and physical world while in community houses and clan houses. We've learned from aunts and uncles, from cousins, from grandparents. We've learned from chiefs and whaling captains. We have learned how to live and grow as communities, in places where others would have perished—and often did so. I always think about how tough the Vikings were—their reputation is that they were so bad. They went to Greenland and folded. Think about it. Think about it, Minnesota, there might be a reason.

We've lived in places with such efficiency and grace that later people who have come to our homelands have considered them to be empty of human beings; and they've called this a wilderness because they didn't see us in those places. They couldn't imagine that a people could live so well in a land that it would appear untouched by them. And we live with the dilemma of that to this day.

We have a challenge, and it's called schools. Alaska Natives have largely embraced the promise of school. The promise was, and continues to be, to prepare our young people to become contributing members of our communities, our state, and our nation. But schools for Alaska Natives are like a meal laced with an unintended, poisonous effect. Along with the promise of preparing us for the future was this poisonous idea—and Byron Mallott has already referred to it—that our Native cultures, our ways of life, our languages, our traditions, our ideas, our understandings of the world, the very societies that were keys to living here for thousands of years, should be stripped from the minds of our children in order to prepare them for a future that will not include Alaska Native cultures. We live with the consequences of this to the present day, and we see the after-effects reverberating through our communities.

Now, I need to emphasize—and we all need to emphasize—that we ask no one in this room to have a sense of guilt. None of us were a part of the policy that told us that, in order to become educated, we had to give up being Alaska Natives. That was a policy that was set in place about a hundred years ago, and it will end hopefully within our lifetime. We need to acknowledge publicly and to accept the fact that this policy was a terrible dilemma. It was a poisonous idea that has tainted the promise of education for Alaska Natives. And we have to root it out, sort through it, and redirect the kind of education that our people are going to experience.

What are we experiencing right now? What do we see? Well, there's good news and bad news. Statistically, we have some of the finest people in formal education that we have ever had in Alaska Native history. We have some amazing successes. We now have a fairly firm second generation of Alaska Native college graduates. On the test scores that the state of Alaska is using—the benchmark exams and the high school qualifying exam—we have some of the highest-scoring individuals in the state. Good news. But the part that we are concerned about and that we're also going to try to deal with here is that overall, Alaska Natives as a group are in the lowest levels of performance on the benchmark and high school qualifying exams.

This is a circumstance that we could turn into an opportunity for finger pointing, and blaming, and defensive postures. You know, I'm a certified teacher. I've been in the teachers' lounge, and I've heard teachers say: "Well, if only parents would be more supportive of education, then things would get better." And, as a Native parent, I used to think, well, how can I support something that I don't even get information about? I don't even have a clue about what they're trying to do. As a parent, I once tried to buy my daughter's textbooks for the next school year. Doesn't that seem like a good idea? If my daughter is going to be responsible for learning this, then as a parent, I should buy the textbooks ahead of time and become familiar with them, read them, and then I'll be ahead. It was easier to buy atomic bomb data from Los Alamos than to find out what textbook my daughter was going to study next year. It was impossible, and I'm within the system. Now, what's wrong with that picture? It's something for us to consider.

When we, as teachers, are asking for parental support for the education of kids, we have to think about how informed are we allowing parents to be about the educational structure and about what their children are going to be learning? It's got to be far more visible than it is today. What goes on in those schoolrooms seems to be classified information at times. It's amazing. I remember people asking: Why don't more parents show up at school meetings? And yet, I saw parents who were there. And I saw teachers who were very uncomfortable when I, a Native parent, wanted to sit in on my daughter's classroom and help. It just made them nervous.

Now, as to the overall status of Native people, we can look at any set of numbers you would care to see, good ones or bad ones. Here's a tough one: What happens if you're an Alaska Native male? We have, apparently, about as many Alaska Native males incarcerated as we have in universities. And for those who are incarcerated, the state is paying about five times as much to support their lifestyle as it is paying for those who are pursuing a college education. So, if your money is where your priorities are, there's something to consider in that.

We have a suicide rate for Alaska Native males that is about eight times the national average in the age category from 15 through 24. What does that say? Some people would look at that statistic and say, well, that's not about education—it's not an educational statistic. But I look at that, and I look at the lives of the people who are trapped in it. We are talking about young people who are going through life so ill-prepared for the future, whose opportunities are so narrow, whose sense of the future is so bleak, and whose circumstances are so overwhelming, that death is preferable to the life that lies before them. Isn't that an educational issue? Something for us to consider.

I want this to be a conference in which we put down our guards. As an educator, I want to be candid about our shortcomings, about how we have failed. I have been involved in the education of Alaska Natives for over

20 years, and I personally accept a measure of responsibility that we just haven't done what we should have done, and we haven't done it as well as we ought to have done it. We've failed in so many ways. I look at schools that are little more than life-support systems for athletic teams, that have no academic life, that have little in the way of substantial preparation of our people to take on the challenges we face, and I have to admit that we are falling short.

Look at what we're talking about. We have Native corporations. Think of the transformation that's occurred in our time. If we had looked at Alaska Natives in 1950, would anybody have anticipated that Natives would own the most powerful state-chartered corporations in Alaska? Would anybody have predicted that, given the power structure, the political structure, and the economic structure? Was that in the cards? Was that fate? We take these corporations for granted, but they were no accident. They were not inevitable. The successes that have occurred have come in spite of enormous odds. And yet, I look at those corporations, I look at their employees and staffs. Nine out of every 10 people who are working in professional positions in at least one of the Native corporations that I've looked at are non-Natives—the highest-paying positions in a Native corporation, and they're non-Natives.

Is that because there's a conspiracy among Native corporation people to keep highly qualified Alaska Natives out of those powerful jobs? No. We've got a disconnect between the educational system and the educational opportunities that are being created by our Native communities, and this conference is saying that we need to make those connections. What good will it do for us to have successful corporations if we don't have successful Alaska Natives to lead them? What good will it do? Look at our educational system. We actually have a decline in the number of Alaska Native teachers in this state, at the very time when we need more of them than ever—we're losing them.

So, what are we going to do about it? I'm at the university, and I can assure you with a high degree of confidence that the university is so fragmented that it would make continental drift seem fast before it will ever address the issues facing Alaska Native communities. It's just not going to happen that way, because the primary mission of this university is funding, parking lots for faculty, and winning teams for the alumni. This university is for the rest of the state. It's not primarily focused on Alaska Native communities and the issues we're facing.

Look at our school board associations. Is their primary issue that of solving the problem of Alaska Native education? What about NEA Alaska? I've been a member. I've been a delegate. They're supportive. They're potential allies, along with the university and the school board associations. They're all potential allies. But, who's going to take the lead and say: No, Alaska Native education, that's the issue. That's what we care about. That's what matters. If we want to see—day in, day out—a difference in our children's education, we ourselves have to start making those changes.

So, how do we do it? Well, a part of it is that we must make some sacrifices in order to make a difference. My dad was medivaced out of Kotzebue three days ago. I was with him most of last night, and he's coming around. He's a tough guy. And when I talked to him about whether I should stay with him or attend this education conference, he looked at me, grabbed onto my arm, gave me that look that I'm very familiar with, and gestured toward downtown Anchorage. I think he was saying that there are some priorities to be made. There are some issues that we need to focus on, and there is plenty of work for all of us to do. The issue we have to consider is what are we going to do to ensure that the education we offer will allow our Alaska Native students to come out of our schools—our schools—knowing our history, our traditions, our successes, our challenges, and our opportunities. How will we ensure that they sense that they are a part of powerful societies that care for them, and that this matters?

And if anyone says that it can't happen because it hasn't happened in the past 30 years, then we have only to look at what many of the Native corporations have become in the last 30 years. It's uneven, the successes of those corporations, but where they have been successful, they have been remarkable. And then look at the Native health care system. I remember when my dad's generation was just starting to take over the clinics and hospitals. Some people spoke loudly throughout the state, saying that if Alaska Natives took over their own health care delivery, it would be a travesty, and there would be illness, death, and destruction everywhere. I heard it. My dad heard it. And now he's in ICU in a hospital that is administered by Alaska Natives, and he's getting some of the finest care he could get anywhere in the world. So, anyone who's a naysayer, who thinks that we can't take on the educational system and make it work for Alaska Natives, isn't looking at the same history that we all should know.

Thank you very much.

Decolonizing Western Alaska

Perry T. Mendenhall

Presented at Alaska Anthropology Association 15th Annual Meeting,
Fairbanks, March 25–26, 1988

ALASKA IS ONE-FIFTH the size of the USA and it holds vast untapped natural resources on land and in the sea, and, because of this, the regions, the state, the nation, and the world continue to have a long-standing interest in Alaska. Alaska's regions are diverse in climate, terrain, culture, and economic and natural resources, yet are mostly underdeveloped by Western standards and desires. Alaska is advertised as the land of the "last frontier." To the Native people of Western Alaska, it is home, with the surrounding landscape serving as our front yard and back yard, which, along with the seas, provides a garden that yields the foods we crave and depend upon as a "people."

William A. Oquilluk, author of *People of Kauwerak*, identifies the people of Western Alaska by the following:

> Many White people think that many years ago there might have been some boats that drifted from Japan or Korea to Alaska to start people being here. Our ancestors say we have ancestors that have been here from generation to generation since there was land between Alaska and Siberia. Our grandparents do not believe our ancestors came from other countries and changed to Eskimos. They learned their own ways from the beginning. (p. 223)

Not only did he tell how the Native people become independent and self-supporting in Western Alaska, he told of disasters that killed many of the people, leaving only a few to survive on the land. Those who survived these disasters rebuilt the population and told their story of what happened to the young ones while they were growing up. Briefly the disasters described by Oquilluk are:

1. Climate change: plants, animals, and people died due to an eclipse lasting three days and nights.
2. The great flood.
3. The time summer did not come.
4. The great sickness (1917).
5. The fifth disaster may be happening NOW. The rules and stories of our ancestors are being forgotten. The people do not know who their relations are. Many children lost their parents and grandparents in the 1917 flu epidemic and other sicknesses. They were taken to orphanages and did not learn about their forefathers.

William A. Oquilluk died on January 6, 1972, on the day he was going to be recognized by his people for his book *People of Kauwerak*. He died shortly after the passage of the Alaska Native Claims Settlement Act on December 18, 1971.

Through this presentation today, I hope to enlighten the young ones so that they may learn from our endeavors and mistakes as we attempt to survive and live with the changes that have come to our land and our people. They too must learn to use their "power of imagination" and "power of wisdom" to survive on the land reserved for our use, as we are still endeavoring to do.

This presentation will examine some of the political, economic, and educational efforts of the Native people of Western Alaska that have been aimed at shifting greater control of decisionmaking into the hands of Native people themselves. Attention will be given to the decolonizing intentions and shortcomings of institutions such as the Regional School Districts, Native Corporations, tribal and municipal governments, and various other Native organizations.

POLITICAL

The Indian Reorganization Act of 1936 was an attempt to help the Native people to better themselves through special federal Indian programs. This gave them the opportunity to study, practice, and to implement self-help programs that would assimilate them into the American way of government on the local level. This act also created a means of communication between the federal government and the Native people for the establishment of schools, reindeer programs, tribal ordinances and offices, health and social services, and attempts at commercial enterprises. Success of the tribal council/traditional council largely depended upon either the Bureau of Indian Affairs (BIA) teacher or official who acted as the overseer/diplomat of the federal government. Some tribes were more successful than others and benefited, while others did not. Either way, our people were starting to learn the ways of the federal political system.

Over time a few Eskimo legislators were elected to the territorial legislature, and organizations such as the Alaska Native Brotherhood and Sisterhood became active in local affairs amongst themselves. Each of these proved to be powerful political action committees for Native people. They encouraged their membership to become active politically in local, state, and national affairs during the territorial days.

Percy Ipalook was the first Eskimo legislator from Kotzebue, elected in 1946. Ernest Gruening encouraged and helped him run. "Ice Block" was a term used to identify the state senators from Western Alaska who held the power against the urban legislators until various reapportionments undid their political positions. Ice Block is similar to the "Bush Caucus" of today. This has shown that we do have the political muscle to draw from, and that an active political caucus can help us become more actively involved in the decision-making impacting our own affairs.

We have seen city councils, corporation boards, and village councils deal with their services and the issues that affect them. We have seen the Native people active in these roles in governing their own affairs. They have used their political knowledge on the local, state, and federal levels to pass a "land claims" bill by using the media, political consultants, party platforms, and their own power of imagination and wisdom. By presenting a united front, Native people have taken on major causes such as the "subsistence issue," Marine Mammal Protection Act, as well as ANCSA amendments and educational reforms.

Natives tend to scrutinize their own candidates more than they do non-Natives. They look at their educational background (how they use their education), employment history (stability), local accomplishments, and community trustworthiness. They also consider their ability to communicate their social, economic, educational, and governmental concerns and to be politically astute while in office. Hopefully they will "bring home the bacon" in the process.

The Native political influence tends to break down when they do not present a "united front" when dealing with issues, thus appearing to be fragmented before the media and the general public. To resolve differences, we need to meet together so we can agree on economic, subsistence, social, educational, tribal, and governmental issues and support one another when putting our concerns before the public. We all serve the same membership and have been charged with certain tasks to benefit this membership.

ECONOMICS

The North Slope region shows what can happen when locally driven economic development takes place. In the 1970s the Iñupiaq people there under the leadership of Eben Hopson organized themselves into a borough so that they could tax the oil development, thus creating a revenue stream for their own community and social services, educational needs, and cultural affairs. Their initiative has paved the way for other regions that have economic potential for development, such as the Red Dog Mine in the NANA region, which provided the impetus for forming the Northwest Arctic Borough. This development would not have occurred without the NANA Corporation managing their economic development affairs and putting forth their monies for such a venture. In recent years NANA region had the foresight to develop a regional strategy so that they would have a plan of action to base their borough formation on. They are now preparing social programs for their people to face the changes that come with economic development. They are also supporting educational programs that allow their own people to take part in this economic development.

The economy of the Bering Sea fisheries is always an issue to those villages involved in both herring and salmon commercial fishing, and the people in the region would like to see one of their own on the fishery board, so they would have a voice on gear limitations, open seasons, and the problem of limited permits. The Eskimo Walrus Commission and the Eskimo Whaling Commission have both been very instrumental in managing the walrus and whales by the data they collect for the various agencies. They both have been and still are active in local, state, national, and international political arenas to fend for their right to hunt walrus and whales for subsistence purposes.

EDUCATIONAL

It seems that every few years, as soon as the people become familiar with a school system, it changes: from the BIA to the Alaska State Operated School System to the REAA district formation, and to the small high school programs in each village. It is a wonder that we have any graduates to speak of with all these changes, though we have had an impact on education, first on committees and advisory boards, then on elected school boards with regional control.

Native people have learned to use the constitution of both the state and federal government to assert their rights. They closed down their regional high schools when their people complained about having to send their children away for school, when non-Native students attended local high schools in their home community. The Molly Hootch case provided for high school facilities for village students. They took over the dormitory program and placed their students in homes for closer supervision and attention. They saw the state using federal monies for the schooling of their high school students, so they presented them with the constitution which states that the education of *all* children was the responsibility of the state.

At the higher education level, the Alaska Federation of Natives passed an explicit resolution in support for a "College of Rural Alaska" to be formed so that the rural community colleges would not lose the effectiveness of their tailored postsecondary educational programs. They wanted "fiscal control" for program accountability that was promised by the legislature during their lobbying efforts. Senator Willie Hensley wrote a public report to the media, stating in no uncertain terms that the College of Rural Alaska should go forth as rural Alaska intended it to be implemented, not as the university officials or faculty wanted. For over 50 years, the urban universities have expected rural Alaska Natives to flock to their campuses for a traditional college education. From the point of view of the largest landowners who hold most of the natural resources of Alaska, the university still treats them in a "colonial way" instead of as beneficiaries of a land-grant college.

There is a need for more Native teachers, businessmen, middle managers, and social workers to partake of the American dream of local control, fiscal control, and social-economic development to effect proper change for our own people in today's fast-changing world. We've shown that the Eskimos can obtain observer status in the United Nations as a people through the Inuit Circumpolar Conference, and that our tribal governments and their activities are recognized by the federal government. For those of us who are surviving this "fifth disaster," we are telling our story to our "young ones" to share what we have learned from the beginning of this fifth disaster to NOW. We hope that they are learning well so that they can carry on our endeavors and dream as a "people" for the decolonization of Western Alaska.

Reference

Oquilluk, William A. 1973. *People of Kauwerak*. Anchorage: Alaska Methodist University Press.

EDUCATION AND CULTURAL SELF-DETERMINATION

———◆•×•◆———

Paul Ongtooguk

EDUCATION AND CULTURAL self-determination is an issue central to the future success or failure of Alaska Native peoples. The very existence of Natives as distinct peoples within Alaska depends on the next generation of Alaska Natives being aware of and connecting to their cultural heritage. Knowledge not passed down from generation to generation is at risk of being lost forever.

For the last 30 years, there have been many issues relating to Alaska Natives in the news. In the 1960s the federal and state governments were taking Alaska Native lands—lands and waters that Natives had been living on for countless generations. But in order to make Native land claims legal in the U.S. Native leaders learned all they could about land issues. They reached a first settlement in 1971 with the Alaska Native Claims Settlement Act.

Since then arguments over lands and the regional corporations have received attention. Cultural self-determination is the big issue now. The heart of the issue lies in three questions: What does it mean to be Alaska Native in this world at this time? What is the cultural legacy being passed on to the children? What knowledge is essential to pass on and how will this happen? If these issues are not addressed, then mainstream culture will quickly erode the fragmented knowledge being learned by the next generation, and the Native cultural legacy will be reduced to things like medical cards and museum artifacts.

When American-style schools were started in Alaskan communities, the idea was to wipe out Native culture—to undermine connections with spiritual worlds, lands and waters, and to break the feelings of individuals and groups that are the essence of a culture. The agenda was to "civilize the Natives" and to make them more like the white settlers. Any beliefs that Natives had that involved understanding the world differently, or defining their place in the world as separate and apart from the white settlers, was not allowed in school. English-only language policies were strictly enforced, and anyone speaking in a Native language was punished. Those policies erased Native languages from schools and from some communities as well. Schools disparaged Native language, food, dress, and customs. At the same time the curriculum of the schools and the teachers taught students to view the world from a Western point of view. Policies were aimed at the hearts of students. Feelings of inferiority and shame were associated with things Native. Good grades and rewards were associated with things Western. This was a tough message delivered by a powerful system.

Fortunately for the state, the world, and for Natives, the heart of being Alaska Native could not be erased. In many places the elders—and some very wise parents—ignored the lies about Alaska Natives being primitive or savage. Traditional practices continued. Young people learned very different lessons from school in fish camps, hunting camps, potlatches, traditional feasts and ceremonies. Some youth learned from the lessons of traditional dances. Most of the young people learned through the lives of elders who showed them that giving to the community was more important than gathering for yourself. The elders also taught that there was more to life than what was learned in school. William Oquilluk used the "power of imagination" as a way for Native cultures and people to grow and exist. It is time to return to William Oquilluk's lesson and to imagine more than what is taught in schools and on TV.

When regional education attendance areas (REAAs) were created in 1975, Alaska Native people felt the promise of some degree of self-determination and control over the education of rural students. Alaska Natives celebrated the fact that young people would not have to leave home for boarding schools. Parents hoped that students would also welcome the new opportunity to complete a high school education in their home communities.

But that generation of parents had themselves attended boarding schools outside Native communities. In many cases the youth were not prepared to assume the roles of adults in the communities when they returned, if they returned. As adolescents within the community, they would have learned the political, economic, artistic, and other aspects of their culture. They would have been observing and becoming familiar with the problems, the issues, the changes. While many positive things were learned in boarding schools, it did not include what it meant to be an Alaska Native and how to return to Native communities and assume the roles and responsibilities of adulthood. Between boarding schools and the rapid social changes in all parts of the state, many communities faced serious issues. REAAs, by themselves, could not solve the problems.

Schools, teachers, and Alaska Native individuals must "imagine" how education is related to cultural self-determination and begin to answer a series of questions. By the time young people graduate from high school, what will they be expected to know about Native cultures? What are Alaska Native young people learning from their parents' generation? What should Alaska Native young people be learning from their parents' generation? How many of Alaska Native high school graduates will be familiar with any Alaska Native authors after 12 years in school?

There are young people in Bethel who do not know who Jackson Lomack or Chief Eddie Hoffman were; in the Interior many do not know the names of Morris Thompson or Rosemarie Maher; in Southeast some do not know what Elizabeth Peratrovitch did.

It is the responsibility of parents, leaders, and communities to become more involved in determining the goals and curriculum in the schools. What should Alaska Native young people learn about being Alaska Native? What are the significant organizations, leaders, legends, poetry, stories, oral history, political and social issues? How can the schools support Native cultures? Non-Native professional educators cannot answer these questions. Alaska Natives must.

Schools and communities must come together and ensure opportunities to learn about Alaska Native history, Native leaders, and oral traditions. Cultural self-determination must be seen as integral to the interests of all Alaska Native societies. It should be central to the purpose of the Alaska Federation of Natives (AFN). Websites need to be recognized as places to learn, to inform, and to discuss things relevant to local, regional, and statewide cultures and organizations. The issue of cultural self-determination also extends to those thousands of Alaska Natives who live outside the state. Most Alaska Native adults care deeply about cultural self-determination. The problem is a lack of attention by Native communities directed to dealing with the issue. Cultural camps can address this issue, and students are very enthusiastic about these experiences. But cultural camps are short-term and they happen away from schools. The message being given to students is that school and culture are separate. REAAs provide an opportunity to integrate the community culture, but only if the communities are partners. Young people must know that communities care about who they are as well as what they know. They must know that communities love them enough to share their greatest riches with them. They must know that their cultural heritage is linked, over thousands of years, to who they are today and who they will become tomorrow.

EFFECTS OF MODERNIZATION ON THE CUP'IK OF ALASKA

Lucy Jones-Sparck

Originally published in *Education and Development: Lessons from the Third World*, edited by V. D'Oyley, A. Blunt, and R. Barnhardt. (Calgary: Temeron Press, 1992)

THERE IS A TENDENCY FOR OUTSIDERS who come to work with the Native people of Alaska to define them from their own stance in life—the culture they come from and the viewpoint of their respective career interest. A non-Native social worker sees Alaska Natives as a class of people with poverty and/or emotional problems. A non-Native teacher sees the children and their parents as academically incapable and disinterested people. An anthropologist sees an exciting chance to study and record about a people in a non-Western culture or a culture going through transformation. A missionary sees a group of people who need to embrace Christ and His teachings within the values of a Western culture. The Native people, however, see themselves differently, and after a period of assault from all these outsiders, they are at the dawn of self-reintegration.

THE WAY WE WERE

The Native people of Chevak, a village in southwest Alaska, call themselves "Cup'ik." The Nunivak Islanders down the coast also call themselves Cup'ik, but the two dialects are vastly different from each other. Although this article is written from the Chevak Cup'ik viewpoint, other Cup'ik and Yup'ik Eskimos in the Yukon-Kuskokwim Delta have had similar experiences as a result of the coming of the white man.

For generations before whites came, the Cup'ik were a group of people living life within a culture of their own making. The values, beliefs, and symbols of that culture were consistent and gave rise to affirmations of individual and group self-identity. Expectations of the behavior of all members of the community were consistent and spelled out. Lines of authority were explicit. Expectations of respect and how one displayed that respect to different people were taught. The striving for harmony between self, others, and nature was a basis for all teaching and living.

THE TRADITIONAL EDUCATION SYSTEM

Traditionally, education was a family and community responsibility. Embedded in the teachings were the values, beliefs, and symbols of the culture. The children learned what things were valued, how they were valued, and why they were valued. Great expectations were placed upon the student to learn and understand these teachings. The irresponsibility to heed or learn the teachings was said to affect the family and the community as well as the learner in a negative way. To act contrary to the teachings of the community was to point to yourself as a disrupter of the social and natural harmony, or as one who was not able to learn and be responsible. In this way you showed yourself to be untrustworthy. You were expected to obey the adults, not only to demonstrate responsibility and competence, but as a necessary condition of survival. You had to become quick-witted about securing shelter, food, and clothing in the most economical and efficient way. You were expected to take only what was necessary or else you would be seen to be wasteful and not very sensible.

The adults were expected to fulfill their duty to teach in the best possible way. If they didn't they pointed to themselves as irresponsible, lazy, and untrustworthy. They had been taught how to raise and teach children in a loving way and were not supposed to act with low self-esteem, ignorance, or antisocial ways. There were times for active listening, for lecture-style teaching, times to use storytelling or folk tales, and times for doing, or on-the-job learning. The Cup'ik children had fun and the toys they played with reinforced the learning.

Another way of transmitting and regulating social behavior was through dance and song. Dancing and singing was the acceptable time for adults and young people to clown around, to laugh at one another, and to show off. It also provided a time to tease or challenge others on matters of concern. Some songs and dances were nonsensical, while others were funny or instructional. Still others allowed you to show off your attractiveness and others to appreciate that beauty. Even if you did not stand up to dance, you could select a dancer and identify with him or her and dance through them. All came away with a feeling of having performed and/or entertained. Eskimo dancing was a major avenue for relieving tensions and reinforcing important values in the community.

The women had the responsibility of learning the techniques of teaching the young. The girls played with dolls or with story knives tracing out events in the mud and re-creating the social systems of the community and family. The women taught the young girls the ways of a woman. These teachings included the biological workings and care of the woman's body and the social rituals that accompanied the changes within the female body. For example, for a full year following a young girl's first menstruation she was instructed in every aspect of her dress and manner around others and in the natural environment.

From the accounts of the Cup'ik Elders today, a more intense atmosphere of learning existed in the *qaygiq* (men's house). In the active listening times when an Elder was lecturing, the men reported that they found it difficult to clear their throats or even to scratch an itch on their bodies. This resulted from the high esteem they had for Elders, which bordered on fear. Being a respected Elder was determined by many factors, including age, wisdom, and the ability to make judgments about community matters. The men included all aspects of life in their teachings, even when they were teaching out on the tundra. For example, when they dealt with the subject of survival tools, they included the science of nature, how to read the signs about what nature was about to do or just did, and how to respond in respect. Learning made sense because it dealt with what was essential to the person's being and nourished that identity. This knowledge is still possessed by a few who are now at the dusk of their lives.

Cup'ik men and women taught basically the same types of subjects to the young, whether it was in the home or the *qaygiq*. Each employed tried -and-true methods of teaching. Both taught about the ways of the culture, the ways of relating to one another, and the man and woman's place in the society, all of which shaped their spiritual, mental, psychological, and physical being. The way they taught, participated in recreational activities, went about their work, and related to one another was connected to their philosophy of harmony with all things. Even how they secured, cured, stored, and ate food was interconnected to the well-being of the self, others, and the world. Nature was an integral part of that striving, as were the spiritual, physical, and mental aspects of living.

THEN THE WHITE MAN CAME

When the first white men arrived, the Cup'iks were a self-sufficient people with a strong society that was well suited to the harsh environment in which they lived. When the next wave of whites came, they declared that Cup'ik ways were wrong and that they should drop their ways and do as the white man (Napoleon, 1991). Schools and churches were set up to teach the new ways and still later laws were established, to be followed by an enforcement system so that wrongdoers would be taken care of by the whites, because Cup'iks did not know the ways in which whites took care of justice. Cup'iks were represented by the whites in the legislature, because only whites understood the white legislative system. Within the educational system there was no question who would teach the Cup'ik children about the ways of the whites.

Much later the whites listened as a handful of urban Natives, who finally saw that the Alaska Native people were no longer in control of their own destiny, demanded that their rights as original inhabitants of the land be recognized. The whites responded with the "gift" of the Alaska Native Claims Settlement Act (ANCSA), passed by the United States Congress in 1971, returning control of selected lands to the Native people and compensating for those taken away. To manage the land and money, Native-run corporations were established in every village and region in the state and every Native person was made a "stockholder." Up to the time of ANCSA, the Native people had little knowledge of the white man's corporate world—the backbone of the white culture. Yet knowing this, the Natives were given a lot of money and told to operate a corporation and earn profits in the white man's way. If the Natives did not operate in the white man's way, they could be held liable for malpractice. The Natives had no choice but to comply, as all this was made legal by the United States Congress.

So the Cup'iks did the best they could, but the corporate world was not well suited to village Alaska. They found that the usual Cup'ik ways of sharing and caring were not the ways to operate a business. The corporate businesses that the Cup'ik operated themselves began to threaten the subsistence way of life, the very thing that Native people wanted to protect the most. The corporation, by necessity, feeds off the land by converting the environment into a commodity for financial gain, with its value as a source of physical and cultural sustenance given secondary consideration. The corporate system has forced the Natives to redefine their culture because of the economic imperatives needed to survive in the corporate world.

Cup'iks have had difficulty holding jobs in their own communities, because the jobs have to be held by people who knew about the white man's ways, and since no one knows these ways better than the white man himself, whites get the jobs. Job descriptions demand that things be done in a manner consistent with the white culture. Cup'iks who want to hold a job, say in social work, have to go to school and learn the white man's way, then go back to their village and do social work following the white man's rules and policies. It does not matter that the Cup'iks receiving these services do not respond to the white man's ways, only that the worker has a piece of paper that proves s/he has the proper qualifications according to white standards.

CUP'IKS LEARN DEPENDENCY

At first the Cup'iks were relatively safe in the womb of the village, carrying on the everyday activities of subsistence, but it was not long before the long arm of white policies got hold of Cup'ik life. No matter what they did they now encountered and had to abide by the white policies and laws. It did not matter to the whites that the Cup'iks did not understand these policies or laws. The Cup'ik, like everyone else, was expected to live life according to the white culture. The Cup'ik saw some whites who wanted to help in making life more meaningful, but could not because of the policies and the laws. Seeing this, the Cup'ik further realized that indeed the white ways could not be broken, even though they did not make sense in the context of Cup'ik culture.

The Cup'ik families eventually realized the whites were going to determine how things would be done in the village. The Elders no longer were to be the guiding voice of the village—that power and authority had to be elected. It did not matter that these men who were elected had pre-set relationships with Elders and others in the village, or that Elders were already identified as leaders in the community. The whites identified who was going to enforce laws made by someone far away from the village. The elected leaders had to override the existing lines of authority to make ordinances understandable by the whites. The Cup'iks called these elected leaders in their villages "*angayuquruat*," or pretend authorities.

The whites sent their people to take care of Cup'iks in need. The natural community or family systems were not expected to care for the people as they always had. There was an agency for every type of need to take over the functions of the community and the families. Soon the Cup'iks learned to refer their problems to these agencies and to depend on them. If a family needed assistance with an unruly or deviant family member, they preferred to have the white agency handle the problem. When one family member required help, instead of the others getting involved with this member themselves, they called a white agency to take care of the problem. The unruly or the deviant person came to prefer it that way as well, rather than face the shame of face-to-face conflict with familiar persons.

Gradually, Cup'ik people bought into this new worldview that Western people brought with them. Behaviors changed in the village. It was not the culture that the Cup'iks knew, but what could they do? Time and time again, when they suggested doing it their own way, they were told that they couldn't because it would either not be recognized by the government or be contrary to some policy or statute. If the Cup'iks went ahead and did what they wanted, trying to take control again, the rest of the village would be penalized by the withdrawal of financial help from all the Western agencies and/or from the government which had taken hold of village life. Everywhere people turned, the white man's way was the only legal way to operate. To operate the village school, people had to abide by the white policies and teach the white man's subjects in the white way. Otherwise, they were told they would have to fund their own schools if they wanted to operate them their own way.

Every aspect of Cup'ik life has been affected by the coming of the whites. At the 1987 Elders' Conference in Bethel the Elder Carl Flynn (1987) of Tununak pointed out, "The white man came and changed everything for us in ways we did not and do not understand. They even changed our names with foreign words we cannot pronounce, changed the names of landmarks with words we cannot pronounce." Native ways were being put aside to make way for the new ways. In that same conference another Elder pointed out, however, that for many years now the parents and the Elders were quietly staying on the sidelines because the Native young people were coming home from school with ideas and initiating programs and activities in the white way. The Elders thought that these young people knew what they were doing, but they soon saw that the young did not really know the ways of the whites either, and they were making many mistakes. To their credit the young people started looking to the Elders for guidance, for it was in the subsistence way of life of the Elders that Cup'ik spirituality, which is at the heart of the true Cup'ik culture, still lived.

TWO WORLDS OR ONE?

Ever since the Western culture arrived on the scene in rural Alaska, Native people, including the Cup'ik, have been trying to walk in two worlds. Native people continue to think and behave with one foot firmly planted in their own unique ways, while the other foot is required to walk in the Western way. In some areas, such as legal requirements and procedures, Natives have been skipping along on one leg on the Western side only, because they have had no choice in these matters. In general, however, Native people are struggling to retain their identity while walking in step with the Western educational system, abiding by its social welfare policies, and adhering to its judicial and policing regulations. Living this way is to walk in two worlds.

In education, the Native people are granted a role in running their own schools, but in doing so, they have to abide by the Western policies, guidelines, and regulations. What the Natives don't always understand are the implications of adopting the logistics of the Western system. When they are allowed to offer a Native dance class or put on a Native cultural awareness day as a supplement to the standard curriculum, they begin to think that they have control over the local schools. Another way that the Native people are duped into thinking they have control is through representation on the local school board. Just because they elect their own people to the local boards does not mean they have real control. The duties and responsibilities associated with implementing an educational program are still dictated by the state government, which knows only the Western way of operating a school system. If by chance the superintendent or the principal of the school is a Native, they also have to work within the confines of the Western system. Native educators are trained in the Western way of running schools and colleges. The Western education system has built within it the purpose of making learners conform to the Western way of doing things. As long as Native people are abiding by these rules, guidelines, and policies which are different from the Native cultural ways, they are having to walk in two worlds—one grounded in their community and the other reflected in the school and other related institutions.

This type of walking in two worlds has become a negative way of living, which has led to a confusion of identity and place in the world for Native people. So, what might it mean to walk in one world? First of all, members of long-standing cultures in the different parts of the world have always had a way of operating their daily lives according to how they understand life. These cultural ways are of their own making, and give them a base from which to incorporate new ideas, and on which to build their self-identity and their self-esteem. The Cup'ik people and other Alaska Natives are such cultural people. They once had a strong cultural base for living. This base was the foundation for the society, and out of it the members' intellect was fed, the body was cared for, the emotions were nurtured, and the spirit was upheld. Every new discovery and realization was accommodated into or through the cultural base, therefore being made understandable and useful. The people walked in one world, a world of their own. If given the chance, Alaska Native people could still accommodate the ideas of a different culture, incorporating the modern world into their own cultural base.

The federal government and the State of Alaska have expended a tremendous amount of money over the years to improve the schooling of Alaska Natives. In recent years, Native voices have been raised, stating that the Western styles of teaching have not worked very well with Native students, in spite of better facilities, up-to-date materials, and more teachers. Even removing children from their traditional homes and placing them in an all-Western boarding school environment did not fully achieve the intent of converting them to Western ways. The students still came away walking in, or caught between, two worlds.

In 1987, the U.S. Department of Education released a booklet called *Schools That work: Educating Disadvantaged Children*, in which the Secretary of Education, William Bennett (1987) wrote, "Too often we have spent money on the wrong things and have not achieved good results." Yet, promoters of the Western system have not considered that, in the case of Alaska Native education, this may have resulted from the fact that the system has been administered wrongly by the wrong people and that the wrong programs have been imposed on the Alaska Natives. The traditional education system was well in place for the Native people at the time of first contact. All new ideas and discoveries were put in their proper places so that members could learn of them and incorporate them into their lives. Instead of allowing Alaska Natives to incorporate new ideas into their own cultural system, the Westerners insisted on imposing a whole new system and running it themselves.

Through this imposition of an externally designed and controlled system, the Alaska Natives were subjugated, leaving them little choice but to try to walk in two worlds. However, the Native world was continuously criticized and invalidated so that the Native people themselves started to be ashamed of it. Many even pretended they did not belong to it, yet a part of them was still walking in it. Edward T. Hall (1976) described the resulting frustration as follows: "The source of rage on the part of minority groups in our culture is not only that they are treated badly, but that they can't seem to get the systems to work for them."

Only when Alaska Native people can understand that they have forfeited their self-determination in accepting the Western definition of how education is provided, how the social welfare system is operated, how social deviance is defined and treated, and how the village government and judicial system is implemented, will they really know what to do to reassert themselves in their Native world. If Alaska Natives can educate themselves about the traditional forms and functions of these systems and then go ahead and take control, not within the guidelines, policies, and procedures of the Western system, but through adaptations to their own ways, then they will truly walk in their own world, a world of their own making, a world in which they make the important decisions. The children and college students can then be educated to know this culture and be confident in it. Our feet will then be planted firmly in prideful recognition of the self, feeling comfortable with who we are, and seeing others of different cultures as they are. The late Cup'ik Elder Joseph Friday (1987) of Chevak said, "Get to know yourself as a whole, knowing and living your culture, then you can adopt and adapt to anything new." The Alaska Native cultures can adapt to, participate in, and help to advance modern technology. They can define the elements of living the way they understand them to be—the way of their culture. Rather than walking in two worlds, they can do this walking in one world, a world of their own making and control.

The Cup'iks and other Alaska Native people must be renewed and validated by their own members first. If the Native people do not validate themselves as a unique society, who else will respect and validate them as a living cultural people? Alaska Natives have tried walking in two worlds for a hundred years and it has not worked. It will take years for the Native cultures to stand as firmly as they once did, taking into account the new ways of making a living and the acquiring of new languages and technology. In the meantime, the path from the past leading to the present will have to be made known and understood, for it is the link with tradition that gives a culture a sense of continuity and strength, a sense of the place in that world where one is walking. As John Gardner (1964) has put it, "No society is likely to renew itself unless its dominant orientation is to the future, but not ignoring its past. A people without a history would be crippled as an individual with amnesia. They would not know who they were." Such is the challenge facing the Cup'ik people today.

HEALING FOR THE FUTURE

The whites came to the Cup'ik without guns, but they came equipped with tools stronger than guns. The Cup'iks were slowly choked out of their self-identity with kindness that came in the form of misguided help. Change was imposed on the Cup'ik people with little regard for what it meant to adopt the new culture they were supposed to emulate. The young were taken away to boarding schools and exposed to the ways of the new culture—some of us even went so far as to get master's degrees and more. Yet, for all the years that we spent with the Western culture, we kept coming out with the feeling of being Cup'ik, and this feeling kept our sanity for us. As tattered as we saw our culture, we still belonged to it and identified with it.

We no longer want to see our culture so tattered and battered. We have tried the Western way and yet find that we are Cup'iks first. We find that we can use the Western tools, dress, houses, and other ways of doing things, but still remain Cup'ik, with an identity that feels comfortable for us because that's who we are. We can participate in and contribute to our country as U.S. citizens and still be Cup'ik. Some changes have been good for the Cup'ik—there is always a necessity to change and adapt to new conditions. The Cup'ik must identify the values and beliefs they wish to abide by, for it is in knowing and understanding a consistent set of values to live by that a person is able to build a solid self-identity.

There is no need to recount all the hurtful behaviors the Cup'iks, like other Alaska Natives, experienced after the coming of the white man. What was done is done, but there is the future. It will take years to understand why Cup'iks and the other Native people of Alaska act in self-destructive ways. Harold Napoleon (1991) has made a valuable contribution to this understanding by examining the devastation of our way of life by the "Great Death"—the epidemics that decimated our people at the turn of the century. It takes time to take stock of where we've been, to forgive and to heal. It takes time to rebuild, and it will not be easy, human nature being the way it is. There is a great necessity to bridge that cultural gap, and on either side of the gap are people of all ages—it is not just a gap between the young and the old. The Cup'ik and other Alaska Natives are moving ahead in their own way, working things through for themselves, making their own mistakes and hopefully learning from them.

EDUCATION FOR THE FUTURE

It is time that our education system recognizes that the Native people of Alaska want the schools to contribute to the transmission of Native culture and language. They want the schools to become more relevant to the children as well as to the parents and the communities. They want the schools to help produce adults with a memory of the past. The past history does help a person gain a sense of continuity and a sense of something to build upon. It is time to put an end to the "pseudo-culture" we have tolerated and re-establish our links with our past to understand who we are today. We need to show the difference between material and nonmaterial aspects of culture and how the two have to be merged to make sense. We need to show why we have not adapted to the nonmaterial aspects of Western culture and how our spirituality has survived. We need to show the effects of the dysfunctional period of cultural transition, how we allowed it to happen, and what we need to do to overcome it.

These are complex issues which we are only now beginning to come to terms with in a way that we can understand and discuss amongst ourselves (Kawagley, 1993; Napoleon, 1991), so it is going to take a great deal more work to sort through how these issues can best be addressed in a formal educational program. Given the unique nature of these experiences for Native people, the burden of this work is on the shoulders of Native educators who can bring the necessary range of experience to bear in developing not only new curricula, but new kinds of educational institutions as well. Such work is just now beginning to get underway with the development of tribally run schools and tribal colleges in various parts of Alaska, and in the efforts of a new generation of Native educators who are finding ways to build bridges between the two worlds in their work as teachers, principals, and superintendents in the current educational system. Out of all this is emerging the outlines of an educational system that is capable of preparing students who can create a new world that integrates and respects all the elements of the lives they lead. It is clear from the outset that this will not be an easy task, but it is one of the most urgent tasks facing education today.

Following are some of the elements and features that are likely to need attention as this new one-world, culturally integrated educational system emerges. First of all, we will need to introduce students to contemporary aspects of traditional Alaska Native cultural knowledge, including but not limited to traditional governance structures, education practices, and tribal justice systems; Native spiritual ways, rituals, rites of passage, and the concept of harmony with all living things; traditional healing ways, medicines, and their uses; legends, stories, and songs (including those associated with dances and games), festivals and their significance; and skills in speaking and writing in the Native language. Students need to understand the traditional kinship structure and how it still functions to-day, including kinship lines and ways of relating within them; ways of courtship, childrearing, and family responsibilities; and rules regarding interpersonal relationships in the community. Students should have an understanding of the village history, including original names of villages and major landmarks, warring history, and biographical sketches of village leaders (past and present). To help insure that village life remains viable, students need to understand the nature of the village economy, including men's and women's roles in subsistence hunting, fishing, and gathering, ways to identify edible vegetation and fruits, ways of curing subsistence foods, tools for transportation, and the science of weather. And in today's world, that needs to be complemented with a well-rounded knowledge of the international world of commerce and an awareness of global relations and trends.

If the teachers in the schools are going to be responsible for teaching the kind of curriculum outlined above, they too need to be prepared with cer-tain qualities in mind. Following are some of the considerations that should go into the selection and preparation of teachers for Native communities. Colleges and schools need to approach their educational responsibilities in a way that will insure teachers have both personal and professional experi-ence and familiarity with Native cultures. Important steps in this regard include increasing the presence of Native instructors and students in all education programs, recognizing cultural expertise as being of equal value as academic expertise, creating a climate that is truly accepting of Native culture, incorporating cross-cultural perspectives in teaching methods, and exposing students to classrooms with Native teachers. Teachers need to be able to teach both material and nonmaterial aspects of Native culture, have the capacity to work in multicultural classrooms, and know how to integrate the community into the educational program. To facilitate all of the above, there needs to be more Native counseling and advising staff, Native people need to be carrying out cultural research on an ongoing basis, and Native master teachers need to be hired to put on summer institutes for teachers of Native students and develop teacher education programs for Native communities on an ongoing basis.

With the above steps, schools and teacher training institutions can begin to better address the current educational needs of Native people as they seek to reestablish their place in the contemporary world. As Vine Deloria, Jr. (1987), has said, "You can earn money but you cannot be happy unless you become yourself first . . . traditional education gives us an orientation to the world around us, so that we know who we are and have confidence when we do things."

SOME WORDS OF CAUTION

We Natives of Alaska should learn from the mistakes of the white missionaries. Many of them were so zealous and narrow-minded that they could not see the strengths of the people they sought to convert. We should be tolerant and show a willingness to be open and listen. The bitterness toward the whites should be healed, for it can only hurt the work that needs to be done. We should move ahead and concentrate instead on the steps needed for Native people to move toward greater self-determination. The whites need to understand that the Native people are not anti-American—we just want to redefine our Nativeness and our place in America in a unique way because we are of a unique culture. To deny this to ourselves and for the whites to deny this to us is to continue the same destructive and aimless ways, allowing ourselves to become weak and beaten.

Since we live in the United States and have become citizens, we do need to continue to try to understand the white culture and its technology. We can selectively use the technology in ways that are compatible and enhance our lives within our own cultural outlook. We need to further understand the white culture to be able to relate to it in ways that are beneficial to us. The problems we have are our problems. The state needs to support us in solving our own problems, rather than pouring money into the existing white agencies to solve our problems for us. Instead the monies earmarked for various agencies should be given directly to the Native communities to use in trying to solve our own problems. Native people must be cautious, however, and avoid the temptation to listen to the well-meaning whites and then end up following the same policies that are contrary to our culture and have not worked in the past. This necessarily requires the Natives to organize and plan as a community to find the best ways to use available resources to address the problems as we see them.

A PERSONAL NOTE

At the present time I am an associate professor at the University of Alaska Kuskokwim Campus teaching several courses in the behavioral sciences. I am considered qualified for this position because of my educational and experiential credentials. I admit I feel qualified, until my Native students say to me, "That's the *Gussaq* way, but what's the Yup'ik/Cup'ik way?" Because I am a Cup'ik and do try to interject Native ways where I can, my students feel free to raise such questions. I would feel much better about my role as an educator if I had also been schooled in the Cup'ik way the years I was getting the Western credentials.

The majority of my students do not realize the extent to which dependency and helplessness have affected the Yup'ik/Cup'ik communities they belong to. When it is all around you in every part of your life, these types of realities are hard to see in their true form. The government can promote the involvement of Alaska Natives in planning for improvements in Native communities, but such participation will end up making little difference if the baseline continues to be a white policy framework within which options must be considered. Many of us have worked hard to find solutions through that framework, and only after much frustration have we come to realize the limitations of what we were doing. Many more Native people need to come to this self-realization, so we can start seeing our situation for what it is.

For many years the Cup'ik youngsters begin school with the hope and belief that they can make it in the world of their white teachers. But along the way they come across difficulties that a normal young white student would not experience. The young Cup'ik's normal coping skills break down in the face of the unfamiliar world of the school. In my introductory psychology class, I teach my students that they have many natural skills for learning about and adapting to new situations. However, when the Cup'ik students are in an unfamiliar environment they opt for withdrawal. Too many experiences have taught them to retreat this way, leaving them with feelings of impotence and/or frustration for having "failed." I have tried to identify, through discussions with other Native persons who have been recognized as successful in the Western system, the factors that lead to what we call "success." Our conclusions always point to the fact that our upbringing was strong, traditional, and consistent, with our identity firmly established through the constant teachings of our parents and sometimes reinforced by certain white teachers. For me, I believe that was what I got from my parents and my extended family, which was truly traditional. I was firm in my self-identity when I went off to college, so I was equipped to deal with what came next. Too many of the students I see today do not have that foundation of a strong identity.

Recently I came across the following statement by Frederick Kanfer (1986): "[C]lients' interests must be protected to avoid damage or grief resulting from a helper's ignorance, or exploitation of a client's vulnerability, and the advice and guidance that would force the client into a situation over which he/she has no control constitutes unethical behavior . . . [T]he client should be told about possible aversive or negative outcomes." Well, the Native interest has not been protected, and there was and still is a lot of advice and guidance that is forcing the Cup'ik people into situations over which they have no control. We can see the consequences around us of all that help we have received over the years. I hope we as Native people will try to heed Kanfer's warning when working with ourselves, and as for the whites who will still be working with us, it is never too late to be ethical.

References

Bennett, William. 1987. *Schools that work: Educating disadvantaged children.* Washington, DC: U.S. Government Printing Office.

Deloria, Jr., Vine. 1990. Traditional education in the modern world. *Winds of Change* 5(1).

Flynn, Carl. 1987. *Elders' Conference Report.* Bethel: Association of Village Council Presidents.

Friday, Joeseph. 1987. *Elders' Conference Report.* Bethel: Association of Village Council Presidents.

Gardner, John W. 1964. *Self-renewal.* New York: Harper and Row Publishers.

Hall, Edward T. 1976. *Beyond culture.* New York: Anchor Books.

Kanfer, Frederick H., and Arnold P. Goldstein, eds. 1986. *Helping people change.* New York: Pergamon Press.

Kawagley, O. 1993. A Yupiaq World view: Implications for cultural, educational and technological adaptation in a contemporary world. PhD dissertation, University of British Columbia.

Napoleon, Harold. 1991. *Yuuyaraq: The way of the human being.* Fairbanks: Center for Cross-Cultural Studies, University of Alaska Fairbanks.

APPENDICES

GUIDELINES FOR RESEARCH

♦•×•♦

Alaska Federation of Natives Board of Directors

Adopted in May 1993

AT ITS QUARTERLY MEETING in May 1993, the AFN Board of Directors adopted a policy recommendation that includes a set of research principles to be conveyed to scientists who plan to conduct studies among Alaska Natives.

These principles were sent to all Native organizations and villages in the hope that compliance by researchers will deter abuses such as those committed in the past which lately have come to light.

Alaska Natives share with the scientific community an interest in learning more about the history and culture of our societies. The best scientific and ethical standards are obtained when Alaska Natives are directly involved in research conducted in our communities and in studies where the findings have a direct impact on Native populations.

AFN recommends to public and private institutions that conduct or support research among Alaska Natives that they include a standard category of funding in their projects to ensure Native participation.

AFN conveys to all scientists and researchers who plan to conduct studies among Alaska Natives that they must comply with the following research principles:

- Advise Native people who are to be affected by the study of the purpose, goals, and time-frame of the research, the data-gathering techniques, the positive and negative implications and impacts of the research.

- Obtain the informed consent of the appropriate governing body.
- Fund the support of a Native Research Committee appointed by the local community to assess and monitor the research project and ensure compliance with the expressed wishes of Native people.
- Protect the sacred knowledge and cultural/intellectual property of Native people.
- Hire and train Native people to assist in the study.
- Use Native language whenever English is the second language.
- Guarantee confidentiality of surveys and sensitive material.
- Include Native viewpoints in the final study.
- Acknowledge the contributions of Native resource people.
- Inform the Native Research Committee in a summary and in non-technical language of the major findings of the study.
- Provide copies of studies to the local library.

The Coolangatta Statement on Indigenous Peoples' Rights in Education

◆◆✕◆◆

Adopted at the World Indigenous Peoples' Conference
on Education, Hilo, Hawai'i
August 6, 1999

Preamble

THE COOLANGATTA STATEMENT represents a collective voice of Indigenous peoples from around the world who support fundamental principles considered vital to achieving reform and transformation of education for Indigenous peoples.

The need for such an instrument is self-evident. Over the last 30 years, Indigenous peoples throughout the world have argued that they have been denied equity in non-Indigenous education systems which have failed to provide educational services that nurture the whole Indigenous person inclusive of scholarship, culture and spirituality.

Most all Indigenous peoples, and in particular, those who have suffered the impact and effects of colonization, have struggled to access education that acknowledges, respects and promotes the right of Indigenous peoples to be Indigenous—a right that embraces Indigenous peoples' language, culture, traditions, and spirituality. This includes the right to self-determination.

This Statement speaks to the inherent rights of Indigenous peoples as declared in Article 27 of the International Covenant on Civil and Political Rights:

> In those States in which ethnic, religious or linguistic minorities exist, persons belonging to such minorities shall not be denied the right, in community with the other members of their group, to enjoy their own culture, and to profess and practice their own religion, and to use their own language.

As an instrument which derives its vision and strength from Indigenous Nations and peoples, the Coolangatta Statement on Indigenous Peoples' Rights in Education is and will remain a living document which addresses the educational rights of Indigenous peoples now and into the future.

I. INDIGENOUS EDUCATION: A GLOBAL OVERVIEW

1.1   There exists a proliferation of international charters, conventions and other instruments that recognize the basic human rights of all peoples, amongst which is the right to education. Some of these instruments have been analyzed in the preparation of this statement. These include:

Universal Declaration of Human Rights;

International Covenant on Economic, Social and Cultural Rights;

International Covenant on Civil and Political Rights;

Declaration on the Elimination of all Forms of Racial Discrimination;

Discrimination (Employment & Occupation) Convention;

Convention Against Discrimination in Education;

Working Group on Indigenous Populations—Draft Declaration on Indigenous Rights;

Kari-Oca Indigenous Peoples Earth Charter.

1.2   Indigenous peoples acknowledge that select principles and articles from international human rights instruments provide some basis for recognizing the rights of Indigenous peoples to education.

1.2.1 For example, Article 26 of the United Nations Declaration of Human Rights states:

> i. Everyone has the right to education. Education shall be free, at least in the elementary and fundamental stages. Elementary education shall be compulsory. Technical and professional education shall be made generally available and higher education shall be equally accessible to all on the basis of merit.

> ii. Education shall be directed to the full development of the human personality and to the strengthening of respect for human rights and fundamental freedoms. It shall promote understanding, tolerance and friendship among all nations, racial or religious groups, and shall further the activities of the United Nation for the maintenance of peace.

> iii. Parents have a prior right to choose the kind of education that shall be given to their children.

1.2.2 Article 27 of the International Covenant on Civil and Political Rights further states:

> In those States in which ethnic, religious or linguistic minorities exist, persons belonging to such minorities shall not be denied the right, in community with the other members of their group, to enjoy their own culture, and to profess and practice their own religion, and to use their own language.

1.3 Although the capacity for such instruments provides some basis for recognizing rights of Indigenous peoples, the 1999 WIPCE asserts that such instruments are limited in their capacity to recognize and protect the rights of Indigenous peoples.

Human rights, by definition, are inalienable, inviolable and innate. The freedom to enjoy and indeed celebrate these rights has been, and continues to be, denied and obstructed for Indigenous peoples throughout the world.

Specific limitations include the extent to which these instruments:

Protect the right of Indigenous peoples to equal access to education systems;

Ensure that Indigenous parents have a prior right to choose the kind of education that shall be given to their children;

Promote the right of Indigenous peoples to enjoy their own cultures in community with other members of their group;

Provide conditions that are conducive to the use and maintenance of Indigenous languages.

1.3.1   Historically, Indigenous peoples have insisted upon the right of access to education. Invariably the nature, and consequently the outcome, of this education has been constructed through and measured by non-Indigenous standards, values and philosophies. Ultimately the purpose of this education has been to assimilate Indigenous peoples into non-Indigenous cultures and societies.

Volumes of studies, research and reports dealing with Indigenous peoples in non-Indigenous educational systems paint a familiar picture of failure and despair. When measured in non-Indigenous terms, the educational outcomes of Indigenous peoples are still far below that of non-Indigenous peoples. This fact exists not because Indigenous peoples are less intelligent, but because educational theories and practices are developed and controlled by non-Indigenous peoples. Thus, in more recent times, due to the involvement of Indigenous peoples, research shows that failure is indeed present, but that this failure is that of the system, not of Indigenous peoples.

In this context the so-called "dropout rates and failures" of Indigenous peoples within non-Indigenous educational systems must be viewed for what they really are—rejection rates.

1.3.2   The rights of Indigenous peoples to access education—even when these rights are recognized in treaties and other instruments—are often interpreted to read that Indigenous peoples only want access to non-Indigenous education. Presumably it is considered that the core of Indigenous cultural values, standards and wisdom is abandoned or withering in the wilderness of Indigenous societies.

Yet, Indigenous peoples across the world are demanding and, in some cases, achieving the establishment of systems of education which reflect, respect and embrace Indigenous cultural values, philosophies and ideologies—the same values, philosophies and ideologies which shaped, nurtured and sustained Indigenous peoples for tens of thousands of years.

One of the greatest challenges confronting Indigenous peoples in the final year of the twentieth century is how to promote, protect and nurture Indigenous cultures in an ever-changing modern society. This is of particular concern for Indigenous peoples who are forced into cities and away from their homelands.

1.4   It is of concern to the 1999 WIPCE that many international instruments have a limited capacity to recognize the most fundamental human right of Indigenous peoples—the right to be Indigenous. The right to be Indigenous involves the freedom of Indigenous peoples themselves to determine who is Indigenous; what it means to be Indigenous; and, how education relates to Indigenous cultures.

1.4.1 Recently a number of international documents prepared in response to the limited capacity of international human rights instruments recognize and protect the right of Indigenous peoples to be Indigenous. The 1999 WIPCE acknowledges and supports such documents, which include the Draft Declaration on the Rights of Indigenous Peoples and the Kari-Oca Indigenous Peoples' Earth Charter.

1.4.2 The Draft Declaration on the Rights of Indigenous Peoples, as revised by the members of the Working Group on Indigenous Populations in July 1993, asserts:

> Indigenous peoples have the right of self-determination. By virtue of that right they freely determine their political statutes and freely pursue their economic, social and cultural development. (Article 3)

> Indigenous peoples have the right to participate fully, if they so wish, in the political, economic, social and cultural life of the state, while maintaining their distinct political, economical, social and cultural characteristics, as well as their legal systems. (Article 4)

The draft declaration goes on to add:

> Indigenous peoples have the right to all levels and forms of education. They also have the right to establish and control their educational systems and institutions providing education in their own language. (Article 14)

> Indigenous peoples have the right to have the dignity and diversity of their cultures, traditions, histories and aspirations appropriately reflected in all forms of education and public information. States shall take effective measures,

in consultation with Indigenous peoples, in eliminating prejudice and to promote tolerance, understanding and good relations. (Article 15) [The Draft Declaration was formally adopted by the U.N. Generally Assembly in September, 2007]

1.4.3   The Kari-Oca Declaration entitled "Indigenous Peoples' Earth Charter" (formulated in Brazil in May 1993) includes the following statements on Indigenous education:

Indigenous peoples should have the right to their own knowledge, languages and culturally appropriate education, including bicultural and bilingual education. Through recognizing both formal and informal ways the participation of family and community is guaranteed.

Indigenous peoples must have the necessary resources and control over their own education systems. Elders must be recognized and respected as teachers of the young people. Indigenous wisdom must be recognized and encouraged.

The use of existing Indigenous languages is our right. These languages must be protected. At local, national, and international levels, governments must commit funds to new and existing resources to education and training for Indigenous peoples to achieve their sustainable development, to contribute and to participate in sustainable and equitable development at all levels. Particular attention should be given to Indigenous women, children and youth.

The United Nations should promote research into Indigenous knowledge and develop a network of Indigenous sciences. As creators and carriers of civilizations which have given and continue to share knowledge, experience and values with humanity, we require that our right to intellectual and cultural properties be guaranteed and that the mechanism for each implementation be in favor of our people and studies in depth be implemented.

1.5   Evident from recent international documents on the Rights of Indigenous peoples, the right to be indigenous is an essential prerequisite to developing and maintaining culturally appropriate and sustainable education for Indigenous peoples.

Also evident, the educational struggles of Indigenous peoples of the world involve more than the struggle for access to and participation in both non-Indigenous education systems and culturally appropriate education. The educational struggles of Indigenous peoples are fundamentally and unequivocally concerned with the right of Indigenous peoples to be indigenous.

1.6   Youth and the young have a special place and responsibility in the struggle to nurture and protect Indigenous cultures. It is to them that truth and wisdom is bequeathed. When Indigenous youth and the young are separated from their cultural base and communities, Indigenous cultures and peoples are threatened with cultural extinction.

1.6.1 The forced removal of Indigenous children from their families and communities was a favored policy and practice of colonial powers throughout the world. The pain and emotional scars that are the legacy of this insidious form of cultural genocide continues to torment many of today's Indigenous peoples.

1.6.2 Acknowledging and respecting their role and responsibilities, delegates from the World Indigenous Youth Conference held in Darwin, Australia in July 1993, declared:

> We, Indigenous youth, believe we must maintain our right to self-determination. Our people have the right to decide our own forms of government, the use of our lands, to one day raise and educate our children in our own cultural identities without interference.
>
> We, Indigenous youth must have the freedom to learn our true histories. We make a call to our elders to open the way for us to learn about our heritages--to help us reclaim our past, so that we may claim our future.
>
> We, Indigenous youth, recognize our languages as an important link to maintaining our cultures. Indigenous languages must be maintained at a local level.

1.7   The 1999 WIPCE recognizes an existence of a commonality of purpose and desire amongst the Indigenous peoples of the world for education. It further recognizes that this commonality involves a shared belief that education must be scholarly and empowering whilst at the same time the processes of education must be embedded in Indigenous culture and wisdom.

1.7.1. Meaningful, empowering and culturally sustainable education for Indigenous peoples will be possible only when Indigenous peoples have the control (a fundamental right) and the resources (an inarguable responsibility of States/governments) to develop educational theories, curriculum and practices that are indigenous and are able to determine the environment within which this education can best occur.

1.7.2 Indigenous self-determination involves choice and diversity. If an Indigenous person chooses to access an Indigenous education system, then this is a choice, which must be respected. If an Indigenous person chooses to access non-Indigenous education, then this choice must also be respected. If an Indigenous person chooses to access both non-Indigenous and Indigenous systems of education, then this choice too must be respected. Not to do so is in itself a violation of a basic human right.

II. Rights in Indigenous Education

2.1   The right to be Indigenous is the most fundamental and important of all Human Rights.

2.2   The right to be Indigenous is a precursor to self-determination. The right to self-determination and the achievement of other inherent rights and freedoms for Indigenous peoples is inextricably connected to the physical and spiritual phenomenon of what most call "the earth." The sense of connectedness and belonging to Mother Earth is similar to the special bonds that unite parent and child. As a child's hopes and securities, aspirations and comforts are fundamental to its relationships with its parents, so too are Indigenous peoples' hopes and securities, aspirations and comforts fundamental in their relationship to Mother Earth.

2.2.1 Non-Indigenous peoples and their representative governments must accept this parent relationship with Mother Earth that characterizes Indigenous cultures. This relationship enables Indigenous peoples to negotiate, use and maintain the land, and to build and rebuild the social structures needed for cultural survival.

2.2.2   There are no single, simple or common answers to the question of Indigenous self-determination—only Indigenous peoples who are spiritually focused and land-based.

2.2.3   The provision and application of material and political responses by Nation States to the right of Indigenous peoples to self-determination, governance and control over Indigenous life and futures must cease.

2.2.4   Self-determination in Indigenous education embodies the right of Indigenous people:

> To control/govern Indigenous education systems;
>
> To establish schools and other learning facilities that recognize, respect and promote Indigenous values, philosophies and ideologies;
>
> To develop and implement culturally inclusive curricula;
>
> To utilize the essential wisdom of Indigenous elders in the education process;
>
> To establish the criterion for educational evaluation and assessment;
>
> To define and identify standards for the gifted and talented;
>
> To promote the use of Indigenous languages in education;
>
> To establish the parameters and ethics within which Indigenous education research should be conducted;
>
> To design and deliver culturally appropriate and sensitive teacher training programs;
>
> To participate in teacher certification and selection;
>
> To develop criterion for the registration and operation of schools and other learning facilities; and,
>
> To choose the nature and scope of education without prejudice.

2.3   Indigenous peoples have strong feelings and thoughts about landforms, the very basis of their cultural identity. Land gives life to language and culture.

2.3.1   Indigenous languages in all forms are legitimate and valid means of communication for Indigenous peoples.

2.3.2   Language is a social construct; it is a blueprint for thought, behavior, social and cultural interaction and self-expression.

2.3.3   Language is the medium for transmitting culture from the past to the present and into the future. Acknowledging that many Indigenous languages have been destroyed, the 1999 WIPCE asserts that Indigenous languages are the best way to teach Indigenous knowledge and values.

2.3.4   Languages are the foundations for the liberation of thoughts that provide direction for social, political and economic change and development.

2.3.5   The survival and revival of Indigenous languages is imperative for the protection, transmission, maintenance and preservation of Indigenous knowledge, cultural values, and wisdom.

2.4   Pedagogy is the interrelationship between learning styles and teaching methods. There are pedagogical principles shared by all Indigenous peoples, but there are also those that are characteristic to the specific cultures, languages, environment and circumstances of Indigenous peoples across the world. Indigenous peoples and cultures are not homogenous.

2.4.1   Indigenous pedagogical principles are holistic, connected, valid, cultural, value-based, thematic and experiential. They promote and reward cooperative learning and the unified co-operation of learner and teacher in a single educational enterprise. They describe who teaches, as well as, how and when teaching occurs. Indigenous pedagogical principles, unlike Western paradigms, recognize the important role of non-verbal communication in the learning-teaching process.

2.4.2   Indigenous learning is clothed in the medium of spirituality. Notions of well being/wellness and ethos are important in the process of learning.

2.4.3   The teacher is a facilitator of learning, one who promotes achievement and success. In this context culturally appropriate environments are employed to reinforce knowledge being imparted to the learner, reaffirming the learner's significant place in the world.

2.4.4   The involvement of community in all pedagogical processes is valued.

2.5   Indigenous peoples at the local level must determine how and to what degree non-Indigenous peoples are involved in Indigenous education. Once this role is determined it is the responsibility of non-Indigenous peoples to respect and adhere to the wishes of the local community.

2.5.1   Non-Indigenous peoples come from a different cultural background. Since Indigenous education is centered in Indigenous culture, non-Indigenous people must only be involved in the process of achieving educational objectives as determined by Indigenous peoples. Non-Indigenous peoples should not involve themselves in the processes of Indigenous decision-making.

2.5.2   Non-Indigenous peoples through the various levels of government and bureaucracy have an over-riding responsibility to accept and uphold the educational rights of Indigenous peoples and to know that these rights and freedoms are non-negotiable.

III. CONCLUSION

3.1   Indigenous peoples throughout the world survive policies and practices ranging from extermination and genocide to protection and assimilation. Perhaps more than any other feat, survival is the greatest of all Indigenous peoples' achievements.

3.2   Indigenous peoples have the right to be Indigenous. They cannot exist as images and reflections of a non-Indigenous society.

3.3   Indigenous education, as a medium for both personal development and intellectual empowerment, is critical for the continuance and celebration of Indigenous cultures.

3.4   To be Indigenous is both a privilege and a birthright. It is therefore the responsibility of all Indigenous peoples to ensure that their respective cultures, philosophies and ideologies remain strong and continue to grow.

3.5   We, the Indigenous peoples of the world, assert our inherent right to self-determination in all matters. Self-determination is about making informed choices and decisions and creating appropriate structures for the transmission of culture, knowledge and wisdom for the benefit of each of our respective cultures. Education for our communities and each individual is central to the preservation of our cultures and for the development of the skills and expertise we need in order to be a vital part of the twenty-first century.

UNITED NATIONS DECLARATION ON THE RIGHTS OF INDIGENOUS PEOPLES

United Nations

A/61/L.67

General Assembly

Distr.: Limited
7 September 2007

Original: English

Sixty-first session
Agenda item 68
Report of the Human Rights Council

> **Belgium, Bolivia, Costa Rica, Cuba, Denmark, Dominican Republic, Ecuador, Estonia, Finland, Germany, Greece, Guatemala, Hungary, Latvia, Nicaragua, Peru, Portugal, Slovenia and Spain: draft resolution**
>
> ## United Nations Declaration on the Rights of Indigenous Peoples
>
> *The General Assembly,*
>
> *Taking note* of the recommendation of the Human Rights Council contained in its resolution 1/2 of 29 June 2006, by which the Council adopted the text of the United Nations Declaration on the Rights of Indigenous Peoples,
>
> *Recalling* its resolution 61/178 of 20 December 2006, by which it decided to defer consideration of and action on the Declaration to allow time for further consultations thereon, and also decided to conclude its consideration before the end of the sixty-first session of the General Assembly,
>
> *Adopts* the United Nations Declaration on the Rights of Indigenous Peoples as contained in the annex to the present resolution.

A/61/L..67

Annex

United Nations Declaration on the Rights of Indigenous Peoples

The General Assembly,

Guided by the purposes and principles of the Charter of the United Nations, and good faith in the fulfilment of the obligations assumed by States in accordance with the Charter,

Affirming that indigenous peoples are equal to all other peoples, while recognizing the right of all peoples to be different, to consider themselves different, and to be respected as such,

Affirming also that all peoples contribute to the diversity and richness of civilizations and cultures, which constitute the common heritage of humankind,

Affirming further that all doctrines, policies and practices based on or advocating superiority of peoples or individuals on the basis of national origin or racial, religious, ethnic or cultural differences are racist, scientifically false, legally invalid, morally condemnable and socially unjust,

Reaffirming that indigenous peoples, in the exercise of their rights, should be free from discrimination of any kind,

Concerned that indigenous peoples have suffered from historic injustices as a result of, inter alia, their colonization and dispossession of their lands, territories and resources, thus preventing them from exercising, in particular, their right to development in accordance with their own needs and interests,

Recognizing the urgent need to respect and promote the inherent rights of indigenous peoples which derive from their political, economic and social structures and from their cultures, spiritual traditions, histories and philosophies, especially their rights to their lands, territories and resources,

Recognizing also the urgent need to respect and promote the rights of indigenous peoples affirmed in treaties, agreements and other constructive arrangements with States,

Welcoming the fact that indigenous peoples are organizing themselves for political, economic, social and cultural enhancement and in order to bring to an end all forms of discrimination and oppression wherever they occur,

Convinced that control by indigenous peoples over developments affecting them and their lands, territories and resources will enable them to maintain and strengthen their institutions, cultures and traditions, and to promote their development in accordance with their aspirations and needs,

Recognizing that respect for indigenous knowledge, cultures and traditional practices contributes to sustainable and equitable development and proper management of the environment,

Emphasizing the contribution of the demilitarization of the lands and territories of indigenous peoples to peace, economic and social progress and development, understanding and friendly relations among nations and peoples of the world,

Recognizing in particular the right of indigenous families and communities to retain shared responsibility for the upbringing, training, education and well-being of their children, consistent with the rights of the child,

Considering that the rights affirmed in treaties, agreements and other constructive arrangements between States and indigenous peoples are, in some situations, matters of international concern, interest, responsibility and character,

Considering also that treaties, agreements and other constructive arrangements, and the relationship they represent, are the basis for a strengthened partnership between indigenous peoples and States,

Acknowledging that the Charter of the United Nations, the International Covenant on Economic, Social and Cultural Rights[1] and the International Covenant on Civil and Political Rights as well as the Vienna Declaration and Programme of Action,[2] affirm the fundamental importance of the right to self-determination of all peoples, by virtue of which they freely determine their political status and freely pursue their economic, social and cultural development,

Bearing in mind that nothing in this Declaration may be used to deny any peoples their right to self-determination, exercised in conformity with international law,

Convinced that the recognition of the rights of indigenous peoples in this Declaration will enhance harmonious and cooperative relations between the State and indigenous peoples, based on principles of justice, democracy, respect for human rights, non-discrimination and good faith,

Encouraging States to comply with and effectively implement all their obligations as they apply to indigenous peoples under international instruments, in particular those related to human rights, in consultation and cooperation with the peoples concerned,

Emphasizing that the United Nations has an important and continuing role to play in promoting and protecting the rights of indigenous peoples,

Believing that this Declaration is a further important step forward for the recognition, promotion and protection of the rights and freedoms of indigenous peoples and in the development of relevant activities of the United Nations system in this field,

Recognizing and reaffirming that indigenous individuals are entitled without discrimination to all human rights recognized in international law, and that indigenous peoples possess collective rights which are indispensable for their existence, well-being and integral development as peoples,

Recognizing also that the situation of indigenous peoples varies from region to region and from country to country and that the significance of national and regional particularities and various historical and cultural backgrounds should be taken into consideration,

---

[1] See resolution 2200 A (XXI), annex.
[2] A/CONF.157/24 (Part I), chap. III.

Solemnly proclaims the following United Nations Declaration on the Rights of Indigenous Peoples as a standard of achievement to be pursued in a spirit of partnership and mutual respect:

Article 1

Indigenous peoples have the right to the full enjoyment, as a collective or as individuals, of all human rights and fundamental freedoms as recognized in the Charter of the United Nations, the Universal Declaration of Human Rights[3] and international human rights law.

Article 2

Indigenous peoples and individuals are free and equal to all other peoples and individuals and have the right to be free from any kind of discrimination, in the exercise of their rights, in particular that based on their indigenous origin or identity.

Article 3

Indigenous peoples have the right to self-determination. By virtue of that right they freely determine their political status and freely pursue their economic, social and cultural development.

Article 4

Indigenous peoples, in exercising their right to self-determination, have the right to autonomy or self-government in matters relating to their internal and local affairs, as well as ways and means for financing their autonomous functions.

Article 5

Indigenous peoples have the right to maintain and strengthen their distinct political, legal, economic, social and cultural institutions, while retaining their right to participate fully, if they so choose, in the political, economic, social and cultural life of the State.

Article 6

Every indigenous individual has the right to a nationality.

Article 7

1.   Indigenous individuals have the rights to life, physical and mental integrity, liberty and security of person.

2.   Indigenous peoples have the collective right to live in freedom, peace and security as distinct peoples and shall not be subjected to any act of genocide or any other act of violence, including forcibly removing children of the group to another group.

---

[3] Resolution 217 A (III).

A/61/L.67

Article 8

1.   Indigenous peoples and individuals have the right not to be subjected to forced assimilation or destruction of their culture.

2.   States shall provide effective mechanisms for prevention of, and redress for:

(a)   Any action which has the aim or effect of depriving them of their integrity as distinct peoples, or of their cultural values or ethnic identities;

(b)   Any action which has the aim or effect of dispossessing them of their lands, territories or resources;

(c)   Any form of forced population transfer which has the aim or effect of violating or undermining any of their rights;

(d)   Any form of forced assimilation or integration;

(e)   Any form of propaganda designed to promote or incite racial or ethnic discrimination directed against them.

Article 9

Indigenous peoples and individuals have the right to belong to an indigenous community or nation, in accordance with the traditions and customs of the community or nation concerned. No discrimination of any kind may arise from the exercise of such a right.

Article 10

Indigenous peoples shall not be forcibly removed from their lands or territories. No relocation shall take place without the free, prior and informed consent of the indigenous peoples concerned and after agreement on just and fair compensation and, where possible, with the option of return.

Article 11

1.   Indigenous peoples have the right to practise and revitalize their cultural traditions and customs. This includes the right to maintain, protect and develop the past, present and future manifestations of their cultures, such as archaeological and historical sites, artefacts, designs, ceremonies, technologies and visual and performing arts and literature.

2.   States shall provide redress through effective mechanisms, which may include restitution, developed in conjunction with indigenous peoples, with respect to their cultural, intellectual, religious and spiritual property taken without their free, prior and informed consent or in violation of their laws, traditions and customs.

Article 12

1.   Indigenous peoples have the right to manifest, practice, develop and teach their spiritual and religious traditions, customs and ceremonies; the right to maintain, protect, and have access in privacy to their religious and cultural sites; the right to the use and control of their ceremonial objects; and the right to the repatriation of their human remains.

A/61/L.67

2.   States shall seek to enable the access and/or repatriation of ceremonial objects and human remains in their possession through fair, transparent and effective mechanisms developed in conjunction with indigenous peoples concerned.

Article 13

1.   Indigenous peoples have the right to revitalize, use, develop and transmit to future generations their histories, languages, oral traditions, philosophies, writing systems and literatures, and to designate and retain their own names for communities, places and persons.

2.   States shall take effective measures to ensure that this right is protected and also to ensure that indigenous peoples can understand and be understood in political, legal and administrative proceedings, where necessary through the provision of interpretation or by other appropriate means.

Article 14

1.   Indigenous peoples have the right to establish and control their educational systems and institutions providing education in their own languages, in a manner appropriate to their cultural methods of teaching and learning.

2.   Indigenous individuals, particularly children, have the right to all levels and forms of education of the State without discrimination.

3.   States shall, in conjunction with indigenous peoples, take effective measures, in order for indigenous individuals, particularly children, including those living outside their communities, to have access, when possible, to an education in their own culture and provided in their own language.

Article 15

1.   Indigenous peoples have the right to the dignity and diversity of their cultures, traditions, histories and aspirations which shall be appropriately reflected in education and public information.

2.   States shall take effective measures, in consultation and cooperation with the indigenous peoples concerned, to combat prejudice and eliminate discrimination and to promote tolerance, understanding and good relations among indigenous peoples and all other segments of society.

Article 16

1.   Indigenous peoples have the right to establish their own media in their own languages and to have access to all forms of non-indigenous media without discrimination.

2.   States shall take effective measures to ensure that State-owned media duly reflect indigenous cultural diversity. States, without prejudice to ensuring full freedom of expression, should encourage privately owned media to adequately reflect indigenous cultural diversity.

07-49830

A/61/L.67

Article 17

1.   Indigenous individuals and peoples have the right to enjoy fully all rights established under applicable international and domestic labour law.

2.   States shall in consultation and cooperation with indigenous peoples take specific measures to protect indigenous children from economic exploitation and from performing any work that is likely to be hazardous or to interfere with the child's education, or to be harmful to the child's health or physical, mental, spiritual, moral or social development, taking into account their special vulnerability and the importance of education for their empowerment.

3.   Indigenous individuals have the right not to be subjected to any discriminatory conditions of labour and, inter alia, employment or salary.

Article 18

Indigenous peoples have the right to participate in decision-making in matters which would affect their rights, through representatives chosen by themselves in accordance with their own procedures, as well as to maintain and develop their own indigenous decision-making institutions.

Article 19

States shall consult and cooperate in good faith with the indigenous peoples concerned through their own representative institutions in order to obtain their free, prior and informed consent before adopting and implementing legislative or administrative measures that may affect them.

Article 20

1.   Indigenous peoples have the right to maintain and develop their political, economic and social systems or institutions, to be secure in the enjoyment of their own means of subsistence and development, and to engage freely in all their traditional and other economic activities.

2.   Indigenous peoples deprived of their means of subsistence and development are entitled to just and fair redress.

Article 21

1.   Indigenous peoples have the right, without discrimination, to the improvement of their economic and social conditions, including, inter alia, in the areas of education, employment, vocational training and retraining, housing, sanitation, health and social security.

2.   States shall take effective measures and, where appropriate, special measures to ensure continuing improvement of their economic and social conditions. Particular attention shall be paid to the rights and special needs of indigenous elders, women, youth, children and persons with disabilities.

A/61/L.67

Article 22

1.   Particular attention shall be paid to the rights and special needs of indigenous elders, women, youth, children and persons with disabilities in the implementation of this Declaration.

2.   States shall take measures, in conjunction with indigenous peoples, to ensure that indigenous women and children enjoy the full protection and guarantees against all forms of violence and discrimination.

Article 23

Indigenous peoples have the right to determine and develop priorities and strategies for exercising their right to development. In particular, indigenous peoples have the right to be actively involved in developing and determining health, housing and other economic and social programmes affecting them and, as far as possible, to administer such programmes through their own institutions.

Article 24

1.   Indigenous peoples have the right to their traditional medicines and to maintain their health practices, including the conservation of their vital medicinal plants, animals and minerals. Indigenous individuals also have the right to access, without any discrimination, to all social and health services.

2.   Indigenous individuals have an equal right to the enjoyment of the highest attainable standard of physical and mental health. States shall take the necessary steps with a view to achieving progressively the full realization of this right.

Article 25

Indigenous peoples have the right to maintain and strengthen their distinctive spiritual relationship with their traditionally owned or otherwise occupied and used lands, territories, waters and coastal seas and other resources and to uphold their responsibilities to future generations in this regard.

Article 26

1.   Indigenous peoples have the right to the lands, territories and resources which they have traditionally owned, occupied or otherwise used or acquired.

2.   Indigenous peoples have the right to own, use, develop and control the lands, territories and resources that they possess by reason of traditional ownership or other traditional occupation or use, as well as those which they have otherwise acquired.

3.   States shall give legal recognition and protection to these lands, territories and resources. Such recognition shall be conducted with due respect to the customs, traditions and land tenure systems of the indigenous peoples concerned.

07-49830

Article 27

States shall establish and implement, in conjunction with indigenous peoples concerned, a fair, independent, impartial, open and transparent process, giving due recognition to indigenous peoples' laws, traditions, customs and land tenure systems, to recognize and adjudicate the rights of indigenous peoples pertaining to their lands, territories and resources, including those which were traditionally owned or otherwise occupied or used. Indigenous peoples shall have the right to participate in this process.

Article 28

1.   Indigenous peoples have the right to redress, by means that can include restitution or, when this is not possible, just, fair and equitable compensation, for the lands, territories and resources which they have traditionally owned or otherwise occupied or used, and which have been confiscated, taken, occupied, used or damaged without their free, prior and informed consent.

2.   Unless otherwise freely agreed upon by the peoples concerned, compensation shall take the form of lands, territories and resources equal in quality, size and legal status or of monetary compensation or other appropriate redress.

Article 29

1.   Indigenous peoples have the right to the conservation and protection of the environment and the productive capacity of their lands or territories and resources. States shall establish and implement assistance programmes for indigenous peoples for such conservation and protection, without discrimination.

2.   States shall take effective measures to ensure that no storage or disposal of hazardous materials shall take place in the lands or territories of indigenous peoples without their free, prior and informed consent.

3.   States shall also take effective measures to ensure, as needed, that programmes for monitoring, maintaining and restoring the health of indigenous peoples, as developed and implemented by the peoples affected by such materials, are duly implemented.

Article 30

1.   Military activities shall not take place in the lands or territories of indigenous peoples, unless justified by a significant threat to relevant public interest or otherwise freely agreed with or requested by the indigenous peoples concerned.

2.   States shall undertake effective consultations with the indigenous peoples concerned, through appropriate procedures and in particular through their representative institutions, prior to using their lands or territories for military activities.

Article 31

1.   Indigenous peoples have the right to maintain, control, protect and develop their cultural heritage, traditional knowledge and traditional cultural expressions, as well as the manifestations of their sciences, technologies and cultures, including human and genetic resources, seeds, medicines, knowledge of

A/61/L.67

the properties of fauna and flora, oral traditions, literatures, designs, sports and traditional games and visual and performing arts. They also have the right to maintain, control, protect and develop their intellectual property over such cultural heritage, traditional knowledge, and traditional cultural expressions.

2.   In conjunction with indigenous peoples, States shall take effective measures to recognize and protect the exercise of these rights.

Article 32

1.   Indigenous peoples have the right to determine and develop priorities and strategies for the development or use of their lands or territories and other resources.

2.   States shall consult and cooperate in good faith with the indigenous peoples concerned through their own representative institutions in order to obtain their free and informed consent prior to the approval of any project affecting their lands or territories and other resources, particularly in connection with the development, utilization or exploitation of mineral, water or other resources.

3.   States shall provide effective mechanisms for just and fair redress for any such activities, and appropriate measures shall be taken to mitigate adverse environmental, economic, social, cultural or spiritual impact.

Article 33

1.   Indigenous peoples have the right to determine their own identity or membership in accordance with their customs and traditions. This does not impair the right of indigenous individuals to obtain citizenship of the States in which they live.

2.   Indigenous peoples have the right to determine the structures and to select the membership of their institutions in accordance with their own procedures.

Article 34

Indigenous peoples have the right to promote, develop and maintain their institutional structures and their distinctive customs, spirituality, traditions, procedures, practices and, in the cases where they exist, juridical systems or customs, in accordance with international human rights standards.

Article 35

Indigenous peoples have the right to determine the responsibilities of individuals to their communities.

Article 36

1.   Indigenous peoples, in particular those divided by international borders, have the right to maintain and develop contacts, relations and cooperation, including activities for spiritual, cultural, political, economic and social purposes, with their own members as well as other peoples across borders.

2.   States, in consultation and cooperation with indigenous peoples, shall take effective measures to facilitate the exercise and ensure the implementation of this right.

07-49830

Article 37

1.   Indigenous peoples have the right to the recognition, observance and enforcement of treaties, agreements and other constructive arrangements concluded with States or their successors and to have States honour and respect such treaties, agreements and other constructive arrangements.

2.   Nothing in this Declaration may be interpreted as diminishing or eliminating the rights of indigenous peoples contained in treaties, agreements and other constructive arrangements.

Article 38

States in consultation and cooperation with indigenous peoples, shall take the appropriate measures, including legislative measures, to achieve the ends of this Declaration.

Article 39

Indigenous peoples have the right to have access to financial and technical assistance from States and through international cooperation, for the enjoyment of the rights contained in this Declaration.

Article 40

Indigenous peoples have the right to access to and prompt decision through just and fair procedures for the resolution of conflicts and disputes with States or other parties, as well as to effective remedies for all infringements of their individual and collective rights. Such a decision shall give due consideration to the customs, traditions, rules and legal systems of the indigenous peoples concerned and international human rights.

Article 41

The organs and specialized agencies of the United Nations system and other intergovernmental organizations shall contribute to the full realization of the provisions of this Declaration through the mobilization, inter alia, of financial cooperation and technical assistance. Ways and means of ensuring participation of indigenous peoples on issues affecting them shall be established.

Article 42

The United Nations, its bodies, including the Permanent Forum on Indigenous Issues, and specialized agencies, including at the country level, and States shall promote respect for and full application of the provisions of this Declaration and follow up the effectiveness of this Declaration.

Article 43

The rights recognized herein constitute the minimum standards for the survival, dignity and well-being of the indigenous peoples of the world.

A/61/L.67

Article 44

All the rights and freedoms recognized herein are equally guaranteed to male and female indigenous individuals.

Article 45

Nothing in this Declaration may be construed as diminishing or extinguishing the rights indigenous peoples have now or may acquire in the future.

Article 46

1.   Nothing in this Declaration may be interpreted as implying for any State, people, group or person any right to engage in any activity or to perform any act contrary to the Charter of the United Nations or construed as authorizing or encouraging any action which would dismember or impair, totally or in part, the territorial integrity or political unity of sovereign and independent States.

2.   In the exercise of the rights enunciated in the present Declaration, human rights and fundamental freedoms of all shall be respected. The exercise of the rights set forth in this Declaration shall be subject only to such limitations as are determined by law, and in accordance with international human rights obligations. Any such limitations shall be non-discriminatory and strictly necessary solely for the purpose of securing due recognition and respect for the rights and freedoms of others and for meeting the just and most compelling requirements of a democratic society.

3.   The provisions set forth in this Declaration shall be interpreted in accordance with the principles of justice, democracy, respect for human rights, equality, non-discrimination, good governance and good faith.

07-49830